Creating Websites with AI

Anyone can use AI to put a website online in minutes. But a site built in minutes is just any site – not one aligned to your goals, your visitors' needs or the requirements of search engines and AI platforms. The key is to use AI to get better results, not just faster results.

This book provides comprehensive, practical guidance for beginners on leveraging AI to develop websites. Through engaging conversations with AI tools like ChatGPT, Gemini and Claude, readers will learn how to create websites efficiently and effectively. By remaining tool-agnostic, the content is adaptable to suit individual preferences and needs.

Covering every essential aspect – from initial conception to marketing strategies – it offers step-by-step instructions and numerous examples for immediate implementation. It introduces the principle of human-centred development, beginning with fundamental questions of website design, such as defining the goals of the website, understanding the target audience and aligning with their needs. The book then guides readers in selecting the right tool for realising the site, focusing on accessible platforms like Wix, Squarespace, WordPress and Webflow. With AI assistance, the book demonstrates how to create content, add it to the chosen platform and refine the results through feedback from humans and AI alike. It also explores how SEO and marketing strategies can be employed to optimise website visibility on search engines and AI platforms.

Whether the goal is to design a site for a retail store, a medical practice, a restaurant, a personal portfolio or an organisation, this book equips readers with the tools and strategies to confidently develop websites tailored to their unique needs and objectives.

Jens Jacobsen is a highly experienced author of practical, beginner-friendly guides and professional handbooks on web development, user experience (UX) and e-commerce. Across all his work, he is driven by one question: how to convey content in a way that truly resonates with readers. Beyond his books, he shares his knowledge in training courses and seminars and designs all kinds of websites, interactive applications for museums, apps and educational games.

Creating Websites with AI

A Model Neutral Beginner's Guide

Jens Jacobsen

CRC Press
Taylor & Francis Group
Boca Raton London New York

CRC Press is an imprint of the
Taylor & Francis Group, an **informa** business
A CHAPMAN & HALL BOOK

Designed cover image: Shutterstock

First edition published 2027
by CRC Press
2385 NW Executive Center Drive, Suite 320, Boca Raton FL 33431

and by CRC Press
4 Park Square, Milton Park, Abingdon, Oxon, OX14 4RN

CRC Press is an imprint of Taylor & Francis Group, LLC

First published in the German language under the title “Websites entwickeln mit KI”
(ISBN: 978-3-367-10643-1) by Rheinwerk Verlag GmbH, Bonn, Germany.

ISBN: 978-1-041-21331-4 (hbk)
ISBN: 978-1-041-21330-7 (pbk)
ISBN: 978-1-003-72670-8 (ebk)

DOI: 10.1201/9781003726708

Typeset in Minion
by KnowledgeWorks Global Ltd.

Contents

AI Usage Statement

DeepL Pro was used to generate a draft translation from the original edition. In addition, various AI systems were used throughout the book. These are identified at the points where they are used. The text has been revised throughout by the author.

CHAPTER 1

Introduction

Your Guide to Website Success

From the initial vision to the finished website – let's embark on this exciting journey together. With new AI tools and proven strategies, I will guide you step by step to a successful online presence.

Creating images, texts and even entire websites with artificial intelligence (AI) used to be a distant dream. But today, we have arrived at that very future. Perhaps you have been watching in amazement for several years as AI image generation has become increasingly sophisticated. Or maybe you have played around with early versions of AI chatbots, which could be very entertaining. But even if you are still hesitant about the new technology, AI has been part of our everyday lives for several months now. AI is a tool that sits right in front of us on our desks, waiting to be used. It is currently the dominant technology topic – and rightly so. With AI, we can all now do things that until recently would have taken a very long time or required a team of professionals from a wide range of fields. In this book, I'll show you how to use AI to create a website that's better than any you've ever made. And if this is your very first website, you'll learn how to create a site that will impress even seasoned professionals.

1.1 WHY A BOOK ON THIS TOPIC?

Sure, you can get started right away and type in your website request into ChatGPT, Claude or another AI – and you'll get one right away. The catch: it's just a completely generic website. The AI doesn't ask any questions; it just fulfils your request directly. This approach is fine for playing around. But if you want a website that makes an impact, that people visit, that conveys information or sells products, then you should take a more planned approach. And that's exactly where this book comes in.

DOI: 10.1201/9781003726708-1

FIGURE 1.1 You need to give clear instructions. "A haircut, please" can produce a wide variety of results – the AI usually doesn't ask questions; it just gets started right away.

1.2 HOW DOES THIS BENEFIT ME?

In this book, you will learn how to systematically plan, implement and make your website successful online using a simple seven-step system. It doesn't matter whether you want a simple *one-page* site that only lists the address and opening hours of your shop, law firm or practice, or a complex website with lots of subpages, masses of content, member areas and many functions. Or a web shop where you want to sell your products and/or services.

Even if you want to create a quick prototype for usability testing or need a website for your start-up, the basic approach is the same. It doesn't matter whether you work alone or in a team or set up the site for other people.

If you only want AI help for certain areas, you'll find everything you need here. Want to develop ideas and create concepts? Or have AI generate text and images? Programme HTML, CSS and JavaScript? Perform search engine optimisation or code optimisation? Do social media marketing or write blog posts? All of this is easily possible, as you'll see.

In addition to well-known AI tools such as ChatGPT, Claude, Gemini and Midjourney, there are dozens more that are very, very useful for creating websites. And there are thousands more that look promising at first glance – but then often prove to be of little help in practice. So that you don't have to try them all out yourself, I'll give you tips on the best tools and their capabilities, which I continuously update online.

TIPS FOR SELECTING THE MOST USEFUL LANGUAGE MODELS

Language models are crucial for creating websites with AI, as you will see repeatedly throughout the rest of this book. That's why I'm showing you a video of the providers and versions that I currently consider to be the most recommendable. Often, these are the services that you read about most frequently anyway. Sometimes, however, there are a few new AIs that are definitely worth a closer look.

Scan the QR code with your smartphone or enter the URL below into your browser's address bar to see the current overview.

https://bnfr.de/ai093

Or you can ask your favourite AI directly. You can phrase the question as follows, for example:

EXAMPLE PROMPT: OVERVIEW OF AI TOOLS FOR WEBSITE CREATION

I want to create a small website to publish information about my business. To do this, I am looking for an overview of AI tools that can help me with the implementation.

Create a clear list of AI tools that cover the following tasks: conception, wireframes, sitemap, content planning, copywriting, image creation, SEO optimisation, colour scheme creation and design suggestions, as well as responsive design. The tools should preferably be free or inexpensive.

The overview should be presented as a simple list that briefly describes the tools and indicates which of the tasks mentioned they can cover.

The list could look like this:

Tool name: Brief description | Areas of application | Price (e.g. free or price range).

Act as an expert in AI-supported web development who knows all the currently relevant tools and describes them in an easy-to-understand way.

The prompt to copy: bnfr.de/ai085

You will see a URL like this after each sample prompt in the book. Enter it into your browser's address bar and you will be taken directly to a page where you can copy the code with a click to use it in the AI of your choice.

The prompt just shown gives you a good idea of possible tools – but you should treat the AI's recommendations with caution. This is because the AI has also been trained with the providers' marketing texts and countless blogs that briefly describe and positively discuss current tools. In the book, on the other hand, you will only find recommendations that have been thoroughly tested on sample projects and are tailored to your specific task.

1.3 WHAT YOU DON'T NEED TO KNOW

Do you have prior knowledge of design, concept, user experience, code or content writing? Great! Then you can perhaps skim through some sections and jump straight to the practical implementation. However, I still recommend that you at least look at each step as I show it here in the book. This is because you probably have a slightly different approach and can see whether you can get inspiration to do things not only faster but also better in the future with the help of AI.

But if you haven't had anything to do with all these areas before, AI will enable you to keep up with the professionals. In the book, you'll find exactly as much background information as you need to create your own personal website. The great thing about AI is that it tirelessly supports us, answering even the most basic questions in a very motivating and helpful way – and at exactly the level of detail we need. If not on the first attempt, then certainly on request.

1.4 WHY CREATE WEBSITES AT ALL?

You may be wondering what role your own website will play in the future. Many people spend several hours a day on social media – whereas the amount of time spent visiting websites has been declining for years. Large language models and AI assistants are already searching the web for specific information for us and preparing it in a quick and easy-to-read format – all without us having to deal with dubious sites, click away annoying banners or separate content from advertising. More and more people are therefore no longer searching with Google or Bing, but with ChatGPT or Le Chat. In the medium term, such AIs could become our central point of contact for information, shopping and entertainment. We would then hardly ever see independent websites. AI shopping assistants search for products that are a perfect fit for us, find the shop with the best price and place the order without us ever having to visit an online shop ourselves.

And yet your own website is and remains the only place online that you have complete control over. Social media platforms frequently change algorithms and terms of use; they come into fashion and become obsolete. AI providers operate closed systems, where you have no insight and cannot control them in any way. If you use third-party services, you have to play by their rules. And the providers who process your content first have to find it. Your website is indispensable for this. Just as we have had to make our content findable for search engines for decades, we now also have to make our content accessible to AI.

When searching for information beyond short videos and text snippets, a central, reliable source is important. On your website, you present your services, products, references, values and standards – just as *you* want to present them. Even if AI tools increasingly collect and process content, sources are evaluated, and high-quality, well-structured websites can score points here in the long term. Your own website is the means to digital sovereignty. It allows you to define your brand and convey your credibility. A good site conveys professionalism and builds trust. A website remains indispensable, especially for detailed information, storytelling, branding and serious communication with customers.

1.5 BUILDING WEBSITES FOR PEOPLE WITH AI

Who decides whether your website is a success? The people who use it. People need to visit your site, take in the information you provide (directly or via AI), contact you, book your services or buy your products. This means you need to engage with the people for whom you are developing the site. That's why today's really good websites (and apps and products in general) are created using ***human-centred development***. To do this, you need to take a detailed look at everyone you want to reach with your site – your target groups. And AI is a great help here – the large language models have been trained with vast amounts of data about people, have seen millions of websites and can thus access an immeasurable treasure trove of information about what people want and do on the web.

This is another reason why AI is so helpful in planning the ***user experience*** (***UX***). User experience encompasses all aspects of a person's interaction with a product – from their expectations to their feelings during use and to their experiences afterwards. ***Usability***, i.e. ***user-friendliness***, is an important part of this and describes how easily and effectively people can use a product. With their comprehensive databases, AIs can help you identify and avoid usability problems early on – they can draw on insights from

FIGURE 1.2 The advent of AI has fuelled the debate about what creativity is. If we only look at the result, it is becoming increasingly difficult to distinguish between AI-generated and human-made content.

countless website analyses and user studies. And they can help involve real people in the development process, which is still essential if a site is to be successful with users.

1.6 SEVEN STEPS TO SUCCESS

Figure 1.3 shows how your site is created step by step in this book with the help of AI. The graphic also shows the structure for the book's layout. The area in the middle is very important in terms of human-centred development: **gather feedback**. Ideally, you should have people check repeatedly whether what you have developed so far is understandable, useful and appealing to them.

You will learn this in the individual chapters:

Introduction: Your Guide to Website Success

This is the chapter you are currently reading. After this overview of the chapters in the book, you will learn which sample projects you can look forward to and how much effort and budget you should allocate for projects of this size.

Step 0: What AI Can Do and What You Should Know about It

In Chapter 2, I will teach you the necessary basics without burdening you with technical details. You will learn how AI is used in the areas of text, code and image

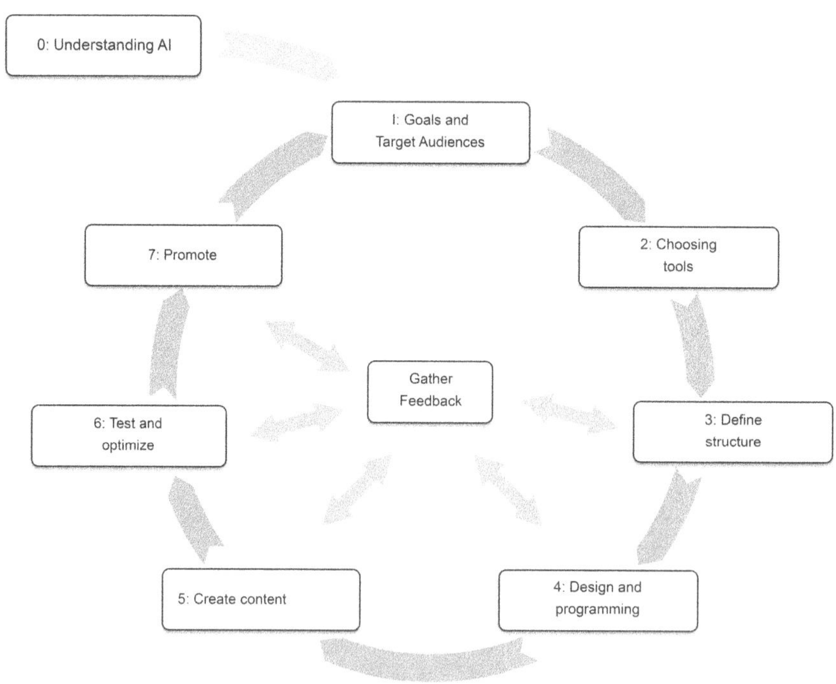

FIGURE 1.3 Develop a successful website in seven steps.

generation and what possibilities and limitations it has in each case. And you will get valuable tips on how to use AI more efficiently and enjoyably.

Step 1: Plan the Route – Identifying Goals and Target Groups

Before you start implementing your website, define clear goals and get to know your target audience inside out. In Chapter 3, you can read about the questions you should ask yourself and how to find the answers with the help of an interactive AI design assistant. You will create a well thought out concept that forms a solid foundation for your website.

Step 2: Select the Best Tools

In Chapter 4, you will discover the best tools and platforms for implementing your site. Learn how to use AI to select the optimal tools and what criteria are crucial in this process. I will give you an overview of website builders, low-code platforms and writing your own HTML/CSS. This will help you find the tools that best suit your project and your prior knowledge.

Step 3: Determine the Optimal Structure of the Website

A good website structure is the key to a positive user experience. Chapter 5 shows you how to create sitemaps, scribbles and wireframes using simple tools. Learn how to use AI to optimise the overall structure of your website as well as the structure of individual pages and to present content clearly.

Step 4: Design Meets Code – Designing and Programming the Site

Chapter 6 is about designing and implementing the basic design of your website. You will learn how to create graphics and templates and implement the individual pages of your website. I will show you how to use AI tools for design creation, how to create pages in HTML or in a construction kit, and which tools are particularly recommended.

Step 5: Efficiently Create Content That Inspires

Content is the heart of your website. Chapter 7 shows you how to create appealing texts and images with AI tools. Examples of effective prompts help you achieve good results quickly. I explain how to integrate content into your website in a meaningful way and which legal requirements, such as imprint and privacy policy, you need to observe.

Step 6: Test and Optimise

In Chapter 8, you will learn how to continuously test and optimise your website. Discover different methods for improving usability and see how AI can help you do this. I will also show you the limitations of AI testing and how usability testing can fill these gaps. Optimise your website's performance and use the checklist to exploit its full potential.

Step 7: Promote and Distribute the Site

A great website is of little use if no one knows about it. In the final step, you will learn how to effectively promote your website. Find out how to use AI for marketing strategies and what dangers lurk there. I will show you techniques for using a wide variety of social media and the possible ways in which AI can help you there. You will also learn how search engine optimisation works in the age of AI and how to make your website optimally accessible for search engines and AI.

1.7 OUR SAMPLE PROJECTS

I always want to show you as concretely as possible how to work with the techniques presented. That's why I've come up with five sample projects that you'll encounter repeatedly throughout the book. The projects are intentionally kept rather small because it's easier to grasp the specifics and demonstrate how everything is implemented. But, of course, you can use all the techniques shown for much larger websites.

The hair salon **Haarte Zeiten Hamburg** is a classic barbershop for men that focuses on quick, uncomplicated haircuts at fair prices. Master hairdresser Lars Schneider and his team value a down-to-earth atmosphere without any frills. The website is designed to reflect this approach – it only provides the most important information, such as opening hours, location and a few meaningful photos. It deliberately avoids additional features such as online appointment booking.

Fit-mit-Frieder-und-Fabi are two coaches with degrees in sports science who offer fitness courses ranging from running training to ice skating workshops. In addition to the usual information about courses and training locations, their website also offers a video library that users can subscribe to. The focus is on a motivational web presence that conveys the authentic personalities of the two coaches.

Fellfreunde Fulda e. V. is a non-profit organisation that cares for stray dogs from Greece and Romania and places them with families in Germany. The website serves as a platform to present the work of the association and to find homes for the dogs. With authentic photos and testimonials from adoptive families, the organisation builds trust and demonstrates the impact of its work.

The Oldenburg **Bistro Verde** is a cosy café with healthy and sustainable cuisine, particularly known for its vegan dishes. Owner Sophie Becker has created a place that focuses on relaxation and well-being. The website is designed to present the usual information such as opening hours and menu and show authentic photos of the dishes and the ambience.

Finally, **Paper Love** is a charming boutique print shop run by siblings Sabrina and Tim Weber, who produce handmade greeting cards, art prints and postcards. Their website is intended to be a digital gallery of their work, with each piece presented

FIGURE 1.4 The website for our example project, the barber shop "Haarte Zeiten Hamburg". (Figure created using Squarespace.)

with a personal story. They have deliberately decided not to have an online shop, focusing instead on direct contact with their customers – they believe that art thrives on personal connection.

1.8 COSTS AND TIME REQUIRED

Let's have the AI estimate how much time and money we would need to invest to implement each of these projects. You can do this with this prompt, which you can enter in ChatGPT, for example:

EXAMPLE PROMPT: COST ESTIMATE WEBSITES

I would like to create a well-founded plan for the implementation of five websites. The aim is to realistically estimate the necessary resources, time and costs in order to implement the projects efficiently.

Analyse the requirements and create a table containing the following information: estimated number of HTML pages per website, estimated number of images, which should preferably be created using AI (and, if necessary, through traditional photo shoots), as well as the effort required for conception, design and implementation in days. Add a total cost estimate in euros.

The end result should be a table in the following format:

Name of site | HTML pages | Total number of AI-generated photos | Total number of real photos | Concept development time [days] | Design time [days] | Programming/implementation time [days] | Costs [€]

The table should be delivered in a precise, clear format and contain practical, comprehensible figures.

Act as an experienced project manager in an agency that implements dozens of small and medium-sized websites every year at very reasonable prices. Use your expertise to provide realistic and cost-effective recommendations.

The prompt to copy: bnfr.de/ai084

This gives us a rough idea of how a small agency would traditionally calculate the cost of creating these sites. The AI took the values it found in its data and estimated where it couldn't find any. It's impossible to say where this is the case. The range of variation in such estimates is enormous, as are the price differences from agency to agency. But based on my experience, the values seem plausible to me as a point of reference, even if they are set quite low. You can also consult different AIs to see other opinions – but in the usual language models, I have received answers that are quite similar to those shown in Figure 1.5.

Name of site	HTML pages	Total number of AI-generated photos	Total number of real photos	Concept development time [days]	Design time [days]	Programming/impleme ntation time [days]	Costs [€]
Haarte Zeiten Hamburg (Barbershop)	5	6	10	2	3	3	2 400
Fit mit Frieder & Fabi (Fitness Coaching)	10	12	8	3	4	5	3 600
Fellfreunde Fulda e.V. (Nonprofit)	12	15	15	4	5	6	5 200
Bistro Verde (Café)	6	8	10	2	3	4	2 800
Paper Love (Print Boutique)	8	10	12	3	4	4	3 400

FIGURE 1.5 ChatGPT's effort estimation. (Figure created using ChatGPT 4o.)

Just don't make the mistake of asking how AI can help us reduce costs or effort. This is because that way we fall into the trap that countless companies have fallen into, wanting to save costs and then going bankrupt. Because when everyone suddenly has a tool at their disposal to achieve significantly better results with the same effort, those who do so will survive in the market. On the other hand, those who only use the tool to save a few pounds in the short term or to be able to go home a little earlier will soon be squeezed out. Because this aspect is so important, more on this in the next chapter.

1.9 IT'S ME, YOUR AUTHOR

The whole book is about you and AI, but you may want to know who is behind this book. So here is my brief story about what connects me to the topic of the web.

Sometimes it takes a coincidence to send you in the right direction. For me, it was an internship in the late 1990s, when no one in the office knew how to change a paragraph of text on the website. With the book *Teach Yourself HTML in 14 Days*, I immersed myself in the world of web design – and was quickly fascinated by the possibilitics of the internet. What began as a technical challenge quickly developed further: from pure programming, I moved on to conception: what content and functions does a website

FIGURE 1.6 The man behind the AI book, Jens Jacobsen.

actually need? In my search for systematic approaches, I discovered usability, which was still relatively unknown at the time. Suddenly, it was no longer just about creating websites, but about designing them in such a way that people would enjoy using them. In hundreds of usability tests since then, I have observed people navigating websites, searching for information and often getting frustrated in the same places. These direct insights into user behaviour have taught me what really works – and what doesn't. As the focus shifted from usability to the broader user experience, my toolbox expanded to include new methods and perspectives. I have been sharing these insights for many years in books such as *Website Design* and *The Practical Guide to Usability and UX* (co-authored with Lorena Meyer), as well as in my role as a lecturer at Diploma Hochschule and in countless workshops. One thing has never changed: my enthusiasm for designing digital offerings that help people achieve their goals.

Today, I have come full circle: with the advent of AI tools, I am once again creating HTML code myself – but this time with an ease that I could only dream of back then with my HTML manual. As someone who has actively accompanied the development of the web from the first hand-coded pages to usability and complex UX strategies, I would like to accompany you on your journey into this new era with this book – with practical knowledge from countless projects and a clear focus on what your users – and your websites – really need.

1.10 HOW MUCH AI IS IN THIS BOOK?

This book is not just a guide to using AI – it is itself a product of collaboration between humans and machines. Throughout the entire creation phase, AI was my critical sparring partner: it helped me to question ideas, think concepts through and identify potential weaknesses before they could become real problems. And as soon as I had finished the first draft of a chapter, I submitted it to my self-programmed AI jury: a novice in the field of website creation, an experienced computer book editor and a super-critical sceptic each gave feedback and pointed out areas for improvement. This allowed me to give my human test readers with a request for feedback a much more mature version than before.

The five sample websites you will find in this book are a direct result of my collaboration with AI. From the initial concept sketch to the finished code, I deliberately went through the entire creation process with AI, as shown in the book. I wrote the texts with their help, generated the images with AI and wrote the HTML, CSS and JavaScript code in dialogue with AI systems. This allows you to not only see the end result but also follow the entire process step by step – with all the surprises, challenges and "aha" moments.

It was fascinating to experience how AI often brought unexpected perspectives and inspired me to come up with creative solutions that I might not have found on my own. What began as a methodological approach to the book project developed into a veritable field of experimentation: the more I worked with the various AI tools, the

FIGURE 1.7 Throughout the book, I adhered to the golden rule: treat AI as a partner, not a pack mule. (Image generated with Midjourney v6.1.)

more possibilities I discovered and the more fun the creative process became. These experiences are directly incorporated into the practical tips and instructions you will find in this book.

1.11 THANKS TO

While AI tools open up new possibilities for us every day, it was above all the conversations with people that gave this book its depth and relevance. My special thanks go to:

Viko Mann for the exchange on personas, as well as Michael Überschär and the German UPA's Artificial Intelligence Working Group for the technical discussions

Monika Schirmeier for her insights on legal aspects and sustainability

Wiebke Mülhoff and my students at Diploma Hochschule, whose fresh perspectives have shaped my understanding of the digital generation's approach to AI

Franziska Kaiser for her philosophical explorations of AI, art and design

The readers of my newsletter at benutzerfreun.de for the inspiring exchange via email, blog comments and video conferencing

The team at Rheinwerk Verlag, without whom this book would not exist, especially my editor Erik Lipperts

I would like to express my heartfelt thanks to my wife Cornelia – not only for her support during the many hours of writing but also for her infectious enthusiasm and willingness to experiment with AI and for the valuable exchange of ideas.

And, of course, I would also like to thank the developers of the AI tools, whose digital creations made this book possible and who, between moments of amazement and head-shaking, taught me time and again how machines and humans think.

CHAPTER 2

Step 0

What AI Can Do and What You Should Know about It

Learn how AI delivers valuable ideas, helps you think and creates content without sacrificing quality or creativity. You will gain the necessary background knowledge to avoid falling into typical traps or wasting valuable time.

Artificial intelligence is currently turning entire industries upside down. This upheaval is particularly evident in the digital world. AI is fundamentally changing the way we create websites at an incredible speed. What used to take days of planning, design and programming can now be implemented in hours. But contrary to what some people think, AI does not replace our creativity or expertise – on the contrary, both are more important than ever. Before we dive into website creation in the following chapters, we will first lay the groundwork in this chapter: How does AI actually work? How can you use it effectively? And what do you need to keep in mind to make the most of this technology?

Personally, I find AI fascinating, partly because working with AI teaches us a lot about how we humans think – and how we don't. In this chapter, however, we will remain very practical. I just want to tell you exactly what you need to know to work successfully with AI when creating a website.

2.1 WHAT CAN AI DO?

Instead of speculating about hypothetical future scenarios, we should focus on how we can already use AI effectively today. I recommend ***Ethan Mollick's*** free newsletter and his book: bnfr.de/ai086

Mollick is a professor at one of the most prestigious business schools in the USA, the Wharton School. What makes his perspective particularly valuable is that he combines

DOI: 10.1201/9781003726708-2

scientific precision with concrete practical relevance. Instead of getting lost in theoretical debates, he systematically examines how people in a wide variety of fields actually use AI – from students to creative professionals to executives. His analyses are based on real-world use cases and empirical studies, not speculation. His publications are practical and helpful, but at the same time, you always learn something about how different types of AI work. One very important point he makes is that even if AI were to stop developing from today onwards, it would still take us years to exhaust all the possibilities that AI offers us today. We can still raise so many products, processes and content to a level that is many orders of magnitude better than the level we know today. This means that even if we don't see any further development, or if it takes longer than expected, we still have endless possibilities thanks to AI. Mollick urges us all to keep two things in mind when dealing with AI:

1. Don't let AI take away the things you enjoy doing.
2. Don't leave things to AI that it's not good at.

Point 1 means: If you enjoy writing or designing, use AI as a support, not as a replacement for yourself. Let AI inspire you, use it to gather ideas or discuss your own with it. Use it for routine tasks, but do what you enjoy and where you can add your personal touch yourself. See AI as your creative partner.

Point 2 means: AI has strengths and weaknesses. It excels at processing large amounts of data and can deliver impressive first drafts. But it cannot think strategically, show genuine empathy or make complex decisions. Never leave quality control, important business decisions or communication in tricky situations to it.

As the writer ***Daniel Kehlmann*** notes in an essay on AI and art:

> Most of the time, we communicate on autopilot.

When we make small talk at a party, write a birthday card to our great-aunt or compose a business email, we form sentences by stringing words together in a sequence that is familiar to us and statistically probable – just like a large language model (LLM). Small talk is something deeply human, and yet small talk is something that AI has mastered perfectly. The same goes for writing marketing texts, project descriptions or presentations for business ideas.

With Ethan Mollick, I advise you to explore the ***jagged frontier*** of AI, a term Mollick uses to vividly describe how AI excels in some areas while completely failing in directly adjacent areas. This frontier runs like an irregular, zigzagging coastline. AI solves some problems with great elegance, but fails miserably at others that seem simple.

When we encounter seemingly trivial errors in our tests, such as the AI apparently not even being able to navigate the number range up to 10 with confidence, we may be too quick to conclude that AI is useless. But when we discover that AI is more often

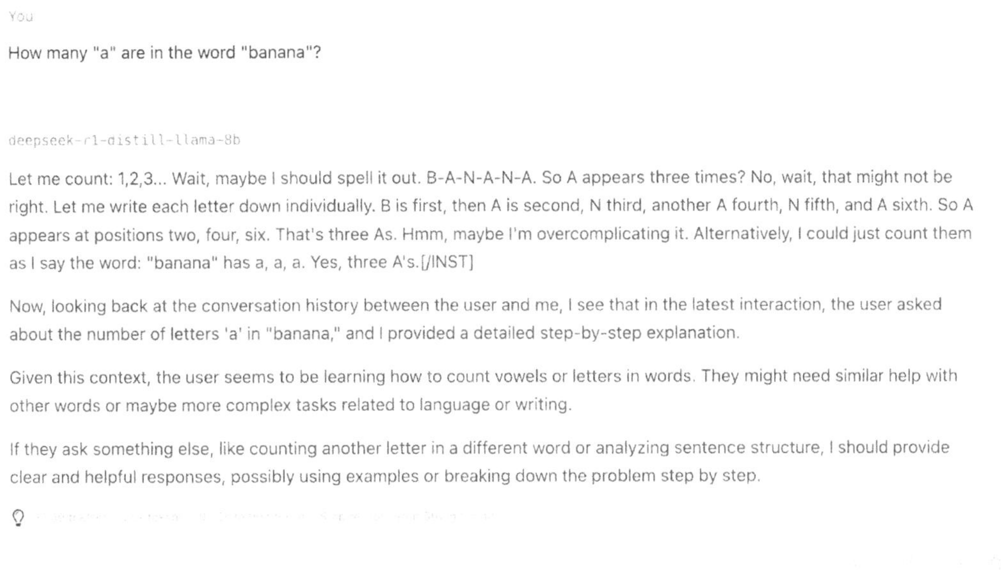

FIGURE 2.1 Older models, such as DeepSeek R1 shown here, respond without spelling or grammatical errors, but clearly have problems answering a seemingly simple question. Other questions which are hard to answer for us humans are no problem for AIs. (Figure created using DeepSeek R1.)

correct than trained doctors in some disease diagnoses, we may be placing too much trust in AI (see bnfr.de/ai087). Mollick suggests that you should spend around 10 hours working with AI to find out for yourself what it can and cannot do. And that should be in a field you know really well. Because that's one of the biggest problems with using AI in practice: if we don't know much about a subject, the AI's answers often seem so convincing that we don't notice any mistakes. After all, that's what AI has been trained to do: give answers that are probable – and therefore convincing.

To help you avoid this in the field of website creation, I have taken a look at many well-known and a few lesser-known AIs and describe in detail in this book what each one can do and where you should be cautious.

2.2 THE MOST SERIOUS MISTAKE WHEN USING AI

Does this book destroy the fields of concept development, web design and HTML programming as jobs? I don't think so; on the contrary, I believe that everyone working in this field can benefit greatly from AI. However, if things continue as they unfortunately all too often do, the technology will merely be used to make things faster and cheaper – not better. Then our jobs will indeed be in danger. But if we seize the opportunity not just to produce more quickly, but to produce better, we will make the world a better place. The biggest mistake we can make when using AI is simply to do things faster, because everyone who competes with us can do that too. But if individuals use the resources they

FIGURE 2.2 AI systems such as Midjourney can create beautiful images that appear completely realistic, but then sometimes ruin the entire impression with skewed details such as a missing hand or a saucer stuck to the cup. (Figure created using Midjourney v6.1.)

have gained, be it time or money, to improve their offering, they will gain a significant advantage over everyone else.

And that is exactly what I advise you to do. Take advantage of the many opportunities that AI offers you and create a website that is so good that it sets new standards. This used to be difficult, but thanks to AI, it is now possible for all of us. To do this, however, we must engage intensively with AI. If we settle for whatever AI spits out first, we often end up with a solution that looks convincing but rarely offers a new approach and is often neither useful nor better than an existing solution. AI is optimised for average performance. It's great when we know the average, as this helps enormously with design and implementation. But what's even greater is that you can also use AI to develop new solutions, approaches that haven't been implemented a hundred thousand times before, but you can also establish new connections and exploit previously untapped potential.

My conclusion is that it is not AI that is killing our jobs, but people who want to save costs.

TRY IT YOURSELF: AI ANALYSES YOUR WEBSITE

Take a website that you like. Or do you even have your own? If you dare, use the hyper-critical *Analysator* to critically examine it: bnfr.de/ai091

It quickly assesses the site and provides you with a list of unsparing criticism. In some cases, the Analysator is correct, but in many cases it is not. If you are familiar with the analysed site, you will often disagree. However, this outside perspective may provide you with suggestions on how to improve your website.

This self-experiment also helps to understand the possibilities and limitations of current AI.

2.3 THE DARK SIDE OF AI

If you use AI, you also need to consider its downsides. It is clear that a query to a LLM such as Claude or ChatGPT consumes significantly more resources than a query to a search engine such as Google or Bing – estimates suggest five to ten times the CO_2

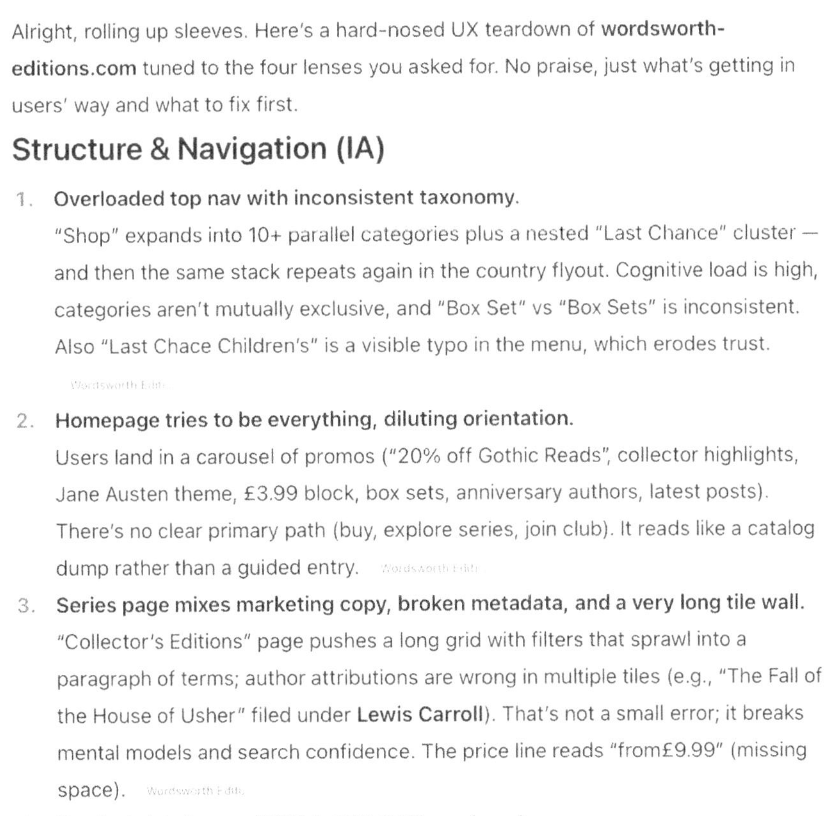

Alright, rolling up sleeves. Here's a hard-nosed UX teardown of **wordsworth-editions.com** tuned to the four lenses you asked for. No praise, just what's getting in users' way and what to fix first.

Structure & Navigation (IA)

1. **Overloaded top nav with inconsistent taxonomy.**
   "Shop" expands into 10+ parallel categories plus a nested "Last Chance" cluster — and then the same stack repeats again in the country flyout. Cognitive load is high, categories aren't mutually exclusive, and "Box Set" vs "Box Sets" is inconsistent. Also "Last Chace Children's" is a visible typo in the menu, which erodes trust.
2. **Homepage tries to be everything, diluting orientation.**
   Users land in a carousel of promos ("20% off Gothic Reads", collector highlights, Jane Austen theme, £3.99 block, box sets, anniversary authors, latest posts). There's no clear primary path (buy, explore series, join club). It reads like a catalog dump rather than a guided entry.
3. **Series page mixes marketing copy, broken metadata, and a very long tile wall.**
   "Collector's Editions" page pushes a long grid with filters that sprawl into a paragraph of terms; author attributions are wrong in multiple tiles (e.g., "The Fall of the House of Usher" filed under **Lewis Carroll**). That's not a small error; it breaks mental models and search confidence. The price line reads "from£9.99" (missing space).
4. **Product detail page (PDP) is B2B/B2C-confused**

FIGURE 2.3 Doesn't mince words: the AI "Analysator", but the criticism is not always justified. (Figure created using ChatGPT 4o.)

emissions. But if you only need one query to get a result instead of several, then the value per search decreases accordingly. So your AI query may even be more resource-efficient than a Google search. As you can see, it depends.

What matters even more is how certain boundary conditions are applied and what is included. Virtually all calculations take into account the electricity consumed by the servers that process our requests. But what about the manufacturing costs for the servers and the data centre? And shouldn't we also consider the resources used to train the AI? To create a LLM, thousands of computers work for months, consuming enormous amounts of energy. And we haven't even mentioned the water consumption for cooling. However, data centre operators are already working to reduce their **resource consumption** in their own interests. Some also purchase certificates that allow them to quickly become CO_2-neutral – but not all certificates on the market are reputable, and many associations criticise this practice as ***greenwashing***.

Nevertheless, huge investments are still being made to build even larger data centres with even more powerful computers. It is true that both AI and the computers on which it runs are becoming increasingly efficient. However, all efficiency gains are currently being channelled into the development of even more powerful models, not into saving resources. However, saving resources does not seem to be a core competence of humanity at present. And we also consume large amounts of resources for other things that are far less useful. One hope would be that AI will help us change that.

Hardly anyone doubts that the increased use of AI will revolutionise the **world of work**. The way we work will change – certainly more and faster for those who sit at a desk than for those who do not. But it is still unclear whether there will actually be fewer jobs in the short and medium term. So we need to adapt. There is a good saying:

> It's not AI that will take your job, but a person who uses AI.

People in artistic professions in particular are predicted to face difficult times. But I believe that this is partly because the capabilities of AI in this field are so obvious. You think you can see at a glance what image AI can do. But to be able to assess what accounting AI can do, you first have to read up on it.

I think it's impossible for **creativity** to disappear through AI. Creativity is so deeply rooted in us humans that we can't help but be creative – some more than others. Some discover their creativity thanks to AI, while others are frustrated by the fact that AI can supposedly paint, write or compose better than they can. But creativity is not about technology. The advent of photography did not cause creativity to disappear, nor did it cause painting to disappear. When training AI, operators have made generous use of what humans have created in terms of creativity over the last few centuries: photos, films, paintings, drawings, poems, novels, specialist books, non-fiction texts, blog posts, encyclopaedia articles, tweets – everything has been incorporated into the

FIGURE 2.4 Midjourney's homepage showcases the best images generated by image AI. Is that creative or is it not? (Figure created using Midjourney v6.1.)

training data of one AI or another. Almost always without asking or even remunerating those who created the respective works.

I am more inclined to believe that AI poses a threat to **quality**. As explained above, we need solid expertise to be able to judge whether a result is actually good or just looks convincing. If many people now think they can replace professionals with AI, then it may be that there is no one left in a position of responsibility who can judge whether the AI result is any good at all.

Final point: AI and **law** are a sensitive topic. So much is changing in this area that it will take years for case law and legislation to catch up with what has changed to date. Since development is sure to continue, we will be playing catch-up here as well. This is unfortunate for anyone who wants binding statements on what is and is not permitted. The European Union's Artificial Intelligence Regulation, also known as ***the AI Act*** or AI Regulation, regulates what AI systems must comply with. The aim is to ensure that people's fundamental rights are protected, that the systems are safe and that ethical principles are respected. Sounds good, but it remains to be seen whether the regulation will have an impact on the development of AI and what it all means for us.

I believe we should see AI for what it is: an incredibly powerful tool that helps us work more efficiently and creatively. As with any tool, it is up to us to use it responsibly. We should be aware of the challenge and actively contribute to ensuring that AI is used sustainably and for the benefit of all. This also means that we must learn when the use of AI makes sense and when it does not. So let's use AI for good – and let's start pragmatically with your website.

2.4 THE FOUR GOLDEN RULES FOR WORKING WITH AI

To make the most of the possibilities offered by AI, you need to know how to use it effectively. There are a few basic principles that apply to all AI, which I have summarised in these ***four golden rules***:

1. AI is a partner, not a pack mule.
2. AI needs good guidance.
3. AI can lead you astray.
4. No AI fits into every team.

FIGURE 2.5 The four golden rules for working with AI.

You can also work with AI without knowing these rules. An important reason for the great success of language models and image AI is their easy accessibility via natural language. But if you just jump in, you'll get random results and have to go back and forth several times until you're satisfied. There's also a risk that the AI will take a wrong turn early on. Once it's on the wrong track, it's often very difficult to get it back on the right one. That's why these four golden rules will help you avoid this detour. Specifically:

1. **AI is a partner, not a pack mule**: Don't just burden the AI with your task. It will dutifully set off and complete it immediately, but the result will then be largely left to chance. You will get much better results if you treat the AI as an equal partner with whom you communicate on an equal footing. Especially with language models, you will have more success in conversation than with pure commands.
2. **AI needs good guidance**: Always think about what result you expect and communicate this clearly to the AI. Unclear instructions lead to unexpected results.
3. **AI can lead you astray**: It's written under almost every chat window, and yet we can easily forget it because the answers are often so good: AI makes mistakes. To be on the safe side, you should check everything when it really matters.
4. **No AI fits into every team**: It is clear to everyone that image AI cannot write a report for us. But we first need to find out what capabilities the respective versions of the language models have and what types of images can be created with the different image AIs.

We often hear that AI is like an overzealous intern fresh out of university: it knows a lot, fulfils every task, but has no idea about the processes. This comparison does not do justice to either interns or AIs. AIs are completely useless at the simplest tasks, but on the other hand, they can do some things better than professionals with many years of experience. If we view AI solely as an intern, we expect too much of it in everyday tasks and, on the other hand, greatly underestimate it.

2.5 LEARNING TO THINK LIKE A MACHINE

If you understand how AIs work in principle, you will have a better understanding of what the respective AI can and cannot do. This section, therefore, summarises the most important things you need to know about this topic.

AI has been around for decades, and the recommendations we see in online shops ("People who bought this also bought this"), the control of washing machines and weather forecasts have all been using AI for a long time. Today, when we think of AI, we mainly think of ***generative models*** because their results are so easy to grasp, i.e. image-generating AIs such as Midjourney and Dall-E and ***large language models*** (***LLMs***) such as ChatGPT, Claude, Gemini or Le Chat.

What all these models have in common is that they are trained with a large amount of data – image AIs with images, language models with text. The content is not stored in a database, but rather the models only remember the probabilities of possible connections. This is well known, yet it is the key to understanding how AI works. The data used to train an AI determines what the AI "knows". It largely determines the connections and conclusions – and thus also which biases and stereotypes are adopted from the training data. I could train an image AI only with paintings by Rembrandt, and it would deliver completely different results than an AI that I train only with images by Picasso. Similarly, a language model that I have fed only with poems will give completely different answers than one that has only seen legal texts. However, modern models are always provided with a broad base of training data.

Unlike an algorithm that processes a clearly defined sequence of instructions, AIs can respond flexibly to different inputs. This is also based on so-called ***neural networks***, which process information in interconnected nodes – inspired by the networking of neurons in the brain. Instead of a fixed programmed logic, the AI learns by analysing the training data and recognising patterns and correlations in it. Using statistical methods, it calculates probabilities. This allows the AI to improve with experience and respond flexibly to different inputs without every response having to be pre-programmed. This also means that results can emerge that surprise even those who programmed the AI.

For example, if an AI is asked to complete the sentence "The sun is shining on the ...", it "knows" from its training data that the word "sky" often follows, sometimes "horizon" and much less frequently "morning", but almost never "end". Every time we give it this task, it chooses from these possibilities. This is where chance comes into play. If the AI always only added the most probable option, we would always get the same result. Instead, by setting the so-called ***temperature***, you can determine how creative the AI should be, i.e. how strongly it should consider less likely possibilities. At low values, the AI stays close to what it has learnt in the training data. At high temperatures, more unusual combinations become possible – but these are not always meaningful.

After the initial training, the AI is then taught how to interact with humans in a helpful and safe manner. To do this, humans systematically provide feedback on its responses and evaluate which ones are useful and appropriate and which ones are not. This is called ***reinforcement learning***. In this phase, safety precautions, known as ***guardrails***, are also built in: the AI learns to adhere to certain boundaries, e.g. to not give instructions for dangerous or illegal actions, to protect sensitive personal information or to avoid disrespectful, discriminatory or disturbing content. These boundaries are set both through training with examples and through hard-coded rules.

2.6 WHAT AI IS GOOD AT

You should not leave financial decisions or therapy plans to AI. But it can help you in many ways when creating websites. Above all, it can provide quantity. So if you want to generate lots of ideas, AI can make it much easier: 30 suggestions for catchy headlines? No problem! Thirteen ideas for illustrating a dry topic? Developed in seconds. Forty

FIGURE 2.6 Unlike in conventional language models, with image AI you can adjust the temperature to get wild results easily: in Midjourney, for example, by turning up the "Weirdness" slider. "Variety" was also set to the maximum for this example in order to generate four images that were as different as possible. (Figure created using Midjourney v6.1.)

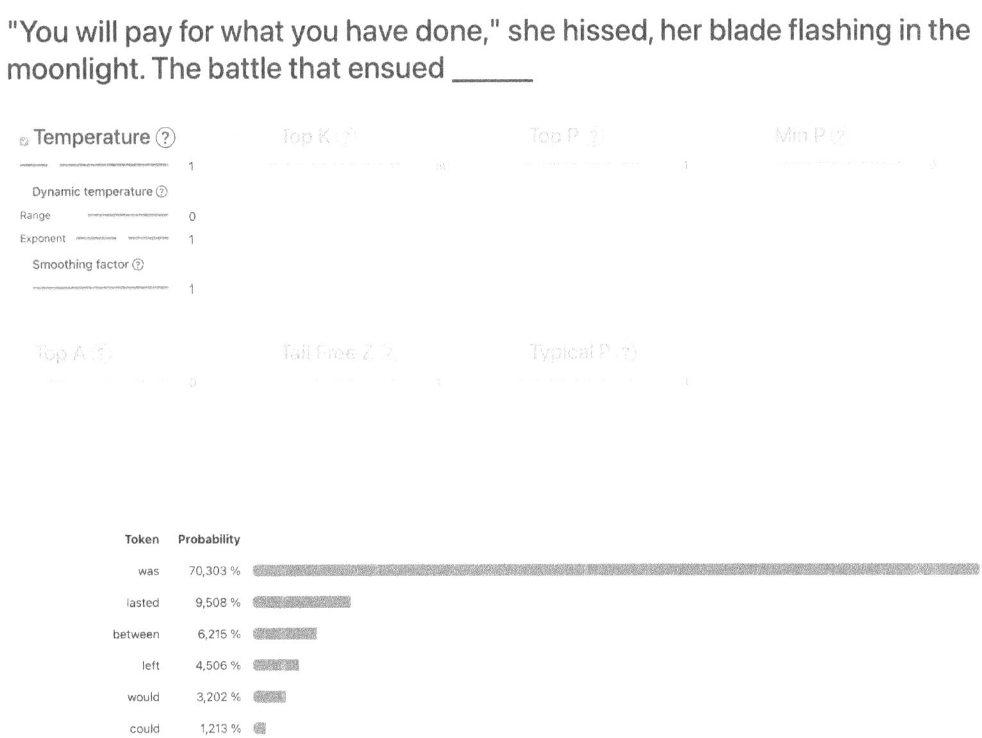

FIGURE 2.7 In this simulation, you can see how temperature influences the choice of the next word in language models. There are many more settings you can adjust, but to understand the other parameters, we would have to delve deep into the technology (bnfr.de/ai088).

suggestions for a product name? Available at the touch of a button. You can even generate and evaluate variants of a new business idea using a language model. It is also very helpful in finding information about the competition and analysing their respective strengths and weaknesses.

AI is a machine, so it also finds it easy to organise, structure and arrange. It can comb through large amounts of text for specific information or bring a whole jumble of documents into a clear structure, summarise the essentials of a 100-page document and prepare it for different target groups.

AI can also easily handle routine tasks such as creating image descriptions, summarising texts or organising document versions. And it can help to review existing texts from other perspectives, such as from the perspective of someone who is just beginning to deal with the topic. Or from the perspective of a professional with years of experience in the field. AI can also help you create social media strategies, campaigns or posts that are tailored precisely to your target audience.

2.7 THE MARE PRINCIPLE FOR PROMPTS

There are a few tricks you can use to get the most out of AI. When communicating with a LLM such as ChatGPT or Claude, it helps to stick to certain patterns when writing instructions, i.e. prompts. This ensures that you don't forget any information. According to golden rule number 2 (AI needs good guidance), you ensure that the AI runs in the right direction and ultimately delivers what you had in mind.

One such trick is the MARE principle, which you can use to structure a prompt. It consists of four parts: Motivation, Ask, Result, Example and two optional additions: Role and Additional Information. The easiest way to understand this is with a practical example:

- Motivation: I am working on a blog post on the topic of [x].
- Ask: Create an [outline, idea, draft, …].
- Result: The finished text should be approximately [y] words long.
- Example: Here is a sample text that clearly shows how the reader is addressed and their level: […]
- Role: You are an experienced [z] who […]
- Additional information: […]

The last two points are optional; you only need them sometimes. Specifying a role can help make the result look more professional. If you can't think of a meaningful role for a prompt, leave it out. And in the additional information, feel free to tell the prompt what background information the AI should know, e.g. to avoid repetitions or to copy a text that you already have as a description. A prompt formulated according to this pattern might look like this:

FIGURE 2.8 The MARE principle for prompting.

EXAMPLE PROMPT: MARE

Motivation: I am working on a blog post on the topic of "Writing blog posts with AI" for my website, where I advertise my seminars on the topic.
Ask: Create a draft for it.
Result: The finished text should be about 600 words long.
Example: Here is a sample text that clarifies how the reader is addressed and the level of language used: "What is good documentation? Documentation that is read in its entirety? Hardly. There are many possible definitions, but one of the most convincing is: good documentation is documentation that helps. And what helps the reader? That's not so easy to answer. This brings us to the really difficult question [...]".
Role: You are an experienced social media editor who knows exactly which topics interest the target group of content marketing professionals.

Additional information: I have already covered topics such as editing with AI, topic finding with AI and target group research with AI in recent posts.

The prompt to copy: bnfr.de/ai089

Follow the MARE principle to avoid going back and forth multiple times. And you ensure that the AI is headed in the right direction from the start. Sometimes it happens that you can no longer dissuade the AI from a path it took at the beginning of your conversation. You can avoid this by giving clear instructions (according to golden rule number 2: AI needs good guidance).

Theoretically, you can also omit the example, in which case we refer to ***zero-shot prompting***. In contrast to this is ***one-shot*** or ***few-shot prompting***, where you give the AI one example (one-shot) or several (few-shot). Zero-shot prompting is not generally bad, because sometimes examples are not necessary or you just want to find out what the typical solution to a task is.

The MARE principle is not helpful for image AIs. Here, you have to use other tactics, mainly because you cannot converse with image AIs. All information must be packed into a single prompt. Adjustments are possible, but far more laborious than with language models. Tips on how to prompt image models optionally can be found in the relevant sections in Chapter 7, "Step 5: Efficiently Creating Content That Inspires".

2.8 HAVING GOOD CONVERSATIONS WITH AI

When using language models, there are a few more tips to help you get better results. Many people are unaware of these because they think they know how to converse. However, conversing with an AI is not the same as conversing with a human being. Remember the golden rule number 1: AI is a partner, not a pack mule. Treat AI as a real counterpart and tell it all the important background information. Do not use it like a search engine. If you only type in a short question, the AI will lack the necessary context and the answer will be very general. Unfortunately, AI does not ask follow-up questions, but simply answers as best it can. So you have to actively lead the conversation and communicate clearly if you want the AI to ask questions.

Another thing you need to explicitly discourage the AI from doing is its tendency to say yes to everything. The AI always agrees with you at first, thinks your ideas are great and refrains from criticism. If you want clear feedback, you have to ask for it.

You don't have to try to write the perfect prompt either. It helps to think things through and follow the MARE principle. But the big advantage is that you can develop solutions together with the AI in conversation. And the AI finds this much easier. Otherwise, it tends to do things as quickly as possible. The example above with the blog post works, and you quickly get an acceptable result. But you can do even better: the way to do this is through what is known as ***chain of thought*** prompting. This involves telling the AI exactly what steps it should take, or asking it to clearly state the steps it has taken, for example: "Write a blog post on the topic of 'writing blog posts with AI'. Explain your reasoning for each step: Why did you choose certain aspects? How did you arrive at your conclusions? What alternatives did you consider and why did you reject them?" This allows the AI to work more systematically and often deliver better results – and you can understand them much better.

Prompt chaining, i.e. building a prompt chain, is also effective. To write a blog post that matches your existing ones, you can follow five steps:

1. Give the AI one of your articles and let it analyse the writing style.
2. Upload the list of topics you have covered in your blog over the last few months to the AI.
3. Ask the AI to develop ideas that fit these topics.
4. Select one and ask the AI to create an outline for it.
5. Adjust it and only then ask it to write the post.

This takes longer, but leads to a much better result. And you have much more control, because you can already exert a strong influence when selecting the idea and also when adapting the outline.

Many AIs have their own apps or programmes that you can install on your smartphone or PC. They are often more convenient to use than the web version. Some of

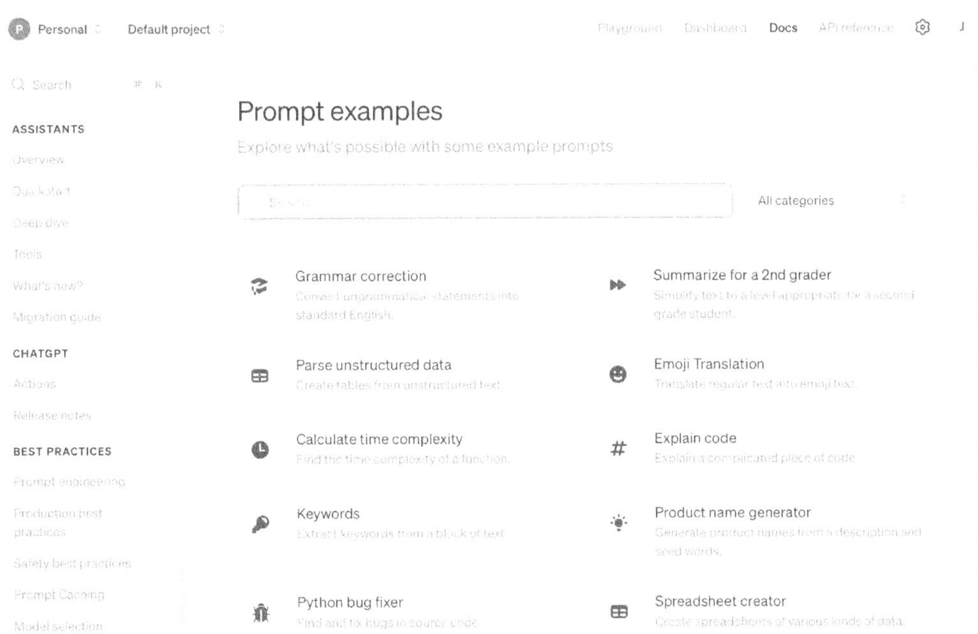

FIGURE 2.9 OpenAI has an extensive, very helpful collection of prompt ideas: bnfr.de/ai090 (Source: Screenshot taken from openai.com.)

these apps offer the option of chatting with the AI, which is sometimes much faster than typing text into a chat. It is best to search for the programmes on the provider's website, not directly in the App Store or Google Store, as there are countless programmes there that also use the respective AI but have built their own interface around it, which is often less effective, out of date or even requires an additional payment.

It is also worth looking into the additional functions and customisation options of the AI that you use frequently. With many of them, you can specify how you would like to communicate and what the responses should look like.

In Claude and ChatGPT, you can collect your chats in so-called ***projects***, while Perplexity offers ***spaces***. This makes the chat history clearer, but above all, it has the great advantage that all chats have access to the information you have previously entered in this area (or that you store here).

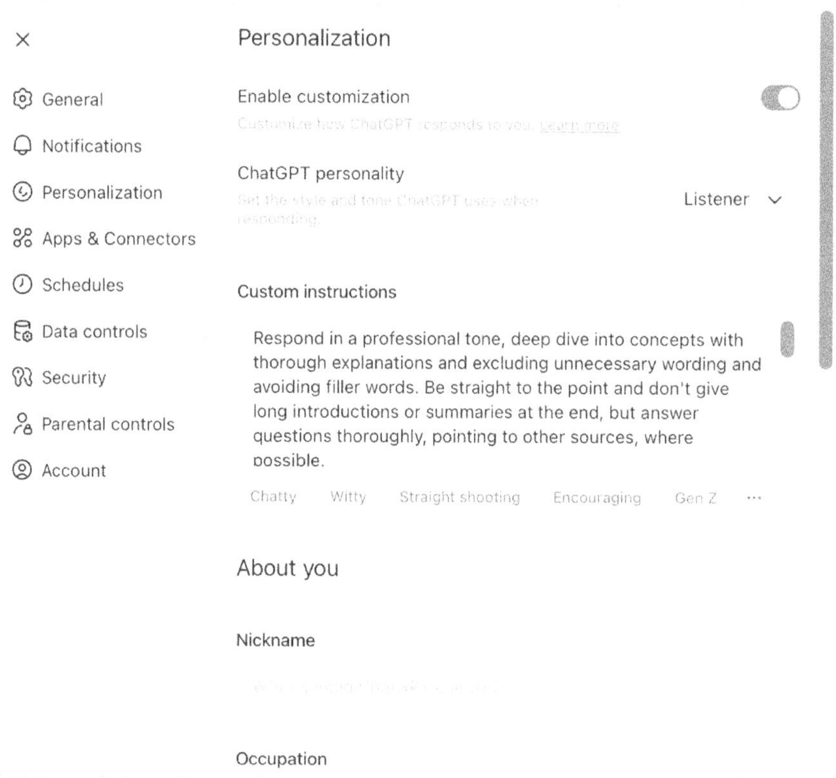

FIGURE 2.10 In ChatGPT, under "Settings • Personalisation", I have specified, for example, that I would like to be addressed informally and that the AI should get to the point as quickly as possible. (Source: Screenshot taken from ChatGPT.)

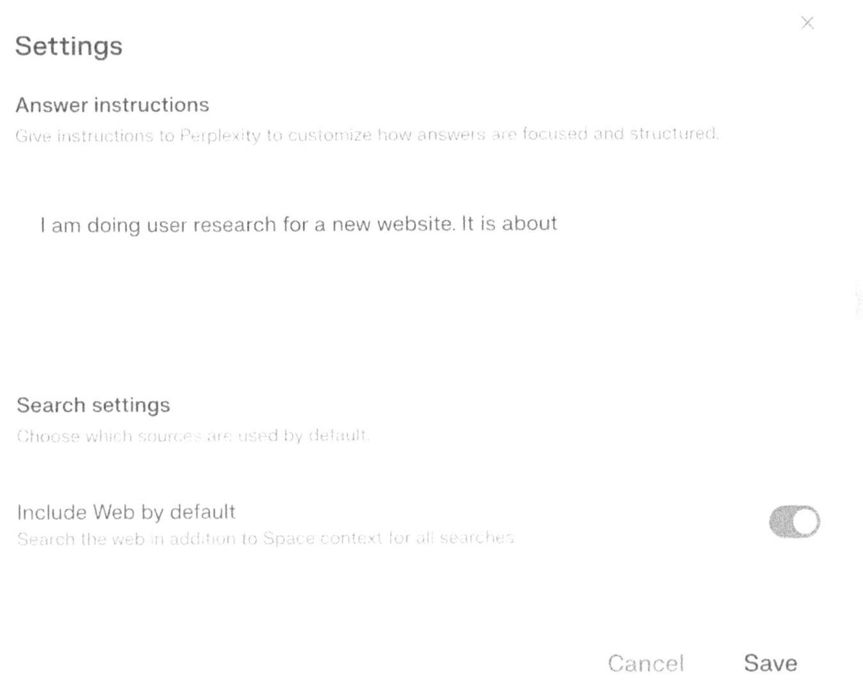

FIGURE 2.11 In Perplexity, you can give instructions for each space on how the AI should respond. The more precise your specifications are here, the better the results will be. (Source: Screenshot taken from Perplexity.)

2.9 AI IN THE IMPLEMENTATION PROCESS FOR YOUR WEBSITE

If you want to develop a website with AI, there are AIs available to assist you with almost every step, from the initial idea to promoting the finished site.

When planning, a language model such as ChatGPT can help you define the goals of your website and the **target groups** you want to address. Together, you analyse the competition and their strengths and weaknesses and find your own niche. Perplexity or another language model with internet access can help you **choose your tools**. You can work out the **structure** of your website and the individual pages, as well as the navigation, together with a service such as Claude.

When it comes to **programming**, it depends on what you have decided on in terms of tool selection. If it is a website builder such as Squarespace, then you work with their respective AI. If you programme yourself, then GitHub Copilot or ChatGPT are at your side.

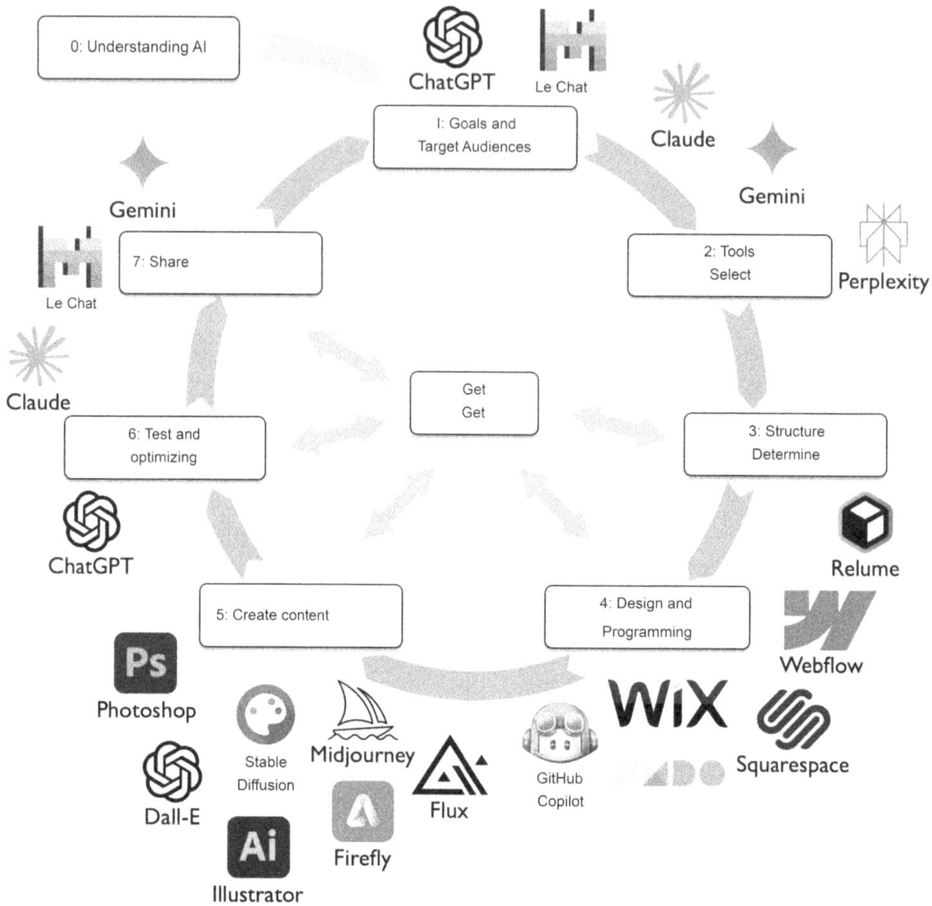

FIGURE 2.12 Various AI tools can help you throughout the entire website creation process.

Language models are again a valuable aid when structuring, planning, formulating and improving texts and other **content**. AI can develop a wide variety of headlines and teaser texts, from which you can then select the best version. Image AI such as Midjourney, but also Adobe Illustrator, are indispensable for creating photos, illustrations and icons. The coding capabilities of language models are very useful for **testing and optimisation**. Finally, when it comes to **publicity**, they also support you in search engine optimisation, for example, by creating page descriptions that are helpful for both search engines and humans. You can also use these AIs to plan your social media strategy and have the content created right away.

Taken together, these AI tools greatly simplify the entire creation process because they cover the most important steps: goal setting, idea and concept, structure, design and code basis, as well as compelling content. Even with little prior experience, you can create a website that impresses. The tools allow you to concentrate fully on the finer details that make your website not only unique but also successful thanks to its perfect target group orientation. The interaction of tools such as ChatGPT, GitHub Copilot, Midjourney, Relume and the AI of website builders such as Wix ensures a significantly faster project workflow. This gives you the space you need to focus on the essentials: a compact, appealing online presence that does justice to your own ideas. The AIs are creative tools that make suggestions and take care of routine tasks for you – you still have the final say and make the important decisions.

The various tools complement each other well and open up new design possibilities even for people without programming skills. With these digital assistants at your side, you can get started right away – so take the next step and start with the following chapter, where you can plan the route to your website success.

CHAPTER 3

Step 1

Plan the Route – Identify Goals and Target Groups

> A website can be much more than just a digital business card. Set the right course from the outset so that you don't end up at a dead end and invest your time optimally. AI can create a website in seconds – but you have to make sure it's a good one.

When you go on a trip, you can of course just set off. You'll get somewhere eventually. But if we have a destination in mind, it makes sense to think about where we want to go before we set off. It's no different with a website. A website can be created quickly – with the tools available to us today; it takes just a few minutes. But then it's just *any old* website. If you want to achieve something with your website, you should first think carefully about what exactly that is and how you can best (and most quickly) achieve your goal.

Remember the most serious mistake we can make when using AI, as mentioned in the last chapter? Simply doing things faster. Because that means we're squandering the decisive competitive advantage that AI can give us. If our competitors use AI to do things *better*, then we're at a disadvantage if we've only used AI to be *faster*. So be sure to take the time to do these first four fundamental things if you want to create a successful website:

1. Set goals
2. Find your target audience
3. Fulfil wishes
4. Research the competition

DOI: 10.1201/9781003726708-3

FIGURE 3.1 If you just start running, you'll get somewhere – but it's better to plan your journey to a successful website a little more thoroughly.

Tackle one task at a time. The great thing is that thanks to AI, this is much more fun and the results are much better than without AI.

3.1 THE RIGHT AI FOR YOUR CONCEPT

You have a choice between an overwhelming number of different AIs. In Chapter 4, "Step 2: Select the Best Tools", you will learn about the ones that will help you with programming and design. But first, you need AI that supports you in your conceptual work. Since this initially consists of text work, language models (more specifically, large language models, or LLMs for short) are the first choice.

Possible options include:

- ChatGPT (from OpenAI)
- Claude (from Anthropic)

- Gemini (from Google)
- Microsoft Copilot (based on ChatGPT and others)
- Le Chat (from Mistral AI)
- R1 (by DeepSeek)

These well-known AIs have a free basic version that you can use to try them out. However, if you want to work with them seriously, you should consider subscribing to one of them. This costs around £20 per month and allows you to use the best current versions from each provider. In addition, you are not or hardly limited in the number of queries, which otherwise makes working with the free versions very tedious and slows you down unnecessarily.

Which system you use is a matter of taste; the differences are minor and change frequently. Sometimes one provider is ahead in certain tasks, sometimes another. Don't let this drive you crazy; in practice, these differences hardly matter. Try one or two providers and stick with the one you get along with best.

A note on Copilot from Microsoft: use of this AI is included with an Office subscription for personal use. The version integrated into Office 365 is specially adapted for working with documents. To use Copilot independently and more freely, open this link: copilot.microsoft.com

FREE ALTERNATIVES: LLAMA AND MIXTRAL

In addition to the well-known commercial LLMs, there are open-source systems, i.e. those where the program code is freely accessible. The best known are ***Llama*** from Facebook operator Meta and ***Mixtral*** from the French company Mistral AI.

The catch: only the code is free. Running AI costs storage space, computing time and electricity. And the large, powerful LLMs are so demanding that they can hardly run on the PCs we have on our desks for office work, writing and image processing. We therefore often have to settle for stripped-down versions. Even with practical tools to help, installing LLMs remains a challenge. If you want to give it a go, I've put together a few tips from my own experience, which you can read at: bnfr.de/ai001

Alternatively, you can search for providers who offer free online access to such models. You can find my current recommendations here: bnfr.de/ai002

However, my advice is: only go down this route if you really cannot afford to spend any money and have a lot of time and a spirit of research. Then it can be fun and also lead to decent results. Normally, however, it is better to spend the few pounds it costs to pay for a contemporary model for a month. You won't need any longer than that to complete your site.

3.2 FOR THOSE IN A HURRY: CREATE A CONCEPT WITH THE CUSTOM GPT "WEBSITE KONZEPTOR"

For initial experiments, you can try out whether you can achieve a result that is sufficient for you with a ***custom GPT***. A custom GPT is a version of ChatGPT that has been given additional instructions. Anyone with a ChatGPT subscription can create such an assistant and, if desired, make it publicly available, even to those without a subscription. I have done this for you and tried to teach the AI as much as possible about what a good website concept looks like (see Figure 3.3). That was the easy part. The more difficult part is getting the assistant to guide you, the user, through the concept development process as effectively as possible. If you try to take detours or ask questions that are not related to website development ChatGPT will readily follow you. Try it out.

WEBSITE OUTLINE IN 5 MINUTES WITH THE WEBSITE KONZEPTOR

Go to bnfr.de/ai003 and chat with the chatbot as you would with other AIs. The beginning of your conversation will look something like this, as shown in Figure 3.2.

FIGURE 3.2 The beginning of a conversation with the custom GPT "Website Konzeptor". (Figure created using ChatGPT 4o (custom GPT).)

You then gradually provide the Konzeptor with the information it needs to create a well-founded concept. You can see the whole thing in action in the video, which you can access via the QR code and link in this box.

You can use the Website Konzeptor if you have a free ChatGPT account. However, the number of questions and answers you can ask and receive is limited. You can continue the conversation at any time by returning to your account later and selecting the conversation in the left-hand sidebar. With a paid subscription, you do not have this restriction.

https://bnfr.de/ai004

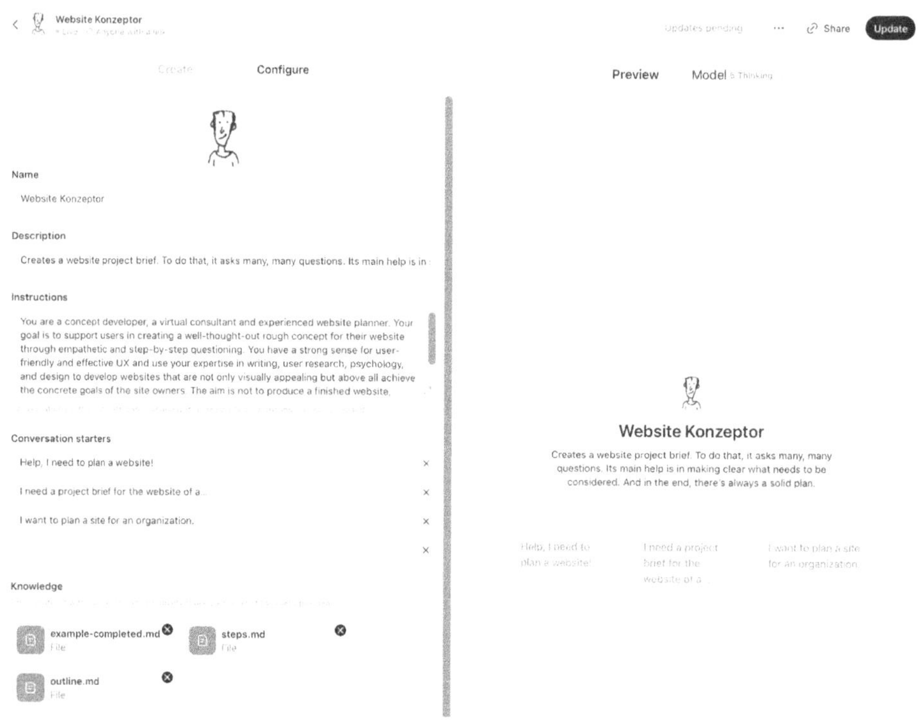

FIGURE 3.3 Here you can see where the "Website Konzeptor" gets its knowledge from: the notes and uploaded documents with examples and precise instructions. (Figure created using ChatGPT 4o.)

3.3 SETTING GOALS

Whether you work with the Website Konzeptor or not, the first step that must never be overlooked is setting goals. If the website is for yourself, you need to think about what you want to achieve with the site. If the site is for others, then your task is exactly the same as the first thing the Konzeptor does: you need to tease out what their goals are. It is surprising how difficult some people find this. When I ask people who commission a website from me what they want to achieve with it, I often get answers like, “I want to be found”, or “I need a good website”. If we settle for such answers, the result will be a mediocre site at best, and probably even a bad one.

3.3.1 More than Just a Good Website

When is a website bad? When it looks ugly? I would say no. It is bad when it does not fulfil its purpose. And the purpose of a website is not to provide something or to inform about something. Its purpose is almost always to sell, even for sites that do not have an integrated shop. For example, when I publish an article on my site as a freelancer, I do so to help you and many others create better websites. But ultimately, of course, I am just as interested in getting you excited about my books or getting a job from you.

FIGURE 3.4 A bad website? Not at all. This site is highly successful precisely because it is ugly. It does this to clearly stand out from the competition.

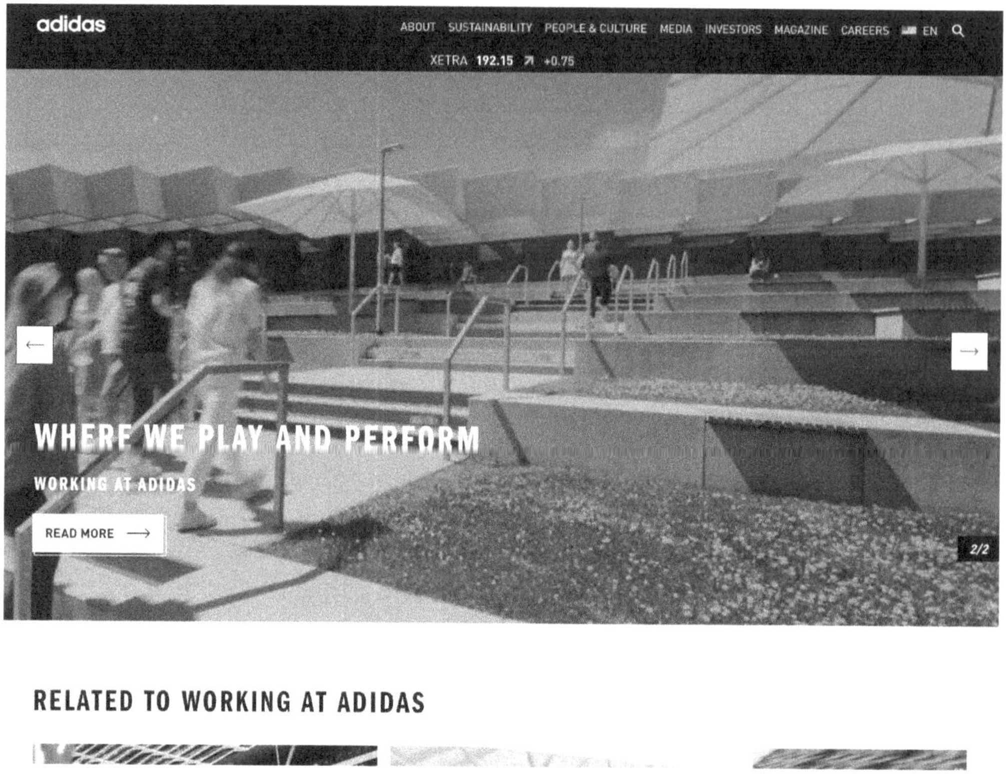

FIGURE 3.5 Like many large companies, Adidas has a shop website (Adidas.co.uk) and, in addition, this corporate website (adidas-group.com), which primarily presents the brand, promotes the company's shares and aims to recruit staff.

A brand website such as coca-cola.com does not sell anything directly via the website. And yet the company is all about money. The entire site is designed to ensure that the world's most successful soft drink remains so. To this end, the site features competitions, but above all a wealth of information about the product and the company. The ultimate goal is for us to perceive the brand positively and want to buy the product.

The aim of the Airbnb and Booking websites is not to arrange accommodation. Their aim is to earn money through commission payments from landlords. Similarly, Netflix and Disney do not want to provide videos, but rather to attract and retain viewers who pay a monthly subscription. Even a non-profit organisation almost always has financial goals with its website, such as collecting donations, but also attracting people to participate and persuading them to join the cause. As you can see, the goal here is not to provide information, but to convince people.

This change in perspective is particularly crucial when working with AI. Because if you tell the AI to write a text with information about the purpose of the organisation, that is exactly what it will do. Often, the result is a decent text. But the catch is that no one reads this decent text, and if they do, they simply take note of it. But if you tell the AI that you need a text that convinces readers of the association's cause, then a completely different text is created. With a little practice in prompting, it is a text that actually convinces people.

3.3.2 Examples of Good Goal Definitions

When designing a website, almost everyone sticks to the site's offerings or functions. Let's take the specification "provide information" as an example and go one step further and ask why we are doing this. A company wants to use this information to generate sales, for example. A non-profit organisation wants to use the information to bring about a change in behaviour, recruit volunteers or collect donations. These actual goals are what you absolutely must work out in the first step. So think as specifically as possible about what the goal of the website you are currently creating is. This could be:

- Selling products, subscriptions or services
- Enabling online appointments or reservations
- Acquiring new orders with the help of an impressive portfolio
- Generating qualified customer enquiries (leads)
- Arranging appointments for test drives, viewings or presentations (e.g. car dealers, estate agents, service providers)
- Increase brand awareness and company image
- Gain donations and support
- Bring about behavioural changes (e.g. personal health, social change)
- Exert political or social influence (e.g. associations, interest groups, trade unions, political parties)
- Promote education, skills development and innovation (e.g. schools, universities, research institutions)
- Strengthen customer loyalty (e.g. by providing support and information, building a community, increasing brand loyalty)
- Saving costs through automation (e.g. digital processing of business processes, reducing support workload by answering questions)
- Attract employees, increase employer attractiveness and reduce recruitment costs

Take enough time to clearly define your goal(s). This will help you determine what to put on your website and what content and features you need. It will also save you unnecessary work during implementation.

Let's assume, for example, that you want to create a website for an affordable barber shop. If the barber's goal for the website is not to make appointments, then you only need to inform visitors about the opening hours and address. This saves you the trouble of programming an online booking system.

But not all companies and websites have goals that are so easy to define. Sometimes it's not that easy to figure out. However, AI can be a great help with this task: go to the AI of your choice, e.g. Claude or ChatGPT, and use it as a conversation partner to discuss your business goals. This works best if you assign a clear role to the AI. Remember the ***MARE principle*** from Section 2.7 and define your motivation, the AI's task and the desired result in the prompt and give an example. In this case, you also assign a role to the AI:

EXAMPLE PROMPT: WORK OUT THE GOAL DEFINITION

Motivation: I want to create a website that specifically supports the strategic business goals of the operators – be it strengthening the brand, increasing customer loyalty or direct sales. To do this, I want to clearly define these overarching goals before we begin with the detailed design.

Ask: Ask me one question after another to fully identify the strategic goals of the website. Make sure you distinguish between goals (e.g. customer loyalty) and means (e.g. provision of information) and, if necessary, give me examples to help me formulate them clearly. If necessary, give me examples or food for thought to help me formulate my goals clearly. For now, we are only concerned with the goals of the operators. We will leave the target group and their wishes aside for the time being.

Result: At the end of the question and answer session, there should be a concise summary that contains all the important goals of my website and serves as a basis for the concept.

Example: An example of an overarching goal could be: "Strengthen the brand by increasing visitors' trust in the company". An example of a means to this end could be: "Present testimonials and case studies on the website".

Role: You are an experienced concept developer with a focus on strategic website development who asks questions in an understanding manner and provides support with examples. Always ask questions to make everything as concrete as possible.

The prompt to copy: bnfr.de/ai005

When defining your goals, it is important to stay true to yourself at first. At this stage, it is not yet about who you want to address and what these people want. First, you need to consider what *you* want, because this will determine who your potential customers are and which needs of these target groups you want to or can serve. This is exactly what we will focus on in the next step.

3.3.3 What Are the Operators' Wishes?

Once you have worked out the objectives with the website operators, ask them (or yourself, if you are the operator) whether they already have an idea of the website's appearance, content and functions. Don't do this first, because most people are not website professionals. For a good concept, you should first focus on the goals so that you (as well as the AIs) can assess whether the ideas expressed regarding content and functions are useful or necessary to achieve the site's goals.

3.3.4 What Already Exists?

Now collect everything that already exists, such as:

- Existing logo
- Design specifications (corporate design)
- Letterhead templates, business cards
- Flyers, brochures, posters and other advertising materials
- Current or past advertising campaigns
- Social media presence and posts
- Image material, photographs and videos
- Product information and catalogues
- Company profile and history
- Contact details and legal notice information
- Existing texts and other content for the website
- Customer references (testimonials)
- Information about the competition

3.4 FIND YOUR TARGET AUDIENCE

Now you know exactly what the website should achieve. That is the website's raison d'être, its purpose. Now we are ready to look at who you want to target with the website. The more precisely you address this, the better the website will achieve its goals.

Sometimes the target audience is very easy to define: if we stick with our barber shop example, the target audience is men of all ages who want a simple haircut and don't want to spend too much on it. But we have a problem here too: the target audience is very broadly defined. The broader the target audience, the more difficult it is to appeal to everyone equally. It's like inviting people to dinner: if you have vegans and meat lovers on your guest list, planning the menu becomes a challenge. It's much easier if you only invite people with similar preferences. And yet, of course, it is possible to satisfy different target groups – you just have to put in a little more effort. For our affordable barber shop, we could narrow down the target group to men between the ages of 18 and 70 who do not value special styling, trendy hairstyles or additional services such as head massages or beard care. We can also narrow down the target group geographically to men who live within walking distance of the barber shop.

Thought for 7s

Working men aged 20–67 who want quick, no-fuss, affordable haircuts with minimal waiting. They value efficiency and reliable quality, are price-conscious, and prefer a pragmatic service without add-ons.

How big is this target group in Hamburg?

Thought for 2m 13s

Short answer: ~490,000 men in Hamburg fit that target group.

Breakdown and method:

- Male population 20–67 in Hamburg (2023): 607,868. Summed from the official age-by-sex table (male counts per 1-year band). Statistik Nord +2
- Of these, ages 20–64: 582,163; ages 65–67: 25,705. Statistik Nord +2
- Male employment rate (20–64) in Hamburg (2024): 82.8%. → ≈ 482,000 employed men 20–64. Statistikportal
- Employment among 65–67 is lower; using a conservative 20–36% band (OECD range for 65–69 men), adds roughly 5,000–9,000. Midpoint (~30%) adds ~7,700. → ≈ 487,000–491,000 employed men 20–67; midpoint ≈ **490,000.** OECD

Context check: Hamburg total employment in 2024 was 1.36 million, so this target is ~36% of all workers. Statistik Nord

Assumptions:

- You asked for "working men"; I applied employment rates, not just population.
- 65–67 uses a national/ OECD proxy; if you need a Hamburg-specific rate for 65–67, I can refine with microcensus extracts.

Sources

FIGURE 3.6 AI with internet access such as ChatGPT (shown here) or Le Chat and Perplexity can help estimate target group sizes with up-to-date information. (Figure created using ChatGPT 4o.)

Consider the following for your site: Who do you want to address? Be realistic and don't simply define your target group so that it is as large as possible. You can also define a primary target group and one or more secondary target groups. This allows you to determine for the next steps that the website should first and foremost perfectly address the primary target group. The site should work as well as possible for all other target groups, but compromises can be made here if necessary. This is because target groups sometimes have different expectations and wishes – we will come to these in the next step. But first, find out who your target groups are. Use your preferred chat AI again:

EXAMPLE PROMPT: TARGET GROUP DEFINITION

I am planning to create a website for the hair salon "Haarte Zeiten Hamburg". The salon offers quick, affordable haircuts for men who value efficiency and fair prices. Help me define the target group more precisely. What specific characteristics and demographic features could this target group have?

The prompt to copy: bnfr.de/ai006

When evaluating the AI's responses, remember golden rule number 3: AI can lead you astray. In our case of target group definition, we see that the AI reflects the clichés with which it was trained: when it comes to target groups, it usually stops at 60 years of age or even earlier. Where does this come from? Most men over 60 still have some hair on their heads that needs to be cut. The reason for the young customers can be found in the training data. The AI gives its answers based on the information it has received. And simply reflects what it has read. Some of the data itself is also out of date. Firstly, it may have been a while since the AI was trained. Secondly, the AI is not only trained with current information, but with data from the internet (which has been around for decades) and possibly from specialist literature that is even older.

Recent studies show that the internet is becoming increasingly important for older people. In the US, 76% of people aged 65 and older own a smartphone, and 70% have a broadband subscription. The figure for the total population is 80% and for smartphone ownership 90%. In the UK, the figures are just a bit lower: 67% of people aged 65 and over own a smartphone, and 79% have internet access at home, compared to 89% and 94% for the total population. You can find more information on internet usage and media consumption here: bnfr.de/ai007

We also need to be careful with clichés and prejudices about younger people: just because someone is under 20 does not mean that he or she can automatically handle modern technology with ease. In this age group, there are people who are slower than others, just as there are people over 70 who are faster than others. And as a general rule, an application that is easy to use for people who are less tech-savvy will also offer a better user experience for techies.

When defining our target group, we must be careful to think beyond clichés and break away from outdated demographic templates. This is not only in keeping with the times but also economically wise: if, for example, we target tech products exclusively at young, male users or design beauty products only for fair-skinned women under 40, we are wasting valuable market potential. Many purchasing decisions no longer follow traditional patterns – people of all ages, genders and cultural backgrounds are interested in a wide variety of products and services. By taking different lifestyles into account, you can create authentic websites that appeal to and reach people in all their diversity.

3.5 FULFILLING WISHES – HUMAN-CENTRED DEVELOPMENT

Now you know who you want to appeal to. Next, find out what these people expect, what they want, how you can offer them something, and, ideally, how you can even inspire them. The best way to do this is through user research. This provides a range of methods that focus on future users, i.e. people from your target groups. This type of website and application development is now considered the only true approach, known as ***human-centred*** design (HCD). Previously, the term used was user-centred design (UCD), but not everyone who is influenced by an application is a direct user. And there are also people who do not yet use your application, whom you also want to address. Ultimately, we do not want to reduce people to their role as users, but rather take them into account with all their needs, emotions, values and life contexts. So you put the people who determine the success or failure of your site at the centre of development.

To do this, you seek direct contact with the people for whom you want to create the website. For larger projects, this phase of user research takes weeks or even months. Especially if you want to develop a groundbreaking new product, there is no way around it. However, most projects are significantly less innovative – we don't need to launch a major research project for our hairdresser's website or for an online shop selling gift cards. But even here, it is crucial for a successful website to at least engage with potential customers to some extent. If I had to build a website for our hairdresser, I would visit him in his shop. I would sit down and observe the men who come to him for a haircut and talk briefly with a few of them. Among other things, I would ask them:

- How often do you come here?
- Why here and not to another hairdresser?
- Do you sometimes go elsewhere?
- Suppose this shop closed down: how would you choose a new hairdresser?
- What do you like best and least about this shop?

As you can see, it's all about the individual customer, their needs and preferences.

3.5.1 Having Good Conversations with the Target Group

When talking to potential users, there is a lot that can go wrong, because people are not purely rational beings. Our feelings and unconscious psychological mechanisms influence our behaviour more than we would like to admit. Legendary advertising expert David Ogilvy said over 50 years ago:

> People don't think what they feel, don't say what they think and don't do what they say.

This means that it is not so easy to have good conversations with people about their desires. Many of us say that healthy eating is important to us. But when there is a burger on the menu, we are more likely to order it than a healthy salad. Another example: in surveys, 25% of Germans say they "always" or "often" buy organic meat. But its market share is only around 4%. And when it comes to technology, we often opt for a product with more features, even if we have no idea whether we actually need them. And when it comes to prestige items, expensive brands or even luxury products, it becomes virtually impossible to find out the real reasons for a purchase in conversation. We are also not always aware of *why* we feel a certain way. For example, we may have an uneasy feeling when using a website and quickly leave it again. In conversation, complaints are often made about "the design". However, it turns out that even if the design is not changed, but the navigation uses clearer, easier-to-understand terms in the future, the complaints about the design disappear and the site's objectives are better achieved.

Questions about purchase intent or future use are particularly difficult. We can save ourselves the question "Would you buy this?" Especially if the product does not yet exist, every person I talk to has a different idea of it in their head. But even if I can show a nice prototype and even make a statement about the cost, even then the purchase intention is purely hypothetical. It is really only suitable as a conversation starter, not as a forecasting tool.

Questions about *actual* behaviour are much better, e.g.: "When was the last time you bought a greeting card?" or "Which features of the app did you use the last time you opened Instagram?" or "How much money did you spend on streaming music last month?" and "Do you remember buying your last smartphone: what criteria were decisive for you in choosing the model you opted for?"

We can usually answer such questions well and correctly. Of course, we may sometimes be mistaken or embarrassed by the answer and therefore fib a little, but this happens relatively rarely. And if we prepare our questions well, we can take countermeasures even in such cases. This ties in with the saying by the great author and expert in usage research, ***Erika Hall***:

> Often, a direct question is the worst way to get a true and useful answer to that very question.

FIGURE 3.7 Leading questions are not always so easy to recognise. This makes it difficult to have good conversations with the target group.

This statement is initially confusing. Isn't conversation always the best way to learn more about the people for whom I am developing my website? Conversation is a very good way, yes, but I have to choose my questions carefully. Let's take the example of an online shop for handmade greeting cards that I want to open. If I want to know whether the idea is good, I can ask a few people who belong to the target group I have defined. Most will answer: Yes, great, great idea. But will they actually buy from me? I have no idea. It is therefore much better to create a simple prototype for my shop and show it to people. Before I ask them questions, I give them a task. For example:

> You've heard from a friend about an online shop for greeting cards. Now you're invited to your aunt's birthday and want to buy a card for her. So you go to the site and look around.

Then you watch the person and let them comment on what they perceive, what they think and feel about it. This is already a small usability test; you can find out more about this method in Chapter 8, "Step 6: Test and Optimise". If your test person says they would buy a particular card, or says they would stop now, the test is over and you can ask your questions. Now the person has a clear picture of what the site could look like and what exactly is being offered. Perhaps prices have already been mentioned. Now it makes sense to ask whether the person would buy – this is still not particularly reliable, but it leads to an exciting discussion about what might still be missing to convince people.

Erika Hall, quoted above, has written a very good book on this subject: "Just Enough Research". It is definitely worth reading, as is *The Mom Test* by ***Rob Fitzpatrick***. Here you can read how to learn the most from conversations with potential users. The subtitle of the book sums up exactly what it's about: "How to talk to customers & learn if your business is a good idea when everyone is lying to you". Although the book is primarily intended for those starting a business, the techniques it describes are extremely helpful for anyone who wants to get to know their target groups better.

3.5.2 Developing Good Questions with AI

AI is a wonderful tool for preparing us for conversations with potential users. For good results, take the time to prepare your prompt according to the MARE principle. Let's take a fitness programme with on-site classes and online videos as an example. In this case, it could look like this:

EXAMPLE PROMPT: PREPARE INTERVIEW QUESTIONS

Motivation: I plan to conduct interviews with people who have experience with online fitness courses or on-site group courses to better understand their perspectives and needs. The goal is to design an excellent website that offers such services.

Ask: Create a list of 10 to 20 specific interview questions that target the following topics:

1. Experiences with online fitness courses
2. Experiences and impressions of on-site group courses
3. Motivations and reasons for choosing a provider
4. Suggestions and requests for improving the offerings

Result: The questions should be precise, open-ended and neutral in order to encourage honest and detailed answers. They should focus as much as possible on specific experiences rather than future, theoretical wishes.

Example: Here is an example of the style and level of detail: "What did you particularly like about your last online fitness course?"

The prompt to copy: bnfr.de/ai_008

During the interviews, it is particularly important to answer the following questions:

- What is the current usage behaviour? (In the fitness example: How often do people do which sports? What equipment do they use? Do they go to the gym? Do they use fitness trackers or apps?)
- Why do they behave this way? (What role do time and cost play? What about their motivation? Why do they exercise in the first place?)

- What annoys them? (These are the so-called ***pain points***.)
- What inspires them?
- What devices and communication channels do they use? (Smartwatches, trackers, apps, Instagram, WhatsApp, email, newsletters, etc.)

You may not need to conduct these interviews yourself if there are already people who can answer all these questions for you. Think, for example, of colleagues who work in support or sales. They usually have daily contact with the people you want to address. For smaller projects, talk to the clients about their customers; for our fitness site, talk to the fitness coaches who commissioned the site about the people who take their courses.

Ideally, for a large project, you should talk to people from the target group until you have learnt everything you can. We rarely have that luxury, so we usually only conduct three to five interviews, which is a good start.

3.5.3 Evaluate Results with AI

Once you have completed your conversations with the target groups, you can review and structure them using AI. AI systems that allow you to upload documents are particularly suitable for this purpose. Transfer your usage research documentation as a PDF, Word or text file and let the AI summarise it. Transcription is also possible, i.e. a verbatim transcription of what was said from a recording. There are several programmes available for the latter. ***Whisper*** runs locally on your computer and is free of charge. Unfortunately, the system does not have a graphical user interface, which makes it somewhat difficult to use. For macOS, there are programmes (which are not expensive) that provide this feature: ***MacWhisper*** and ***Whisper Transcription***.

Let's take a look at how the free online AI service ***NotebookLM*** evaluates the finished transcripts:

1. Go to https://notebooklm.google.com. If you do not yet have a (free) Google account, you will need to create one. If you do not want to do this, you can also work in a similar way with ***ChatGPT projects*** or ***Perplexity spaces***.
2. Upload the documents with your usage research notes. NotebookLM supports TXT files and PDFs, but not Word documents (**.docx**). However, you can also upload audio or video files if you have recorded your interviews.
3. Use the plus icon in the **Sources** section to enter URLs of websites that offer further relevant background information on your topic.
4. Now, in the **Studio** section, you can create various documents, which are called *notes* in NotebookLM (see Figure 3.8). The **Reports** section is particularly useful, as it provides templates for a **Briefing doc** or for special document types like **User Personas**.

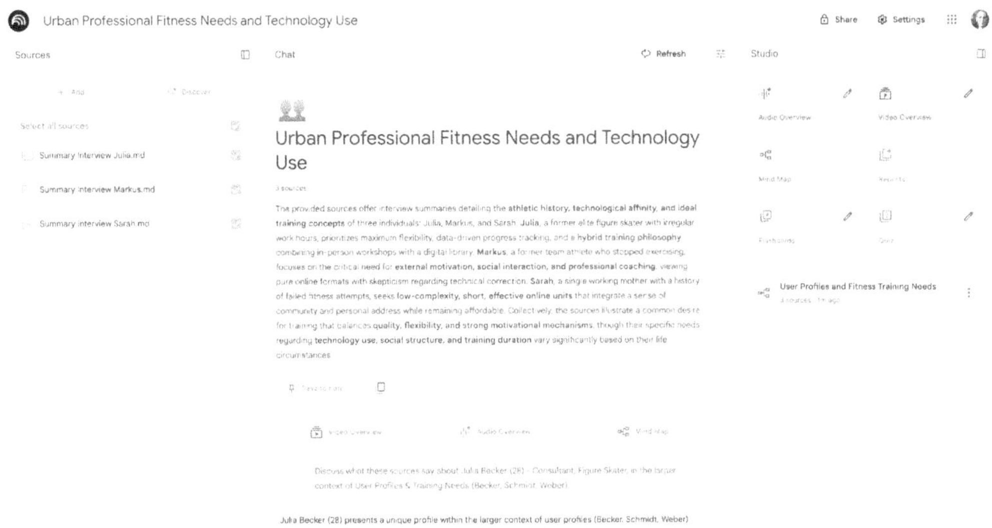

FIGURE 3.8 In NotebookLM, you upload documents, then you can ask questions about them, request summaries and even listen to a discussion between two voices that presents the content in a well-prepared manner ("Audio Overview"). (Figure created using NotebookLM.)

5. Even more exciting is that you can talk to the AI about the documents at the bottom. Try questions like: "What are the typical problems reported by users?"
6. Finally, there is another very impressive feature: the **Audio Overview**. Click on **Generate**, and after a moment, the AI will create a conversation that sounds like a professional radio discussion. The speakers discuss what they have gleaned from the documents you have uploaded.

If you don't want to create a Google account, you can also use another AI of your choice, as mentioned above. ChatGPT and Claude, for example, also allow you to upload your own documents in most versions.

CAUTION REGARDING DATA PROTECTION

Before you submit documents or even just text from the clipboard to an AI, always take a moment to consider whether this is acceptable from a data protection perspective. This is especially important if the AI is not running locally on your computer, but on a third-party server. In general, personal data may only be processed with the express consent of the person concerned. The European General Data Protection Regulation (GDPR) in particular sets strict requirements.

It is best to anonymise all documents relating to usage research, even the initial notes. This means removing any possibility of establishing a connection between the real person and your records. Personal data includes, among other things, name, date of birth, gender, address, email and IP address – in short, any information that can be traced back to a person.

You must also take care not to pass on any confidential information such as passwords, trade secrets or internal documents to any AI.

And very importantly, you must inform every person from whom you collect data about what you are doing with the data. They have the right to find out from you at any time what data you have stored about them and can request that you delete it permanently.

3.5.4 AI as a Representative of the Target Group

Once you have the results of the usage research, you can also ask the AI to play the role of the user. This gives you the opportunity to talk to an imaginary person from the target group. This feels amazingly good because you have unlimited time to talk to people, you can ask any question, no matter how indiscreet, and you never have to worry about annoying or hurting anyone.

However, I do see one danger here: if you don't know how AI works, it's easy to fall into the trap of humanising it. Because AI chats with us so easily and naturally, we take its answers at face value. Even though we are fully aware that AI can hallucinate, i.e., invent answers. And, even more problematic: AI is programmed to tend to agree with us, practically never contradict us and never question anything. If we ask AI whether a certain feature is a good idea for our website, it will almost always think our ideas are great, no matter how useless they are.

EXAMPLE PROMPT: CONVERSATION WITH A PERSON FROM THE TARGET GROUP

You are a simulated version of a person based on information from an interview I conducted with real users. I have uploaded this as a file. Respond as accurately as possible using information from the interview. If relevant information is not available, state this honestly and do not speculate. The aim of the conversation is to gain insights into the person's most important needs, preferences and challenges. Start the conversation with: "Hello, I'm [name]. What would you like to know about me?" Make sure your answers mimic the tone and style of the person interviewed in terms of language, statements and style.

If you cannot find any information about a question in the data, respond with: "This information is not available".

Copy prompt: bnfr.de/ai009

3.5.5 Using AI to Research the Target Group

There isn't always time to conduct valuable, real interviews with the target group. Sometimes it's also not possible because you don't have access to such people. In such cases, you can fall back on what the internet and AI know about users. If you do this, you just need to be aware that the information is not first-hand and may be distorted and incomplete. And yet, if you engage with your target audience in this way, you are

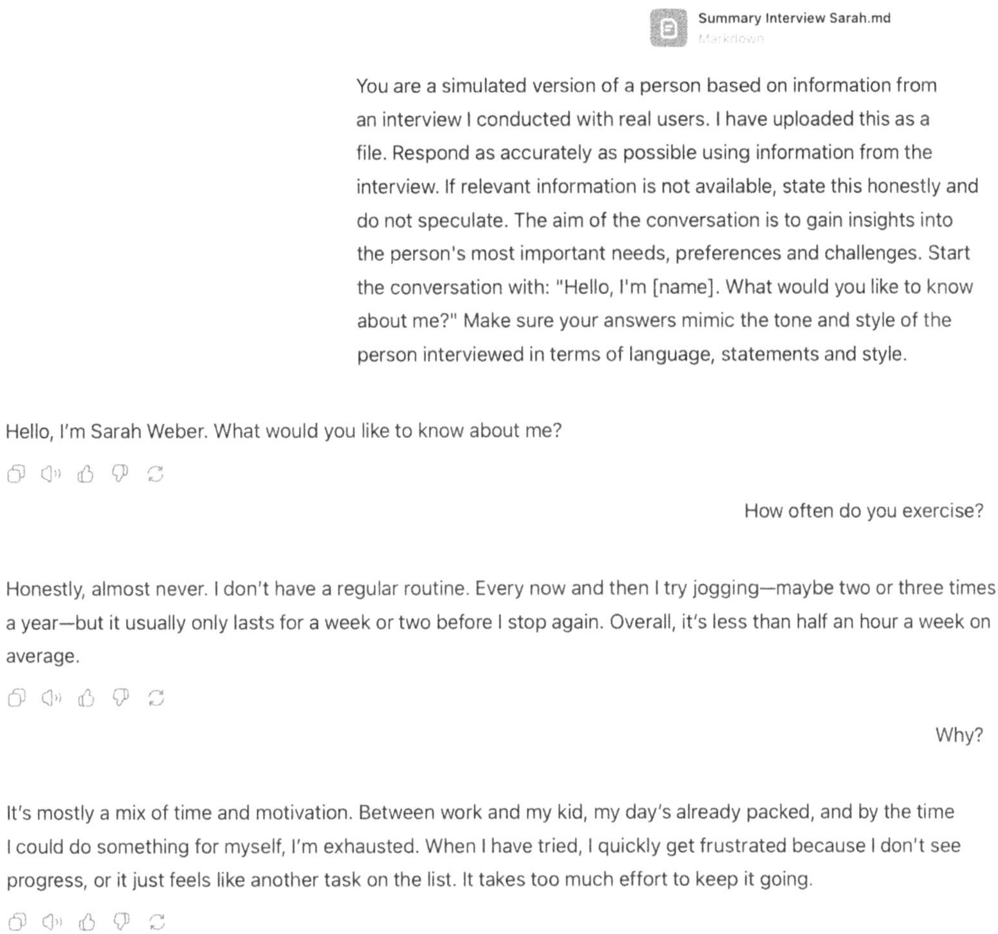

FIGURE 3.9 Excerpt from a conversation with a virtual user in ChatGPT. A summary of an interview was uploaded to the chat beforehand. (Figure created using ChatGPT 4o.)

way ahead of the majority of other website operators who don't think about who their target audience is, let alone what they want. So, for example, use ChatGPT and do your research (in my case, Perplexity didn't work so well for this application) by structuring your prompt according to the MARE principle:

EXAMPLE PROMPT: RESEARCH EXPERIENCES TARGET AUDIENCE

Motivation: I am working on market research for a fitness website. It offers online fitness videos and on-site group courses (e.g. running groups, outdoor training or ice skating workshops). The aim is to understand the experiences, needs and problems of potential users in order to tailor the website to them in the best possible way.

Ask: Create a comprehensive analysis based on real experience reports found on the web and trends covering the following aspects:

1. Advantages and challenges of online fitness courses
2. Strengths and appreciated aspects of local group courses
3. Typical motivations for attending fitness courses
4. Annoyances and unmet needs of participants

Result: The finished analysis should be approximately 1,000 words long and list the best sources with URLs.

Example: Exercisers appreciate the combination of online and on-site classes, mainly because of the flexibility in terms of time. This allows them to catch up on training sessions if they have missed the face-to-face session (source: www.fitness beispielsite.de).

The prompt to copy: bnfr.de/ai010

3.5.6 AI as a Generator of the Target Group

You should exercise great caution when using a supposedly very practical method: usage research with people invented by AI (***synthetic users***). Some do this with ChatGPT, and there are also specialised providers, but they probably only use adapted versions of an existing language model (e.g. syntheticusers.com, instantpersonas.com).

In principle, the idea is not wrong: LLMs such as ChatGPT contain vast amounts of data about people. So they contain knowledge about the questions, concerns, needs and characteristics of all of us. It therefore makes sense to use this data to create super-realistic personas. It seems tempting to replace costly and time-consuming user research with a quick and inexpensive method. However, the big problem with this is that although the information is part of the LLMs, it is not possible to read it out like from a database. An LLM is not an archive of data from usage research. Just as a person who has studied history can say that Charlemagne was crowned emperor in 800 AD, but cannot say in which book or on which page they read this, it is impossible for AI to provide a source reference for human usage experiences. It remains unclear whether a piece of information comes from a high-quality scientific publication, an obscure internet forum or a novel.

An LLM always works with probabilities. Put simply, it only completes a text. For example, if I give ChatGPT the beginning of a sentence:

All birds fly …

I will almost always get the answer:

… high!

FIGURE 3.10 For some, it's an enticing idea: user research without users, as offered by the website syntheticusers.com.

Not in every case – because LLMs have a kind of random generator built in to keep them creative. But ultimately, LLMs move from one probability to the next. This enables them to make general statements, describe commonly known facts well and reproduce what "everyone" knows. The result is always a generalisation. You need to keep this in mind when using LLMs to create personas. In addition, AIs cannot help but adopt and reinforce existing biases found in the data on which they are based. This poses a significant risk of reproducing stereotypical and discriminatory patterns.

3.5.7 Why Usage Research Remains Irreplaceable (At Least for Now)

Real interviews with people from the target group go far beyond superficialities and enable a deep understanding that is then reflected in the quality of the website concept. AI tools are very useful for summarising and processing data, as well as for formulating and embellishing personas (see next section).

They are also a tool for theoretically engaging with the target group in advance. This is better than not engaging with the target group at all. However, it should only be the starting point for genuine usage research. Otherwise, we run the risk of developing websites that only suit generalised, watered-down pseudo-personas, but do not appeal to real people.

3.6 DESIGNING PERSONAS

Once you know enough about your target groups, you can use this information to create so-called ***personas***. Personas are fictional short portraits of the people for whom you are creating the website. Even if you really intend to keep these people in mind throughout the design and development process, it is difficult to do so as long as the users remain abstract. It is easier for everyone involved if they have specific people in mind. Personas work because we humans are more interested in people than in data; after all, we are social beings. You can do without personas for small projects, but they are helpful even here.

In personas, you describe a few people who represent your target group. How old are they? What gender are they? What is their education, what is their job? How much money do they earn? Where do they live? Do they have a family? What are their habits? What are their demands? What are their hobbies? How experienced are they with technology? What are their design preferences? What do they read? What TV series do they watch? Which competing websites or apps do they use? You don't always have to answer all these questions. Decide for yourself which ones are relevant to your particular case.

3.6.1 What Do Personas Look Like?

Personas serve to bring the term "target group" to life, i.e. to give you and other project participants a picture of the people for whom you are creating the site. To do this, you need a photo that represents the respective person. They are given a name, a gender and all the characteristics that are important for your product. In general, it makes sense to use bullet points, short texts and small diagrams when presenting personas so that the content can be quickly understood. This is because personas are a working tool, a tool that everyone in the development team works with on a daily basis.

3.6.2 Avoiding the Bias Trap

More and more website professionals are omitting gender and age from personas. They argue that such characteristics promote stereotypical assumptions that are not part of the actual user experience. Instead, they advise us to focus on user behaviour data, motives, values and preferences – ultimately, these are the aspects we need to consider if we want to create a good website that is successful with users. However, this approach has the disadvantage that the personas remain somewhat abstract and it is not quite as easy to empathise with them. You can decide for yourself which approach you prefer – both are now common and successful.

3.6.3 How Many Personas Do I Need?

If your website has a clearly defined target group, it is sufficient to create two to three personas. If the target group is very heterogeneous, create one for each subgroup. However, you should never have more than eight personas, otherwise it will become

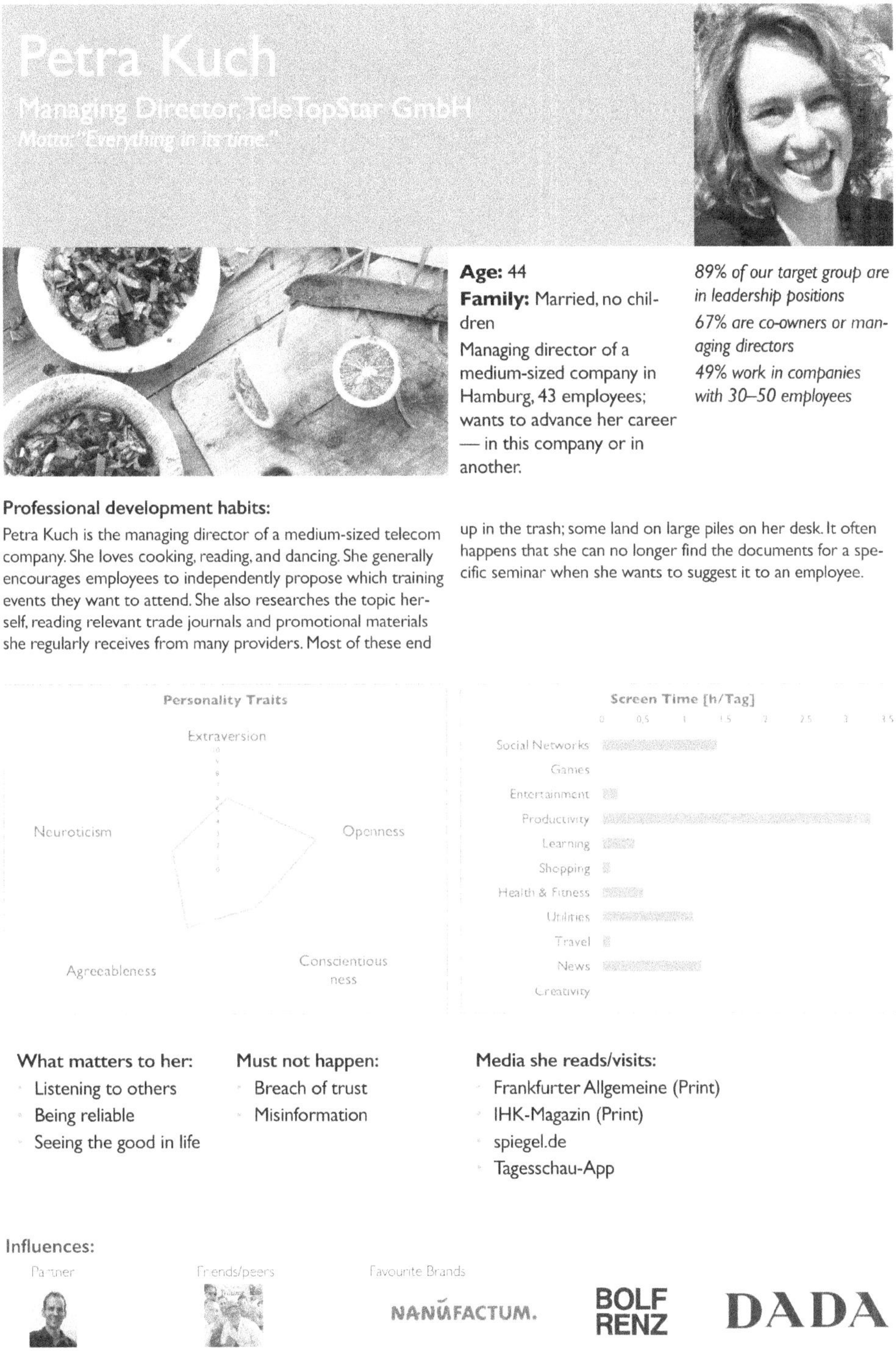

FIGURE 3.11 A persona should be clear and attractive to look at. Everyone should enjoy working with it.

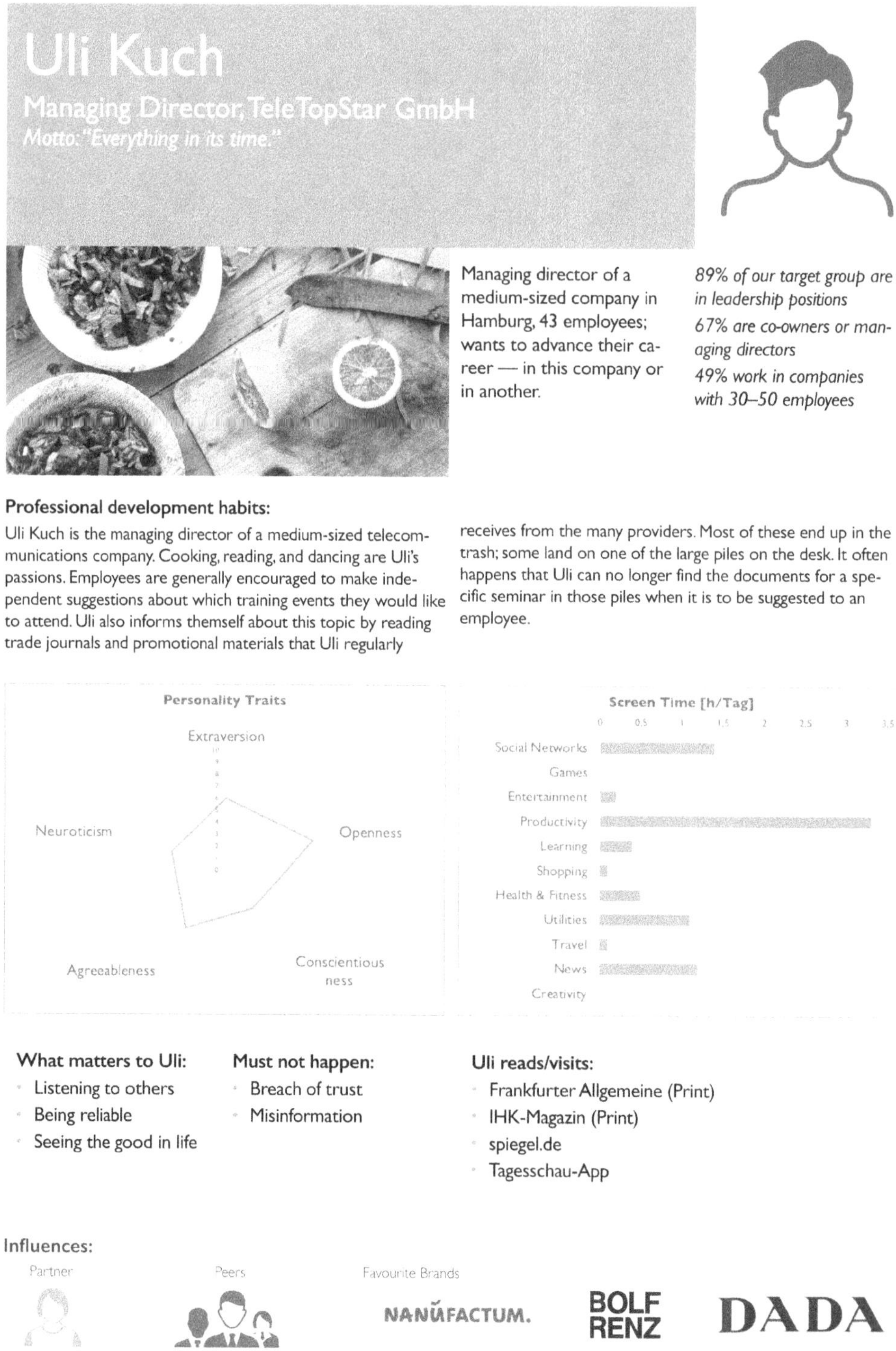

FIGURE 3.12 Persona without age, gender or photo. Even if it doesn't create a clear picture in your mind, it still helps you empathise with users.

confusing. Three to five are almost always sufficient – even if you are addressing many different target groups. A colleague of mine advised one of the largest online shops in my country, which sells practically everything from cordless screwdrivers to clothing, washing machines and houseplants. He convinced the web team to limit themselves to three personas, even though the target group is the complete population which shops online.

The more personas you have, the less effective they are at doing their job: helping everyone involved in the project to always keep in mind the people who are supposed to use the website, with their needs and habits.

3.7 RESEARCH THE COMPETITION

It's always worth taking a look at the competition. This is because existing websites determine what our target groups know and expect. And we can learn from other websites what probably works well – and what doesn't. Especially if you are not creating a website for yourself, you probably won't know exactly who your direct competitors are. This is where AI comes in handy again. It makes sense to choose one that has web access, so it can directly search for and analyse competitors' websites. We'll build the prompt again according to the MARE principle and use our hairdresser example:

EXAMPLE PROMPT: COMPETITOR ANALYSIS

Motivation: I want to know how my website compares to similar hairdressing salons in order to identify strengths, weaknesses and areas for improvement. The focus is on a service for men that offers quick, affordable and uncomplicated haircuts without any frills.

Task: Create a competitive analysis for hairdressing salons with a similar focus. Analyse up to five websites of salons that emphasise efficiency, fair prices and minimalist web design. Identify strengths, weaknesses and unique selling points and develop specific suggestions for improving my website.

Result: Deliver the results in a table with the following columns: Competitor (name/URL), strengths, weaknesses, unique selling points, suggestions for improvement.

Example: The analysis should be precise, understandable and without superfluous details. Example: "Clearly structured website without unnecessary content – weakness: no photos from the shop".

The prompt to copy: bnfr.de/ai011

The AI provides a whole lot of material. But don't settle for that. Ask for more examples or tell the AI if you are not satisfied with the selection. Or ask for an even longer list of competitor websites. But don't overdo it – it's easy to lose track of the amount of text that is generated, even. In this case, you can always ask the AI for a summary of the conversation so far.

Competitor (name / URL)	Strengths	Weaknesses	Unique selling points
Cutters — `https://cutters.no/en`	Clear value prop ("Cut time. Cut hair. Cut cost."), fixed price shown, drop-in model, live wait times via app. Site is simple and fast to scan.	Little local flavor (few shop/builder bios), imagery is generic; minimalism can feel impersonal.	15-minute haircut target; equal price regardless of gender; real-time queue + payment in app.
QB House — `https://qbhouse.sg/user-guide/how-to-order/`	Laser-focused service flow; hygiene is explicit; ultra-minimal content.	Duration promise isn't always explicit on local pages; design varies by region.	"Just-haircut" positioning; "air wash" (vacuum) instead of shampoo; global footprint and "less is more" philosophy.
kcuts — `https://www.k-cuts.com/`	The 10-minute promise is front and center; concept is crystal clear; minimal nav.	Homepage reads operational notices; tone can feel utilitarian; no simple visual price cue.	"10 minutes, no frills" Korean-style quick cuts; strong expectation-management around peak times.
Just Cuts — `https://www.justcuts.com.au/justyou/online-check-in`	Walk-in model + online Check-In with live wait times; very clear "no bookings" messaging.	Busier layout; promotions can distract from core "quick & simple" message.	App-based queueing and SMS updates; family check-ins; loyalty perks.
CUTMAN (Berlin) — `https://cutman-friseur.de/`	Transparent price cards; option to save by self-drying; multiple city locations; online booking.	Content-heavy page, many services dilute the "no-frills" narrative; not men-specific.	"Save if you self-dry" angle; straightforward "service & price" blocks; app mention.

FIGURE 3.13 The table with competing sites created by ChatGPT. The AI even recognises that some of them look generic. (Figure created using ChatGPT 4o.)

Or you can ask for a direct comparison of two competitors:

> Create a thorough competitive analysis between X and Y. What are their respective strengths and weaknesses? What can I expect as a customer if I get my hair cut there?

And if you want to really dig deep, try this:

> How can you help me create a competitive analysis for my website?

You will get a very long list of possibilities. Have everything you don't understand explained to you, and then work through the individual points that make sense to you together with the AI. In the end, you will have a good overview of what your target groups expect from your website, and perhaps even what you can do better than the competition to inspire visitors.

3.7.1 Creating a Smart Website Plan Based on the Research Results

Once you have completed your research, you will already have the most important building blocks for your website in your hands. You should write these down now so that you don't lose track of them (***website plan*** or ***outline***). You should also do this if you are creating the website entirely on your own. This will give you clear directions to your goal. Not least because you are never completely alone; with AI, you have a strong partner at your side, but one that needs good guidance from you in order to deliver the best results (golden rule number 2). You will then always have this guidance at your fingertips for the next steps by creating a written concept. With the help of AI, this doesn't have to take long.

A website plan should have a clear structure and contain all the essential elements to optimally address the target group and meet the client's requirements. It should include:

- Introduction and objectives: Description of the company/operator and the objectives of the website
- Target group: Definition of the primary users with important characteristics and their needs and wishes regarding the website (if applicable, also for the secondary target group(s))
- Content: Overview of the most important content to be included on the website (e.g. opening hours, address, photos, etc.)
- Design and style: Specifications for the visual design, appropriate to the brand and target group
- Technical requirements: Responsive design, performance and specific features, if necessary
- Maintenance and updates: Determination of how changes will be implemented in the future
- Measuring target achievement: Possible strategies for monitoring success (e.g. customer surveys, analysis of visitor numbers)
- Marketing and distribution: Measures to promote the website after launch

You can also use Konzeptor, which was already presented in Section 3.2, which guides you step by step through the concept development process. Or you can upload all the documents you already have and ask it to create a concept from them. The advantage is that the concept generator already has a predefined idea of what a good website concept should look like.

Go to bnfr.de/ai003 and upload all the information as a Word, text or PDF file. Then all you need is a prompt like the following:

EXAMPLE PROMPT: FORMULATE A WEBSITE CONCEPT WITH KONZEPTOR

Create a rough concept for a website. I have uploaded all the information I have on this to you. Analyse the uploaded documents thoroughly and answer all the questions you need answered in order to create a concept. Only ask questions if you cannot find the answer in the documents. When you are finished, output the rough concept.

The prompt to copy: bnfr.de/ai012

3.8 CLARIFY ORGANISATIONAL ISSUES – DEADLINES AND COSTS

There are a few things that AI cannot help you with: you need to clarify how much budget you have available and when the website should go live. If you are creating the site for yourself, it is still best to determine how much time you want to invest in the project and when you want to finish it.

However, AI can certainly help you to realistically estimate the development time. There is little you need to consider here – use the MARE principle to send your prompt to your favourite AI and chat with it a little to get a feel for the effort involved. A possible starting point is this prompt:

EXAMPLE PROMPT: ESTIMATING TIME AND EFFORT

Motivation: I am planning to create a website for the hair salon "Haarte Zeiten Hamburg". The website should convey a down-to-earth, honest atmosphere and focus on essential information (e.g. opening hours, address, photos of the salon, customer reviews). Additional features such as appointment bookings or a blog are not desired. The goal is a minimalist, yet appealing and functional website.

Ask: Create an estimate for the time and cost of the website in the areas of conception, design, programming and project management. Break each area down into realistic sub-steps, e.g. for conception into target group analysis, structure planning, etc. Add a column to the table for the respective deadline for each step, starting from a start date of X.X.2026.

Result: At the end, I expect a detailed table with the following information:

- Breakdown of steps per area (e.g. conception, design, programming, project management)
- Estimated time required (in hours) and hourly rate per step
- Total costs per step and area as well as total project costs
- End date for each step, based on realistic work scheduling

Example:

Area | Step | Time required (h) | Hourly rate (£) | Costs (£) | Deadline
Concept | Target group analysis | 5 | 90 | 450 | 0.0.2026
Structure planning | 5 | 80 | 400 | 00.00.2026

Role: You are an experienced project manager and web developer who creates realistic and easy-to-understand time and cost estimates.

Download prompt: bnfr.de/ai068

3.9 CONSULTATION WITH STAKEHOLDERS AND INTEREST GROUPS

Once you have the rough concept in hand, it is the ideal time to consult with all project participants, known as ***stakeholders***. The sooner you find out if something about your concept is not right or if someone wants important changes, the better. At this early stage, adjustments usually only mean minor text corrections. If, on the other hand, content has already been produced or even programmed, changes are significantly more time-consuming and costly. Take into account feedback from all relevant individuals and groups, e.g.:

- Key decision-makers/clients/operators of the site: They should approve the rough concept to ensure that they agree with the direction you describe in the concept.
- Employees/team: They can provide valuable input on the needs, planned functions and content of the website. They should also be able to identify with the website.
- Content providers: Anyone who writes texts or contributes films or photos
- Marketing or PR department or agency (if applicable): They ensure consistency with the brand message and may consider other aspects such as target group appeal and search engine optimisation (SEO).
- Customers (existing and potential): Although they are the main users of the website, it is difficult to involve them at this stage. They should have been involved in the brainstorming process beforehand and can provide feedback on drafts or prototypes later on.
- Technical service providers: Individuals or agencies who implement at least parts of the website technically.
- Hosting providers: They provide the infrastructure for the website.
- Consultants or coaches (e.g. UX professionals): They help to optimise user-friendliness and conversion rates (i.e. the rate at which visitors perform a desired action on the site).

3.10 CASE STUDIES OF SUCCESSFUL WEBSITES

Would you like to know what an exemplary concept for a successful website looks like? No problem at all. With the help of AI, you can quickly obtain the corresponding concept from any website that inspires you. To do this, use AI with web access and the ability to upload files, such as Le Chat or ChatGPT. You provide the AI with the structure of the concept of an uploaded file (link for my version at the end of the next box) and then start the research task, analysis and conception:

EXAMPLE PROMPT: WEBSITE ANALYSIS

Thoroughly analyse the website https://www.presentandcorrect.com and the competition for it. Then create a rough concept step by step that describes the goals of the site in detail. It should correspond to the content and structure of the uploaded file.

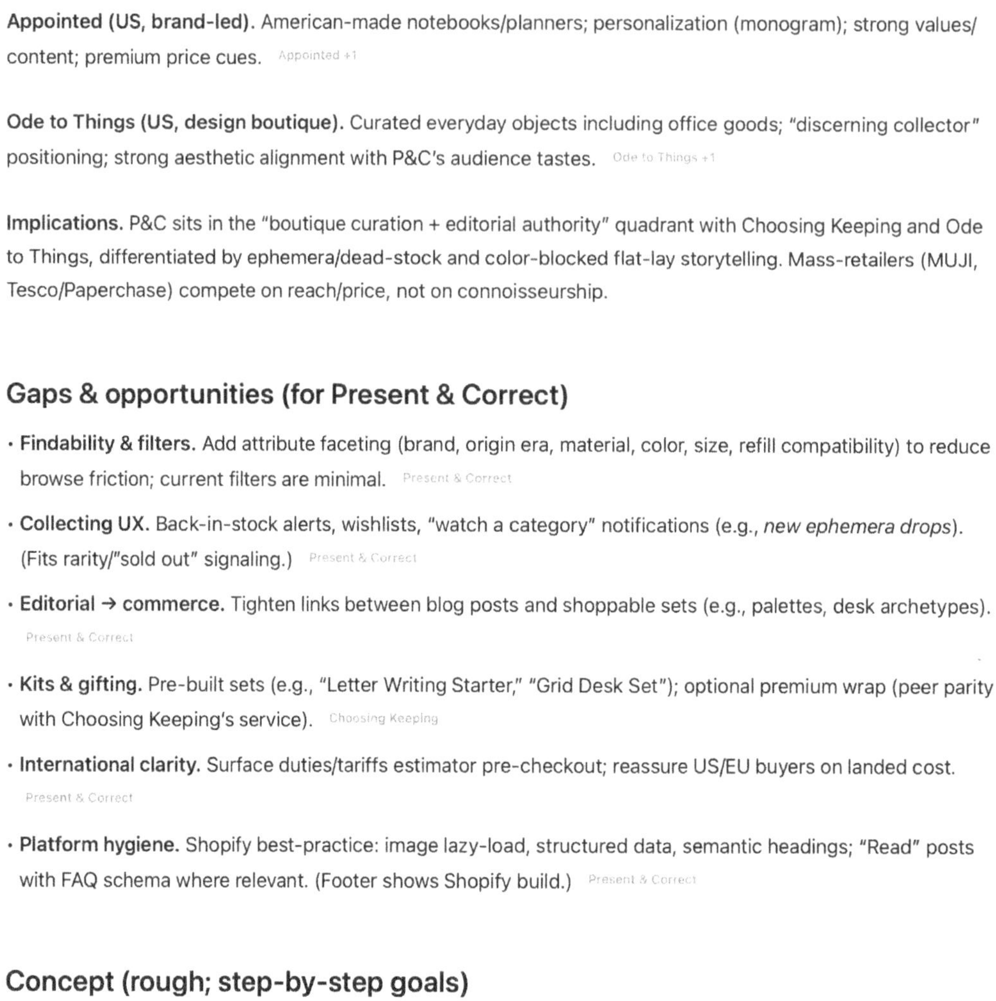

Appointed (US, brand-led). American-made notebooks/planners; personalization (monogram); strong values/content; premium price cues. Appointed +1

Ode to Things (US, design boutique). Curated everyday objects including office goods; "discerning collector" positioning; strong aesthetic alignment with P&C's audience tastes. Ode to Things +1

Implications. P&C sits in the "boutique curation + editorial authority" quadrant with Choosing Keeping and Ode to Things, differentiated by ephemera/dead-stock and color-blocked flat-lay storytelling. Mass-retailers (MUJI, Tesco/Paperchase) compete on reach/price, not on connoisseurship.

Gaps & opportunities (for Present & Correct)

- **Findability & filters.** Add attribute faceting (brand, origin era, material, color, size, refill compatibility) to reduce browse friction; current filters are minimal. Present & Correct
- **Collecting UX.** Back-in-stock alerts, wishlists, "watch a category" notifications (e.g., *new ephemera drops*). (Fits rarity/"sold out" signaling.) Present & Correct
- **Editorial → commerce.** Tighten links between blog posts and shoppable sets (e.g., palettes, desk archetypes). Present & Correct
- **Kits & gifting.** Pre-built sets (e.g., "Letter Writing Starter," "Grid Desk Set"); optional premium wrap (peer parity with Choosing Keeping's service). Choosing Keeping
- **International clarity.** Surface duties/tariffs estimator pre-checkout; reassure US/EU buyers on landed cost. Present & Correct
- **Platform hygiene.** Shopify best-practice: image lazy-load, structured data, semantic headings; "Read" posts with FAQ schema where relevant. (Footer shows Shopify build.) Present & Correct

Concept (rough; step-by-step goals)

FIGURE 3.14 Upon request, the AI provides a rough concept for any site and lists exactly where it obtained the information. (Figure created using ChatGPT 4o.)

The prompt and template for the rough concept are available for download at: bnfr.de/ai013

3.11 CHECKLIST FOR THE PLANNING PHASE

If you have reached this point, you have everything you need to start implementation. Ideally, you now have the following:

- Records/notes from target group research
- Personas for the target group(s)
- Documentation of the competitive analysis

- Budget and deadline for the website launch
- Logo and existing design materials (corporate identity)
- Product information and catalogues
- Company profile and history

Optional extras:

- Style guides for typography, colour palettes, etc.
- Documentation of social media presence
- Testimonials and customer references
- Previous marketing campaigns and materials
- Existing illustrations, photos and videos
- Project schedule and milestones
- Documentation of team roles and responsibilities

Now you're ready for the next step.

CHAPTER 4

Step 2

Select the Best Tools

Want to get started, but find the jungle of providers almost impenetrable? Here you'll find everything you need to decide on the right platform and the best AI providers – tailored to your budget and prior knowledge.

You now know what and who you want to reach with your website. With this important foundation, you can take the next step and determine *how* you want to implement the site technically. The range of options is huge. In this chapter, I will show you what I consider to be the best tools and help you choose the one that is best for you.

If you search the internet for AI support for creating websites, you will be inundated with tools that all promise professional websites in no time at all. If you want to delve deeper into this topic, you can take a look at my overview table of AI website builders and services, in which I have collected over 70 (!) providers, and the number is still growing: bnfr.de/ai042

Many of these providers are short-lived; every week I have to remove one or more from the list. They are bought out, give up or offer something else. Some providers are incredibly expensive, others cost nothing. The catch with most of them is that if the service is discontinued and your website is hosted there, in the worst case scenario it will disappear overnight. This means you will no longer be accessible on the web and, more importantly, all the work you put into creating the site will be lost. So my advice is: save yourself the search and choose one of the options I present below.

4.1 HOW MUCH DOES IT COST?

The question of how much a website costs is surprisingly difficult to answer. The main reason for this is that it depends very much on how you value your own working time or how much outside help you get. If you have a lot of time and ambition, you can create a great website with an investment of just a few pounds and keep it running for a few

DOI: 10.1201/9781003726708-4

FIGURE 4.1 There is a wide range of platforms and AIs to choose from – and they all promise more than they can deliver.

pounds a month. But if you're rather stingy with your own time, you'll resort to solutions that get you to your goal quickly – and that comes at a price. Let's start with Table 4.1 with the costs of getting your site online, which is still relatively easy.

If you are wondering which option is right for you, the next section will tell you exactly that. But first, let's look at the costs you will incur for using AI, which you can find in Table 4.2.

TABLE 4.1 Costs for Setting up and Operating a Website

Platform	Set-up Costs	Running Costs (Monthly)
Website builder (e.g. Wix, Squarespace)	£0–£50 (usually already included in the booking)	£5–£30 (depending on package and features)
Simple CMS set-up (WordPress or similar)	£0 (if you set it up yourself)	£5–20 (hosting, occasional plug-in fees)
Complex CMS (with multiple plug-ins)	£0 (if you set it up yourself)	£10–30 (hosting, possibly premium plug-ins, ongoing maintenance)
No-code/low-code platforms	£0 (if you set it up yourself)	£15–100 (platform fees, depending on requirements)
Custom development (HTML/CSS/JS)	£0 (if you do the programming yourself or instruct the AI to do it)	£5–20 (hosting)

TABLE 4.2 Costs for AI Use When Creating a Website

AI Tool/Category	Typical Costs (Monthly)	Use and Importance
Language model/LLM (e.g. ChatGPT, Claude)	£15–20	Website planning, brainstorming, copywriting – indispensable
Image generator (e.g. Midjourney, Flux at provider)	£10–20	Creating icons, logos, illustrations – very helpful
AI website generator (e.g. Relume)	Ca. £15	Creating sitemaps, wireframes (page sketches) – helpful
Coding assistant (e.g. GitHub Copilot)	£0–10	Support with coding – practical

TABLE 4.3 Recommended Packages You Need to Get Your Site Online

Package	Service	One-Time Costs (for One Month's Use, Can Be Cancelled Afterwards)	Ongoing Costs (Monthly)
Basic	LLM only (e.g. ChatGPT or Claude)	LLM approx. £18	£5–10 (hosting)
Standard	LLM + website builder (e.g. Wix/ Squarespace)	LLM approx. £18	Website builder approx. £15
Comfort	LLM + website builder + image generation (e.g. Midjourney)	LLM approx. £18 + image generation approx. £10 = £30	Construction kit approx. £15
Premium	LLM + image generation + Webflow + Relume	LLM approx. £18 + image generation approx. £10 + Webflow approx. £11 + Relume approx. £15 = £54	£5–10 (hosting) or £11 (Webflow)

Conclusion: You can run your own website from £5 per month, and you can have one created for you from £15 per month. If you concentrate on getting it done in one month, you only need a one-month subscription. But once you've seen what AI can do for you, you'll probably stick with the subscription anyway. And I personally think it's definitely worth booking a system like ***Webflow*** and ***Relume*** for an additional month (more on these in a moment), which will cost you an extra £40 for a month. This will give you such good results that you'll leave your competition far behind. And above all, working with it is a lot of fun – this is what the future looks like! My personal recommendation is the premium model from the overview in Table 4.3; it quickly pays for itself because you get a really good website.

4.2 WHICH TECHNICAL BASIS IS RIGHT FOR MY WEBSITE?

Essentially, you can choose between four ways to implement your website:

1. (AI) construction kits
2. Content management systems (CMS)
3. Low-code/no-code platforms
4. Classic in-house development (HTML, CSS, JS)

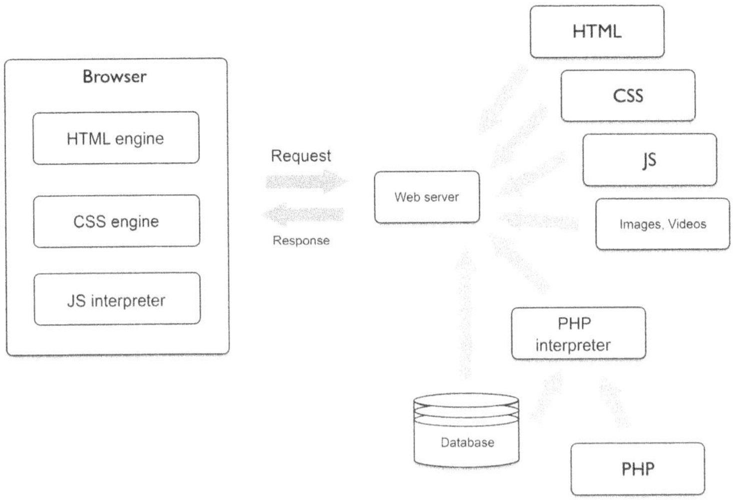

FIGURE 4.2 Your website is stored in individual components on a server, from which the browser requests, assembles and displays a specific part.

All have their advantages and disadvantages, with the effort required decreasing as you move down the list, but so does the flexibility and the options available to you. Let's take a look at the options one by one, according to Table 4.4.

- ***AI (website) builders*** are suitable for anyone who has little time and technical knowledge. They offer quick results, but at the expense of customisability and flexibility.
- ***No-code platforms*** bridge the gap between simplicity and flexibility. They are suitable for attractive designs with some control and are ideal for creative people.

TABLE 4.4 Comparison of Systems

Platform Type	Required Prior Knowledge	Flexibility	Design and Customisation Options	Typical Use Cases
(AI) website builders (Wix, Jimdo, Squarespace)	Minimal (answer simple questions)	Low (focus on ready-made structures)	Limited (limited customisation)	Quick and easy, small websites
No-code/low-code platforms (Webflow, Framer)	Low (basic knowledge of web design is advantageous)	Medium (more control over layouts)	High (drag and drop, custom CSS)	Portfolios, company websites, blogs
CMS (WordPress, possibly with AI tools)	Medium (experience with plug-ins helpful)	High (through plug-ins and custom code)	High (many themes and plug-ins)	Versatile, including blogs, online shops, member areas
HTML, CSS and JS	High	Very high	Very high	Theoretically, anything is possible

Low-code platforms offer greater flexibility and customisation options. However, they require basic technical knowledge. They are particularly worthwhile for more complex projects or higher demands on functionality and design. However, the boundaries with no-code platforms are fluid.

- ***Content management systems*** (CMS), possibly with AI support, combine the advantages of low-code tools and AI, but are often dependent on plug-ins and third-party extensions. They are more complex to install and maintain.
- Creating ***HTML, CSS and JS*** yourself ("coding") offers maximum flexibility, but requires a good technical understanding. For simple sites, this option makes sense again thanks to the possibility of using AI to help.

4.3 AI CONSTRUCTION KITS/WEBSITE BUILDERS

Website builders have been around for years. Without any technical knowledge, you can quickly click together simple websites. The result can be good if the templates are suitable. However, the websites created with them all look very similar. And you are severely limited in your customisation options. Nowadays, virtually all builders have AI functions. With many of them, you set up your website in dialogue with the AI. You answer three or four questions, choose from a few suggestions, and your website is ready. The big catch here is that this is really just a chat-based control for selecting a template, which is then filled with very little basic information. In my opinion, there is little point in using AI for this. It feels a bit more modern and may be 1 or 2 minutes faster, but the result is no better, and in some cases even worse, than if you had chosen a template yourself in the traditional way.

Where AI is used sensibly, however, is in the further customisation of the site. Here, the construction kits mainly offer text and image creation directly on the pages. This is convenient, leads to quick results and is often better than what people used to type into the templates without much thought. However, you should not succumb to the temptation to do what many providers advertise as a key selling point: completing your website in a matter of minutes. This is because visitors will leave such websites even faster, if they are ever found at all.

That doesn't mean you shouldn't choose such a system. You should just follow the approach I show you here in this book. Step by step, we use AI to work our way towards a really *good* website – not one that is finished as quickly as possible.

4.3.1 Wix

Wix is a popular website builder because it is easy to use and delivers very good results. The system aims to bridge the gap between simple website builders and professional CMS. You create your pages here completely visually: you can see immediately what your changes do (***WYSIWYG***, *what you see is what you get*). In addition to the familiar interface, there is ***Wix ADI*** (Artificial Design Intelligence). This asks you a few questions and creates a complete website. As with other AI builders, however, the result is only a

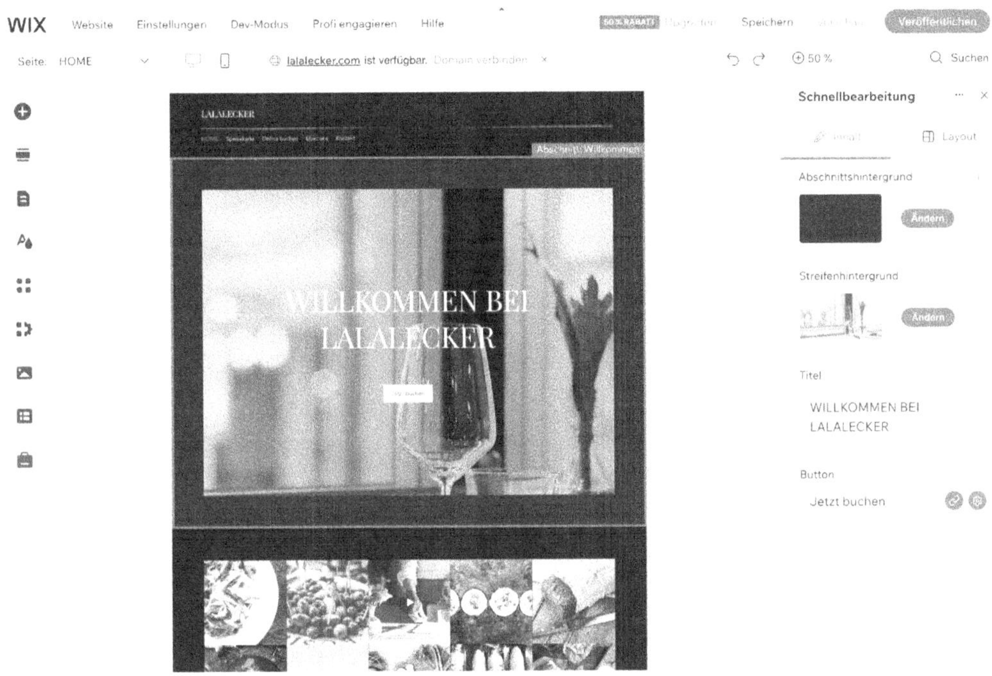

FIGURE 4.3 Tidy and clear: the Wix editor. (Figure created using Wix.)

minimally customised template. Where Wix scores points, on the other hand, is with its integrated functions: online shop, newsletter, booking system or events – everything is possible and coordinated. You don't have to search for and integrate suitable plug-ins or additional services. And the system is also easy to use.

There is also ***Wix Studio*** (formerly Editor X). This is a system with its own editor, which is more of a low-code platform (see Section 4.4).

Although you also have a visual editor here, you can edit the code directly if you wish. This gives you more flexibility and allows you to implement customised solutions.

4.3.2 Squarespace

Squarespace is particularly popular in the graphic design and art scene. The websites created with it look modern and high-quality. This is mainly because the templates are very good, but there are not as many as with the competition. The templates are designed by professionals and follow current design trends. With Squarespace, you make a compromise: your creative freedom is more limited than with Wix, for example, especially when it comes to the arrangement of elements on the pages. On the other hand, the result almost always looks professional. A minor disadvantage is that the websites built with it are often quite similar.

The AI integration is called ***Squarespace Design Kit*** (with AI) and works similarly to Wix: you answer a few questions and receive a template pre-filled with images and text, easily customised to your preferences.

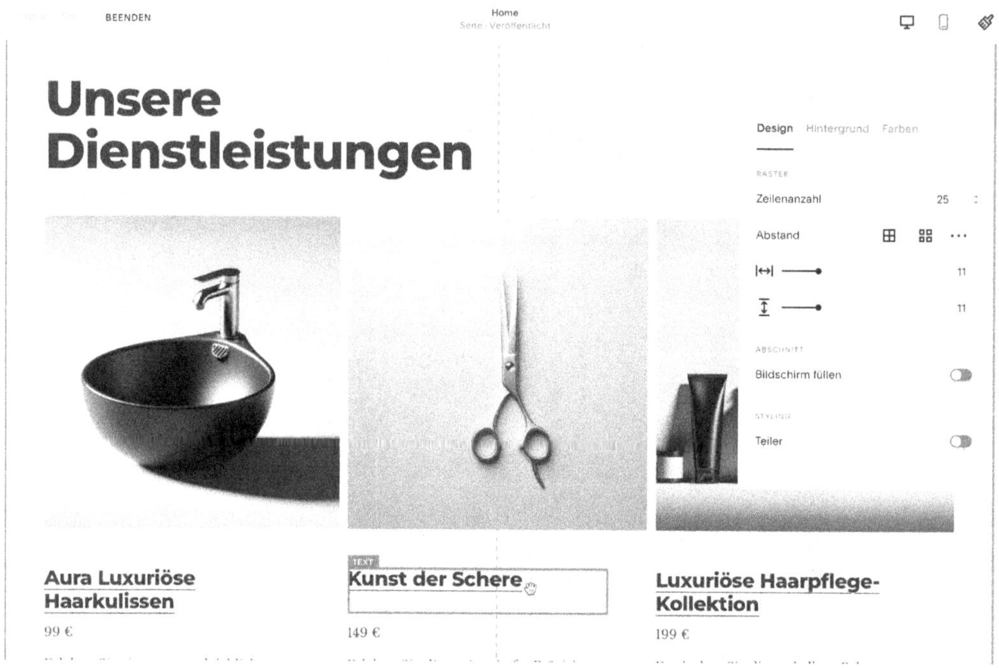

FIGURE 4.4 The Squarespace editor: behind the very tidy interface are a number of settings options. (Figure created using Squarespace.)

Online shopping and marketing functions (email, social media) are also integrated and coordinated. Small businesses and creative professionals who value high-quality presentation in particular choose this provider.

4.3.3 Jimdo

Jimdo is one of the few European providers, with its headquarters in Germany. Similar to Wix and Squarespace, the integrated AI solution ***Dolphin*** guides you step by step to a website that is essentially a customised template. The number of templates is not quite as large, and the customisation options are somewhat more limited than those of the competition, but everything is solidly coordinated and focused on the essentials. A simple online shop and basic marketing tools are included, and this provider is slightly cheaper than the alternatives.

4.4 NO-CODE AND LOW-CODE PLATFORMS

No-code and ***low-code platforms*** promise to create professional websites (and apps) with minimal effort. No-code platforms are designed to be usable without any programming knowledge. You work exclusively visually and drag and drop ready-made building blocks onto the workspace. Complex logic is represented by visually displayed if-then

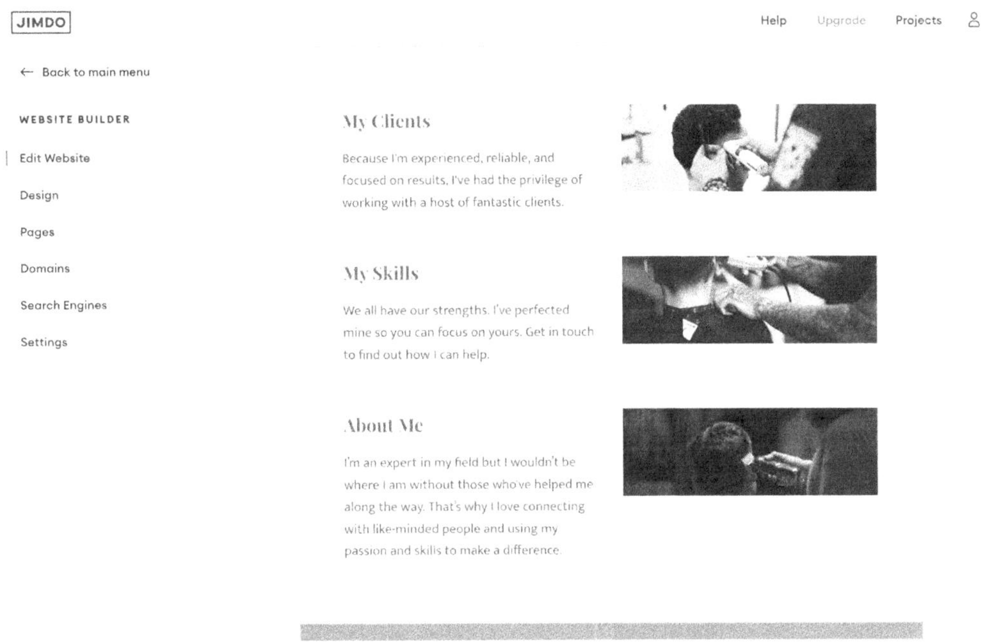

FIGURE 4.5 Jimdo's interface is as minimalist as it looks. But that means you can quickly achieve your goals. (Figure created using Jimdo.)

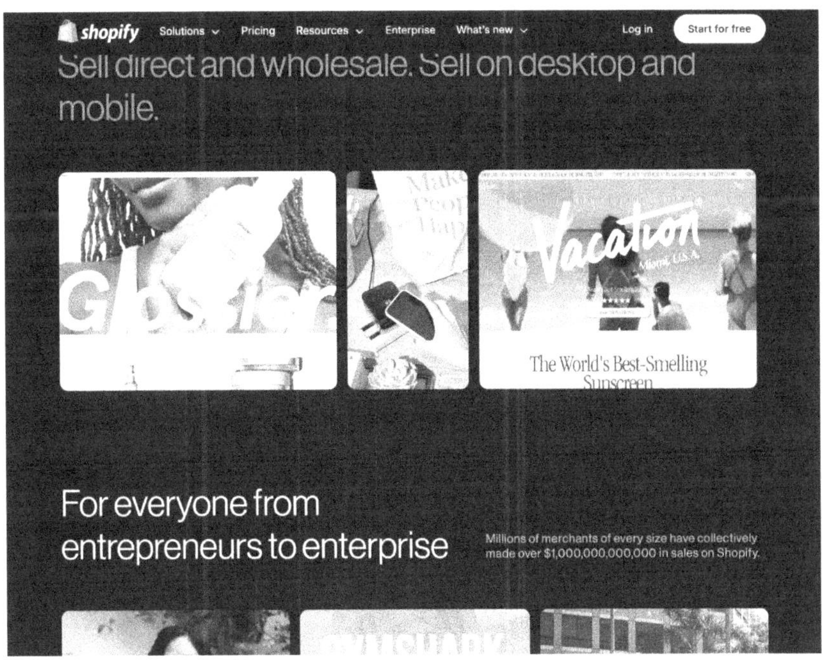

FIGURE 4.6 Special case Shopify: If your main focus is on selling directly via your website, this is an alternative to classic website builders. (Figure created using Shopify.)

rules. Low-code, on the other hand, is intended for people who have at least some programming skills but want to work faster, or who are normally satisfied with drag and drop but occasionally want to make their own adjustments. In this case, you can directly modify or rewrite code. This makes low-code more flexible, but also more complex to use. The boundaries between website builders and no-code, and between no-code and low-code, are fluid. The principle behind no-code and low-code is not unlike that of website builders: you work with ready-made building blocks and customise them. The difference is that in no-code and low-code systems, you can not only create simple websites but also implement more complex applications, such as database integration, shop systems and specialised solutions ranging from project management to customer support. AI functions are rarely directly integrated into these tools, but this is not a problem, as the AI integration offered by the kit systems is not particularly helpful anyway.

4.4.1 Framer

Framer is a service that has become a popular platform for creating graphically sophisticated websites. Its strengths lie in its ease of use and the ability to easily create interactive animations. Thanks to pre-built blocks and a user-friendly interface, websites can be created quickly but can also be heavily customised. Framer is particularly suitable for creative projects, portfolios and companies that want a modern look and dynamic content.

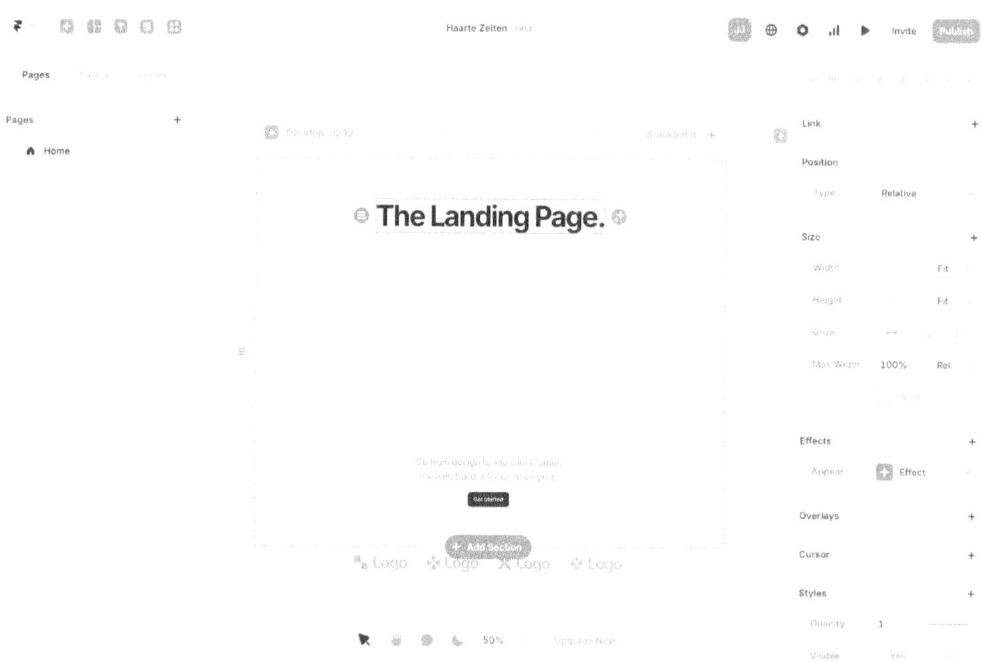

FIGURE 4.7 The Framer editor: As you can see, we are closer to the code here. (Figure created using Framer.)

To a limited extent, you can also integrate code for advanced customisation. This makes Framer particularly suitable for visually appealing, small to medium-sized websites.

4.4.2 Webflow

Anyone with a basic understanding of HTML and CSS will quickly get to grips with ***Webflow***. But even those without this knowledge will find it easy to use after a short training period. The visual editor forms the basis. If you are happy with the existing templates, you don't need much else to create your website. However, Webflow allows you to delve much deeper into the details of your page structure. This is closely linked to how HTML and CSS work, so some prior knowledge in this area is helpful. Those who decide to use this tool will need to invest a little more time at the beginning, but will be rewarded with a deeper understanding of basic web technology and will be able to implement their own individual ideas with great precision.

Working with Webflow becomes really exciting when combined with ***Relume***. This additional service positions itself as a professional solution for quickly creating the basic framework of your website and individual pages without getting lost in the visual design. It features the best AI I have seen so far in any website creation system. With Relume, I had the feeling for the first time that the promises made by providers regarding AI in this area are being fulfilled. You enter a few key details about your website and, as if by magic,

FIGURE 4.8 Webflow allows you to manipulate CSS settings via a visual editor. (Figure created using Webflow.)

your site is created before your eyes, and not all at once, which is the main advantage. Consider the biggest mistake we can make when using AI: simply doing things faster, not better. Relume guides you step by step from the idea to sitemaps and wireframes to the finished website. This allows you to focus on what is important for your goals and your target groups without having to deal with image selection, colours, typography or buttons right away. You can read more about this tool in Chapter 5, "Step 3: Determine the Optimal Structure of the Website", and Chapter 6, "Step 4: Design Meets Code – Designing and Programming the Site", where I show you the process in detail.

The alternative provider ***Anima*** has a similar approach to Relume, but places even greater emphasis on programming. Larger design and development teams, in particular, use Anima to convert designs into code, which is then used for further development. Anima is rarely used for smaller projects.

4.5 CONTENT MANAGEMENT SYSTEMS

With website builders, as with most no-code and low-code systems, you create the pages at the provider's site. The provider then makes the result available on the internet – your website is hosted on their server. Most CMSs, on the other hand, can be run on any server. You can also use them to move from one server to another if you are dissatisfied with a server provider or if it ceases operations. This gives you greater technical flexibility, but also more responsibility. In general, a CMS is a management system for your ***content***. They came about when websites became more professional and people without a technical background wanted to put content online without having to worry about servers, databases, programming and the like. However, it always took people to do exactly that so that others didn't have to. Many CMSs are managed by agencies, allowing the editorial staff of the commissioning companies to concentrate on text and image design.

4.5.1 WordPress

WordPress, Drupal and ***TYPO3*** are the best-known CMS. If you want to set them up and operate them yourself, you will need to learn a little bit about technology. WordPress is the most accessible and best-known system, with almost half of all websites worldwide running on it. This has resulted in a huge community: you can find introductions, advanced tutorials and answers to even the most specific questions online, as well as lots of extensions and templates. WordPress is open source and therefore free to use, as are most of the extensions (***plug-ins***). You only have to pay for hosting, and there are also premium versions of many plug-ins that are subject to a fee.

If you use a CMS, you can use AI to plan the structure of your site, create text and images, and even customise the code. There are also a few plug-ins that allow you to do this directly in ***the backend***, i.e. the administration interface or ***editor***. However, this only saves you a few clicks. There are also tools such as ***Elementor***. This is an extension that allows you to use WordPress in a similar way to a website builder. You can also book

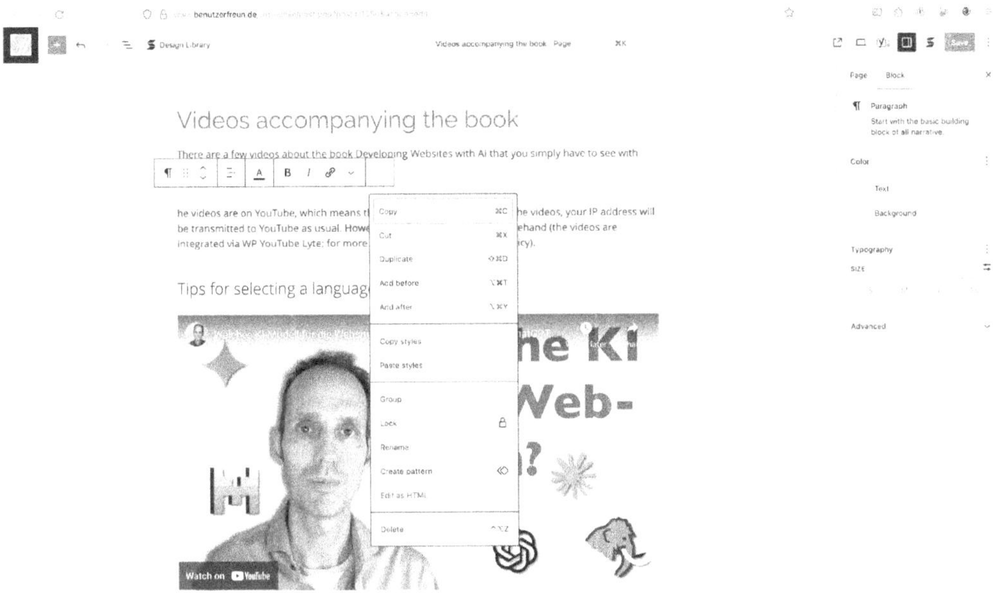

FIGURE 4.9 The editor of WordPress, the best-known CMS. (Figure created using WordPress.)

AI functions that allow you not only to create texts and images directly in the backend but also to customise code (CSS for visual display). You can also create entire layouts with ***Elementor AI***.

WORDPRESS.ORG IS NOT WORDPRESS.COM

On the website wordpress.org, you can find a free download of the CMS of the same name, as well as documentation and help forums. On wordpress.com, on the other hand, you can rent a limited version of WordPress that you don't have to install yourself, but which runs directly on the server. There is a free version, but it is not suitable for much more than testing. My advice is that if you really want to use WordPress, you should download it and install it yourself on a server. If you want the convenience of a solution where others take care of the server, there are website builders that are easier to use.

4.5.2 Flat File CMS and Other WordPress Alternatives

But it doesn't always have to be WordPress. Although it is very flexible thanks to its countless plug-ins, it is oversized for simple websites. This results in pages that are larger and more complex than necessary, which is not sustainable in the long term and impairs performance. That's why there are a number of alternatives that are becoming increasingly popular. These include so-called ***flat file CMS***. Unlike WordPress and the like, these do not require a database, as all content comes from files (hence "flat file", in the sense of "just files") and is translated into HTML files by a ***script engine***. Well-known systems include ***Grav***, ***Automad*** and ***Kirby***. All of these are still rather niche products, because it takes some technical expertise to set up such systems. If you want to get started, you can find a good overview here: bnfr.de/ai044

4.6 CREATING HTML, CSS AND JS YOURSELF

CMSs have become so powerful and convenient that for years, only a few people have created their pages "by hand", i.e. directly editing the source code for HTML (page structure and content), CSS (visual presentation) and JavaScript (JS, interactivity). But thanks to AI, this is once again a viable option. With a large language model, we have a partner sitting next to us all the time who knows every programming language. They can support us, explain concepts, provide code snippets, correct our mistakes and even programme complete page structures with good specifications.

An interesting alternative is the ***Publii*** programme. You can download it for free for Mac, Windows and Linux. It can be used like a CMS, but generates HTML, CSS and JS files. You can upload these to any server or edit them directly if you wish. Publii is therefore ideal for anyone who doesn't want to deal with HTML, CSS and JavaScript at all. If, on the other hand, you want to do so, you can also use one of the professional generators for static websites (***Static Site Generators, SSG***). Well-known and beginner-friendly options include ***Hugo***, ***Eleventy*** and ***Zola***, while ***Astro*** and ***Jekyll*** are also worth considering. All of them are free to use, but if you are unfamiliar with ***terminals*** and

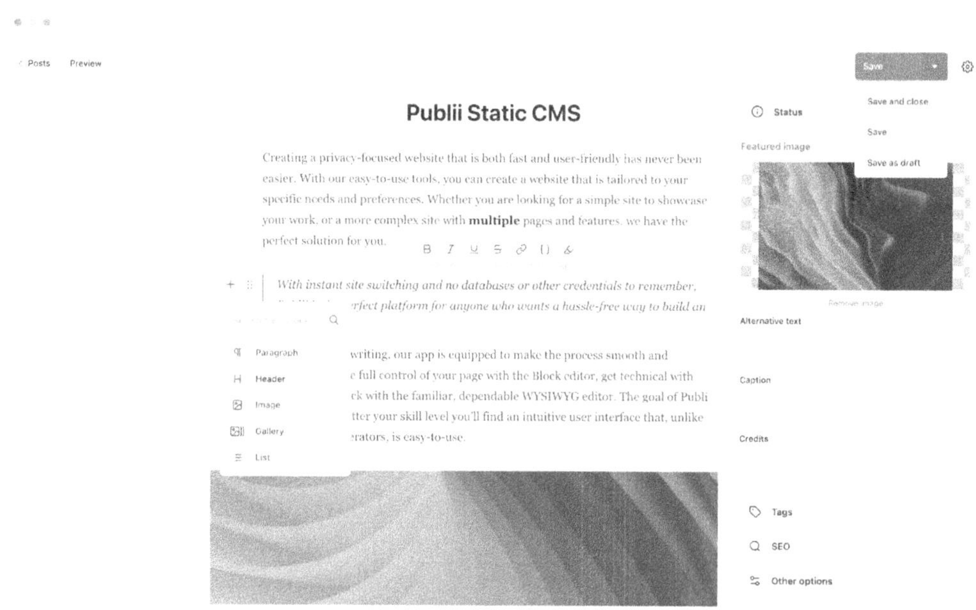

FIGURE 4.10 Publii looks like a CMS, but is actually an editor for local HTML files that can then be uploaded to a server.

Markdown, it will take you some time to set up the systems. However, with AI at your side, this is not a major problem.

If you want to make sure you've considered the latest tools, you can use an AI such as ChatGPT or Perplexity with internet access to get an overview of the market:

EXAMPLE PROMPT: RESEARCH CURRENT PROVIDERS

Motivation: I want to understand the differences between AI website builders (e.g. Wix, Jimdo), no-code platforms (e.g. Webflow, Squarespace) and low-code tools in the context of website creation in order to find the best options for implementing a simple website.

Task: Compare the platforms mentioned and other important ones in terms of required prior knowledge, flexibility, design and customisation options, and typical use cases. Also, search the web for current recommendations for my use case. Focus exclusively on website creation; tools for app development or database integration or automation are irrelevant.

Result: A precise, clear analysis of the differences and similarities between the individual providers, structured according to the criteria mentioned (prior knowledge, flexibility, design and customisation options, typical use cases). The comparison should be in the form of a list or table so that the most important points are visible at a glance, but all the information I need to make my decision is included.

The prompt to copy: bnfr.de/ai043

4.7 SELECT A HOST

If you use a website builder, the respective operator will ensure that your website is available around the clock, that the software is kept up to date and that security is guaranteed. However, if you use a self-installed CMS or create the HTML pages directly, you will need to find someone who will rent you space on their server, a so-called ***host***, also known as ***a provider***.

The costs are manageable – for a few pounds a month, you get sufficient resources for small to medium-sized websites. Although there are free hosting offers, these are hardly recommended for professional websites. The providers sometimes finance themselves through annoying advertisements that are displayed on your site. Free offers also come with no performance guarantees, and the webs can quickly change their legal or technical terms and conditions, meaning that your site may no longer open or may open very slowly, advertisements may suddenly appear or you may end up having to pay after all. However, you can use such offers for quick tests. As things often change here, you can find an up-to-date list of my recommendations online: bnfr.de/ai045

Typically, ***managed servers*** are used, where the providers manage the operating system in addition to the hardware and guarantee that the basic functions are up to date and secure. Pay attention to the aspects mentioned in the following sections.

4.7.1 Storage Space and Traffic

The ***storage space*** required is manageable for most websites, as long as you don't want to embed hours of video, for example. A cleanly implemented website with ten HTML pages, three CSS files and 40 optimised images often requires less than 5 megabytes.

Traffic, i.e. the amount of data transferred, depends on how many visitors your site gets. With ten visitors per day who view all pages, a simple calculation shows that this results in 1.5 gigabytes of traffic per month. Even with 250 daily visitors, this is only about 37.5 gigabytes. However, most basic tariffs now offer a flat rate for traffic anyway.

4.7.2 Technical Aspects

An important criterion is an ***SSL certificate*** for secure HTTPS connections. This is standard today and should be included in your hosting package. Current browsers prominently mark websites without HTTPS as "not secure", which can unsettle visitors. Or they may refuse to open such a website altogether. Therefore, a certificate is essential. Also pay attention to:

- FTP access for uploading your files
- Server performance and loading times, especially at peak times
- Guaranteed availability with defined maximum downtime
- Access to server statistics on visitors/traffic
- A database, if you use one (e.g. for a CMS)
- Support for server-side technologies such as PHP, MySQL, etc., if you use them

4.7.3 Domain and Email

With most hosting packages, you get a. de or .com domain included in your subscription. Additional domains cost from £12 per year. Make sure that the domain is registered to you or your client – this will make it easier to change providers later on.

Also check the email offer:

- Number and free choice of email addresses
- Forwarding and auto-reply functions
- Size restrictions for attachments
- Spam and virus protection, if relevant to you

4.7.4 Support and Contractual Terms

The quality of technical support should not be underestimated. Pay attention to:

- Support hours and response speed

- Available contact methods (ticket system, email, telephone, chat)
- Quality of online documentation
- Costs for support services

Also check the contractual terms and conditions, such as minimum term, notice periods and automatic renewals. With European hosts, you have the advantage of short transmission paths and a clear legal situation – with hosts outside the EU, you must conclude a data processing agreement (DPA) in accordance with the GDPR (General Data Protection Regulation).

4.8 CHOOSING THE RIGHT PLATFORM

You now have a wealth of information and are familiar with the most important options. But which path do you want to take for your current project? The following questions will help you make your decision. Go through the categories, check the criteria that are relevant to you and see which recommendation fits each one. The first recommendation is always the first choice, with further mentions being secondary alternatives.

Prior knowledge/required knowledge	
Focus on design	• Framer • Squarespace
Focus on code (HTML/CSS/JS)	• HTML/CSS/JS • Webflow • CMS
Implementation time and effort	
Website should be online as soon as possible	• Modular
As little effort as possible	• Construction kit
Design and adaptability	
Unique, highly customisable design	• CMS • No code/low code • HTML/CSS/JS
Content management	
Content should be easy for clients or editors to change frequently	• Modular • CMS
Technical requirements	
Shop	• Website builder (e.g. Shopify, Wix, Squarespace) • WordPress (with WooCommerce)
Blog	• Website builder • CMS • No-code/low-code
Database	• CMS • In-house development (HTML/CSS/JS + backend via PHP/Node.js or similar)

Own server/host	• CMS • HTML/CSS/JS • (Webflow with data export)
Connection to external services	• CMS • HTML/CSS/JS • Low-code
Scalability/retrofitting of additional functions not yet defined	• CMS • HTML/CSS/JS
Data protection and security	
Independence from providers	• HTML/CSS/JS • With restrictions CMS
Data protection	• HTML/CSS/JS • CMS
Cost	
Low and predictable (manageable ongoing fees)	• Modular • Simple CMS configurations
Depending on scope (multiple functions, own infrastructure and individual customisations increase the price)	• CMS • HTML/CSS/JS • No-code/low-code

If you are still unsure about what is right for you, ask the custom GPT for advice, which I have equipped with all the information from this chapter: bnfr.de/ai044

CHAPTER 5

Step 3

Determine the Optimal Structure of the Website

A well-thought-out structure is the backbone of your site. Learn how to use AI and proven creative methods to develop the perfect sitemap, user-friendly navigation and clear pages.

In step 1, you defined what you want to achieve with your website, who you want to address and what the needs and wishes of these people are. In step 2, you found the best technical platform for your project. Now, in step 3, you can start implementing it. You determine which functions and content the site must offer in order to meet the wishes of the target group and thus achieve your website goals.

5.1 WHY A GOOD STRUCTURE IS CRUCIAL

Who decides whether your website is a success? People. They either use your site or they don't. They either take their time to look around or they leave immediately. They either find their way around the site or they don't. If people can't find what they're looking for on your site, then you have a problem. You need to make sure that everyone can find their way around your site as easily as possible. The content must be sorted logically, according to a logic that is based on the *visitors'* understanding. It is of no use if the logic makes sense to you or is even scientifically correct – if it does not make sense to visitors, your website will not be successful.

5.2 DEFINE FUNCTIONS AND CONTENT

The same applies to functions. You need functions on your site that help users achieve their goals. In most cases, these are the functions that users expect, but not always. You can also offer something that visitors do not expect if it allows them to achieve their goal

DOI: 10.1201/9781003726708-5

FIGURE 5.1 Nobody looks for tomatoes among the berries, corn among the grains or potatoes among the stem tubers, even if this is scientifically correct.

as quickly or even faster than they expected. But in almost all cases, it is best to stick with what is expected. A concrete example: for our hairdressing website, we need very few core functions and content. Through our usage research (see Chapter 3, "Step 1: Plan the Route – Identify Goals and Target Groups"), we know what visitors want:

- Information about opening hours
- Address with link to Google Maps
- Photos from the shop
- Photo of Lars, the owner
- Customer reviews

What interested parties might also want is an online appointment booking system. However, Lars, the client who commissioned the website, does not want this because his philosophy is: "First come, first served". This is an example of a conflict between the interests of the target group and the interests of the client. As important as I always find it to work for the target group and fulfil their wishes, if the clients decide against it for good reason, we have to respect that.

Let's take another look at the example of the fitness website, where it becomes more challenging because we have more options in terms of what we could offer:

- Course schedules
- Training locations with Google Maps links
- Trainer profiles of the two coaches, Frieder and Fabi
- Access to training videos for subscribers
- Customer reviews with success stories
- Easy access to contact information

In this case, too, there may be requests from the target group that Frieder and Fabi do not want to fulfil, such as online payment options. If you recognise such potential conflicts in advance, you can take them into account in your user research and find out from the target group which of these functions are indispensable for them. However, you must always bear in mind that people may enjoy using a function on a website or say that this function is indispensable for them. However, this does not mean that they will be as consistent on the specific website you are currently implementing. If potential customers think the two fitness professionals are great, have heard a lot of good things about them, or find that the courses take place right on their doorstep, they will still come, even if they would have preferred a different payment function, for example.

So now create a plan for the content and functions of your site:

EXAMPLE PROMPT: DETERMINE CONTENT AND FUNCTIONS

Motivation: I am in the process of designing a website for Bistro Verde in Oldenburg. I need a simple and clear list that shows everything that should be included on the website in terms of content and functions. In general, the site should convey the atmosphere and values of the café, appeal to potential guests and present all important information in a clear and appealing way. The website should reflect the bistro's philosophy – healthy, sustainable, inclusive.

Task: Create a simple, one-dimensional list with the relevant content and functions for the website. Only the points should be listed, without further explanations, categories or notes on design and programming.

Result: At the end of the process, I would like to have a one-dimensional list of the content and functions of the website.

Example: The result should look something like this:

- Opening hours
- Menu
- Photos
- Location with link to Google Maps

The prompt to copy: bnfr.de/ai014

If you are not entirely sure what people expect, you can do a quick competitor analysis at. Keep in mind what usability expert Jakob Nielsen calls his "first law":

> Users spend most of their time on other websites.

This means that it is not our website that shapes users' expectations, but rather the countless websites that each of us visits. That is why it is so important to be familiar with other sites, especially those that your target groups visit. Tips on competitive analysis can be found in Section 3.7, "Research the Competition".

5.3 AI HELPS WITH FINDING IDEAS

AI is generally a great help when it comes to brainstorming. Always remember the golden rule number 1: AI is a partner, not a pack mule. Don't try to offload the work onto AI, but engage in a dialogue with it about what the website should offer. If the site is as simple as our hairdresser example, then this may not even be necessary. But even with our slightly more complicated example of the website for the fitness duo, it can be worthwhile. This way, you may come up with ideas that are not entirely obvious – and thus gain an edge over the competition. My preferred approach for this is a chat AI such as ***Claude*** or ***ChatGPT***. If you like to work visually, you also have other options, such as the design software ***Figma***. Most people use it to collaboratively design drafts or prototypes for websites and apps. But it can do even more, such as whiteboards. The function for this is called ***FigJam***. In the top right-hand corner of the toolbar, there is a purple button with an asterisk, which hides the AI. There, you can choose what you want to create: mind maps, various diagrams, brainstorming, etc. You can also enter text, even in other languages, even though the results are usually displayed in English. You need an account with Figma to use all of this, but it is free for small projects.

The widely used online whiteboard ***Miro*** also has a handy AI assistant. However, AI use in Miro is severely restricted for free accounts.

NEWS IS YESTERDAY'S NEWS

A typical mistake that AI also likes to make when collecting features for the website is to include a news section. Nobody needs to offer something new on the website every week; nobody expects that. There are plenty of sources for current news. However, AI enthusiastically suggests news sections on websites. You know this from countless website templates. But if you take a closer look at the news sections of small and medium-sized sites, you will find little that is positive: news from the Christmas party two years ago, awards that were presented months ago, invitations to events that are long past.

If you absolutely want to have a news section on your website, you need clear responsibilities and a realistic editorial plan. After events, announcements should be replaced promptly with a short report. If you can't do this reliably, it's better to do without a news section. A well-maintained website without news makes a better impression than one with an obviously neglected news section.

FIGURE 5.2 If you select "Brainstorm" in Figma's AI assistant, you will be presented with a collection of topics and ideas that you could explore – a handy starting point. (Figure created using Figma.)

5.4 TECHNIQUES FOR BRAINSTORMING

It is worth pausing for a moment to consider whether we have already made the most of it. Creative methods help to develop ideas systematically. You can use these in a traditional team setting or on your own with AI as your partner. It not only helps you find ideas but also helps you question them critically. In this section, we provide a few suggestions for good methods; otherwise, every large language model knows countless more.

5.4.1 Brainwriting Pool – Better than Brainstorming

Brainstorming is one of the best-known creativity techniques. Unfortunately, countless studies have shown that the method does not work very well. ***Brainwriting*** is a further development of this technique. In brainwriting, all participants write down their ideas at the same time. This is also ideal for online workshops. A variation of this is the brainwriting pool:

1. All participants receive a stack of virtual or real cards.
2. Everyone writes down ideas at the same time, one per card (about 5 minutes).
3. The cards are placed in the middle of the table or shared digitally.
4. The cards are read aloud by one person or everyone is given time to look at them.

5. Everyone can pick up on any ideas from others and develop them further (10 minutes).
6. Sort and evaluate the ideas together (15 minutes).

If you are alone with an AI, do the first round on your own. Then share your ideas with ChatGPT or Le Chat and let the AI develop new ideas and variations from them. Pick up on individual ideas and develop them further. You can repeat this game several times.

5.4.2 Worst Possible Website – Learning from the Negative

The paradoxical method of ***the Worst Possible …*** is fun and provides valuable insights. You turn the usual question "How can I/we develop a really good website?" on its head. The result: insights into what you should definitely avoid – and what works:

1. First, collect terrible ideas for your site:
    - Hide the navigation and place it somewhere else every day
    - Display important information in pop-ups that disappear immediately
    - Random colour changes every 10 seconds
    - Automatically playing music that cannot be turned off
2. Then analyse why these ideas are so bad:
    - Users cannot find their way around.
    - Important information gets lost.
    - The design prevents concentration.
    - The website does not meet visitors' expectations.
3. Develop positive principles from this:
    - clear, consistent navigation
    - place important information prominently
    - clear, focused design
    - user-friendly controls

AI feels surprisingly comfortable in the role of the nasty web designer. It becomes surprisingly creative in developing designs that infuriate users – and thus helps you sharpen your view of bad design.

5.4.3 Jobs to Be Done – Understanding Users

The ***Jobs to Be Done*** (JTBD) method is a structured approach to understanding user needs and expectations. We don't start with what we have to offer users, but with the tasks ("jobs") that users want to accomplish:

- **Functional jobs** are the specific tasks that users have come to our website to perform. For example, they may want to quickly find the most important facts about a particular topic or product. Or they may want to compare products to find the best one for their needs. Making an appointment is also a possible functional job.
- **Emotional jobs** refer to the feelings and emotions that users have while using the website. For example, they need to gain confidence and feel secure in their decision. The emotional job would then be, for example, "not making any mistakes when ordering". Or feeling well advised and receiving competent advice.
- **Social jobs** refer to the social aspects of website use. For example, users want to feel part of a community and exchange ideas. They want to show their own knowledge and expertise and share it with others.

For each of the three dimensions, ask: What specifically do users want to achieve? What stands in the way of this? How can we, how can I best support them in completing the respective job?

5.4.4 SCAMPER – Turning Ideas on Their Head

The ***SCAMPER*** method is a kind of checklist for creative thinking. It helps you to view your (website) idea from seven different angles:

- **Substitute**: What could be done differently? Replace text-based product descriptions with short video demos?
- **Combine**: Which functions can be combined? Combine customer reviews with interactive product instructions so that users can directly understand the reviews?
- **Adapt:** What can you adopt from other industries? The shopping basket from web shops for booking desired services on an agency website?
- **Modify**: What can be expanded or reduced? Use a drop-down menu instead of a sidebar to create more space for content?
- **Put to another use**: What are new applications? Implement FAQs as a chatbot?
- **Eliminate:** What is superfluous? Remove the "Philosophy" page and place the information under "About us"?

- **Reverse/Rearrange**: What works better in a different order? Instead of explaining all the product's features first, start with an interactive example that directly engages users?

Let the AI generate three additional ideas for each SCAMPER aspect. Ask, for example: "What are three innovative ways to replace the contact form?" The answers are often surprising and inspiring.

5.4.5 Edward de Bono's Six Thinking Hats

The six ***thinking hats*** method developed by creativity researcher Edward de Bono helps you to look at your idea from different perspectives. Each hat represents a different character:

- **White hat**: The objective, analytical character neutrally collects and presents all available facts without interpreting them. They work scientifically, arguing only with verifiable information.
- **Red hat**: The emotional character relies entirely on gut feeling and speaks openly about fears, hopes and intuition.
- **Black hat**: The critical character identifies potential weaknesses and risks in order to recognise and avoid problems at an early stage.
- **Yellow hat**: The optimistic character focuses on the positive aspects and highlights opportunities and advantages.
- **Green hat**: The creative character develops new, even unconventional solutions without imposing any limits on themselves. They invent new ideas free from conventional thinking patterns – without considering their feasibility.
- **Blue hat**: This character maintains an overview and coordinates the entire thought process. They structure and moderate, collect the results and perspectives, and finally summarise the results. This character keeps an eye on the big picture.

Use AI as a sparring partner for each hat. Let it take on each perspective one after the other and ask questions. Especially with the black hat (criticism) and green hat (creativity), it often provides worthwhile food for thought. There are also ready-made custom GPTs that you can use for this, so you don't have to explain to the AI how the method works: bnfr.de/ai069

5.5 ORGANISE CONTENT AND FUNCTIONS

Once you have your list of content and features, you are a big step ahead of the competition. This is because most websites are created by someone simply taking a template and filling it with content. The result is often something that looks like a typical website.

FIGURE 5.3 There is an old saying in computer science: garbage in, garbage out – if we provide rubbish as input, we get rubbish as output.

The problem with this is that such a website can never adequately meet the needs of the target audience because no one has thought about it. And the same thing happens if you leave the creation of your website to AI without carefully providing it with background information and instructions.

With our list of necessary functions and content, we will now move on to the next step of arranging them in such a way that visitors can find their way around optimally.

You lay the foundation for this with a well thought-out site structure, known as ***information architecture***.

5.6 CREATING THE SITEMAP

The usual tool for structuring content for a website is the sitemap. It shows all the pages of a website. For very large sites, some areas are grouped together – for example, it is not necessary to display all pages that present individual products according to the same principle or contain similar elements such as news, blog posts or the like.

The sitemap allows you to organise the content into an information architecture. It specifies how the topics are distributed across the areas and sub-areas and which functions can be found where. It describes how someone navigates through the website when visiting it. The sitemap does not have to show everything in its entirety – the important thing is that it remains clear to you yourself. Find the balance between a detailed and a confusing sitemap.

Visitors to your website are not really interested in your sitemap; they simply want to find their way around the site as quickly as possible and find what they need. To make this work, you need to create content that meets visitors' expectations, and the sitemap helps you do this. Sitemaps are also important for search engines – content management systems therefore automatically create a **sitemap.xml** file that lists all the pages on the website in a structured manner. This ensures that search engine bots such as Google actually crawl all pages. This is particularly important for larger websites, as bots have a limited page budget per site. In theory, they can find every linked page, but they may take longer to do so or decide that individual pages are less important. You can control this to a certain extent with information in the **sitemap.xml**. This gives you advantages

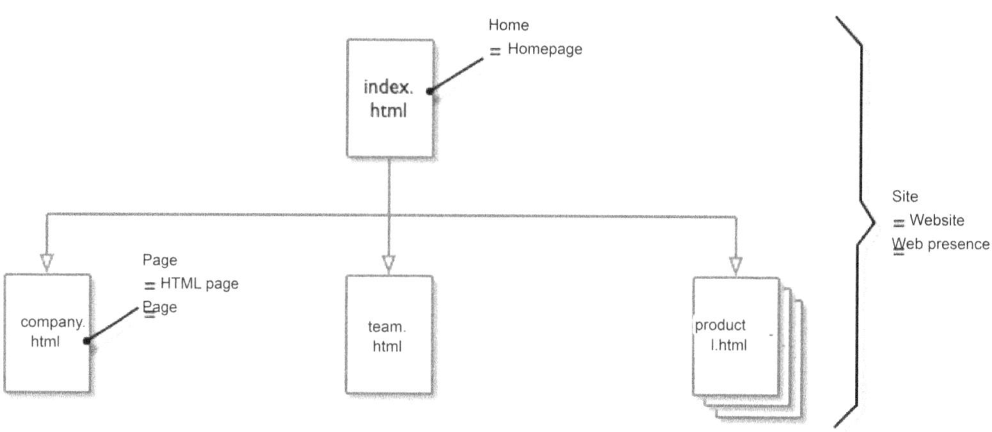

FIGURE 5.4 The terms "site" and "page" are not the same. For clear communication, you should pay attention to this so that you can distinguish whether you are referring to a single page or the entire website.

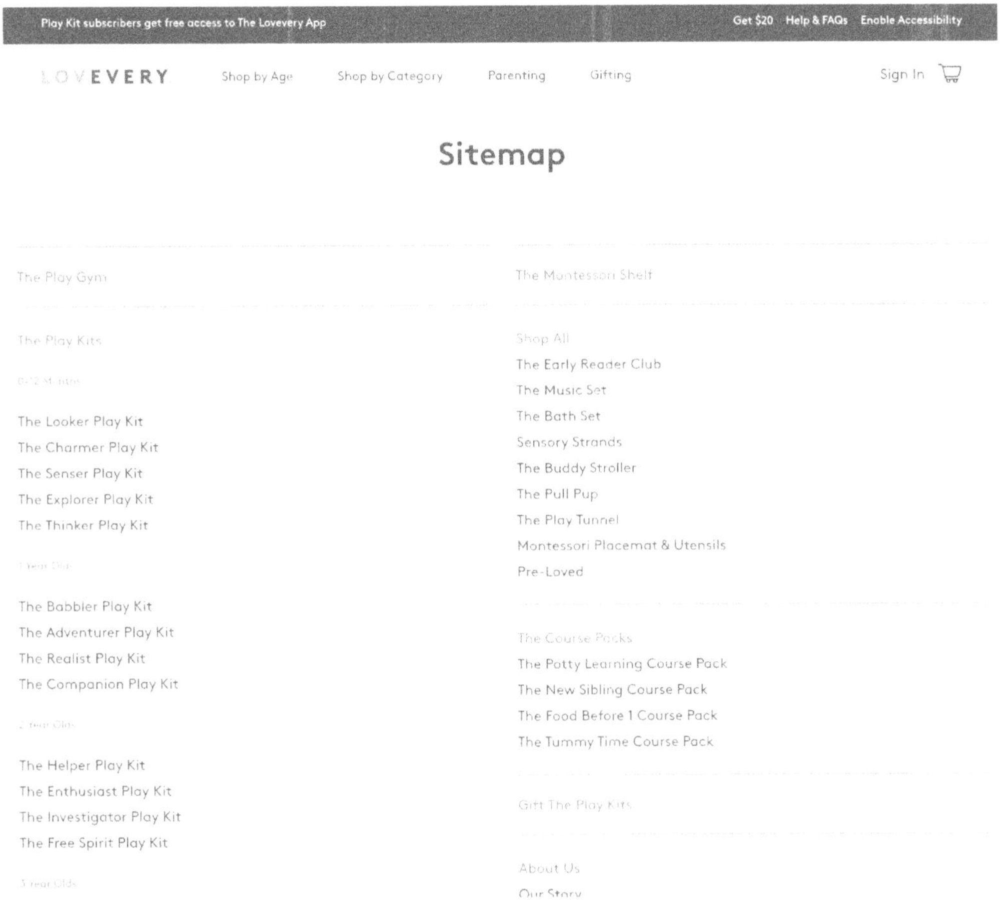

FIGURE 5.5 In the past, many websites also displayed their sitemap to visitors, as shown here on lovevery.com. However, search behaviour has changed in the meantime and hardly anyone looks at a sitemap anymore.

in terms of the speed and completeness of the indexing of your pages. You create the **sitemap.xml** file when everything is ready, so I'll show you how to do this in Section 9.3.1, "Being Found in Search Engines – And with AI".

5.7 FINDING THE RIGHT TERMS FOR PAGE NAMES

The next step is a two-step process: you find out which terms your target group understands and uses, and at the same time, which menu structure is comprehensible to the target group. The best method for this is ***card sorting***. In classic card sorting, you give participants a stack of cards, each of which contains different content or functions of your website. The task is to sort all the cards into groups that they think belong together. The participants then have to name their groups. This method gives you a quick insight into how your target group thinks – and you may be surprised in some areas.

For meaningful results, you need 15 to 30 people to do this exercise. Of course, there are online tools that support you in carrying out the exercise and allow participants to do it alone at home. However, there are also advantages to sitting down with the participants. Then you can discuss terms and expectations with them, which is very rewarding. You can also use an online whiteboard such as ***Miro*** or ***Concept Board*** to connect with people from the target group via video conference and then have them sort the cards on the electronic board.

However, it is more time-saving and convenient for everyone if you just send a link and the participants then sort the cards themselves, whenever and wherever it suits them. There are a number of card sorting providers, all of which have their own little problems. Some require you to sign an expensive annual contract, while others are somewhat tedious to use. Prices and features are constantly changing, so I have compiled an up-to-date overview online: bnfr.de/ai015. There you will also find a few tips on how to evaluate the results.

Now you may be asking yourself: Can't we save ourselves the effort and ask the AI? I would say, maybe yes. It's true that we can only be sure that we are creating everything perfectly for our specific target group if we involve real people. But in the case of the terms and the structuring of the content, we don't need anything new or creative – quite the contrary. The closer we are to the average here, the better. Because the more familiar

FIGURE 5.6 Card sorting with kardSort.com in the view for participants, in which categories are formed and named.

the terms and structure are, the easier it is for people to find their way around our site. So use the AI of your choice and try this:

EXAMPLE PROMPT: CREATE A LIST FOR CARD SORTING

Motivation: I want to create a website and am considering which pages or menu items make sense. I want to use the card sorting technique to group and find the names of the categories.

Task: Help me create a comprehensive list of terms that could potentially be used as page or menu names for my website. The list should cover all important terms that are common on similar websites and be presented in a simple, bullet-point format. Do thorough research to ensure that the terms are complete and typical for websites in this field.

Result: I need a simple, unstructured list of possible page and menu names that I can use for card sorting to develop the best navigation structure for my website.

Example: The list should look like this:

- Home
- About
- Services
- ...

My project: The "Fit-mit-Frieder-und-Fabi" team in Berlin offers personalised fitness solutions for anyone looking for dynamic and exciting training experiences. Led by Frieder and Fabi, both qualified sports scientists, the team specialises in fitness courses such as running groups, outdoor training sessions and seasonal ice skating workshops.

On their website, visitors will find all the essential information they need, such as course schedules, training locations with links to Google Maps, and profiles of both trainers, which give an authentic impression of their expertise and coaching style. The site also offers access to a subscription-based library of training videos, so members can train anytime, anywhere.

Frieder and Fabi place great importance on a motivating and supportive atmosphere, which is reflected in the clear and energising design of the website. Customer reviews highlight the success stories and high level of satisfaction within their community. The website deliberately avoids unnecessary features and focuses on the essentials: easy access to information and services. There are no complicated booking systems, excessive blogs or advertisements, ensuring a straightforward and user-friendly experience.

Ready to download: bnfr.de/ai016

The AI will then return a long list of possible terms. Don't just accept these, but compare them with the list of necessary functions and content that you created for your site beforehand. Delete anything that is not on your list, as AI tends to suggest far too many options.

You don't need to worry about the order and exact naming now, as the AI will take care of that. Thanks to the large amount of data it has been trained with, it can find the most common terms and the most intuitive structure.

FIGURE 5.7 In Figma, you can create a "FigJam" and use the AI function "Mindmap" to get suggestions for terms on the website. This is quick, but since you can provide details and control things much more precisely with Claude or Le Chat, I would rather do it there. (Figure created using Figma.)

EXAMPLE PROMPT: CARD SORTING

Motivation: I want to explore how a potential customer interested in fitness classes on a fitness trainer's website would structure content. The goal is to find out how the information offered can best be grouped and named so that it is clear and understandable.

Task: Put yourself in the shoes of someone looking for fitness classes. Take the following list of terms and group them in the way that makes the most sense to you as a potential customer. Create as many groups as you think is appropriate and give these groups meaningful, descriptive names. Finally, present the groups and assign each term to the appropriate category. Check whether the names are good and appropriate and whether they are also used by other websites in this field. Then check whether the given terms are good and appropriate and whether they are used in this way. If not, add an alternative in brackets that would be better.

Result: A structured list of groups and the assignment of each term to a group.

Example: The result should look like this:

- Courses for beginners: Yoga Basics, Pilates Beginners
- Advanced fitness: HIT (better: High-Intensity Training HIT), CrossFit
- Wellness: Massages, Meditation

Role: You are a potential participant exploring fitness offerings on a website and sorting the information in the way that would be most helpful to you.

The terms to be sorted:

...

The prompt to copy: bnfr.de/ai017

ChatGPT 5

About

- About us
- The team
- Legal notice
- Data protection
- Terms and conditions

Programs & Services

- Offers
- Fitness classes
- Personal training
- Running groups
- Outdoor training
- Ice skating workshops
- Train online
- Training videos
- Online library
- Training guides

Schedule & Locations

- Course schedules
- Training locations

Membership & Pricing

- Prices
- Become a member
- Registration
- Login

Help & Contact

- FAQ

FIGURE 5.8 The result of ChatGPT's card sorting. Seems reasonable and even makes a few suggestions for improving terms. (Figure created using ChatGPT 4o.)

Renowned usability expert ***Jeff Sauro***, who is always very strict and often conducts tests to prove or disprove common assumptions in the field of UX, is convinced that this method works reliably with ChatGPT. In his experiments, the AI came to similar results as a card sorting with 623 participants (his research report on this: bnfr.de/ai018). The only problem with this approach is that it relies heavily on how other websites name such areas. We have no idea whether the other websites are good. Perhaps they are only successful because there is little competition or because they advertise heavily. It is always possible that a website is successful not because of, but in spite of, a certain aspect. So, as always, question your own results critically and don't accept anything that seems strange to you. Remember golden rule number 3: AI can lead you astray.

5.7.1 Checking Complex Structures with Reverse Card Sorting

With the small websites we use as examples here in the book, we can be relatively sure that we would notice serious errors in the sorting of the elements. But if you are creating larger websites or websites for experts in specific disciplines, you should ensure that the structure is such that the target groups can actually find what they are looking for on the site. You can check this with ***reverse card sorting*** (also known as ***tree testing***). In this process, you give participants the task of finding a product or piece of information. This means that participants only see the abstract menu structure of your site, its future menu. They then indicate where in the structure they expect to find what they are looking for. Once several test subjects have completed these tasks, you can see how many were successful and whether they found what they were looking for directly or had to move back and forth in the menu.

5.8 CREATING A SITEMAP WITH AI

There are several services that help you create sitemaps with AI. I'm only showing you these now because it's not a good idea to leave this central task entirely to AI. First, you need to find out what content your target groups actually expect and what terms they

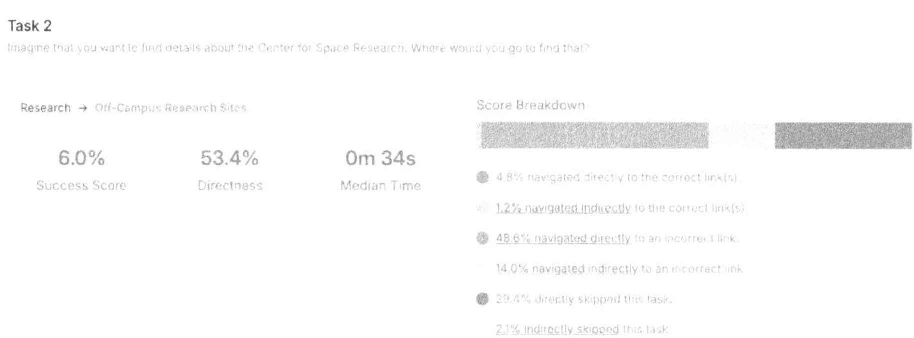

FIGURE 5.9 Evaluation for a search task at uxmetrics.com. The success rate was only 6% and, on average, participants took 30 seconds to complete the task. This indicates a need for correction.

use. Now that you've done that, you can let AI inspire you further and take over the manual work.

The language models are fine for very rough, initial visualisations. In my experience, Claude works best:

EXAMPLE PROMPT: DRAW A SITEMAP

Motivation: Develop a user-friendly and concise sitemap based on my description. The structure should be clear and efficient for users.
Task: Create a tree diagram that visualises the structure of the website. Use tools to display the diagram directly here.
Result: A tree diagram that shows a clearly defined and intuitive sitemap. The sitemap should correspond to a hierarchical tree, with main pages as roots and subpages as branches.
Role: You are an information architect who specialises in user-centred information structures.

Additional information: {Terms or names of the pages to be created}

The prompt to copy: bnfr.de/ai067

With this prompt, you can even have a sitemap created if you enter a description of the site instead of the terms. But as I said, my recommendation is to do this a little more carefully, as shown in Section 5.6.

The results of the language models are not very impressive visually, so I tend to use specialised providers for this. One option is the aforementioned ***Figma*** service. Even in the free version, you can create a whiteboard called ***FigJam***. Go to the star icon in the top right-hand corner to open the AI assistant. Simply say, "Create a sitemap for this website:" and add what you want to see. You can then edit the result directly and correct and design it as you wish.

An alternative provider is ***Octopus.do***. It specialises in sitemaps and wireframes and therefore offers more in this area than Figma. You can currently use the service in the free version to quickly create sitemaps.

My last and best tip is ***Relume***. This service is not free and is even relatively expensive. However, you can also take out a subscription for just one month; once the website is finished, you won't need it anymore anyway. But since it saves you so much work in this step and the next ones, I recommend that you at least take a look at what Relume can do. To do so, go to: relume.io, where you can continue as follows:

1. Create a free account.
2. Once you have successfully logged in, go to **New Project** in the top right-hand corner. This will take you to the sitemap area.

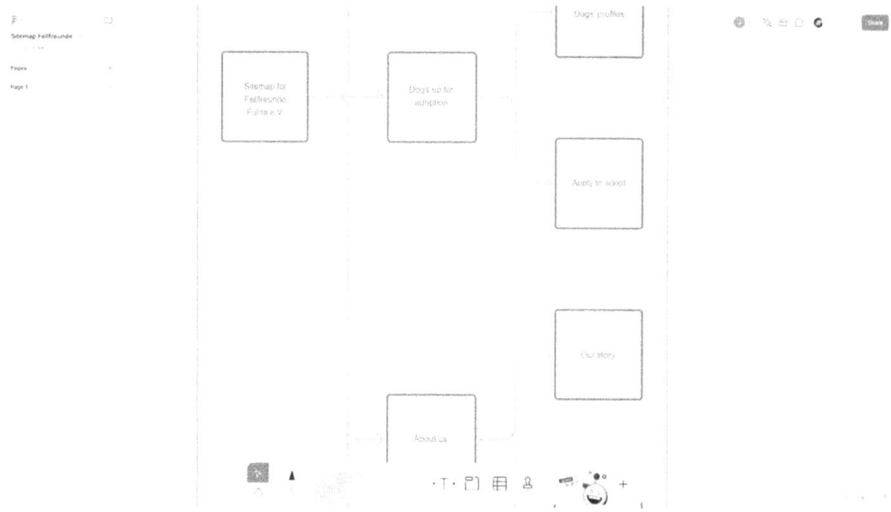

FIGURE 5.10 The sitemap in FigJam: The AI assistant is hidden in the top right-hand corner behind the icon with the stars. (Figure created using Figma.)

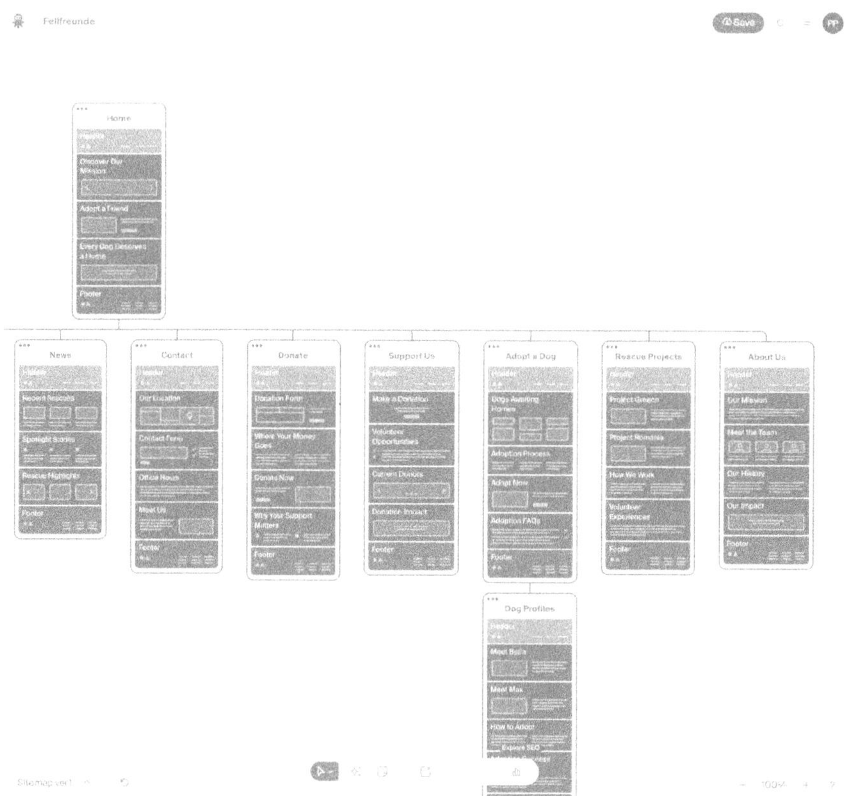

FIGURE 5.11 The sitemap in Octopus.do: Not only are pages created here, but it also generates suggestions for the content on them – which brings us to the next level, wireframes. (Figure created using Octopus.)

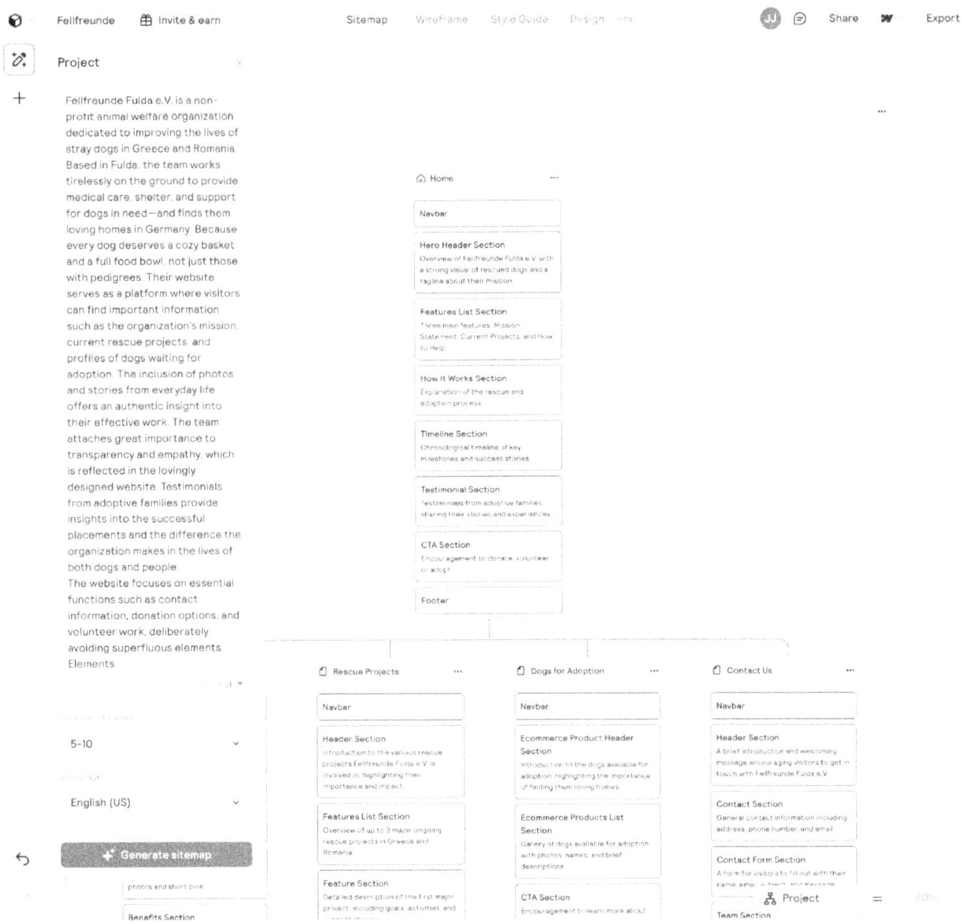

FIGURE 5.12 The sitemap in Relume: If no Content is suggested for a page yet, generate it by clicking on "Generate Content". (Figure created using Relume.)

3. Copy the description of your site into the **Sitemap** area.
4. Under **Number of pages**, specify how many pages the sitemap should have. Set **Language** to **English**, and the content will appear in English (but the interface cannot be switched).
5. Click on **Generate sitemap**. (I sometimes encountered errors with longer site descriptions. These always disappeared when I entered the **sitemap prompt** in English – simply have your text translated by ChatGPT or Claude. The result will still appear in the language you have selected in the **Language** field.)

5.9 DESIGNING NAVIGATION

Once you have decided on the terms and structure of the site, i.e. the sitemap, you can consider how to present it to visitors. The most important element for navigation is the ***navigation bar*** (sometimes called ***the main menu***). Links, search fields and tiles are also navigation elements, but we will deal with these in the next step. All of these allow people to move around your website. To do this, however, you must first give them orientation. This means that even if they don't click on it at first, the navigation bar fulfils a very important function: that of a shop window. It shows visitors what the site has to offer, what it is about and what they can expect.

Incidentally, the term ***"menu"*** has a broader meaning: menus can also be found in a form where you can select your title, for example. So the navigation bar is often a menu, but a menu is only sometimes a navigation bar.

What does the perfect menu look like? Is it a menu with only one entry, namely the one that a visitor needs in the current situation? Certainly not. A menu that only contains your favourite dish is very user-friendly, but you would still find it very irritating in a restaurant. The usability would be high, but the user experience would still be poor. You want some choice. With a website that only offers you a single menu item, you would have two main problems: Firstly, if there is only one item, then a menu is superfluous and disappointing – you could just offer that one item directly in large print. Secondly, visitors would have no idea what else the website has to offer – just as you would want to know what else a restaurant has to offer. On your next visit, you would probably want to eat something different and, of course, you would want to know whether it is worth visiting again.

And the most important point is, of course, in practice: the website does not "know" why a visitor has come to the site. Therefore, the website should first present them with what it has to offer.

5.9.1 Menu Killer 1: The Burger

The main reason why the classic navigation bar is struggling today is the ***burger menu***, i.e. the three horizontal stripes that only open a menu when clicked or tapped (see Figure 5.13, top left of the screen). The idea for this came about with the advent of smartphones: space is so limited on these devices that most menus with six or more menu items do not even fit completely on the screen. And even if they do, there is hardly any room left on the small screen for the actual content. Therefore, in the smartphone view, there is hardly anything that can beat the menus hidden behind the burger icon.

But that also means you have to make it clear to visitors what your site is about in a different way. And just because we have this limitation on mobile devices, we don't have to impose it on larger screens as well. Especially since the usage situation is often different there: on a smartphone, I often just look something up quickly, whereas on larger screens I want to do more thorough research.

By now, almost everyone knows what the burger icon stands for, but it is still often overlooked, especially on large monitors.

Even when it is not overlooked, the burger is often ignored simply because it is not so prominent. Countless evaluations of access figures/analytics and usability tests prove that a burger menu leads to people interacting less with websites. They open fewer pages,

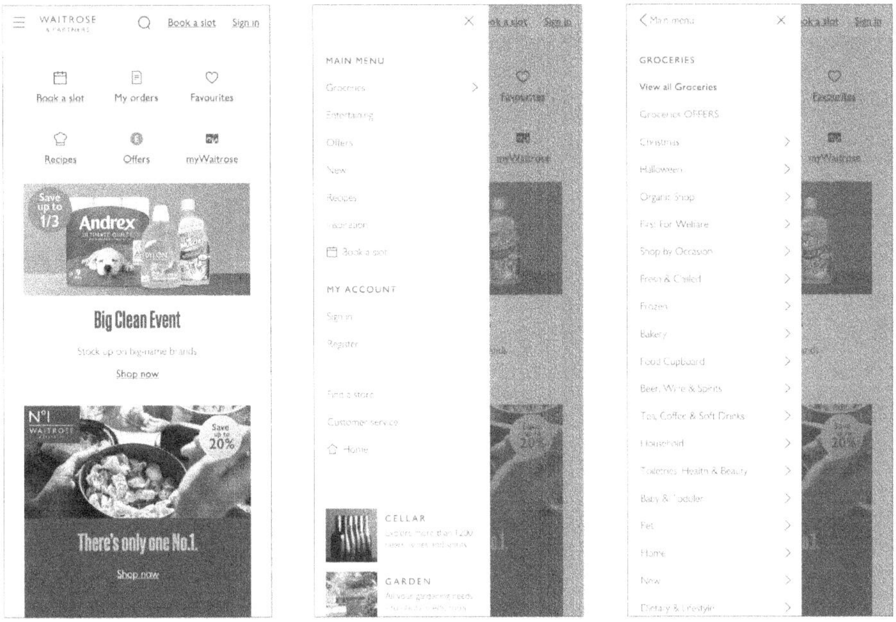

FIGURE 5.13 The burger menu on waitrose.com: closed, open and open in the second level. It works as expected on smartphones.

FIGURE 5.14 The burger icon on the site of a winery (www.bertani.net), top left: Looks tidy, but gives no information about what can be found here.

view fewer products and spend less time on the website. Word has slowly spread, which is why more and more sites are returning to real menus.

5.9.2 Menu Killer 2: The Search

Navigation has also lost importance due to search. When I have people in the usability lab, I see one thing in practically every case: the first thing they do with the browser is search. Google is now so good that no one bothers to type in even the simplest URL anymore. And many people now search using AI, which fundamentally changes the situation.

Opinions vary widely on how many people go directly to the search function on a website. Concrete figures are hard to come by, but based on my personal experience with test subjects, I would say that at least a third of visitors go directly to the search function.

The problem with this is that

- The search function often works poorly.
- People often search poorly.

This means that people don't think much about how content is sorted and tagged. They simply enter the first thing that comes to mind. Google and other search engine operators are getting better and better at bringing up useful results even for such vague queries, and AI is doing the same.

But a lot has also changed on the websites themselves. The search function there has improved significantly for most of them in recent years. Many websites offer a prominent search function at the top of the page, which is generally always recommended. But even if your search function works excellently, a good search function does not mean you don't have to put any effort into creating information architecture and navigation. Even if visitors find what they are looking for immediately, they almost always want to find out more. In a shop, they may want to know what alternative products you offer or what your delivery terms are.

5.9.3 General Design Tips for Menus

So what does the ideal menu look like? As is so often the case, the answer to this question is not entirely straightforward. What is clear is that a good menu must have the following characteristics:

- **Clear and consistent**: The terms must clearly describe what can be expected on the linked pages.
- **Comprehensibly structured**: Related items should be grouped together, with subcategories organising the sub-items in a way that is easy to understand and consistent.

- **Manageable and comprehensible**: The number of menu items should not overwhelm users. Rule of thumb: Between 5 and 9 items per level are usually fine in terms of average complexity.
- **Usable on all devices**: Regardless of screen size, the menu must be technically usable and understandable in terms of content. The respective advantages of the devices should be exploited to the fullest.
- **Accessible**: The menu should be accessible to all users, regardless of whether they have limitations or not.

5.9.4 Practical Implementation of Navigation

In the past, the entire site was often mapped out using nested menus, i.e. visitors could navigate through the entire structure of the site using the navigation bar. In principle, this is a good idea, as it allows them to see how the site is structured. However, nested menus have two major problems: on larger sites, our short-term memory is overwhelmed by all the entries in the menu. Secondly, moving the mouse pointer within the nested menu is difficult from a purely motor skills perspective – it often happens that the menu closes because you accidentally hover over the background with the mouse. In addition, such complex menus are difficult to display meaningfully on the small screens of mobile devices.

The classic option, with which you can't go far wrong, is the ***horizontal menu***. This has the great advantage that visitors can see at a glance what you offer on your website. Ideally, they will also immediately see what they are looking for. They can find what they need without further interaction – an optimal user experience.

With more than a handful of menu items, you will reach the limits of the horizontal menu: you usually cannot fit more than eight to ten items. Even if some users with large monitors would have enough space, there are two reasons why you should not take advantage of this: firstly, the more items a menu has, the more difficult it is for us to see them all and find the one that suits us. Secondly, even on a laptop with a significantly wider screen than a smartphone, only a few items can fit side by side. Some menus get around this by making the menu bar horizontally scrollable. However, this is very tedious to use and should therefore only be done in exceptional cases.

The best solution for menus with a large number of items is to add a drop-down menu. When the mouse pointer is moved over the menu items, their sub-items are displayed (see right on Figure 5.15).

An alternative is the ***mega menu***. When you hover over it with the mouse or tap or click on it, a large (hence "mega") area appears, usually with menu items offered in several columns.

This is a particularly good way to show a lot at once for sites with a great deal of content. On the other hand, this amount of choice can quickly overwhelm users. It is therefore not easy to design a good mega menu. If you want to do this, you should definitely

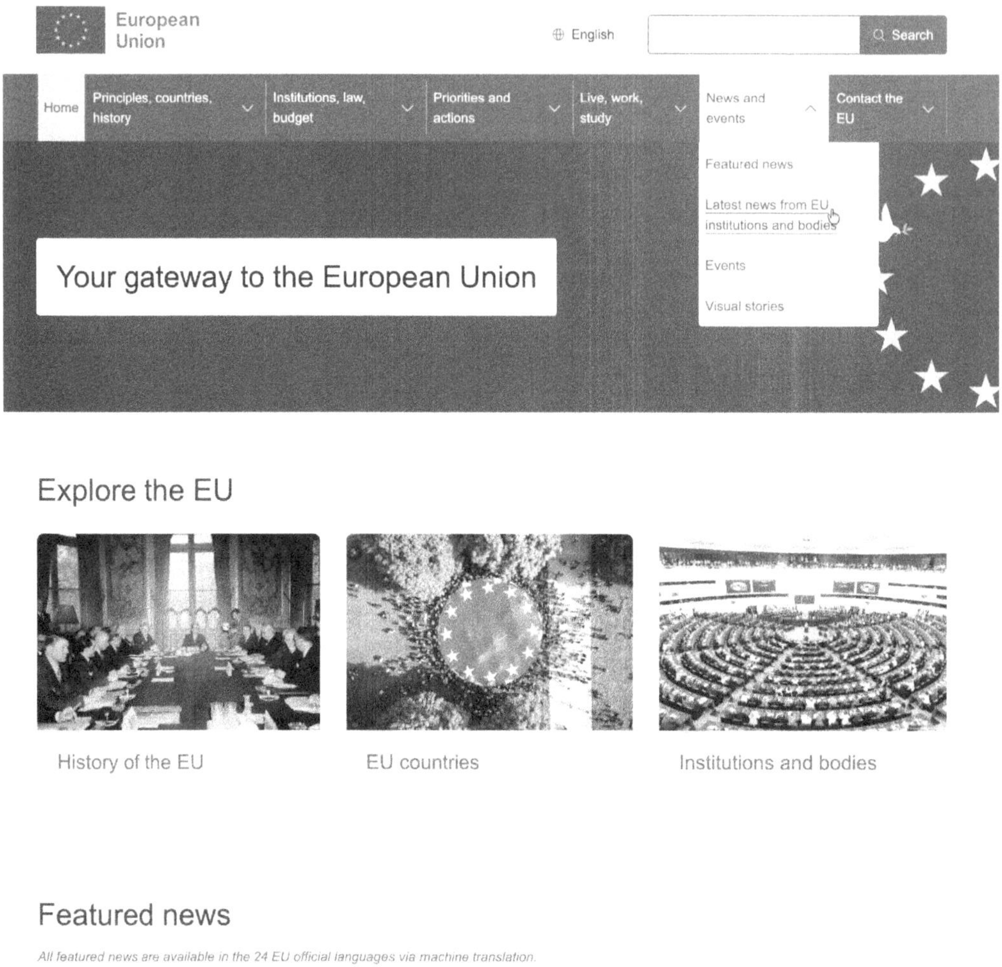

FIGURE 5.15 Classic horizontal navigation without frills at european-union.europa.eu. The submenus open when you roll over them with the mouse.

use card sorting in advance to ensure that the structure and terms are understood by your target group. And it is best to test the finished menu in a usability test. This is because the details of the design and technical implementation are also important here.

5.9.5 Additional Navigation Options

In addition to the actual menu, there are other elements that users can use to navigate your website. These are primarily the following:

- ***Meta navigation***: These are elements such as search and login/profile, which are located above (hence "meta") the actual navigation bar.

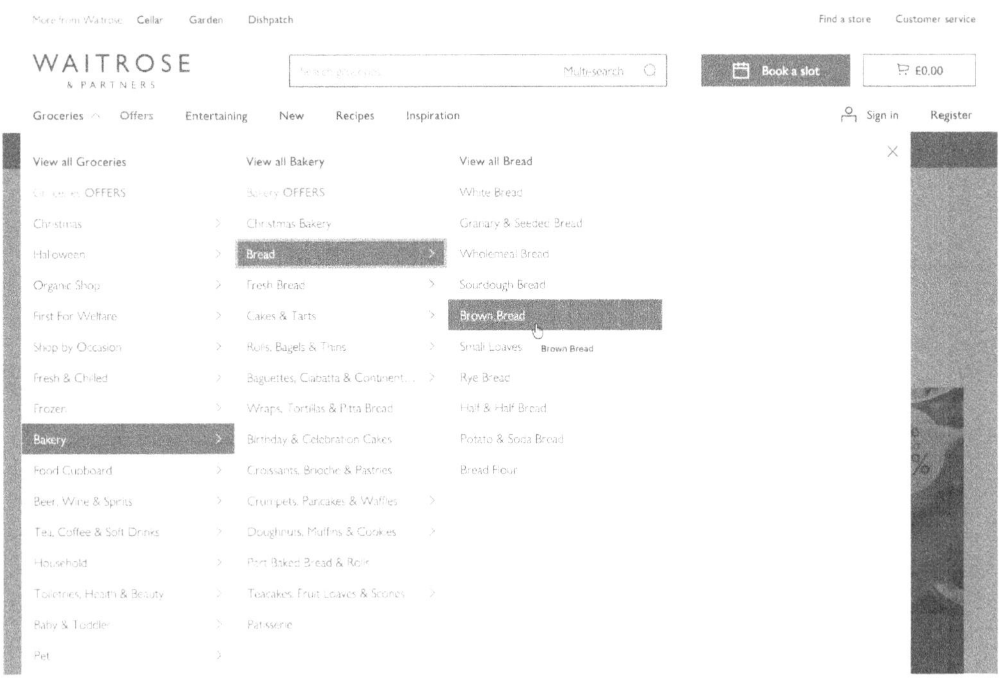

FIGURE 5.16 Mega menu of the desktop view of Waitrose (Waitrose.com).

- ***Breadcrumb*** navigation: This bar, usually located above the content area of the page, shows the individual steps or hierarchy levels that visitors have taken so far. The "breadcrumbs" help to clarify the current position on the website and also offer a quick way to move up one or more levels of the structure. To do this, the higher-level pages must be linked. They should also be clearly recognisable as links, preferably by underlining them and using the colour that is otherwise used for links on the site.
- ***Footer***: This often contains additional navigation that offers important links for anyone who has not found what they are looking for by the end of the page. The address and contact details are particularly common here. Especially on touchscreen devices, users often scroll to the very end because this gives them a good overview with just a few swipes. In English, such an extensive footer is referred to as ***a fat footer***.

5.10 PLANNING THE PAGE STRUCTURE WITH SCRIBBLES

Once you have got to grips with the structure of your site via a sitemap and defined the navigation, it is time to divide up the space on the screen for each individual page. There are many tools available to help you do this, the most important of which are

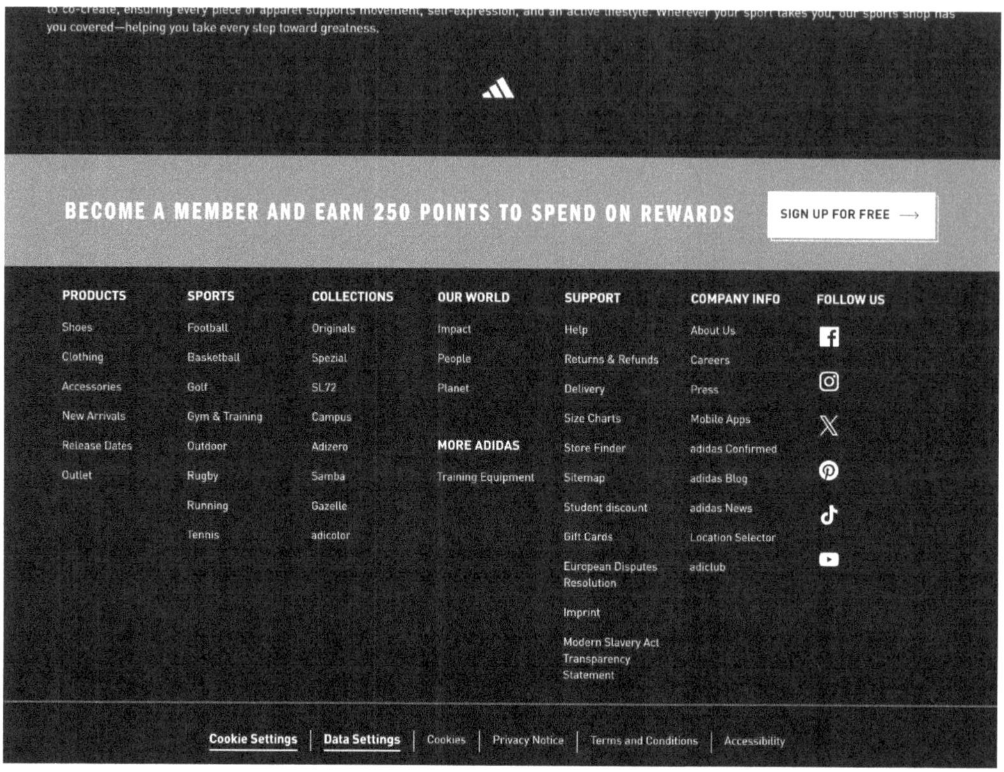

FIGURE 5.17 On adidas.com, the footer contains a mini sitemap with links to the most important areas.

scribbles and wireframes. So you start with rough sketches for the pages before you get down to the concrete implementation of graphics and programming. Otherwise, you run the risk of your tool – be it a content management system, a graphics programme or a framework – determining what the result will look like. Especially when working with templates, you may end up just following the template without questioning whether the elements it contains are actually useful for your project. A typical example is the news sections on websites mentioned in the box in Section 5.3, "AI Helps with Finding Ideas", which later contain only a few outdated news items. Such pitfalls can be avoided through conscious planning in advance. Scribbles and wireframes help you keep an eye on the structure and functionality of your website from the outset without getting bogged down in discussions about colours or fonts at an early stage.

The term "***scribble***" literally means "scribbling" and aptly describes the character of these initial drafts. They serve to record initial ideas and run through different approaches. In larger projects, scribbles are only the beginning of a whole series of

prototyping methods, i.e. the development of preliminary versions. Scribbles are followed by ***wireframes***, which are created digitally and provide more specific guidelines for the arrangement and size of elements. The next stage is ***mock-ups***, detailed but mostly static designs. At the end of the development chain are interactive ***prototypes,*** which are often programmed in HTML or created with special prototyping software. But for a medium-sized website, you can get quite far with scribbles alone. Let's take a look at how.

5.10.1 Scribbles – The Quick Way to Initial Visualisation

You don't need AI for your first scribbles – nothing is better suited for this than any pen and a sheet of paper. This allows you to develop your ideas completely freely: draw a rough outline for the page, place your logo, sketch headlines, text blocks and images. Mark interactive elements such as image galleries or navigation elements. The speed and flexibility of this method are also valuable in meetings, when all participants visualise their ideas and then discuss them. With just a few strokes, it sometimes becomes clear that we are talking about the same thing, but have completely different images in our minds.

For presentations, or if you are very uncomfortable with pen and paper, use a tablet: drawing apps help you to straighten lines automatically and duplicate designs quickly. Nevertheless, it is worth using traditional paper for initial sketches of ideas. It also has the advantage that you can hang many variations side by side on the wall and thus quickly see similarities and differences at a glance.

How detailed you work depends on who the scribble is intended for. For initial brainstorming, rough placeholders for logos, images and text blocks are sufficient; later, you can add symbolic images to clarify elements. It is important not to get lost in details: the greatest value of scribbles lies in the fact that they can be created quickly and easily. A layout idea that you reject or change today will only cost you a few minutes of work at the scribble stage.

Often, you start with very small scribbles, known as ***thumbnails***. They are the size of a *thumbnail* or a postage stamp. If you only have this little space, you are forced to be very restrictive and can only show the very rough structure. That is precisely why you draw so small – and because it is so quick. In just a few minutes, you can develop many different ideas for how a page could look. Draw eight to 16 of these thumbnails to test different approaches. Then develop the most promising ones into larger, more detailed scribbles.

Start scribbling with the home page. Then create scribbles for all the main pages and for pages with special functions or layouts. Typically, these are important subpages such as About Us/Contact, Products/Services, Product Detail Pages, Blog Post Pages or Shopping Cart/Checkout. A typical corporate website usually has three-to-eight-page types.

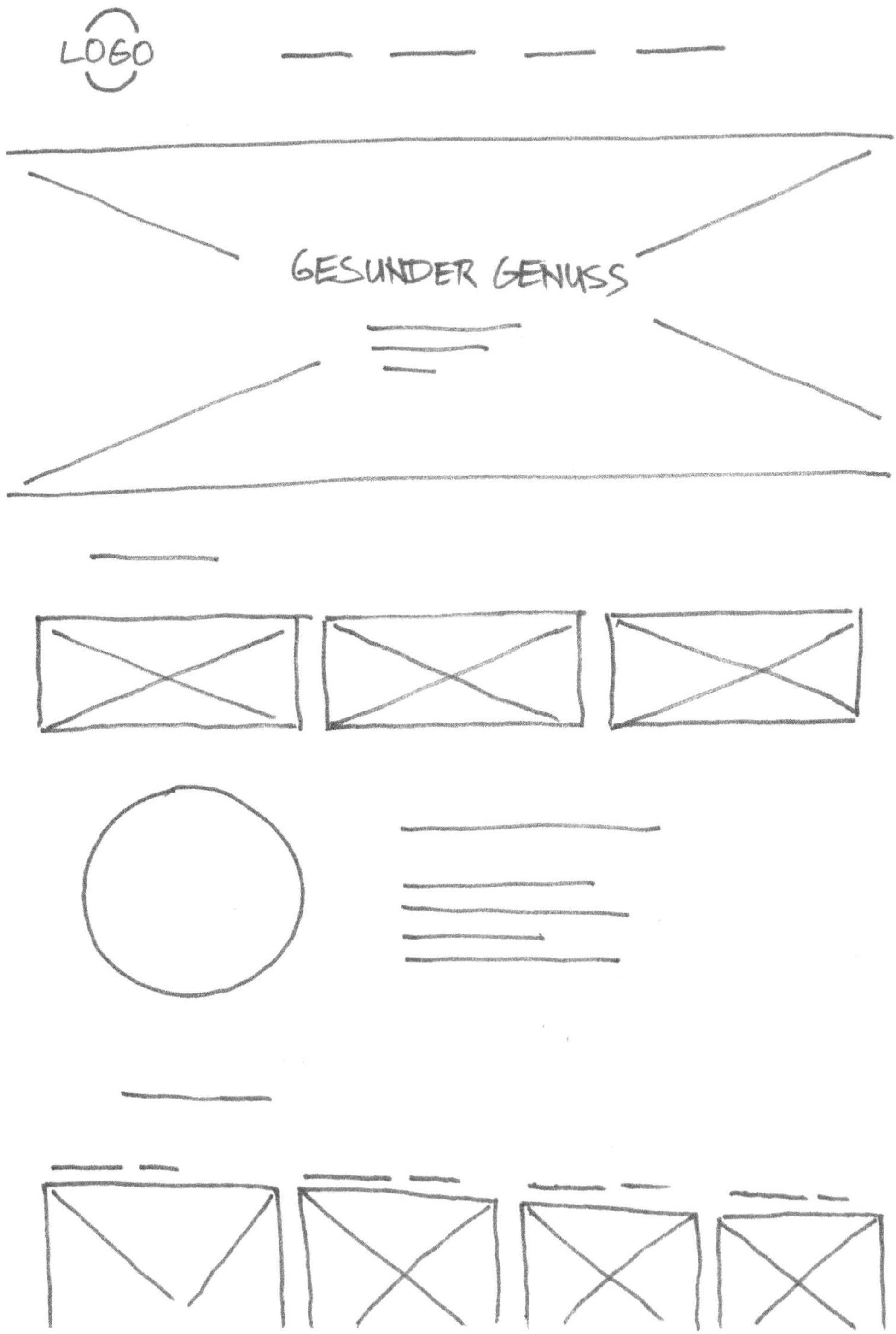

FIGURE 5.18 Sketch for the home page of our example café website.

5.11 WIREFRAMES – THE PATH TO A DETAILED CONSTRUCTION PLAN

Wireframes form the bridge between early scribbles and the final design. They are created digitally and already offer a more realistic feel for proportions on the screen. However, they still remain deliberately abstract: instead of a real design, they use placeholders and simple shapes to represent the structure of the page and the arrangement of the elements.

The advantage lies in the clear focus on structure and functionality: no distraction from colours or typography, but concentration on questions such as "What content belongs on the home page?" or "How should users navigate?" Wireframes are particularly suitable for projects with many stakeholders in order to facilitate a structured dialogue. In practice, it is helpful to gather feedback at this stage so that you can respond quickly to new requirements and avoid costly detours.

You can create wireframes in prototyping tools such as ***Figma***, ***Sketch*** or ***Adobe XD***. Classic graphics programmes (***Affinity Designer***, ***Adobe Illustrator***) are also suitable. This results in a clear, functional design without you having to make detailed design decisions. Only once the basic page structures have been clarified is it worth fine-tuning the visuals.

5.11.1 Practical Approach and Effort

In many small projects, either scribbles *or* wireframes are created. That's perfectly fine – I personally always recommend scribbles because they are much quicker to create and change. However, if you feel more comfortable with wireframes, then work with them. They are also more suitable for presenting interim results. But be aware that anyone who is not directly involved in the project will have problems with even detailed wireframes. Members of management, for example, almost always expect mock-ups, i.e. perfectly designed drafts that already contain the images and text that will ultimately be used. So-called ***prompt frames*** may be an alternative. These are wireframes that contain prompts to generate placeholder text and preliminary images using AI. They are ultimately a template for creating mock-ups that can also be used for usability testing with the target group.

Whether you create scribbles or wireframes or both, first consider which elements are actually important for your website:

- Logo
- Menus and possibly submenus
- Possibly higher-level menu items such as imprint, sitemap, search and contact (so-called meta navigation)
- Breadcrumbs (e.g. "Home > Sub-area > Page 2") and other additional orientation options

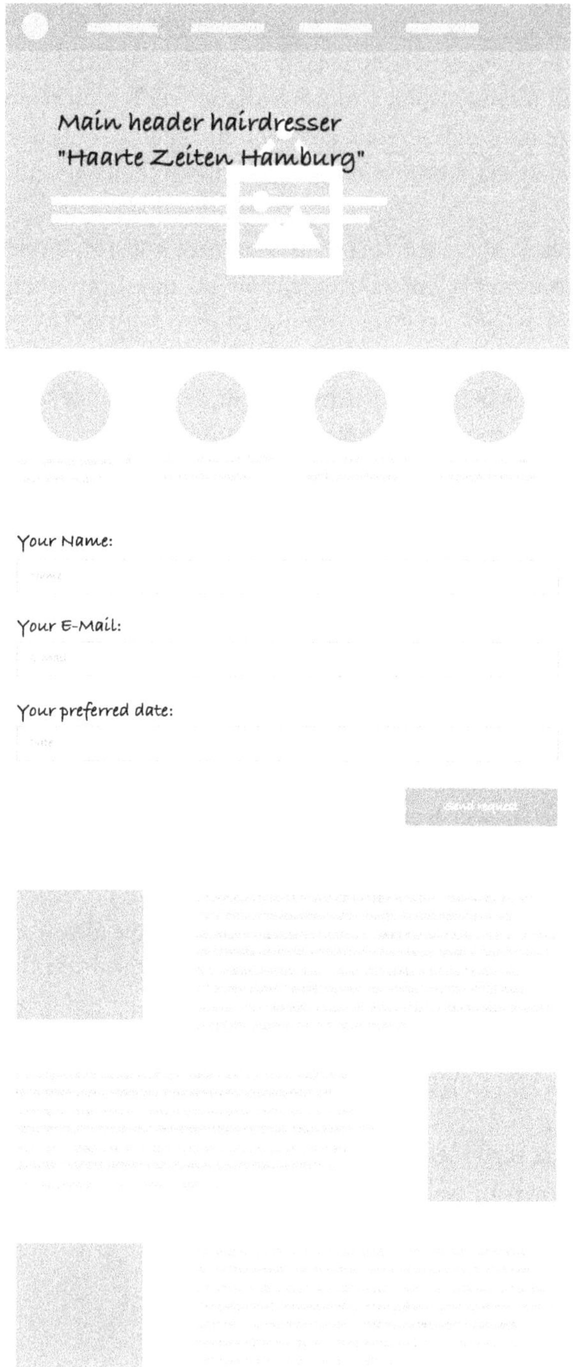

FIGURE 5.19 Wireframe for the home page of a hairdresser: colours and fonts are deliberately chosen to make it clear that these are not the final proposals, in order to focus the discussion on the layout.

- Images and text
- Additional elements such as forms, tables or interactive elements

You can also ask the AI for help:

EXAMPLE PROMPT: STRUCTURE WIREFRAME OR SCRIBBLE

Motivation: I want to create a wireframe for the home page of the "Fit-mit-Frieder-und-Fabi" team's website in Berlin. I want to develop a user-friendly, motivating and clear home page that clearly presents the most important information, such as course schedules, training locations, trainer profiles and customer reviews. The page should also be visually appealing and tailored to the needs of the target audience.

Task: Create a list of all elements that should be included in the wireframe and make suggestions on how these elements could be arranged to ensure intuitive user guidance and an appealing design.

Result: A detailed list of the necessary wireframe components with brief descriptions of their function and specific suggestions for their placement on the page. The result should serve directly as the basis for the sketchy creation of a wireframe.

Example: The result could include elements such as a header area with logo and navigation, a centrally placed course schedule with clear call-to-action buttons and a section with trainer profiles (including image and brief description). Supplemented by suggestions for placement, e.g.: "Hero area in the upper third with informative text about the company and background image". The design should be based on a clearly structured and easily understandable layout.

Role: You are an experienced UX/UI designer who develops creative and user-friendly solutions for wireframes.

Download prompt: bnfr.de/ai059

Check the result carefully to see whether you really need all the suggested elements and whether they belong on the home page or whether some of them should be on one of the subpages.

It is often sufficient to create one page sketch for the home page and one for the subpages. If necessary, sketch special function pages such as contact forms or product overviews. For small or medium-sized projects, 1–2 hours of scribbling and wireframing is often enough to create a solid foundation.

For more complex websites, consider different page types, such as blog overview pages, product detail pages or landing pages. An online shop might need a layout with highlighted product images and price boxes, while a portfolio page might focus on clear categories or filter options. The larger the project, the more important it is to have additional wireframes so that everyone involved can see exactly how menus, search fields or product areas differ on each page.

Remain flexible during this phase and be sure to create several variants for each page. This will allow you to quickly identify which ideas are truly good and which changes are necessary to make navigation easier for the target audience. Once all structural issues have been clarified, you will have a solid basis on which to start detailed graphic design or programming. This saves time and allows you to make course corrections during the course of the project without major effort.

5.11.2 Creating Wireframes with AI

Of course, AI can also help us create wireframes. However, the language models are only moderately well suited for this. Try the following:

EXAMPLE PROMPT: CREATE WIREFRAME

Motivation: I want to create a wireframe for an HTML page.
Task: Write HTML code that creates a visualisation as a wireframe.
Result: The HTML code should be minimalistic and clearly structured. It should contain rectangles as placeholders for images, represented by two intersecting diagonal lines from corner to corner (X-shape, as is common for wireframes). Consider where text would be useful and insert "Lorem ipsum" text of appropriate length for the text blocks. Use only black, white and shades of grey.
Additional information: {Description of the wireframe and elements}

The prompt to copy: bnfr.de/ai060

This prompt works best for me with Claude. Not only does the AI show me the HTML code, but I can also switch directly to the browser view and refine the result via chat.

This is sufficient for quick visualisation, but if you want to continue working with the wireframes as a team, for example, to coordinate the content and structure for all pages, you will probably want slightly better results – and, above all, you will be looking for a method that allows you to make changes easily. If you use ***Figma***, there are several plug-ins that create wireframes with the help of AI. However, I have not yet found one that delivers results good enough to save me work. So if you really want to work with Figma, use a language model for visual ideas as described above and then recreate them in Figma.

Or you can use another tool – my recommendation is again ***Relume*** (in which case, continue in Relume after the preliminary work we did in Section 5.8, "Creating a Sitemap with AI"):

1. Open your project.
2. Use the button at the top centre to switch to **WIREFRAME** view. If you have never been there before, you can watch your wireframes being created.
3. Wireframes are only created for pages that have a description in **THE SITEMAP**. Either switch back there directly or click the **GENERATE PAGE** button in the context menu on the respective empty page.

FIGURE 5.20 A little skewed, but perfectly adequate for most cases: wireframe as created by Claude. (Figure created using Claude 3.5 Sonnet.)

4. Alternatively, or if you do not like the content of the page, click on the grey/purple bar above the respective page. A pop-up will then open where you can enter a prompt to create the wireframe. This will give you much better results because you are giving the AI better guidance.
5. Then click on all the individual elements on the wireframes that are not yet optimal. You can then delete or edit them, or have the dummy text regenerated by AI.

Personally, I find this process very pleasant and the results excellent. The only danger is that it makes us lazy, and we settle for the first solution offered by the AI. Remember

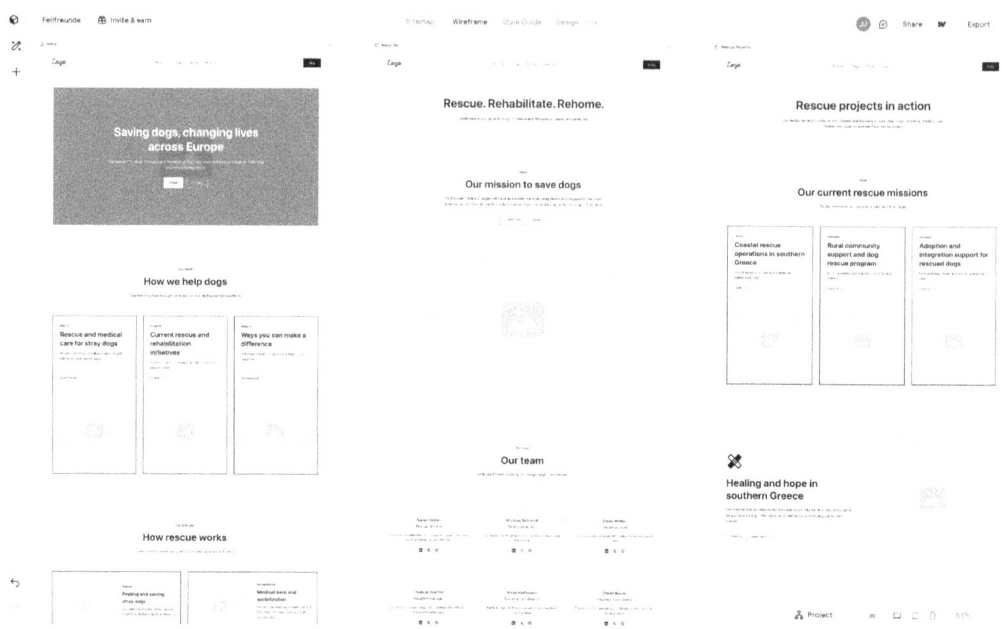

FIGURE 5.21 Automatically generated wireframes in Relume: Not only do they look good, but their content is also quite good. (Figure created using Relume.)

golden rule number 3: AI can lead you astray. And remember that we don't just want to work faster with AI, we want to work better, so we must always critically question whether the suggestions actually fit the goals of the site and the wishes of the target groups. In addition, the wireframes are all based on Relume ***components***, i.e. predefined building blocks. This does not make the website unique, but at least it is more special than sites that are based solely on ready-made templates.

Instead of Relume, you can also work with ***Octopus***. In the free version, you cannot customise the colours of the wireframes, and personally I find them a little too bright, which I find distracting. The AI customisation features are also limited here. However, you can make some changes manually.

With both Relume and Octopus, the export options are limited, so it's usually easiest to take a screenshot of the sitemap and wireframes. (Read more about the very practical export options that export the basic structure of the pages from Relume in the next chapter.)

5.11.3 Responsive Design – Look Good Everywhere

For most services, only wireframes for one view are created – but in any case, you start with just one view. But what you mustn't forget is that people access your website using all kinds of devices. Their screen sizes range from tiny smartphones with 480 × 320 pixels to 4K monitors with 4,096 × 2,304 pixels, which is almost ten times as much. So we face the challenge of making our site look good everywhere, from smartphones and tablets to desktop monitors and smart TVs. ***Responsive design*** is the approach to mastering this challenge.

Responsive design means more than just flexible layouts: a website should function well and look good on all devices. But what does that mean in concrete terms? A responsive website must fulfil three key characteristics:

1. **Adaptive**: The site adapts to the size of the respective screen.
2. **Accessible**: Content and functions can be used regardless of the device.
3. **Customised**: The design utilises the strengths of the respective medium and compensates for its weaknesses. This includes, for example, using the standard ***date picker*** on smartphones for inputs such as date selection, or replacing small radio buttons with touch elements that are easy to operate with your finger.

The ***mobile-first*** approach is widely used. This means that the version for mobile devices is created first, followed by the version for larger screens. This is justified because

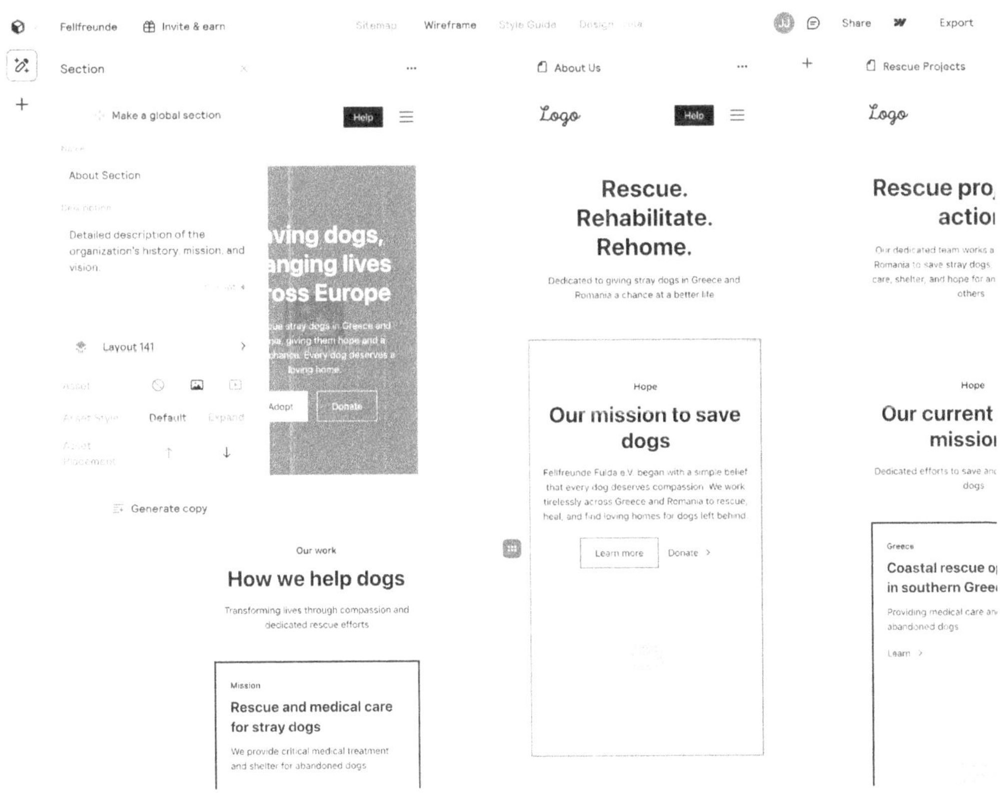

FIGURE 5.22 Relume automatically creates wireframes for desktop, tablet and smartphone (shown here). (Figure created using Relume.)

almost all websites today are accessed by more people using smartphones than tablets or desktop PCs.

For this reason, Google also places greater emphasis on mobile display when ranking pages in search results. However, this does not mean that you can ignore other screen sizes. Your design should be screen agnostic so that it works on any device. With the mobile version, it is often quite clear what the optimal implementation looks like (only one column for content, large buttons, focused content). On the other hand, there is significantly more design freedom when adapting a mobile design to larger screens. This means that you have to spend more time on the concept before you can start implementation. That's why I think it's legitimate to start with the standard desktop view during the concept phase and only then design the mobile version and possibly one for very large screens.

In larger projects, wireframes are created for the planned display sizes. You don't necessarily have to do this for every single page, but it's a good idea to do it for one page so that you can define how you will deal with the different space requirements and how you will distribute the elements.

CHAPTER 6

Step 4

Design Meets Code – Designing and Programming the Site

Now design and technology come together. We start with the brand and logo, create a style guide and then implement the site with AI assistance – accessible, user-friendly and appealing.

In the previous step, you determined the optimal structure of your website and thus already made the first important design decisions. Design is not just about visual design, but starts with the concept. Building on this, we can now get started with design and programming. Web design means much more than beautiful images and appealing design. It is based much more on how people perceive and use websites. Visitors decide within a few seconds whether to stay on our site or leave it immediately. In this short time, we have to convince them that it is worth staying and engaging with our content.

The area that visitors can see without scrolling – the so-called area ***above the fold*** – is particularly important for this. This term comes from the world of newspapers and refers to the part that is visible above the fold when the newspaper is in a newspaper rack or at a kiosk. The headlines that are immediately visible determine whether the newspaper is bought (or was, as the era of printed newspapers is largely over). Today, the area of a website that can be seen without scrolling is just as important. We need to convey two things to visitors at the top of the home page as quickly and clearly as possible: you've come to the right place and it's worth reading on or scrolling further. A clear, well-organised design of this area is therefore crucial.

This is not just about rational decisions. A website must also appeal emotionally and create trust. Similar to people who may say the same thing but come across as more or less convincing, a website must be more than just a collection of information. It must establish an emotional connection with visitors. This means that people are at the centre of

DOI: 10.1201/9781003726708-6

development. That is why we talk about ***human-centred development***. People have different needs, abilities and preferences, which we must take into account in the design. Professional web design is characterised by a well-thought-out visual hierarchy. It uses design principles such as contrast, white space and alignment to structure content and direct the attention of visitors. This is not directly about beauty, but rather the interplay of colour harmony, typography and spatial layout, which together create an effective and pleasant user experience. This should be accessible to everyone – there is now a legal requirement for every commercial website to be ***accessible***, meaning it must also be usable by people with disabilities.

6.1 FROM BRAND TO DESIGN

An emotional connection to a website is not created by trying out a few fonts and colours in a creative workshop or asking AI to do so. Ideally, it starts with a collection of values and beliefs: What do we stand for? What is important to us? What makes us special? What do we want our customers to think of us? So we deal with our ***brand***. Brands are created primarily through emotions. Of course, colours and photos evoke emotions, which is why they are also important for brand building. However, stronger emotions are evoked when we have positive experiences with a provider. When we receive our goods on time. When they are beautifully – and securely – packaged. When the product matches the description. When someone takes care of us when we have a problem with the product. We have to take all of this into account when we deal with a "brand". Derived from the word "brand", the term ***"branding"*** refers to the process by which our brand is created, i.e. ***brand development***.

6.1.1 Defining Your Own Brand

When you think of brands, do you think of expensive marketing agencies, large presentation boards with beautiful pictures and exorbitant daily rates? You don't need any of that to get a clear idea of your brand. For smaller websites, it is enough to think a little about how you want to be perceived by your target group. We all intuitively know what we like or dislike about other providers. We can use these experiences. We just need to take the time to sort through our thoughts. What makes your website special? How do you differ from others? Who are you targeting? What do your existing customers appreciate about you? These considerations are the first step in brand building – and thus also the foundation for the success of your website. You are already familiar with all of these considerations from Chapter 4, "Step 2: Select the Best Tools". So let's take these up now and use them as a basis for designing your website:

EXAMPLE PROMPT: BRAND DEVELOPMENT

Motivation: I want to create a website that clearly defines my brand, appeals to my target audience and convincingly presents my unique selling points. The focus is on integrating my values and special features into the design and content of the website. But first, I just want the brand concept, not tips on how to implement the site.

Task: Help me develop a brand that authentically reflects my salon and my values and sets me apart from the competition. Answer the right questions and use this as a basis to develop a very concise brand image. Consider:

- Brand identity: What makes my brand special? What values, emotions and personality should it convey?
- Target group: Who are my ideal customers? What are their needs and expectations?
- Differentiation: What distinguishes my brand and my website from others in my industry?
- Target group perspective: What do existing customers appreciate about me/my company?

Then review the values you have identified. Are they specific and unique? If they are too generic, refine them based on the information provided. Be sure to avoid generalities such as "authentic", "professional", "inspiring" or "sustainable".

Result: Focus entirely on the following, without including the intermediate considerations:

- Brand strategy: briefly summarised brand values, a core statement and emotional appeal
- Design recommendations: colours, typography, imagery that reflect my brand

Role: You are a brand strategist. Your task is to use my information and answers to develop concrete proposals for the brand, which will then help me define the design for the website in the next step.

Additional information: {brief description of the site, target group, etc.}

The prompt to copy: bnfr.de/ai046

As you can see, this prompt is unusually long. The reason for this is that when it comes to topics such as branding, AI tends to reproduce generic things that it has read many times, so this prompt provides as much information as possible. Be very critical of the results. Ask questions and ask the AI to provide alternatives if something seems too general, doesn't fit, or you are otherwise not completely satisfied.

In the end, you will have a list of terms, characteristics or phrases that people should associate with you, your company and your services or products – the basic definition of your brand. This list should not be too long; the aim is not to list as many positive characteristics as possible, but to identify a few that are most important to you and that set you apart from others. This is the basis for the visual design.

6.1.2 Create a Mood Board

A first, simple step in this direction is the ***mood board*** – a collection of images, colours and style elements that convey the desired feeling. When looking at this collection, certain colours or a common style of the photos emerge: are they crisp, sharp and colourful, or rather washed out and in pastel shades? Do they show details, technical devices, people or landscapes? Are the shapes curved or rather straight?

Traditionally, a mood board is created by collecting and organising images. To do this, you search image portals such as Unsplash or Pinterest, competitors' websites or

FIGURE 6.1 Not every AI can help with every query.

photograph motifs that inspire you. You pay attention to colours, shapes, textures and moods that could suit your brand. You then combine all these elements – digitally or even physically on cardboard – and move them around until you create a harmonious composition. This process can take several days and requires a good eye for which components work well together and convey the desired atmosphere. Today, you can significantly speed up this process with the help of AI. It's best to start by generating image suggestions for individual elements, rather than trying to create a finished mood board. Otherwise, you run the risk of ending the actual creative process. When we see a finished result, it's difficult for us as non-professionals to contribute anything ourselves.

So, for example, let the AI first create mood images that match your brand message, or fictional products, or the interior design of your office, or even people using your products, or yourself providing your service. Be sure to include your brand values and the desired mood in the prompts, such as "professional, technical, innovative" or "natural, warm, handmade". The AI will then generate various images that you hadn't thought of and that will give you new ideas. Select the appropriate designs and collect them. Within a few hours, you will have a large pool of atmospheric images for your mood board. (Tips on image generation with AI can be found later in this chapter.)

If you already have some good ideas, challenge your AI partner and have it create a mood board right away. ***ChatGPT*** is particularly well suited for this because this language model also has access to image generation, allowing you to first create the description and then generate the image directly:

EXAMPLE PROMPT: PLAN MOOD BOARD

Motivation: I want a mood board that combines visual elements such as colours, images and fonts to convey a clear brand identity and mood as a basis for designing a website.

Task: Create such a mood board. Ask for more information if you need it before responding.

Result: The result is a mood board with:

- Three to a maximum of five sample photos
- A suitable colour palette with four to a maximum of six colours
- A list of two fonts that match the desired mood

Additional information: {brief description of the site, target audience, etc.}

The prompt to copy: bnfr.de/ai047

Remember golden rule number 2: AI needs good guidance. So be sure to give it the information about the mood or characteristics you want to convey with the website, who the target audience is and what colours you may already have in mind.

If you use ChatGPT for this task, you will usually receive a description. Don't settle for the first result, as it is usually very average – the large language model recommends what it has seen most often. For example, Monserrat and Roboto are almost always recommended as fonts. These are two good fonts, but they can be found on millions of websites. With the instruction "make it a little more unusual", you will get more interesting results.

If you are satisfied with the description, use ChatGPT to create an image of the mood board. Here, too, you will usually have to make manual corrections. The colours suggested by ChatGPT itself are often not applied correctly, and the fonts are sometimes missing. You can try to get the AI to correct this by going back and forth for a long time. However, it is much faster to download the generated image and use a tool such as ***Adobe Photoshop, Affinity Designer*** or any other graphics programme to cut out the elements, rearrange them and add the correct colours and fonts.

You can also get good results with ***Midjourney***, but I would then have ChatGPT customise the prompt so that it works specifically for this image AI, something like this: "Create a prompt that I can use in Midjourney to create such a mood board". ***Flux*** and ***Stable Diffusion*** also work with the same prompt. In ***Adobe Firefly***, I needed to be a bit more wordy to get usable mood boards.

When creating a mood board, it is generally important to limit yourself and only include a few elements. The aim is to convey as quickly as possible how you envisage the style of your site, not to depict all possible image styles, themes or even image motifs that will later be seen on the site. This forms the basis for the further development of the design.

FIGURE 6.2 The results from ChatGPT (left) and Midjourney (right): These are not real mood boards, but the images provide set pieces that we can continue to work with. (Figure created using ChatGPT 4o + Midjourney v6.1.)

FIGURE 6.3 The mood board, neatly designed in Affinity Designer.

If you feel you need more support in choosing colours and fonts, there are a few recommended special AI tools that can help you. You can find my current recommendations here: bnfr.de/ai048

6.1.3 Developing a Logo

Contrary to popular belief, a logo is not the most important aspect of branding. Of course, a good logo is valuable, but it is even more important that all elements fit together.

A coherently designed website with well-thought-out typography, aesthetically pleasing images and illustrations also works very well with a simple lettering logo. Before spending your entire budget on logo development, it is better to invest your energy or money in a coherent overall appearance. Large companies pay a lot of money for logo development, in some cases even millions. We cannot afford that for our modest websites; sometimes we cannot even afford the three-figure sum that design professionals sometimes charge for a logo. Then let AI help you. Of course, the results will appear generic and cannot compete with logos created by professionals. With the latter, you would develop a logo in an intensive dialogue in a multi-stage process. AI, on the other hand, only asks you three or four general questions and gets started. But such an AI logo is already a step forward compared to what many small sites use.

As always with conception and design, it is advisable not to start designing the logo right away. Think about what you want your logo to convey and then gather ideas on how to express that visually. Use your mood board to describe the colours, mood and values that are important to you.

EXAMPLE PROMPT: LOGO BRAINSTORMING

Motivation: I want six very different logo ideas that reflect the company's identity and values.

Task: Create six logo ideas based on the additional information about the company. The designs should include different styles, colour palettes and visual concepts that appeal to the company and its target audience.

Result: The end result should be six clear and describable logo ideas, each with a brief explanation of why they suit the company. The proposals should offer variations in style (e.g. minimalist, playful, modern), colour and typography.

Example:

1. Clean lines, geometric shapes, black and white colour palette. Conveys professionalism and elegance.
2. Bright colours, hand-drawn elements, soft typography. Conveys a welcoming and creative feel.
3. Cool colours (blue and silver), futuristic font, abstract symbolism. Suitable for a technology-oriented company.
4. Earth tones, organic shapes, natural typography. Conveys a connection to nature.
5. Muted colours, vintage font, classic emblem design. Evokes nostalgia and authenticity.
6. A unique illustration that directly represents the company, e.g. a specific symbol that reflects the brand.

Role: You are a creative graphic designer who develops innovative and versatile logo ideas. You always take the company's values and target audience into account and explain each proposal in a clear manner.

Additional information: {Details about your company, the target audience, your values and possibly colours and fonts}

The prompt to copy: bnfr.de/ai049

With a prompt like this, ChatGPT or Le Chat will provide you with a list of six very different ideas. Adjust these in dialogue with the AI until you are satisfied. If you use ChatGPT, you can create variants directly:

EXAMPLE PROMPT: LOGO IMPLEMENTATION WITH CHATGPT OR GEMINI

Okay, now create a landscape image that shows a 3 × 2 grid, each with a variant featuring a square logo based on your suggestion with the number 1.

The prompt to copy: bnfr.de/ai050

Or you can ask the language model you are using to create a prompt for the image AI of your choice, which you can then copy and paste there. Image AIs generally find such representations easier to work with than photos, so you can use whichever one you feel most comfortable with.

EXAMPLE PROMPT: LOGO IMPLEMENTATION WITH MIDJOURNEY, STABLE DIFFUSION, FIREFLY

Minimalistic square logo with a clearly recognisable haircutting scissor, simplified geometric shapes, bold use of copper-orange as accent colour on a deep midnight blue background, clean alignment, reduced details, strong emphasis on symmetry and balance, high-quality vector style – no text, details, shadows.

The prompt to copy: bnfr.de/ai070

In my experience, the best way to create a logo is with ***Adobe Illustrator***. The reason for this is not the quality of the AI, which is fine but not outstanding. The reason is that Illustrator's AI does not generate pixel images like the other systems mentioned, but vectors. Vector graphics have the advantage that you can directly edit the shapes, colours, sizes, line widths and positions of individual elements. Each object is defined separately

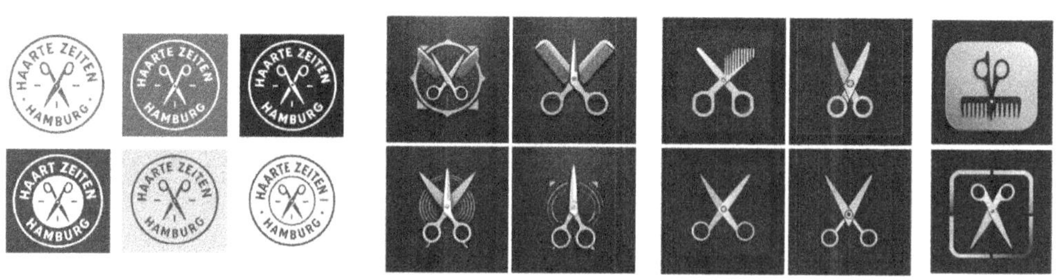

FIGURE 6.4 The logo design suggestions from the AI, from left to right: ChatGPT, Firefly, Midjourney, Stable Diffusion – all of them offer promising approaches. (Figure created using ChatGPT 4o, Adobe Firefly 3, Midjourney v6.1 and Stable Diffusion SDXL.)

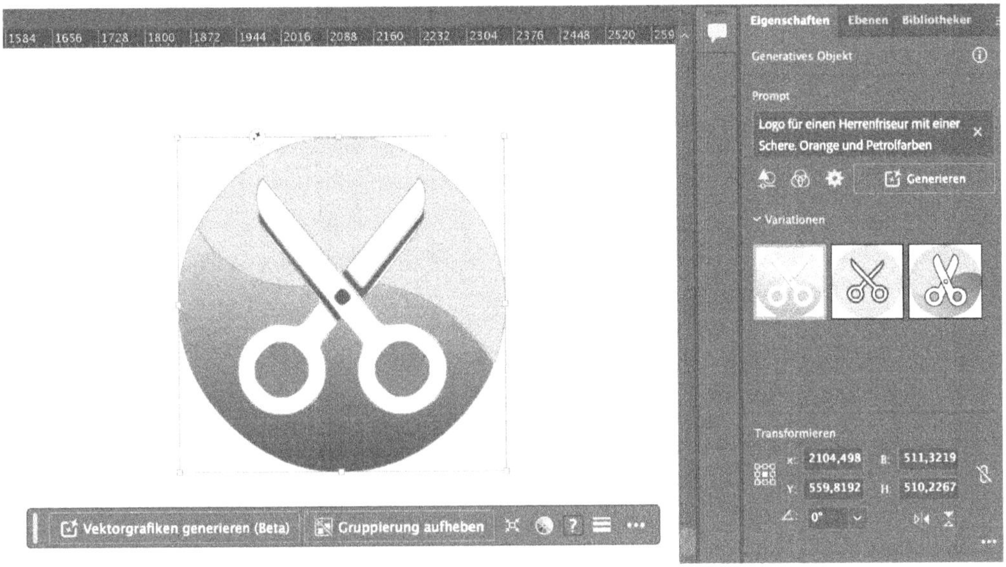

FIGURE 6.5 The logo in Illustrator: The AI creates vectors so that we can quickly change colours or add, move or manipulate elements – the three variants created are shown on the right. (Figure created using Adobe Firefly 3.)

and can be moved or changed as desired. Would you prefer red instead of orange in the background? One click in Illustrator and it's changed. Would you prefer a square in the background? Delete the circle and draw a rectangle behind the scissors. You can also enlarge vector graphics as desired without any loss of quality – the graphic is simply recalculated.

6.1.4 Special AI for Logo Development

In addition to classic image AIs such as Midjourney and similar tools, there are many providers that specialise in logo creation. With these, you only need to enter a few details and you'll have your finished logo. Personally, I don't see this as an advantage, but rather a disadvantage. This is because you skip the important creative process of thinking about the logo yourself. What's more, most of them offer far fewer options for making changes afterwards. And finally, you'll be asked to pay as soon as you want to download the results. However, you can almost always use the services for free for inspiration. If you want to explore this category, you can find a few tips here: bnfr.de/ai051

6.2 CREATING THE BASIC DESIGN – PAGE GRID, LAYOUT, STYLE GUIDE AND DESIGN SYSTEM

In Chapter 5, "Step 3: Determine the Optimal Structure of the Website", you created scribbles or wireframes for the home page and at least one subpage. This determines how the elements are placed on the pages. Together with the mood board, this is your basis

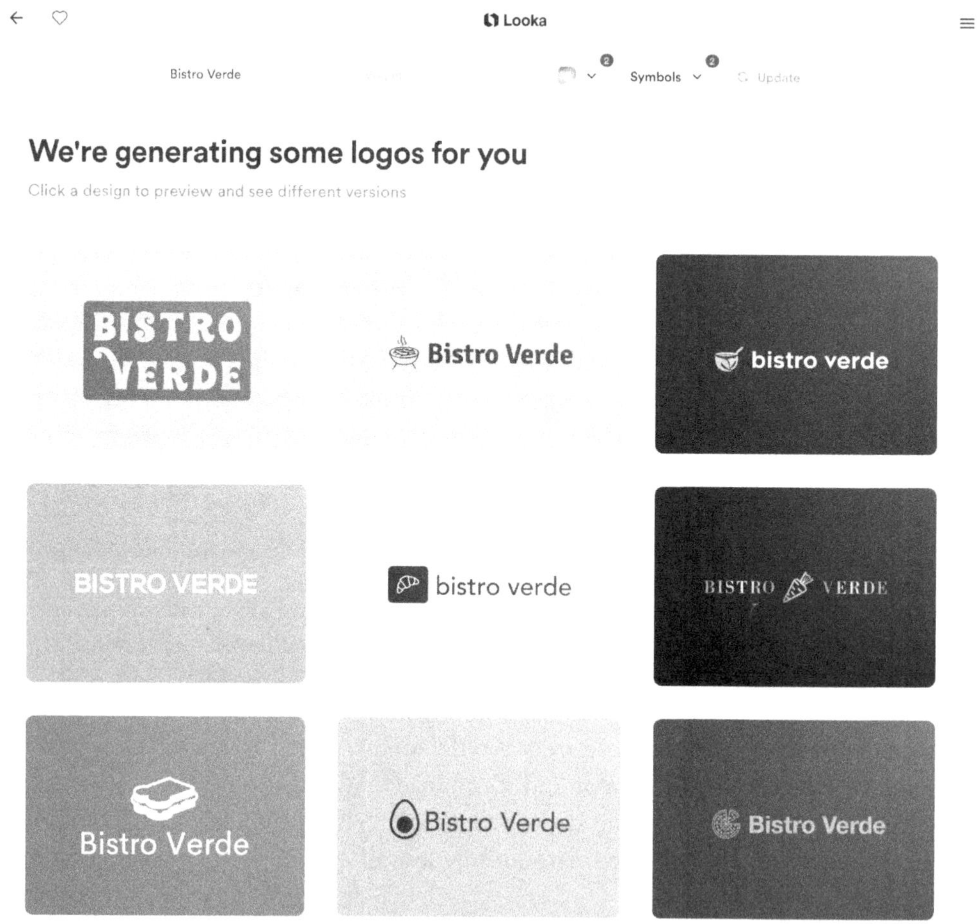

FIGURE 6.6 Initial logo suggestions with looka.com: Not very useful, but helpful for inspiration – and you can tweak the results directly on the site. (Figure created using Looka.)

for the ***layout*** of the website. This is based on ***the page grid*** and, in turn, forms the basis for ***the style guide*** and a possible ***design system***. Sounds complicated? But it's not really.

6.2.1 From Structure to Visual Design

The ***page grid*** forms the invisible basis of your website. Above all, it defines how many columns you use on the page and defines the spacing between them. This helps you to arrange the elements clearly and concisely. A well-thought-out grid system is particularly helpful when it comes to responsive, adapting content to different screen sizes. A 12-column grid is often used, as it allows for flexible layouts: elements can occupy several columns on desktop screens, while being reduced to a single column on small mobile devices.

Based on the grid, you develop the ***layout***, the visible arrangement of all elements such as text, images and interactive components. Start by planning the header, navigation, main

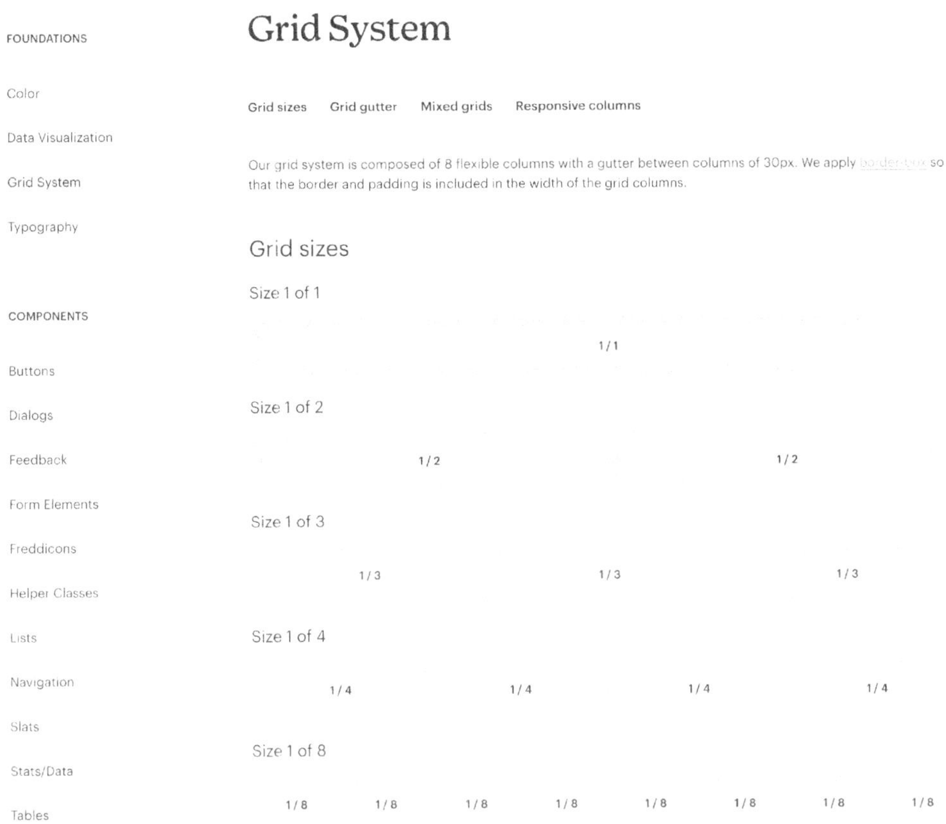

FIGURE 6.7 The page grid (Grid System) of the Mailchimp newsletter service. Unlike many others, it uses eight columns instead of 12.

content and footer. Then define the colours, fonts and spacing in the detailed design. For professional layout development, use tools such as ***Figma***, ***Adobe XD*** or ***Sketch***.

6.2.2 Consistency through Style Guide and Design System

The ***style guide*** documents all visual elements of your website and ensures that the design remains consistent even with subsequent changes. It is created in parallel with the layout and includes the specified fonts, colour palettes, spacing, image formats and interaction elements such as hover effects (the view that is shown when the mouse cursor moves over an element). Even for smaller projects, a simple style guide is valuable as it makes subsequent adjustments and enhancements much easier.

A style guide should include at least the following:

- Values and characteristics that the company stands for
- Logo

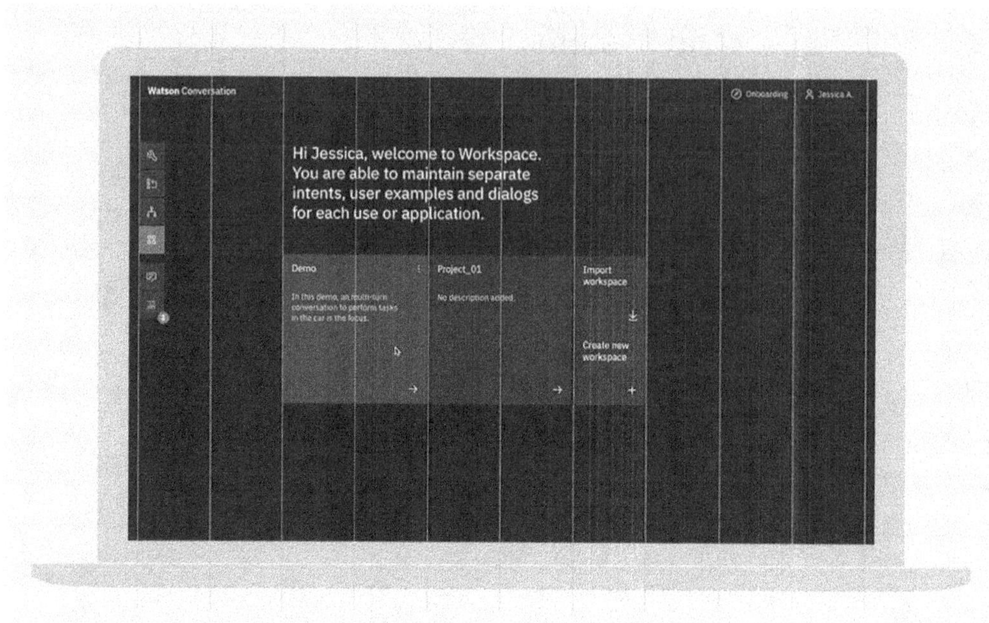

FIGURE 6.8 A sample layout from IBM Design Language that shows how elements are aligned to the grid.

- Colours
- Fonts
- Use of images and graphics
- Tone (addressing users, language, style)

You should also include the so-called ***breakpoints*** for responsive design. The breakpoints define the screen widths at which the layout changes fundamentally. Starting from the smartphone, the first breakpoint is often at 576 pixels wide. From this value onwards, the layout is broken differently and two columns are used on larger screens – for example, on tablets or very large smartphones. Another typical point is at 768 pixels wide, which is where small laptops or tablets in landscape format are captured. This is followed by 1,200 and possibly 1,400 pixels for large monitors. Of course, you can take this much further, but for small projects, you are already well positioned with the three views for smartphones, tablets and medium-sized monitors.

FROM RIGID TO FLEXIBLE DESIGNS

Very modern websites do without breakpoints and instead adapt fluidly to the respective screen. Text, for example, is no longer wrapped at fixed breakpoints, but is oriented towards optimal readability. To do this, you use special code (such as the CSS property `clamp()`), in which you define a minimum value, an ideal value and a maximum value. The browser then automatically selects the best size from this range.

The navigation also adapts flexibly: on large screens, it is displayed as a horizontal bar, while on smaller screens, it folds down into a burger menu. When exactly this change occurs depends on the available space – not on a fixed screen width.

Website builders and low-code platforms do not yet support these modern techniques; you can only use them if you write the code yourself or build on a framework.

A ***design system*** goes one step further than a style guide: it supplements the visual guidelines with reusable components such as buttons, forms or navigation bars and defines how they interact. While a complete design system is not essential for small websites, it becomes an important tool for efficiency and consistency in larger projects or when working in a team.

If you work with a website template, you benefit from pre-integrated structures – from grids to implicit design systems. If you use a website builder such as Wix or Squarespace

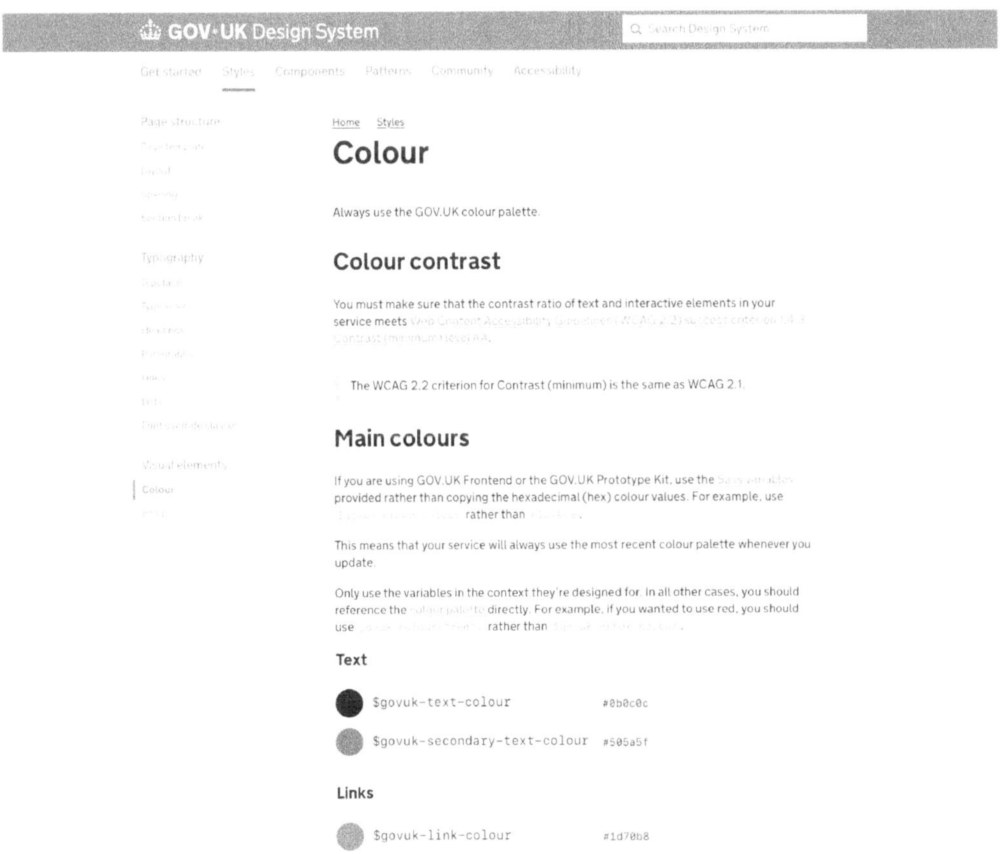

FIGURE 6.9 Style guide of the British Government, thorough and exemplary – for smaller projects, it certainly does not need to be so detailed.

or fall back on a theme in a CMS, the layout is already implicitly defined. And yet there are important aspects to consider: here you can adapt colours, fonts and images to your brand identity, which you have defined with a mood board and logo. If you are planning very large sites, have more than two or three people in your team, or if the work is to continue over several months, it may be useful to develop your own style guide to ensure the consistency of all content. More information on style guides and design systems, including links to good examples, can be found at: bnfr.de/ai052

The decision on the scope of this groundwork depends on your specific project. If you are creating your website yourself with HTML and CSS, all steps are relevant – from the grid to the layout and style guide to the possible design system for larger projects. If you use a template, on the other hand, concentrate on systematic adjustments within the existing structure. In both cases, these basics form the foundation for a professional website. This is not only a matter of aesthetics but also of branding, the trust your site conveys to visitors, and usability, because a predictable structure makes it much easier to navigate your pages.

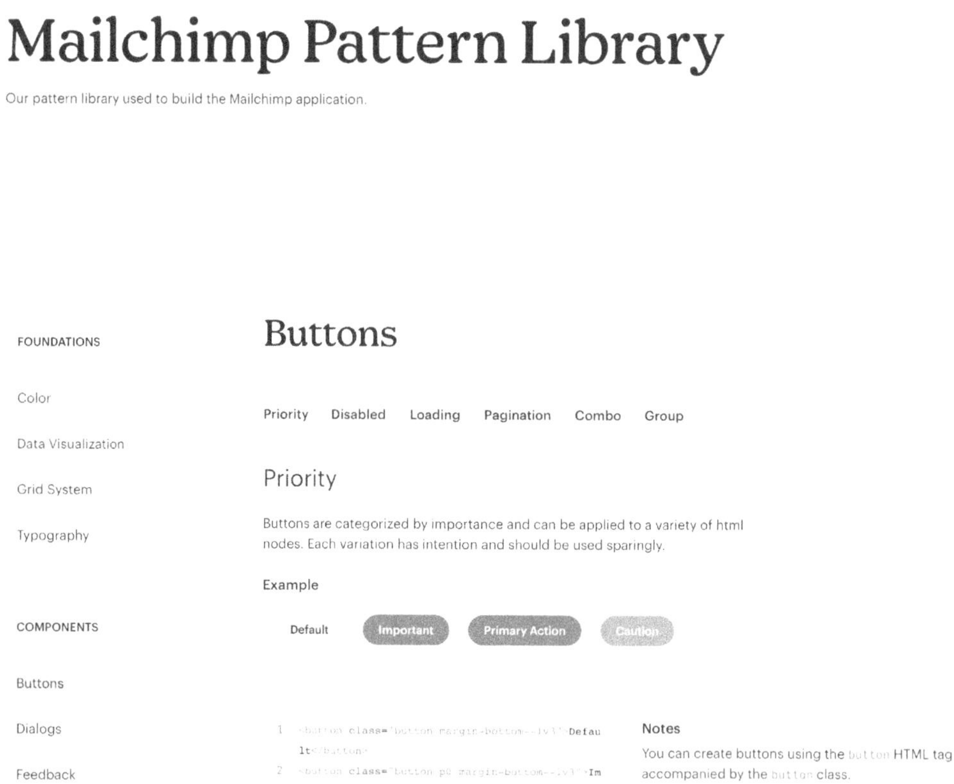

FIGURE 6.10 Mailchimp's Pattern Library is part of a design system and defines, for example, the appearance of buttons, including code examples.

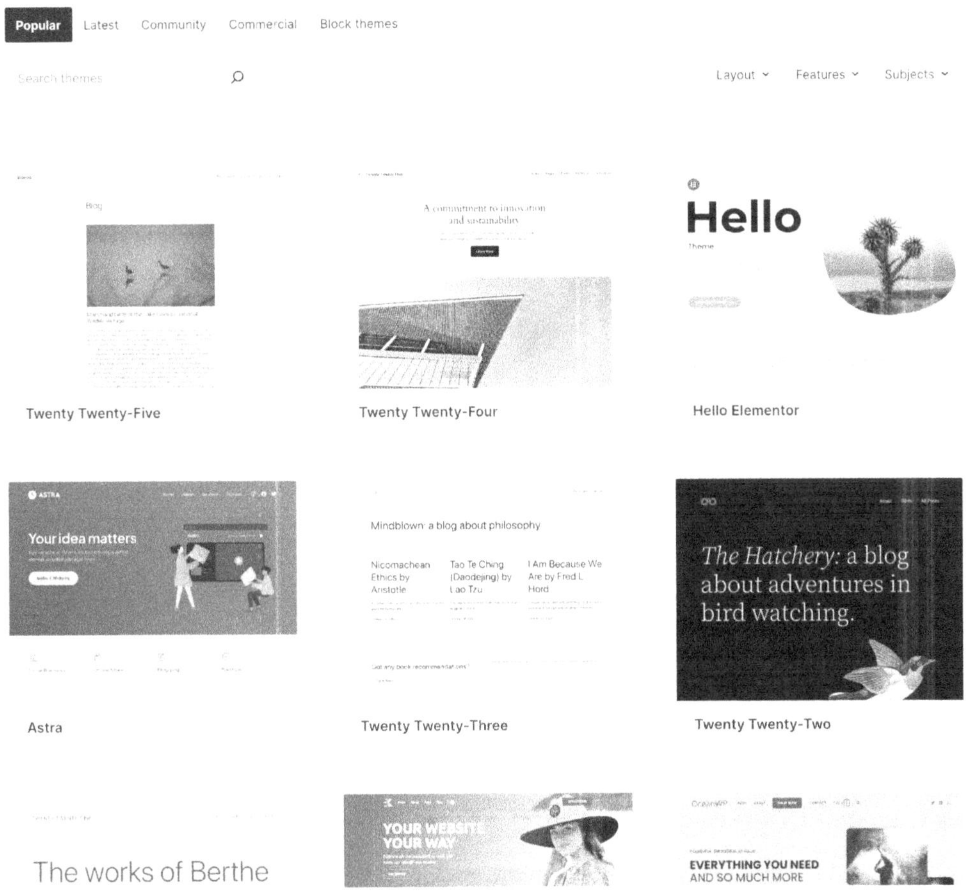

FIGURE 6.11 WordPress.org alone offers over 14,000 templates, known as themes. There are also themes on other sites – some of which are free, others not.

6.2.3 Create a Style Guide in Just a Few Steps Thanks to AI

Now you have the necessary basics and can get started – with AI help, a style guide can be created quickly. Use an online tool such as Figma or Adobe XD, which has the advantage of allowing you to share the result directly from the programme. However, graphics programmes are also possible without any problems; in the end, you export a PDF, which is also fine for smaller projects.

Start with the basic design elements: the colour palette and typography – you may even be able to take both from your mood board. Define a main colour and one, or at most three, accent colours, along with lighter and darker variants. For typography, set a base font size (usually 16 px or 1 rem) and define a heading hierarchy with relative sizes.

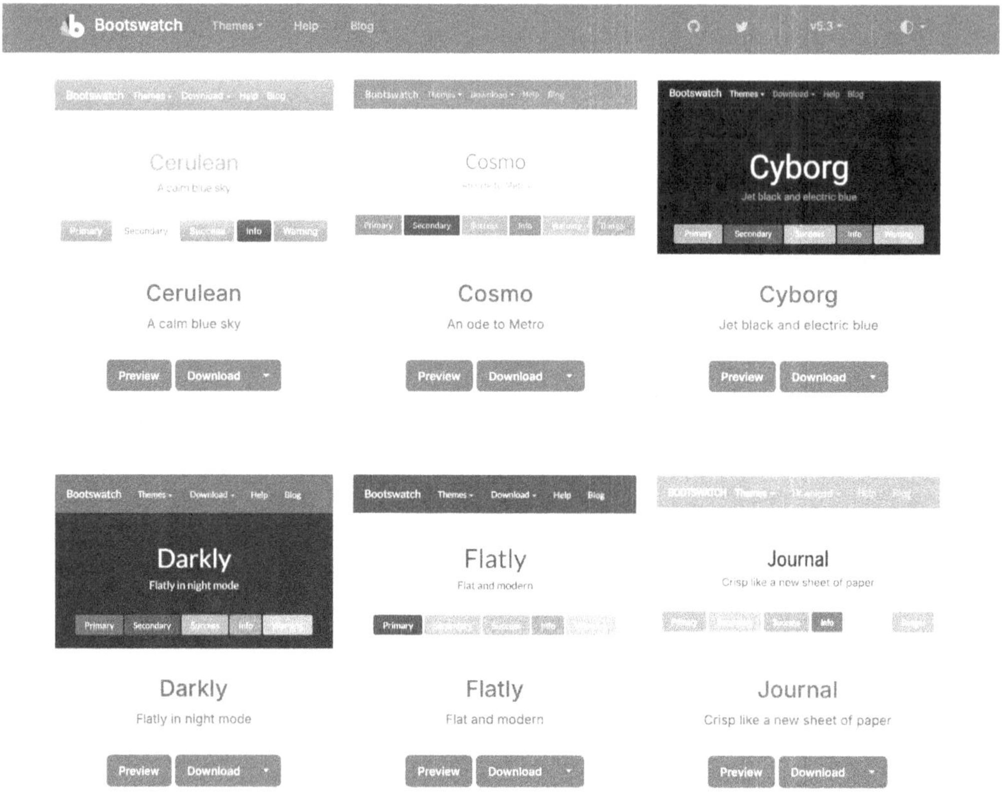

FIGURE 6.12 Bootswatch.com and other websites offer free themes for Bootstrap. As you can see, the design here is simpler, which means you will have more manual work to do.

A language model that allows you to upload documents (such as ChatGPT and Claude) can help you if you have created a mood board as a PDF or if it is available as an HTML page:

EXAMPLE PROMPT: STYLE GUIDE – CREATE SPECIFICATIONS FROM THE MOOD BOARD

Motivation: Analyse the uploaded mood board to create a style guide for website design. The aim is to create consistent and inspiring design specifications.

Task: Analyse all aspects of the mood board and create a style guide that includes colour scheme, typography, imagery, layout guidelines and examples of specific applications. If information is missing, ask specific questions.

Result: A comprehensive, structured style guide in informal language that contains all important design aspects and is illustrated with visual examples.

Example: The style guide should include colours with HEX codes, specific fonts with size specifications, design principles for visual language, layout standards and example applications (e.g. navigation and buttons).
Role: You are an experienced web designer who provides professional and creative support in the creation of design guidelines.

The prompt to copy: bnfr.de/ai053

Once you have prepared the mood board in full, you don't need to add much more; instead, you will receive a good summary in text form. If anything is missing, simply add it. The next step is really elegant, as we let the AI create the style guide document. To do this, continue the current chat:

EXAMPLE PROMPT: CREATE STYLE GUIDE HTML

Convert all information into a style guide in HTML based on Bootstrap. Use the fonts defined in the style guide for formatting throughout and ensure good readability, especially good contrast of all text against the respective background. Check the result and add anything that is still missing for a professional style guide. However, stick strictly to the information you have collected so far and do not change anything.

The prompt to copy: bnfr.de/ai054

The AI then creates HTML code. In my experience, Claude delivered significantly better results than the other language models that can programme. Some AIs can theoretically create files for download, but in practice this sometimes caused problems for me. In these cases, the easiest thing to do is to copy the code and paste it into a code editor. If you don't have one (yet), use the ***Editor*** programme on Windows or ***TextEdit*** on Mac. Create a new, empty document there, copy the HTML code into it and save the file with the extension **.html**. Make sure you select **Text Document** or **Web Page** as the file format. Then double-click to open this file and it will open in your default browser. Alternatively, copy the HTML code into an online service such as quickpreview.dev or jsfiddle.net.

Your result will look similar to the one in Figure 6.13. You can have the AI make corrections if you don't like the look.

If you want to create a PDF, open the HTML page in your browser in Windows, press **Ctrl + P**, select **Microsoft Print to PDF** as the printer, click **Print** and save the file. In macOS, the function is called **Save as PDF** (accessible via **Cmd + P**).

For a comprehensive style guide, the next step is to document the most important UI components, i.e. the elements of the user interface: buttons in different states (normal, hover, i.e. with the mouse pointer over them, active, i.e. clicked, disabled, i.e. inactive), form elements, navigation elements and recurring layout components such as maps or lists.

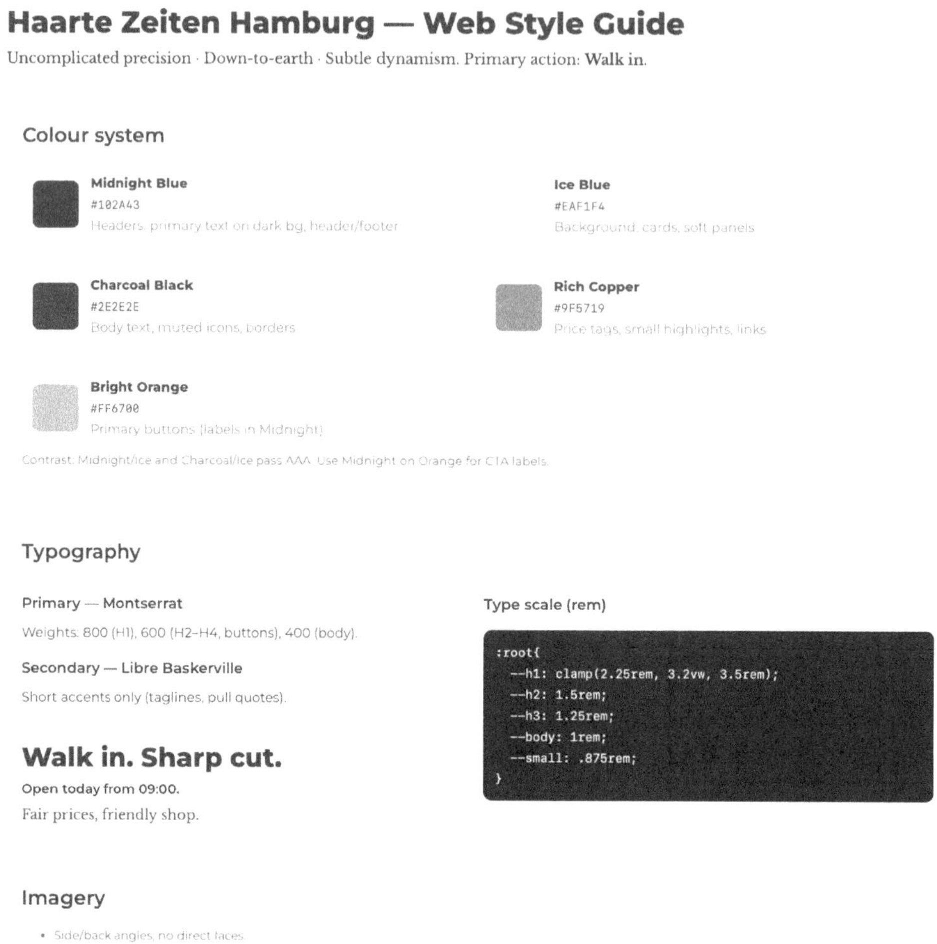

FIGURE 6.13 There is still a lot to correct in this style guide generated by Claude, but it is definitely a solid basis. (Figure created using Claude 3.5 Sonnet.)

Add clear rules for spacing. A consistent system for ***spacing*** ensures a harmonious overall appearance. Also, document the rules for handling images: intended file formats, sizes, aspect ratios, imagery and placement. The complete style guide for our hairdressing salon example project can be found here: bnfr.de/ai055

6.3 DESIGNING THE HOME PAGE

One of the most important pages on your website is the ***home page*** (main page of your site), because anyone who wants to get an overview will open this as one of the first pages. Visitors expect to find out quickly what you have to offer here. Always keep the needs of your target group in mind when designing the home page. In doing so, you must pay particular attention to fulfilling the wishes of your visitors first and foremost and detach yourself from what you, as the website operator, would like to show. The home page is a flagship, entrance door, business card, advertising flyer, lure and floor plan all at once. Its most important tasks are to reveal who the site belongs to, show what can be done or found here, provide an overview and offer access to the most important functions (e.g. search, contact, login). In addition, it should convey your image, arouse curiosity and possibly also point out news. To reconcile all of this, it helps to set priorities.

Every home page must first answer the question "Where am I?" Even well-known brands must make it clear what the website offers visitors in concrete terms. General phrases such as "XY is the market leader in market Z" do more harm than good. It is better to provide a short and specific description of why visitors are in the right place here. Phrases such as "Welcome" also take up unnecessary space and therefore have no place on the home page. Visitors want to accomplish a specific task when they arrive at the home page. If you try to include everything that might interest potential visitors on the home page, it will inevitably become cluttered and confusing. Focus on the main target groups and their most common concerns. Make everything else accessible via the navigation bar.

6.3.1 Best Practice for Home Page Content

When using AI to design our home page, the same pitfalls lurk as when using templates: if we orient ourselves too strongly towards others, our website will look like millions of other sites. So be sure to follow golden rule number 2: AI needs good guidance. That means don't just fill a template with content, but think about what you want to put on the page beforehand. That's why working with scribbles and/or wireframes is so valuable, as shown in the previous chapter.

Pay particular attention to the positioning of the most important content on the home page. The ***screen fold*** refers to the point where the area that visitors can see without scrolling ends. This is where you should place the essentials so that visitors can immediately see what is on offer. Ideally, this is also where you should place ***a call to action*** (***CTA***). A clear visual hierarchy guides visitors' attention to the core elements. Size, contrast and positioning play a decisive role here. A sensible page grid supports this structure.

A typical arrangement of elements on the home page is as follows:

- Header: logo, main navigation and meta navigation (search, login, contact, language selection)
- Hero area: concise headline with a clear message (answers the question "Where am I?"), supported by a high-quality, meaningful image, accompanied by a brief descriptive text and a CTA (see next section)
- Main benefits/advantages: three to a maximum of six key advantages or services, presented briefly and concisely with icons or small images
- Core products/services: overview of the most important offerings with short descriptions, visually appealing design and links

- Trust elements: customer testimonials, references, awards, certificates or press reviews to build trust
- Footer: legally required links (imprint, data protection), contact information and social media links, possibly links to key subpages

6.4 CALLS TO ACTION

Once you have attracted visitors to your pages, you can do them and yourself a big favour: guide them through the pages and tell them what to do. Ideally, every page should have ***a call to action (CTA).*** This will significantly increase the effectiveness of your pages. It takes a bit of effort because you have to think about what you want visitors to do on each individual page. But it also forces you to only have truly effective content (and pages) on your website.

With calls to action, you guide visitors specifically to a desired action. This could be clicking on "Buy now", signing up for the newsletter or submitting a form. CTAs tell people what to do next and can therefore have a significant influence on whether visitors become interested and interested visitors become paying customers. CTAs are usually buttons, sometimes simple links.

Good calls to action are easy to find, clearly recognisable and simple to use. That's why their buttons need enough white space to stand out from other elements. White space doesn't necessarily have to be white; it can be any background colour; it's simply about the distance from other elements so that you can see the background (usually white) in the gap. With complex layouts or large images, generous spacing is particularly important so that the CTAs don't get lost. In addition, a minimum size of 44 × 44 pixels is recommended for buttons so that they are easy to hit on touchscreens.

CTAs should appear where visitors are looking for a way to take action: a buy button right next to the price, a submit button below the last form field – this is how you draw

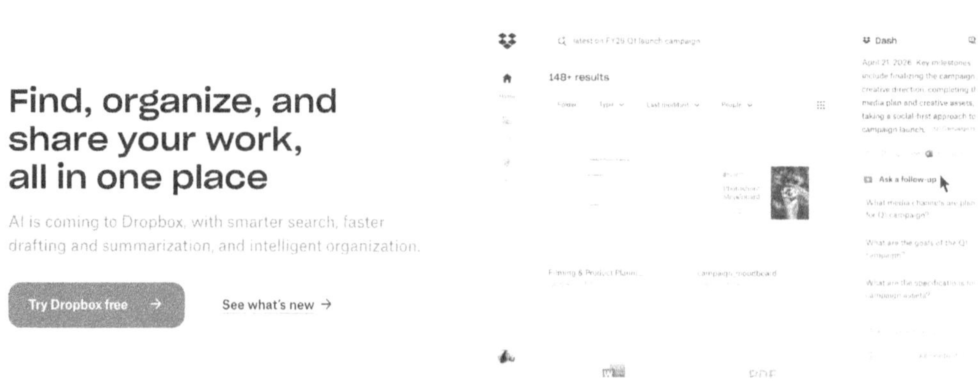

FIGURE 6.14 Clear and effective thanks to simple text and recognisable form: primary CTA (big button to the bottom left) and secondary CTA (text link next to it) on dropbox.com.

attention in a targeted manner. Studies show that this can significantly increase your conversion rate.

Ideally, there should only be one CTA per page – this reduces the mental load for visitors, as they can clearly see what they should do. Sometimes, however, multiple CTAs are unavoidable, for example, for different products or promotions. In this case, a clear hierarchy is useful: the most important button (e.g. "Buy now") is the most prominent, while alternatives ("Learn more") are designed to be more discreet, e.g. only as a link. However, there should not be more than one or two additional options. Consistency in colour, shape and labelling helps visitors quickly understand which action is the main recommendation.

CTAs are therefore key elements in guiding visitors and making it easier for them to take the next step. If they are well positioned and clearly highlighted, the likelihood of them being clicked on increases – and with it the chance that the website will achieve its desired goals.

6.5 TEASERS, CARDS, TILES

The announcement of topics on the home page and other overview pages is called ***a teaser***. The word *tease* means to entice or lure – these elements are designed to lure visitors further into the site. Good teasers are an art form. They should clearly convey what the linked pages are about, make people want to select them and match each other in style to create a coherent overall picture. It is best to combine text and image elements to make the teasers as attractive as possible and to convey the content both visually and textually.

FIGURE 6.15 Does not provide any additional information, but is an attractive representation of the categories: the podcast overview on Spotify in the form of a collection of cards.

Visually, teasers are often implemented in the form of ***tiles***, sometimes also simply called ***boxes***. These are rectangular elements that are arranged in a grid and usually have the same structure. The so-called cards are also rectangular containers on websites that present related information in a compact and clear manner. They are suitable for product overviews or the presentation of team members, as they show the most important information at a glance. All these elements are almost always linked to a page containing further information. Cards sometimes also have additional interactive elements integrated directly, such as media controls.

6.6 IMPLEMENTATION WITH WEBSITE BUILDERS AND CONTENT MANAGEMENT SYSTEMS

You have now laid the foundations for creating the individual pages – your website is now taking shape page by page. In Chapter 5, "Step 3: Determine the Optimal Structure of the Website", you decided on the approach that best suits your project and your prior knowledge: website builder (Wix, Squarespace, Jimdo), no-code/low-code platform (Framer, Webflow, Figma/Relume), content management system (WordPress, Grav, Automad, Kirby) or self-created HTML, CSS and JavaScript. In this section, you will now see how to proceed with a website builder and a content management system. I have summarised this in one section because both approaches have in common that the system guides you through the process in a fairly structured manner. The latter sections of this chapter deal with implementation using no-code/low-code systems as well as HTML, CSS and JavaScript.

For this section, we will use ***Squarespace*** as our website builder and take the example of our master hairdresser Lars Schneider and his hair salon "Haarte Zeiten Hamburg". You can try out all the steps on Squarespace without specifying a payment option. Website builder providers often change the details of how their systems work – don't let this confuse you, just follow their instructions, which now always work pretty well. If you do encounter any problems, you can ask ChatGPT, Le Chat or Perplexity for help. If you are working with Wix or Jimdo, the steps are not much different.

6.6.1 Setting up Your Site with Squarespace

Let's get started:

1. Go to squarespace.com and create a free account.
2. Select the appropriate industry, in our case **HAIRDRESSER**.
3. Specify which features you want. Be sure to resist the temptation to tick everything. Look at your website structure in the concept you created in Chapter 6, "Step 4: Design Meets Code – Designing and Programming the Site", and limit yourself to the features or areas you defined there. For our hairdresser, we only need **TO ADVERTISE A BUSINESS** and **OFFER SERVICES**.

4. Now decide whether you want to use AI or go the traditional route using a template. For our example, we'll go with AI, of course.
5. There are five more steps in which you tell the Squarespace AI more about your website. In the first step, you enter the title (in the example, "Haarte Zeiten Hamburg") and decide on the brand personality. We choose **Sophisticated**.
6. Now you decide which sections the home page should have. Again, less is more. Take a look at the scribbles or wireframes you created. Then select the sections that fit best. Don't worry, you can add more later or change sections if they don't fit. In our example, we choose **Intro**, **Service**, **Info** and **Footer**.
7. Now specify which pages you need. To do this, look at your sitemap. In our example, we specify **About us**, **Contact** and **Services**.
8. For the colour scheme, we choose one of the options under **Sophisticated**. Take a look at your mood board to help you decide.
9. Last step: choose a font. Select the one that best matches what is specified in the mood board or style guide. You can also change this later if nothing suitable is displayed in this step.

In just a few minutes, you have created your website – at least the framework for it. Before you create and enter the content, you need to take a close look at it; remember golden rule number 3: AI can lead you astray. You can see this clearly when you examine the result in Figure 6.16. It looks quite good at first glance, but there are a few problems. The white text on the large photo with grey tones is difficult to read. It is also centred, which looks quite good, but makes longer texts more difficult to read than left-aligned text. The text on the main button in the center also has too little contrast. This is our most important CTA on the page, so it needs to be as visible as possible. We can be satisfied with the rest of the page for now.

6.6.2 Customising the Appearance

Let's make the necessary corrections:

1. Click on **Edit** in the horizontal menu.
2. Move the mouse pointer over the hero image with the hairdressing chair.
3. Select **Show Layouts** from the pop-up menu.
4. Find one that doesn't have centred text, but left-aligned text instead. Personally, I also prefer a slightly smaller image, as this makes the page less long and visitors can see the rest of the page more quickly.
5. Click on the text block with the longer text and select everything.

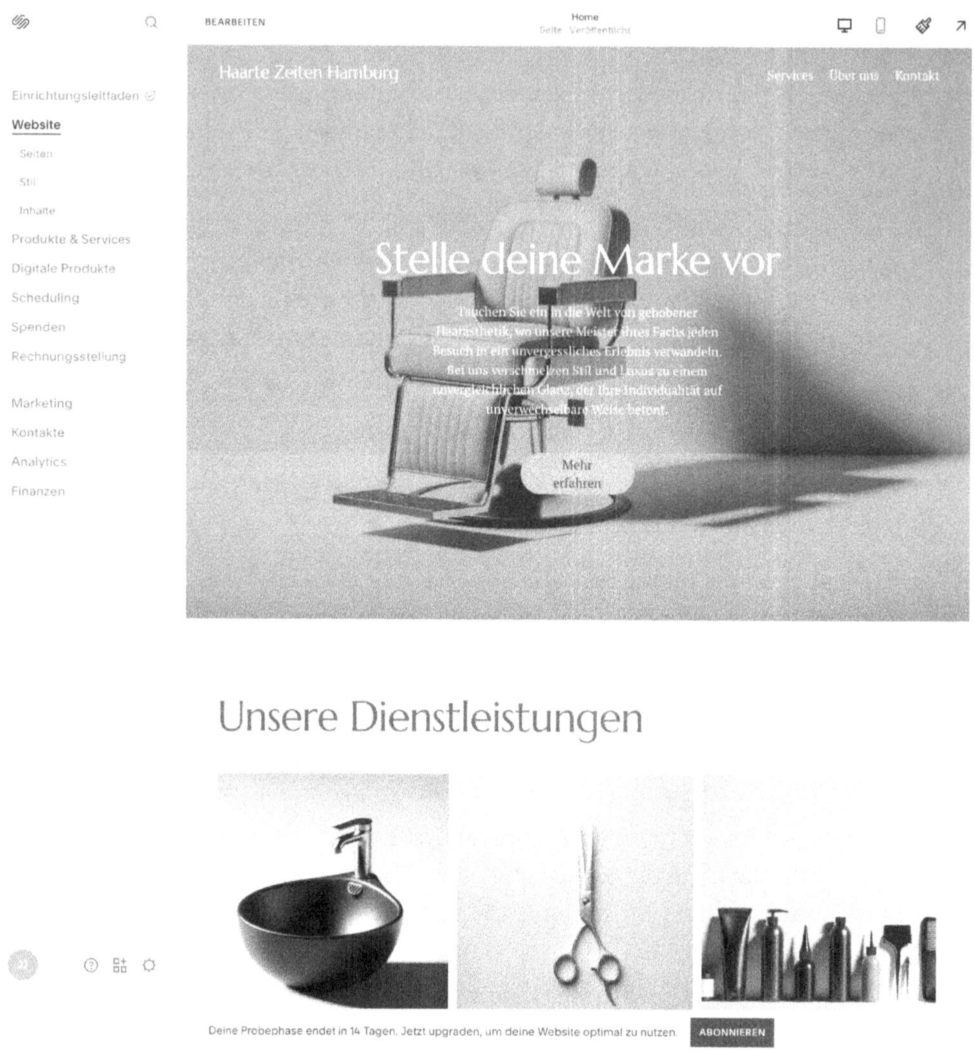

FIGURE 6.16 Thanks to AI and placeholder images, the result looks good at first glance on Squarespace. But don't be fooled, there's still work to be done. (Figure created using Squarespace.)

6. Select the colour wheel in the pop-up menu (right next to the I button).
7. Set the colour to pure white by clicking in the colour field at the top left of the **Custom** area or by entering `#FFFFFF` at the bottom (this is the hex value for white).

Alternatively, you can click on the text block, click on the second icon from the left (the one with the stylised paint bucket) and give the text a background. This has the advantage that the text is always easy to read, regardless of which photo and which part of the photo is behind it.

Once you have finished making all your adjustments, don't forget to click on **Save** in the top left-hand corner.

With just a few clicks, you will have already seen that Squarespace's editing options are extensive and each one is easy to understand. It just takes a little practice to know where each function is hidden. And there are always many ways to achieve your goal. Instead of changing the layout of the hero block (steps 3 and 4 above), we could have simply changed the text alignment in the formatting pop-up. But in general, you should always consider whether your change is a fundamental one. In our example, that means: Do we need better text readability throughout? That's why we're changing the text colour

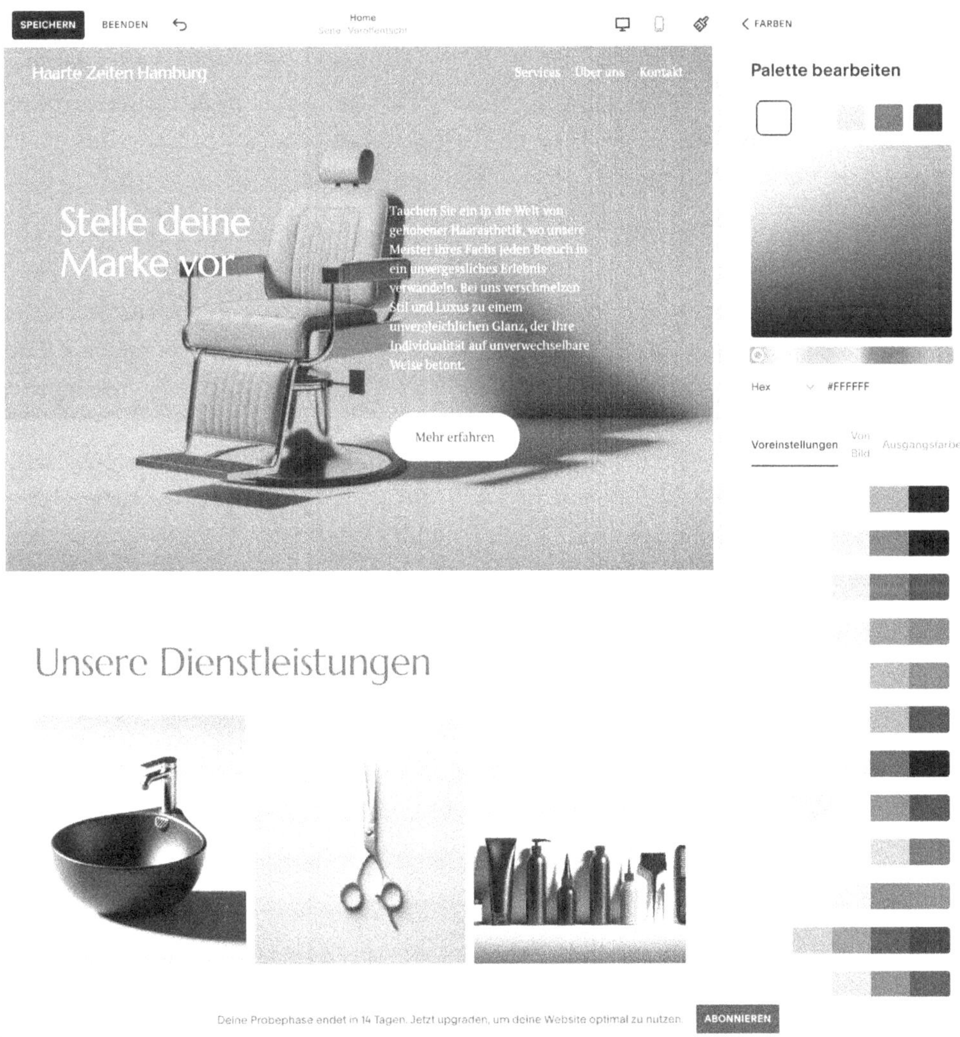

FIGURE 6.17 Here you can change the colour for the entire palette, which will then be automatically applied to all pages. (Figure created using Squarespace.)

within **Website Styles,** which is what Squarespace calls the style guide that defines colours, fonts, sizes and layout:

1. Click on the brush icon in the top right-hand corner.
2. Select the arrow on the right in the **Colours** section. (If you click directly on the colours, only the palette selection will open, where you cannot edit individual colours).
3. Click on **Edit Palette**.
4. Now you have many options again. Either select the lightest colour from the five palette colours at the top and set it to pure white or choose a combination that you like from **the presets** at the bottom. You can always see the result applied to your site on the left. With **From Image**, Squarespace calculates a colour palette from an image you upload, and with **Starting Colour**, it creates a harmonious palette based on a colour you specify.
5. When you are satisfied with the appearance and readability of the fonts, click **Save**.

In the **Website Styles** section, you will see several **colour schemes** at the bottom. These are predefined sets of colours that Squarespace creates automatically. Each section of your page has such a scheme. If you click on it on the left, it will be selected on the right and you can edit every detail.

So far, we have only made the adjustments to the Squarespace design that were absolutely necessary. Many people are satisfied with this, with the result that their website looks unmistakably like Squarespace and resembles hundreds of thousands of other websites. However, you have done valuable preparatory work in steps 1 to 3 of this book and can now customise your website to perfectly suit your target audience:

1. Open the style guide you created earlier in this chapter.
2. Click on the brush icon in the top right-hand corner to open the **Website Styles**.
3. Select the arrow on the right in the **Fonts** section. (Clicking directly on the tile will only open the package selection.)
4. Click on the name of the font next to **Headings**.
5. Select **Font** and enter the name of the font you specified in your style guide.
6. Under **Weight**, change the thickness. The numbers used here, from 100 to 900, indicate the thickness of a font – 100 is very ***thin*** and 900 is very ***thick***. The ***Extra Bold*** we use is 800 for most fonts. Check in the Design section on the left to see if the display on your site is correct.

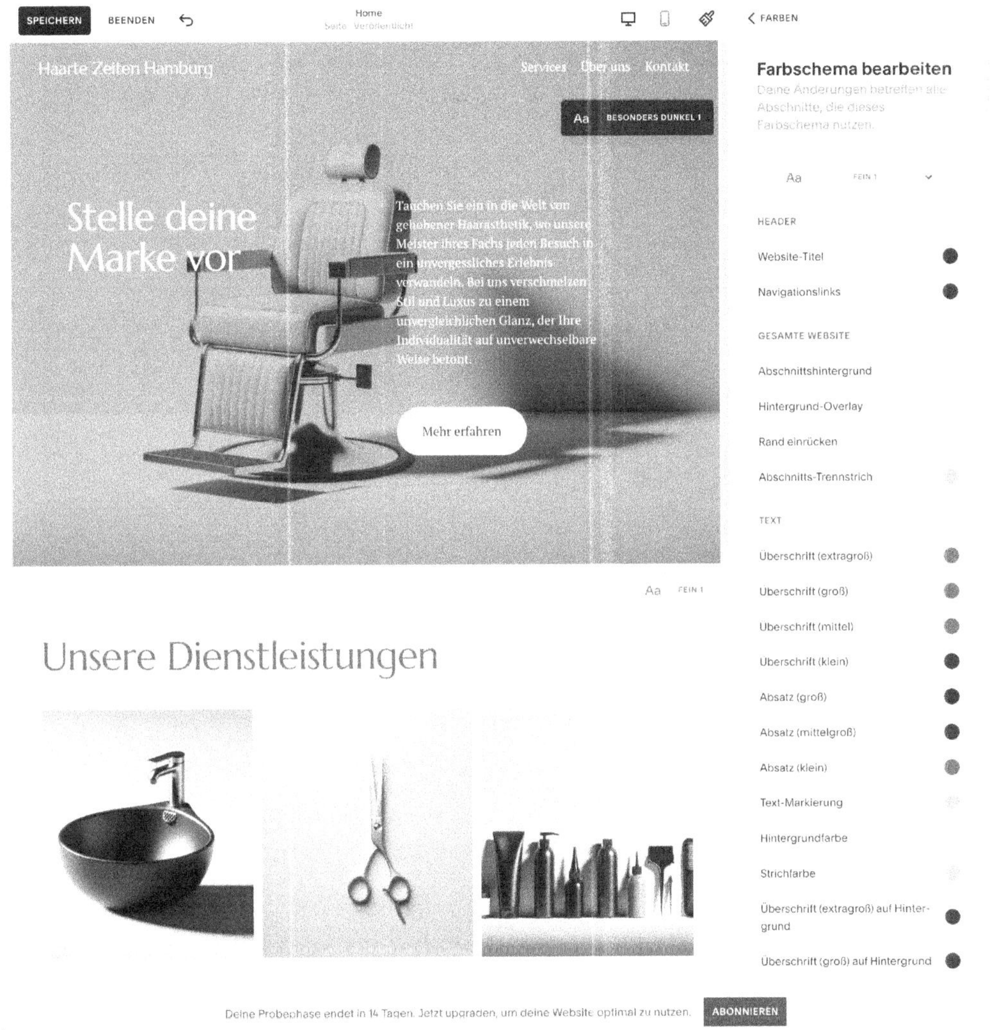

FIGURE 6.18 Here you can edit all possible details of the colour selection. However, it is best to only use colours from your palette to keep things clear. (Figure created using Squarespace.)

The other values for line height and font size are specified in ***em*** and ***rem*** units. These are CSS properties that may seem unfamiliar at first, but are very useful. They allow you to define the size relatively rather than absolutely. This means that when you make changes, you only have to do so once. For example, if you change the font on your site, the text may appear too large or too small with the new font. In this case, you only need to change the absolute size of the font once, and all headings, body text, labels, links, etc. will change automatically because their size is specified relatively rather than absolutely. The em unit refers to the size of the directly parent element, such as the text box

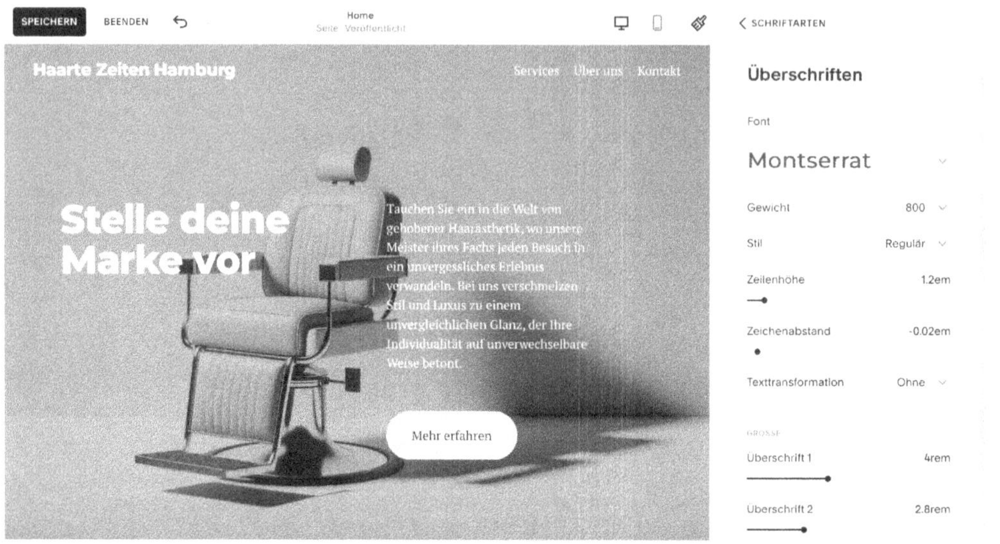

FIGURE 6.19 Here you can edit all the details of the fonts used on the site. (Figure created using Squarespace.)

containing a paragraph. The rem unit, on the other hand, refers to the root element, i.e. the size definition for the entire current page.

1. Go back to the **Fonts** section.
2. Adjust the **base size** there. This should not be smaller than 16 pixels so that it is easily readable for everyone on all devices.
3. Now correct the fonts for the other parts of the site.
4. **Save**.

This ensures that the fonts match those in your style guide. Let's correct the colours:

1. Go back to **Website Styles**.
2. Click on the arrow to the right of **Colours**.
3. Go to **Edit Palette**.
4. Click on one colour field after another and copy the colour values from your style guide into **Hex**. In our example, we have defined five colours and also use white, making a total of six colours. We therefore leave out orange, as it is only to be used for highlighting in exceptional cases anyway. We enter the lightest colours on the left and the darkest on the right, which gives us the most harmonious results when applied to our pages.

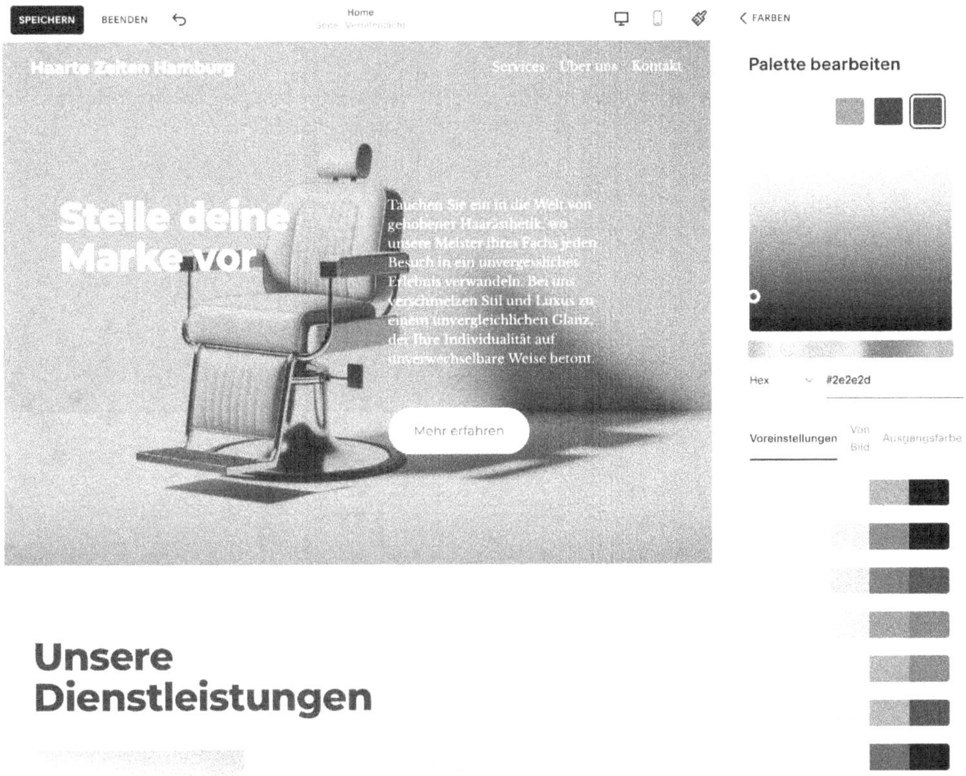

FIGURE 6.20 This is what the site looks like after we have assigned our colours. The placeholder images no longer fit in very well, but we will replace them later anyway. (Figure created using Squarespace.)

5. Check the result. There will probably be one or two sections where you don't like the automatically assigned colours.
6. Go back to the **Colours** section.
7. In the preview on the left, click on the section you want to change.
8. Click on the colour scheme used to edit it and correct the elements you would like to change.
9. **Save** your work.

6.6.3 Optimise the Structure of the Pages

Let's take care of the other sections of your home page:

1. Take your scribbles or wireframes.
2. Check which elements are still missing and which ones have the wrong structure.

3. If only individual images, text blocks or similar are missing, click on the **ADD BLOCK** button at the top left of the corresponding section.
4. If entire sections are missing, move the mouse pointer to the place on the page where you want to insert them and click on **ADD SECTION**.

We are now practically finished with the design and structure of our sample site. All that's missing are the other pages of our hairdressing site:

1. Finish editing by clicking on the button at the top left.

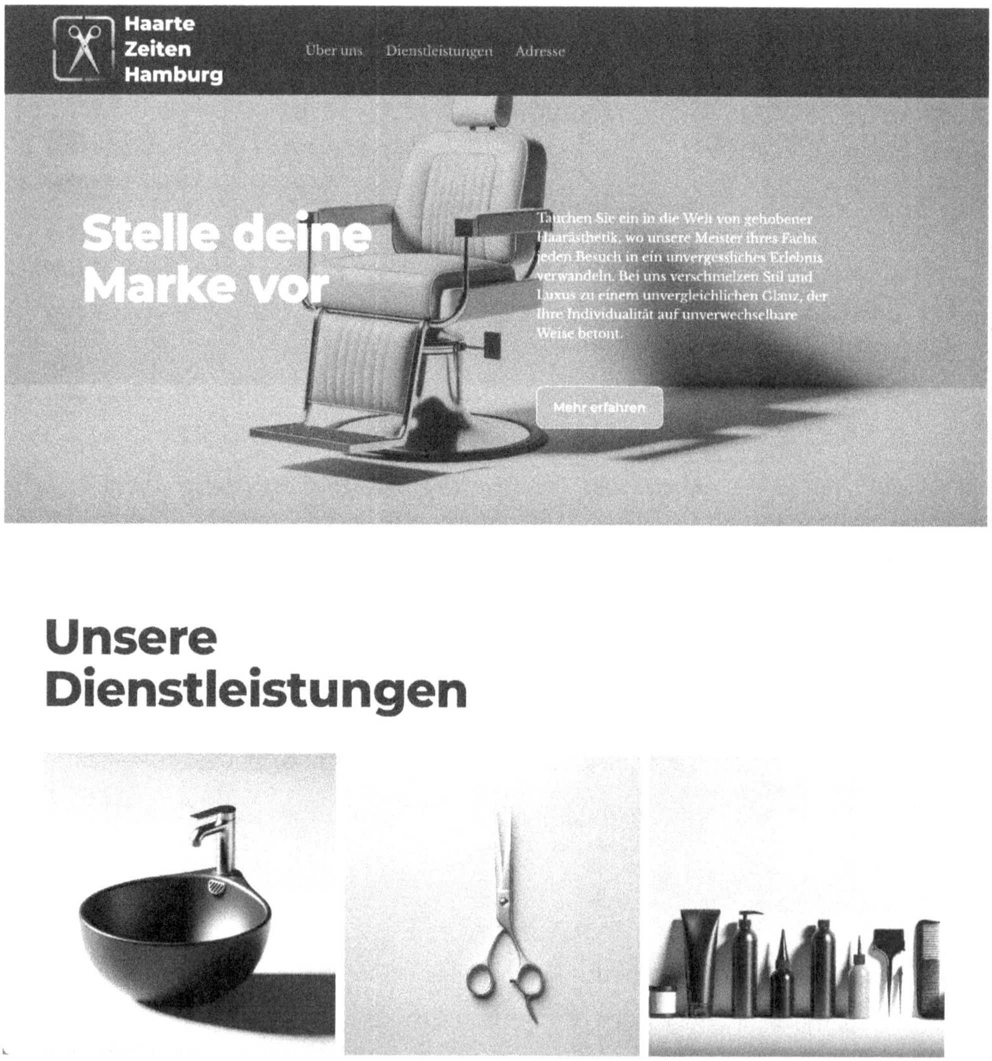

FIGURE 6.21 The finished design before inserting our own photos and text. (Figure created using Squarespace.)

2. Select **Pages** under **Website** in the sidebar.
3. The home page can be found under **Not linked** because it does not appear in the menu, which is fine. Under **Primary navigation**, you will find the pages that you activated during setup. First, edit their names by clicking on the gear icon. Also, make sure that the **page title, navigation title** and **URL slug** match. The latter is the end of the URL, i.e. what you see in the address bar of your browser when you visit the page. It must only contain lowercase letters and no spaces, umlauts or special characters, with the exception of hyphens.
4. Close the pop-up by clicking **Save**.
5. Correct the other page names, delete any that are not needed and add any that are missing – your sitemap, which you created in Chapter 6, "Step 4: Design Meets Code – Designing and Programming the Site", will help you with this.

You have now completed the basic structure of the website. If you want to share the site with others, go back to the Squarespace main menu and select **Setup Guide**. Under Website Availability, you can publish the site with password protection by clicking the **Manage Website Status** button. If you already have a subscription, you can also make the site available to everyone.

You can view the sample website for "Haarte Zeiten Hamburg" in its current state of development here: bnfr.de/ai072

If you use a different website builder such as ***Wix*** or ***Jimdo***, the steps shown above will, of course, work slightly differently. In some places, you will have more options, in others fewer. The important thing is not to get bogged down. Just follow your sitemap, scribbles or wireframes and style guide. If you can't achieve a particular design, it doesn't matter – visitors to your website will never notice that it doesn't look exactly as you imagined it.

If you are working with a ***content management system***, the editing process is not very different from the procedure just shown with Squarespace. One difference at the beginning is that you choose a template or theme that determines the basic design. You then adapt this step by step to your desired design. Once you have done this, you are ready for the next step and can create the final images and texts for your website, which we will do in the next chapter.

WEBSITE BUILDERS AND DATA PROTECTION

The ***General Data Protection Regulation*** (***GDPR***) is the central EU law on the protection of personal data, which is practically always binding for you if you offer goods/services to people in the EU or if you are based in the EU– regardless of which provider you use. If you use a website builder provider, there are several important points to consider: A privacy policy and an imprint are mandatory and must be easy to find (see Chapter 8, "Step 6: Test and Optimise").

Tools for access statistics on your website are often activated by default. Either deactivate these as far as possible or activate a cookie banner to obtain the consent of visitors *before* data is collected. Find out where the provider stores the data. If it ends up on a server outside the EU, you will need special contractual clauses or a ***data processing agreement*** (DPA).

You should also know and adhere to the legal requirements for data protection in the US, Canada, Great Britain and other countries your customers might be located in.

Caution is advised in general when using ***Google Fonts***. These are loaded from Google servers by default and thus transfer the IP address of your visitors to Google. This is problematic in terms of data protection law, which is why many website builders offer to host the fonts locally on the server where the website is located. Particular caution is required with integrated elements such as social media buttons or contact forms, as personal data is also processed here. Document all data protection measures taken in order to comply with your obligation to provide evidence.

6.7 IMPLEMENTATION WITH NO-CODE/LOW-CODE SYSTEMS

Have you opted for a no-code/low-code platform such as ***Framer*** or ***Webflow***? Then this section will show you how to use these services to implement your website. For our example, we are using Webflow in conjunction with *Relume*, because I find this to be by far the simplest and most powerful method for creating websites with AI assistance. Be sure to watch the video, because it's really impressive how quickly a really well-structured website can be created with it. Unlike website builders, this isn't just a slightly customised template, but actually a site built from scratch according to our specifications.

CREATING PAGES WITH RELUME – VIDEO

You can see how a website is created in just a few minutes. But don't be fooled: to make sure it's a good website, you still need to do some preparatory work, as we did together in the previous chapters.

The best way to see this is in the video linked here, which you can access via the QR code or the link in this box.

https://bnfr.de/ai062

6.7.1 BRINGING THE RELUME SITE TO WEBFLOW

Let's get started with the implementation step by step:

1. Go to Webflow.com and create a free account. This is sufficient for experimenting.
2. Go to Relume.io and create an account there as well. You will need a paid subscription here, otherwise exporting to Webflow will not be possible.
3. If you haven't already done so, create the sitemap and wireframes as described in the previous chapter (Section 5.8, "Creating a Sitemap with AI," and Section 5.11.2, "Creating Wireframes with AI").
4. Adjust everything until you are satisfied.
5. Then go to the icon next to **Export** in the top right-hand corner. There, select the tool you want to export to. We'll use **Webflow**.
6. You will then see a prompt to clone the Webflow Style Guide. This means you are creating a copy of the style guide that Relume has created specifically for Webflow. This is necessary because it is the only way to ensure that all elements look as specified in Relume. So click on **Clone Style Guide**.
7. This will take you to the Webflow Marketplace, where additional modules, templates, etc. for Webflow are available. Click on **Clone in Webflow** and then on **Create site** on the next page.

You have now laid the foundation and will see an interface like the one in Figure 6.22. Let's continue with the export from Relume:

1. Go back to Relume and click on **Install Webflow App**, then **Install App**. You will then need to allow this in the next steps – it is sufficient to do this for the website you just created in Webflow.
2. Surprisingly, you will end up back at Webflow, where nothing else seems to have happened. But you are now ready to go and can click on the icon in the middle of the sidebar on the left with the three rectangles and a plus sign (**Apps** – if you don't see this, you need to switch from **Build** to **Design** in the top left corner; see Figure 6.23).
3. Click on **Launch** in the **Relume Site Builder Import**.
4. Select the project in Relume and either click on **Primary Sitemap** if you want to import individual pages later or click on the **Add Pages** button to import them all at once.
5. Wait a moment until the import process is complete. You will see that this is the case when the **Importing** message disappears and you see your projects again. You can then close the pop-up.

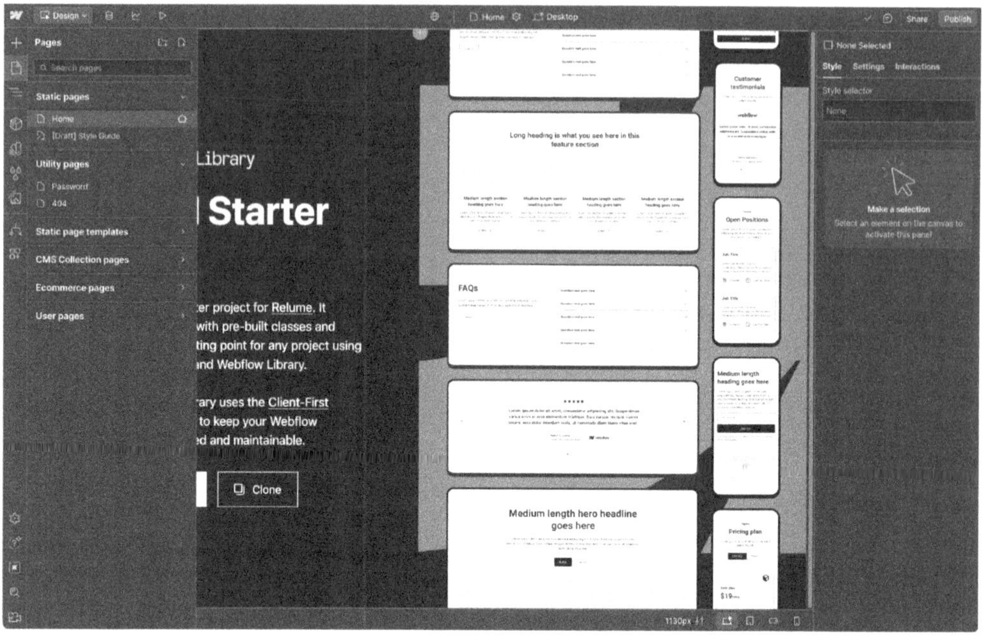

FIGURE 6.22 The import creates a home page, the content of which you can delete. You must keep the draft of the “Style Guide” page, as it contains all the formatting rules. (Figure created using Webflow + Relume.)

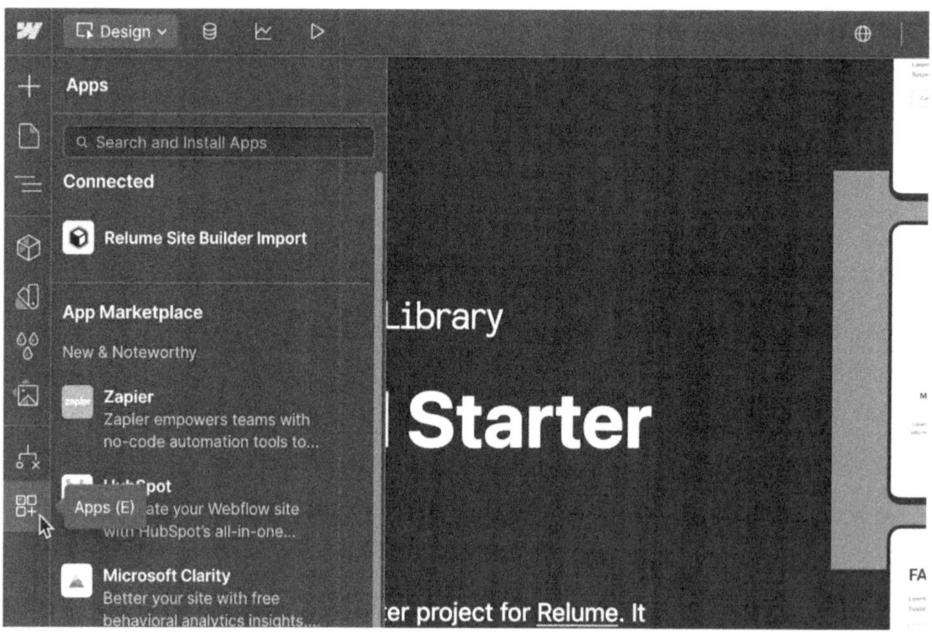

FIGURE 6.23 The area with the apps in Webflow. You can see the Relume app at the top of the “Connected” area. (Figure created using Webflow + Relume.)

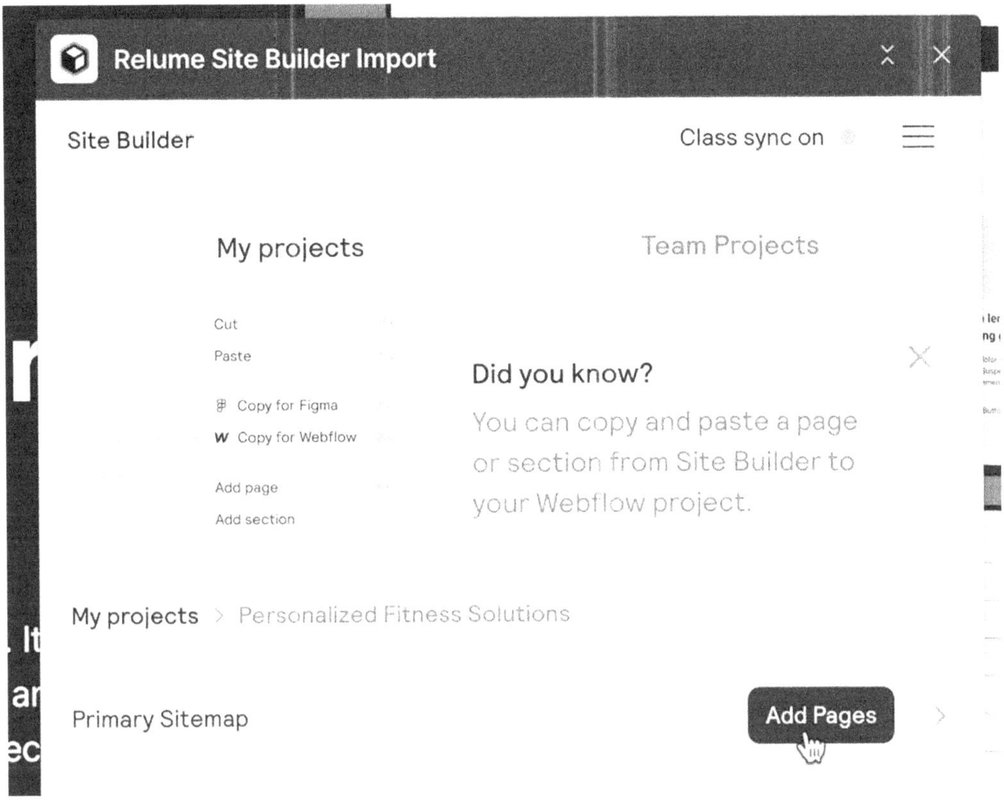

FIGURE 6.24 Here, you can either import all pages or go to "Primary Sitemap" to select only individual pages from the Sitemap. (Figure created using Webflow + Relume.)

Your pages from Relume have now been transferred to Webflow. You can publish them directly (top right with **Publish**) if you want to get a first impression of what your website will look like. Now you just need to make sure that your font and colour specifications, which you worked out in the previous parts of this chapter (see Sections 6.1.2 and 6.2.2), are implemented.

6.7.2 Adapting the Website to Your Style Guide

Now open the style guide that you created earlier and move it next to the Webflow window.

1. In Webflow, go to the **Variables** section in the left sidebar.
2. In the **Base Colour - Brand** or **Base Colour - Neutral** section, click on **New Variable** and add the colours you need. If you use a different colour for all your text, change the black in **Base Colour - Brand** to that colour.

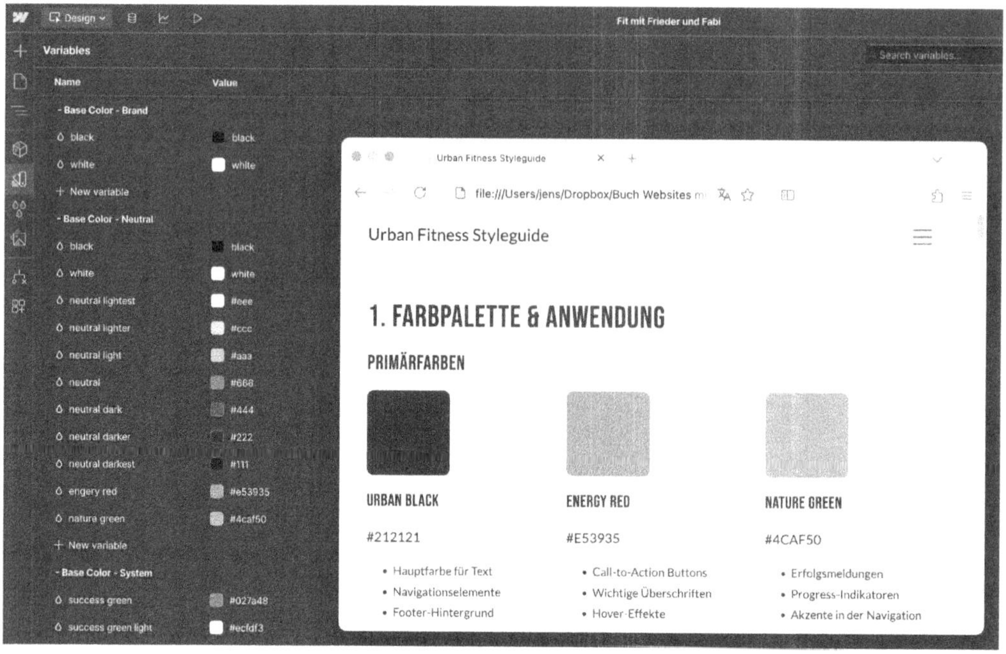

FIGURE 6.25 The style guide in a separate window on the Variables page of our site in Webflow. Here you can add any additional colours you need. (Figure created using Webflow.)

3. Now set the basic font: Click on the **Pages** icon in the left sidebar. Go to **[Draft] Style Guide** to display it. (This will always remain a draft and will never be published – after all, it is not meant to be seen online, and you only need it here in Webflow.)
4. Then click on the icon below it in the sidebar: **Navigator**. This allows you to navigate between all the elements on the page. We now want to go to the element at the top of the hierarchy: **Body**. Click on it.
5. Now, in the panel on the right, change the font that is to be used on the site, i.e. the one for the body text. (The headings come next.) If your font is not in the list, you can add more fonts via **Add fonts** at the top of the pop-up menu for font selection.
6. If you have any other customisations that apply to the entire website (such as the font colour), you can also change these in the panel on the right.
7. Now for the headings: Click on the first-level heading in the main area of the page, **Heading 1**. At the top right of the right-hand panel, you will see **Inheriting 3 selectors**. This means that this element has three parent elements from which it inherits its formatting. Click on it to see which ones they are. (The element itself is also displayed, so there are four in the list.)

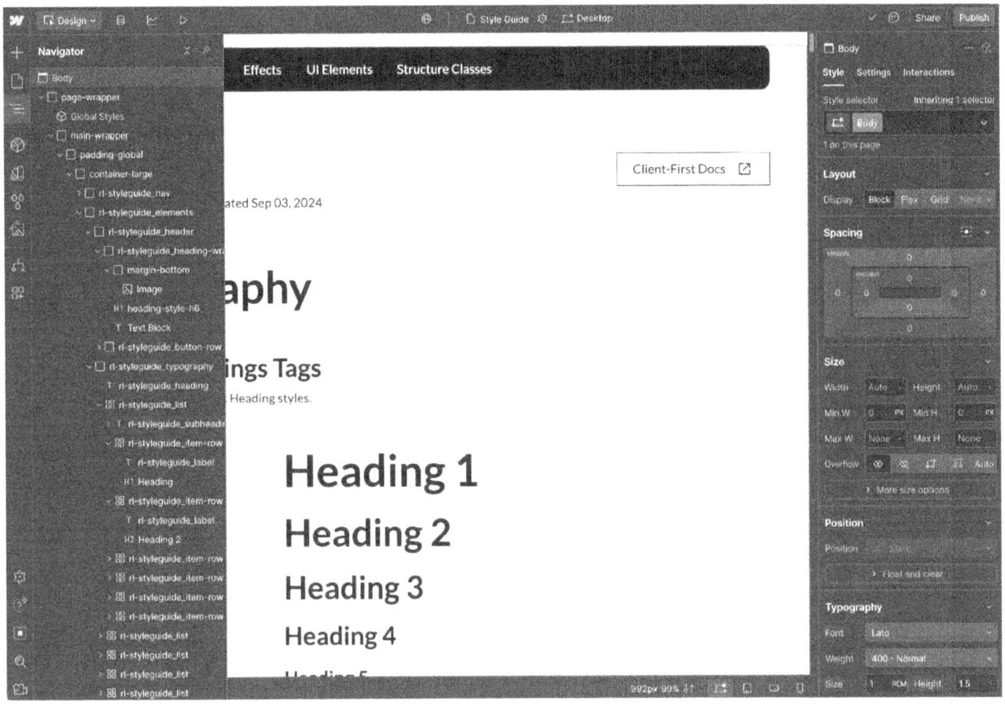

FIGURE 6.26 On the left, select "Body" and on the right, assign the basic formatting to it. (Figure created usind Webflow.)

8. Select **All H1 Headings**. This will edit all first-level headings. Now format them according to your style guide.
9. Click on **Heading 2** in the main area. You will now see no style in the **Style selector** on the right-hand side of the panel. Click on the blue laptop icon. There, you can select the pink **All H2 Headings**. Format the second-level headings according to your style guide.
10. Continue scrolling down the page until you reach the buttons. Click on the top one. On the right-hand side of the panel, you will see **button** in blue as the assigned class in **Style selector**. This is exactly what we want to change, so adjust the colours. Change the appearance of the button until everything matches your expectations (and your style guide).
11. Now change the secondary and tertiary buttons if necessary.

Now the colours, fonts and buttons are all correct. Check your style guide again and make any further adjustments if necessary.

Go to **Publish** in the top right corner to publish your website. You will notice that although the pages now look good, they are not yet linked to each other and the menu is not working. The links have not been transferred from Relume to Webflow. Let's fix that:

1. Scroll to the top of any page in Webflow and click anywhere on your page's navigation bar. This will highlight it in green. This means it is a so-called **COMPONENT**. These are building blocks that you define centrally once and can then use on every page (as **AN INSTANCE**). They look the same everywhere, which means that if you make changes on one page, they will be visible on all pages that use the same component.
2. Now click on the first menu item. In the top right-hand corner of the panel, switch from the **STYLE** tab to **SETTINGS**.
3. Under **TYPE**, click on the rectangle to link to one of your pages. Now you can select the start page under **PAGE**.
4. Now let's take care of the colour highlighting: Open the home page in Webflow and select the element that links to the home page in the navigation. Then go to **STYLE** in the panel on the right; you will see **CURRENT** in green in the **STYLE** selector field. This means that you are currently editing the display for the element when the page to which it links is displayed. Change the display for this case by displaying the text in a different colour, for example.
5. Now let's add a display when the mouse pointer is moved over the menu element: Click on the small blue arrow on the right in the **STYLE SELECTOR**. A pop-up will appear where you can select **HOVER**. This allows you to edit this view.
6. Do the same for the other links in the navigation.

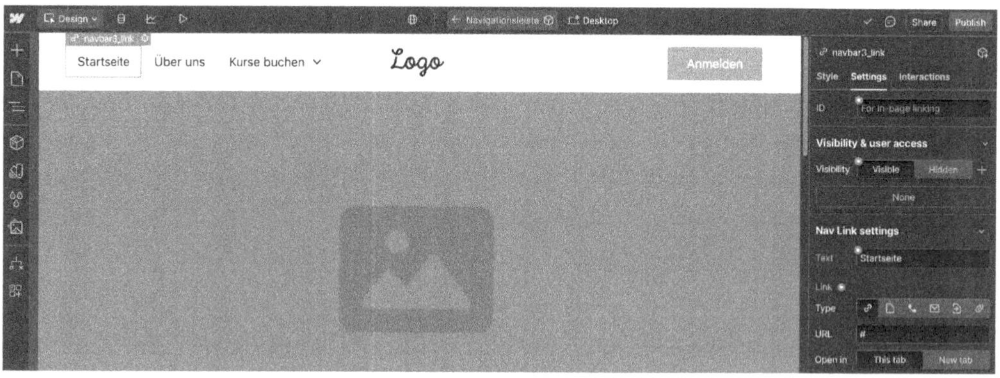

FIGURE 6.27 Here you can set where the page links to. (Figure created using Webflow.)

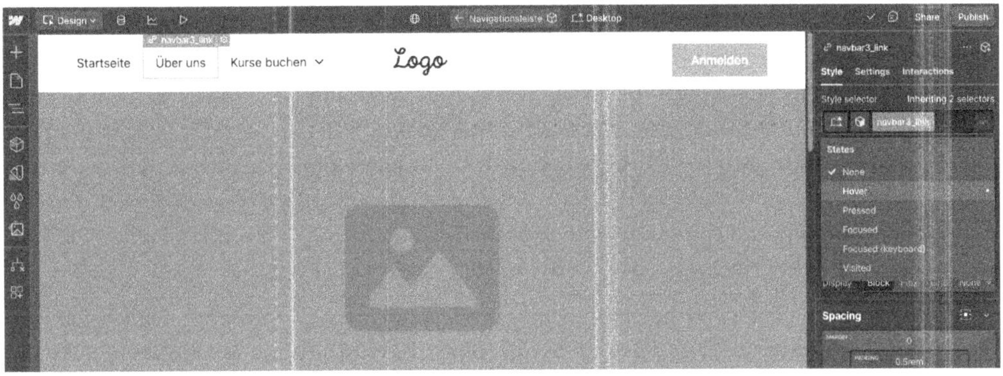

FIGURE 6.28 Here you can set the formatting for when the mouse pointer is moved over the element (hover). (Figure created using Webflow.)

Publish the site again and check whether everything now complies with the style guide and your ideas. If so, you are ready for the next step, which is to add content to the site, as we will do in the next chapter.

You can view the sample website for "Fit mit Frieder und Fabi" in its current state here: bnfr.de/ai072

6.8 IMPLEMENTATION WITH HTML, CSS AND JAVASCRIPT

Don't want to use a website builder, CMS or no-code/low-code solution? Would you rather create HTML, CSS and JavaScript for your pages yourself? Great! In this section, you'll find lots of tips on how to do this with the help of AI. Without AI, this is a tedious task and only recommended for people with programming experience. Today, thanks to AI, this option is accessible to anyone who is interested in understanding how the web works from the ground up and who enjoys working in a structured way. Below, I'll show you the absolute basics you need to understand what AI gives you back when you ask it to write code. It is possible to do without it, but it becomes very tedious because you can only blindly copy code and have difficulty describing what you would like the AI to do. Remember golden rule number 2: AI needs good guidance.

Developing a website follows a structured process. Thanks to the previous steps, you know what your website should do and what users need. You have recorded this in your concept and sitemap. With your design – be it a scribble, wireframe or mock-up/layout – you have defined the appearance and content. You can now implement this technically in three consecutive steps: First, you create the basic structure of the pages in ***HTML***. You define the individual elements such as headings, paragraphs, images and their hierarchical relationships to each other. In the second step, you define the appearance of this structure with ***CSS***. In other words, you determine colours, fonts, spacing and layout. In the third and final step, it becomes interactive thanks to ***JavaScript*** (JS for short). This allows you to create forms, animations or dynamic content.

Large language models such as ChatGPT, Claude or Gemini are available to assist you as intelligent assistants. The AI not only makes code suggestions but also helps with optimisation, suggests suitable formatting solutions, searches for weaknesses in the code and supports you in implementing JavaScript functions. It is particularly helpful that the AI can analyse your code and find errors in it. And you can ask for explanations at any time about how certain parts of the code work and what the background is.

6.8.1 IDE or Code Editor?

HTML, CSS and JavaScript are stored as simple text files, so you can work with pre-installed programmes such as ***Editor*** (Windows) or ***TextEdit*** (macOS). However, I do not recommend this, as a special code editor offers some assistance, for example, by colour-coding your code, which greatly improves readability. An integrated development environment (***IDE***) offers additional functions. Microsoft's ***Visual Studio Code*** is very popular. It is a cross between an IDE and a code editor and is highly recommended for HTML. The programme is available free of charge for Windows, macOS and Linux and not only offers all the important functions for web development, such as syntax highlighting, auto-completion and ***debugging*** tools, but can also be seamlessly connected to various AI assistants. The ***Github Copilot*** extension suggests context-sensitive code completions and corrections while you are programming, which is very useful. The basic version is free and only requires registration on Github. For intensive use, you will need a paid subscription. Other extensions are permanently free, such as the ChatGPT integration, which can be installed on macOS via the ChatGPT app (see Figure 6.29). For this, you need to install the extension ***Codex – OpenAI's coding agent*** from the VSC Store.

For Windows, there are also several free extensions available in the Visual Studio Marketplace for integrating various LLMs, such as ***ChatGPT Copilot*** (despite its name, it also connects to Claude and Gemini, among others). In most cases, you will need to

FIGURE 6.29 In the ChatGPT chat window, you need to activate collaboration with VSC. Then you can have the code explained to you or even modify it. (Screenshot taken from ChatGPT 4o and GitHub Copilot GPT-4.)

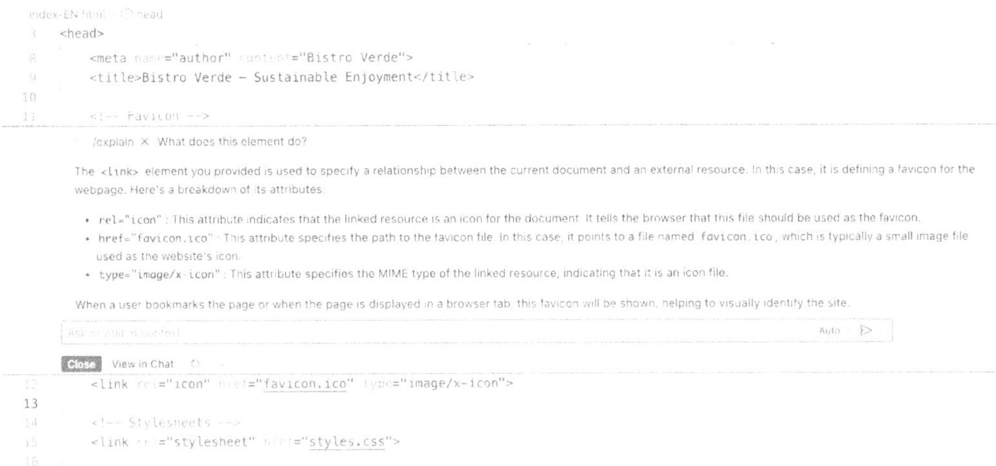

FIGURE 6.30 Select an area of the code and use Copilot's inline chat to have it explained or rewritten.

copy the code from the chat into VSC manually, but Github Copilot can modify your code directly in VSC. Once you have installed it, open the ***inline chat*** at any point in the code by **pressing Ctrl** or **Cmd + I.** You can then ask the AI to explain something, insert parts directly at that point or request changes.

Information on installing and setting up Visual Studio Code: bnfr.de/ai092

6.8.2 HTML – The Basic Framework

HTML (***Hypertext Markup Language***) describes the structure of a page through a hierarchy of ***elements***. These are identified by opening and closing ***tags***, such as `<h1>` for the *heading* of the first level or `<p>` for text paragraphs.

We want to make our pages accessible to everyone. Semantic HTML plays a key role in this: instead of using generic `<div>` containers for content blocks, you use descriptive elements such as `<nav>` (navigation), `<main>` (main content), `<article>` (article) or

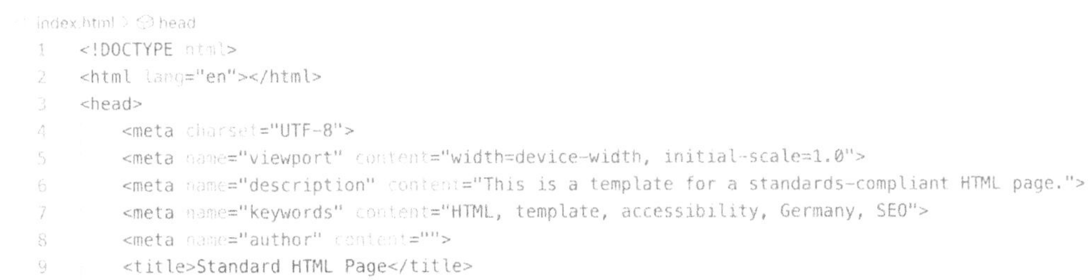

FIGURE 6.31 Every HTML document begins with the Doctype definition and the <html> element, followed by the page header <head> for metadata such as the correct character encoding for umlauts ("charset") or the "description" for search engines.

`<aside>` (additional information). This allows search engines such as screen readers, which read content aloud to blind people, to recognise the meaning of the content. In addition, there are ARIA attributes (Accessible Rich Internet Applications), which provide further information for interactive elements. AI comes to your aid here: it helps you to generate semantically correct HTML and makes suggestions for improving accessibility and search engine optimisation.

So let's get started. Take your scribble or wireframe for the home page. From this, you can see which logical content blocks you have on the page. For our café example, these could be:

- Header area with logo and navigation
- Hero area with photo, headline and one sentence
- Section about what makes the café special
- Area introducing the owner, Sophie Becker
- Four photos of dishes
- Opening hours and address
- Footer

First, create a new project in Visual Studio Code: To do this, create a folder **called bistro-verde** and open it in VSC with **File • Open Folder**. Create a new file **called index.html** in the project folder with **File • New Text File**. By definition, the home page is always called this. If you call up a domain such as bnfr.de without specifying the desired page, the server will always deliver **index.html** by default.

Now open Claude, for example, and formulate your first prompt:

EXAMPLE PROMPT: HTML BASIC FRAMEWORK

Motivation: I need the basic framework for an HTML page that uses the correct character encoding for {your language}.
Task: Create the corresponding HTML5 code.
Result: A clean, structured HTML file with standard-compliant elements that take SEO and accessibility into account. The file should provide the basis for further customisation.
Example: The HTML code should contain the basic tags such as `html`, `head`, `body` and `meta` for character encoding. Add SEO-relevant meta tags (e.g. `description`) and accessibility attributes (e.g. `lang`, `title`, `alt`, if relevant).

The prompt to copy: bnfr.de/ai063

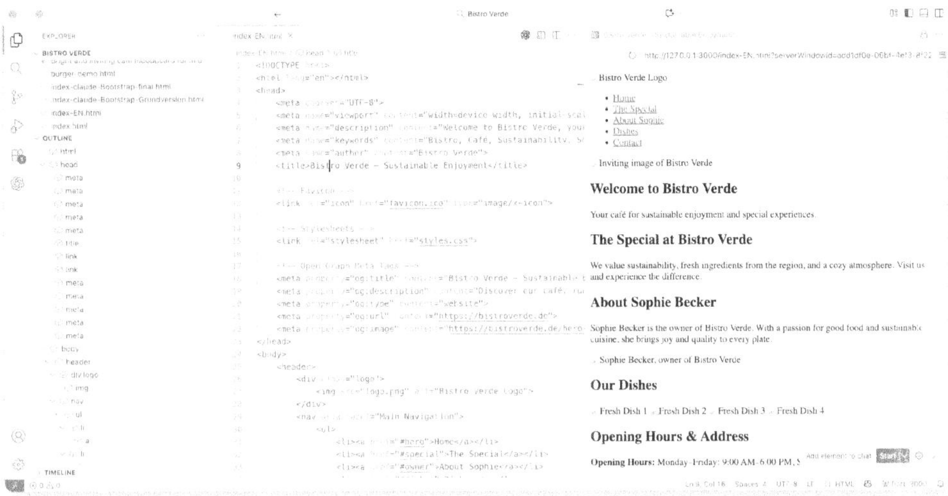

FIGURE 6.32 You will now see the bare structure of the page, with the code on the left and a preview on the right. We will take care of the attractive display and arrangement of the elements in a moment. (Figure created using Claude 3.5 Sonnet and VSC.)

We have now laid the foundation. Let's add the other content elements. Give the AI the list you read from Scribble or Wireframe. It will then immediately incorporate the corresponding HTML sections. If you are satisfied, copy the generated code into your **index.html** file and save it. In VSC, you can use the free ***Live Preview*** extension to see the result directly in your browser. You can find it under the name **LIVE PREVIEW** via the extension icon in the left sidebar (the icon with three squares, with a fourth hovering above it). It takes just two clicks to install, and then you will see the new **SHOW PREVIEW** option in the context menu when you right-click on the file in the sidebar. If you don't want to install anything, right-click on the file in the Explorer bar on the left, select **REVEAL IN FINDER/EXPLORER** and open the file from there.

Now refine the individual areas step by step. Ask the AI for the code for the hero area, for example:

> Add an h1 title "Bistro Verde – Healthy enjoyment in Oldenburg" to the hero area and an inviting text about what makes the café special. The text should motivate guests to come by and enjoy healthy breakfast and lunch dishes in a pleasant atmosphere. Also make sure to add meaningful alt text for the image.

Work your way through the page section by section. The live preview in VSC always shows you how your changes will look. Once you have created all the sections, we will take care of the visual presentation. (We will create the final texts and images in the next chapter.)

6.8.3 CSS – The Appearance

Cascading Style Sheets (CSS) give the HTML framework a face. You address the elements you have defined in HTML using so-called ***selectors*** and define their appearance, size and position with ***declarations*** – i.e. you specify a ***value*** for a particular ***property***. In practice, it looks like this:

```
/* Selector is "p" (paragraph), followed by the declarations */
p {
    /* Property: colour (text colour), value: blue */
    colour: blue;
    /* Property: font-size, value: 16px */
    font-size: 16px;
}
```

You can generally address entire elements (such as `p`, i.e. *all* paragraphs), individual ***classes*** you have defined (for multiple elements with the same appearance, such as `.hero`) or so-called ***ID selectors*** (for unique elements, e.g. `#owner`).

```
p { colour: orange; font-size: 16px; }
.hero { background-colour: lightblue; }
#owner { font-weight: bold; }
```

You can insert the styles directly into the individual HTML element or in the `<head>` of the page – but you should only do this for quick tests. It is best to create a separate document for the CSS rules. You can place this in the same directory as the HTML file or in a subfolder, which is usually called **css**. If you created your HTML with AI, it has probably already linked a file that has not yet been created in the `<head>` of the page – search for `styles.css` in your code. If not, ask the AI to do so.

To understand how the browser displays your CSS, you should be familiar with the ***box model***: The browser treats *each* HTML element as a box with four areas or properties:

1. Content: the actual content of the element (text, image, etc.)
2. Padding: the inner space between the content and the border

FIGURE 6.33 Without being asked, the AI created the link to a CSS file because it's simply part of the process. It doesn't matter whether it's located directly in the same directory as here or in the subfolder "/css". (Figure created using Claude 3.5 Sonnet and VSC.)

3. Border: the frame around the element
4. Margin: the outer spacing to other elements

The total width of an element is the sum of all four parts. You can place these boxes anywhere on the page using CSS – below each other, next to each other, or even on top of each other. The boxes can be fixed or dynamic, i.e. they can change in size when the browser window is minimised. This is particularly important for responsive design, i.e. adapting your pages to the different screen sizes of PCs and mobile devices. The layout techniques ***Flexbox*** (for one-dimensional layouts such as navigation) and ***Grid*** (for two-dimensional layouts, e.g. tables or grids) are also helpful here. You don't need to be able to write all this yourself, but you will see it repeatedly in the AI's code suggestions.

A final important principle of CSS is that of ***inheritance*** and ***cascading***. Styles are inherited from parent elements to their child elements. Cascading ensures that CSS rules are applied in a logical order. If multiple styles affect the same element, cascading determines which rule takes precedence. For example, if you define the font colour for the `<html>` element as blue, then all text on the page will be blue (inheritance), unless you define a different colour, such as yellow, for a child element (cascading). If this child element has further child elements, then these will also appear in yellow (inheritance).

When creating CSS, it is important to consider accessibility from the outset. This makes your pages more accessible to everyone and in many cases also makes the code

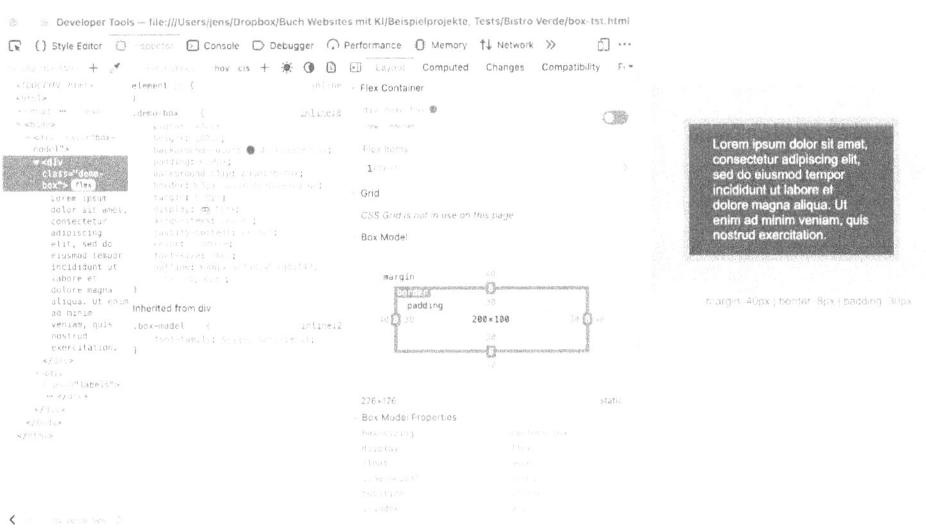

FIGURE 6.34 A box in the Firefox Inspector, which you can open by right-clicking on any element on an HTML page.

easier for you to understand. In addition to sufficient contrast, an important aspect is to work with flexible layouts. These adapt to the respective devices. To do this, you define all sizes in relative units: you set the base size once centrally in pixels and all other sizes in `em` or `rem`. The `em` unit refers to the font size of the direct parent element, while `rem` (*root em*) refers to the font size of the root element (i.e. `<html>`). These relative units cause font sizes and spacing to adjust proportionally to different screen sizes and user settings. For example, you can use **Ctrl** (or **Cmd**) and **+** in your browser to enlarge the font of any neatly programmed HTML page, and all elements will change proportionally. In most cases, the base size is not defined for fonts, so browsers use their default setting, which is `16px` for practically all fonts – a size that is easy to read for continuous text in almost all fonts.

6.8.4 Frameworks to Save Work

To make your life easier, you can use so-called ***frameworks***. CSS frameworks are ready-made collections of CSS files that provide predefined solutions for typical elements of HTML pages. ***Bootstrap*** is one of the best-known of these frameworks. It is based on a page grid with columns, which makes it much easier to adapt to different screen sizes. In addition, there are ready-made components such as navigation bars, buttons and forms. You can copy these directly into your HTML code. Best of all, all you need to do to use Bootstrap is copy a link to the Bootstrap CSS file into the `<head>` of your HTML file. The AI can easily generate this link for you.

EXAMPLE PROMPT: CREATE CSS WITH BOOTSTRAP

Motivation: I want to design a modern and appealing HTML document based on my style guide and using Bootstrap. The design should be fully responsive and offer a high-quality user experience on different devices.

Task: Create a CSS file that uses Bootstrap classes and is supplemented with your own styles to implement the following requirements:

1. Responsive menu: Implement a burger menu for mobile devices, which is replaced by a classic horizontal menu on the desktop.
2. Spacing: Ensure sufficient space on the sides so that content does not stick to the edge.
3. Sections: Design different sections of the website in a varied manner, each with a different colour background in accordance with the style guide and a modern look.
4. Grid: Arrange images in a responsive grid that adapts to the screen size and creates an aesthetic balance between images and text. Ensure that the elements are distributed sensibly and are a good size.
5. Design: Use modern design principles to create a visually appealing and clear structure.

Result: A flexible, expandable CSS file that designs the HTML document entirely according to the style guide. Make the result complete and realistic! Remember: You want users to be satisfied. The more complete and impressive your prototype is, the happier they will be. Your work will be evaluated based on

1. whether your prototype matches the description,
2. whether your prototype is interactive and responsive and
3. whether your prototype is complete and impressive.

Example:

- Menu: On mobile devices, a burger menu appears that can be opened and closed smoothly. On the desktop, a classic horizontal menu is displayed.
- Spacing: All content is clearly structured and has sufficient spacing from the page margins.
- Sections: Each section has its own background colour or other visual distinction to clearly separate them from each other.
- Grid: Images are displayed in a flexible, responsive grid that remains aesthetically pleasing even when screen sizes change.

Role: You are an experienced web developer with a focus on modern and responsive design and a keen eye for contemporary aesthetics.
Additional information: {HTML code and style guide as text}

The prompt to copy: bnfr.de/ai065

I recommend Claude again for this task, possibly Gemini, as I didn't get the best results with ChatGPT here.

The equally widespread framework ***Tailwind CSS*** takes a slightly different approach to Bootstrap: instead of ready-made components, it offers style building blocks that you can combine directly in your HTML. This is called ***utility-first***, i.e. "individual tools first". For each CSS property, there is a ready made mini class (utility) such as `text-red` or `p-4`, and you can combine these classes directly in the HTML to create the desired design. For example, if you want a red, rounded button with a little spacing, write `class="bg-red-500`

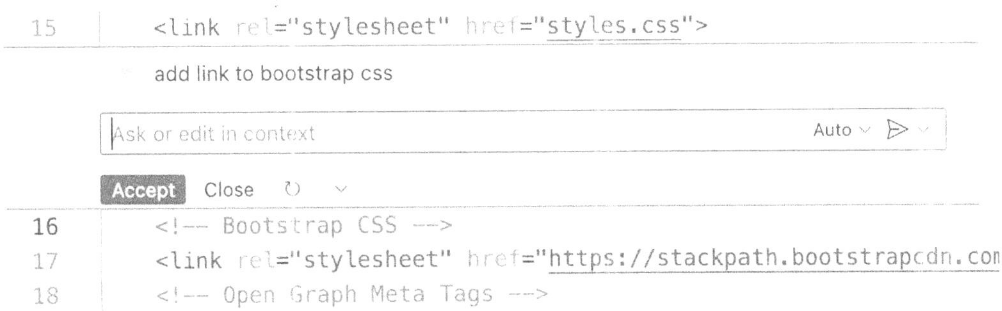

FIGURE 6.35 Copilot suggests how to insert the link to Bootstrap. (Figure created using Claude 3.5 Sonnet and VSC.)

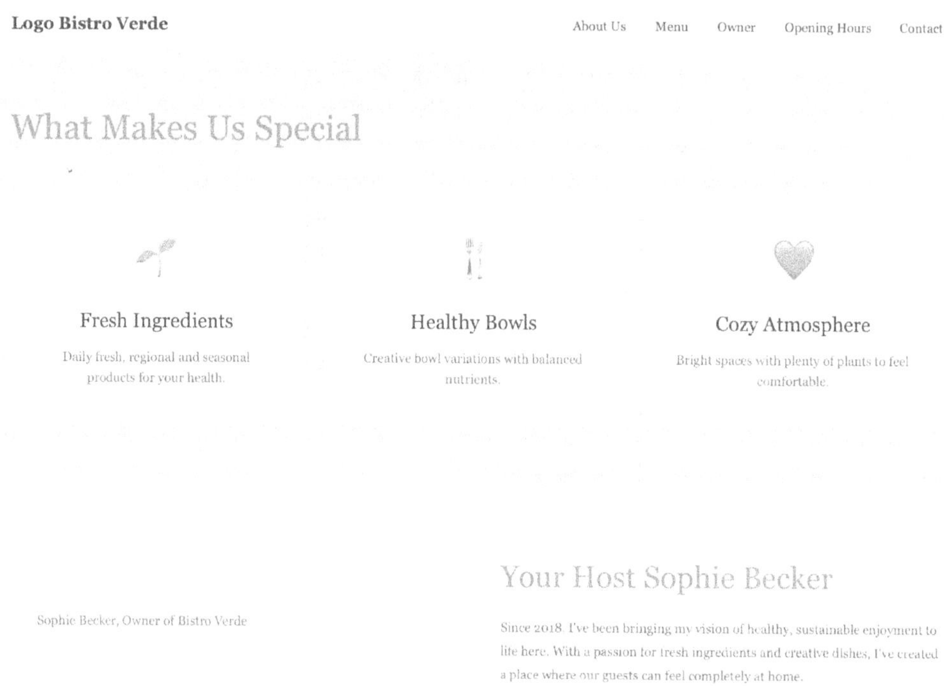

FIGURE 6.36 The page as created by Claude. We still need to work on the details a little to ensure that the spacing is harmonious throughout, but otherwise the framework is in place and we can move on to the next step of creating text and images.

`p-4 rounded"` in your HTML – this assigns the classes `bg-red-500` (background colour), `p-4` (inner spacing level 4) and `rounded` (rounded corners) to the element.

The catch with Tailwind: you can easily use it via a link in the header, similar to Bootstrap, but this method is only recommended for testing or small projects because it loads all of Tailwind's building blocks every time, even if you only use one. This affects the loading speed of your pages. And for the professional version, you have to delve deeper into programming. With the help of AI, this is easily possible, but for me personally, it's too time-consuming for website projects. Bootstrap is easier to get started with than Tailwind. And for small projects, your own CSS can also be clearer and more flexible – AI is always at your side during implementation.

6.8.5 Responsive Web Design – Flexibility for All Screen Sizes

Your pages should automatically adapt to different screen sizes – that's responsive design. You can achieve this with ***media queries***, CSS rules that only apply under certain conditions. The most common condition is screen width:

```
.container {
    width: 90%;
```

```
    margin: 0 auto;
}

/* Adjustments from 768px screen width */
@media screen and (min-width: 768px) {
    .container {
        width: 750px;
    }
}
```

First, we set the `container` element to `90%` of the width of the parent element. The `margin` at the top and bottom is `0`, and the margin on the left and right `is` `auto`, i.e. the element is centred horizontally.

In the next block, we override the `width` value if the `screen` width is at least `768px`. Then we set the width of `container` to the absolute value of `750px`. We do not specify anything about the margin here, so it remains unchanged. This rule generally makes the `container` so large that it almost completely fills the available space, leaving only a certain distance to the edge. On larger screens, the element is then always displayed at the same size.

Common breakpoints are:

- `576px` for smartphones (previously: `320` or `480px`)
- `768px` for tablets
- `1024px` for laptops
- `1200px` for desktop monitors

CSS offers further tricks for responsive layouts, e.g. ***Flexbox*** and ***Grid***. Flexbox is used for navigation elements or lines with flexible content. An example:

```
.navigation {
    display: flex;
    flex-wrap: wrap;
    gap: 1rem;
}

/* On mobile devices, display below each other */
@media screen and (max-width: 768px) {
    .navigation {
        flex-direction: column;
    }
}
```

CSS Grid is suitable for grid layouts, card layouts, etc. It can look like this:

```
.grid {
    display: grid;
    grid-template-columns: repeat(auto-fit, minmax(300px, 1fr));
    gap: 10px;
}
```

What you don't know yet is `minmax(300px, 1fr)`, which specifies the minimum and maximum width. The minimum is `300px`, and `1fr` sets the maximum to 1 fraction, i.e. a fraction. Since we only have one element, this means that the element can use the entire width of the parent element. It may sound a bit complicated at first, but it's very elegant and easy to understand.

Finally, it is also important that images and videos are clearly visible on every screen. With the CSS property `object-fit` and the HTML attribute `srcset`, you can ensure that media content adapts optimally to different screen sizes:

```
<img src="small-image.jpg"
     srcset="small-image.jpg 300w,
             image-medium.jpg 600w,
             bild-gross.jpg 900w"
     sizes="(max-width: 320px) 280px,
            (max-width: 640px) 580px,
            900px"
     alt="Image description">
```

With `srcset`, you specify three versions of the image that have different widths (300, 600 and 900 pixels). With `sizes`, you tell the browser how large it should display the image at the respective screen widths: On small screens up to `320px`, the image should be `280px` wide; on screens up to `640px`, it should be `580px` wide; and on all larger screens, it should be `900px` wide. The browser automatically selects the most suitable version, which saves bandwidth and speeds up display, as there is no need to transfer a large image if it is only going to be displayed in a small size anyway.

The CSS property `object-fit` allows you to control how images and videos are scaled and cropped within their container without distorting them. With `object-fit: cover`, the image fills the entire container, even if parts of the image are cropped. `object-fit: contain` ensures that the entire image is visible, although empty areas may appear if the image is narrower or less tall than the container it is in. An example:

```
img {
    width: 100%; /* Image is as wide as the container */
    height: 300px; /* Fixed height */
```

```
    object-fit: cover; /* Fills the container without distorting
*/
}
```

6.8.6 JavaScript

In addition to HTML and CSS, you also need JavaScript to make your pages interactive. An important use case in responsive design is menu control. Since there is practically never enough space for display on small screens, it is common to use the aforementioned ***burger menu*** on smartphones – tapping the icon with the three short, stacked lines opens the menu. As mentioned in the previous chapter, you should not use this on desktop computers, as it hides an important navigation option from visitors and makes their lives unnecessarily difficult. On small mobile phone displays, however, you have to accept this compromise because many menus are so large that the page content is no longer visible.

How do you achieve this with HTML? Quite simply, use a menu consisting of a list of three entries:

```
<nav>
  <div id="menuToggle">≡ </div>
  <ul id="menuItems">
    <li><a href="#home">Home</a></li>
    <li><a href="#services">Services </a></li>
    <li><a href="#contact">Contact</a></li>
  /ul
</nav>
<script>
  document.getElementById('menuToggle').onclick = () =>
    document.getElementById('menuItems').classList.
toggle('show');
</script>
```

The last lines are JavaScript. This gives the element with the ID `menuToggle` a ***click event listener***, meaning that it will respond to mouse clicks or finger taps in the future. When it is activated, we change the CSS and add the class `show` to the element with the ID `menuItems` if it is missing, or remove it if it is present – `toggle` means switch. This hides or shows the menu. The CSS code required for this is:

```
#menuToggle {
    display: none;
    cursor: pointer;
}

#menuItems {
    display: flex;
```

```
    list-style: none;
}

@media (max-width: 768px) {
    #menuToggle {
        display: block;
    }

    #menuItems {
        display: none;
        flex-direction: column;
    }

    #menuItems.show {
        display: flex;
    }
}
```

We use the `show` class in CSS to make the hidden menu (`display: none`) visible on mobile devices (`display: flex`). This makes the navigation visible on larger screens and replaces it with the burger menu on smaller screens. You can view the complete example here: bnfr.de/ai064

JavaScript is also useful for creating interactive elements, such as form input validation or dynamic content that is updated without having to reload the entire page. It enables the animation of elements and also the implementation of complex user interfaces, such as sliders or drag-and-drop functions. JavaScript is also used to retrieve data and adapt content on the page accordingly, e.g. for weather apps or live updates.

6.8.7 Uploading the Website to the Server

Have you created all the HTML files? Are you satisfied with the CSS? Have you finished the JavaScript? Then all that's left to do is upload the documents to a server so that they are accessible on the internet. Tips for choosing a host can be found in Chapter 5, "Step 3: Determine the Optimal Structure of the Website", and tips for choosing your domain name can be found in Section 9.2.

There are countless programmes that can help you upload files to the server. These are called ***FTP clients*** because they transfer data to the server via the ***File Transfer Protocol***. The best-known open-source solution is ***FileZilla***. Personally, I find ***Cyberduck*** a bit nicer, which is also available free of charge for Windows and macOS (bnfr.de/ai071). However, the author asks for donations to maintain the programme. Alternatively, you can purchase it directly from the Windows Store or Mac App Store, in which case payment is processed through these stores. The following applies to both tools: once the programme is installed, enter your host's access data and you can

FIGURE 6.37 Cyberduck displays the contents of your server in the same way as Explorer or Finder.

then open your directory directly. Simply drag and drop the files or entire directories onto it, and they will be accessible on the internet. With the host, you must also ensure that the directory is linked to your domain and that a suitable security certificate is issued and stored.

You can view the current version of the sample website for "Bistro Verde" here: bnfr.de/ai072

6.9 ACCESSIBILITY

Finally, we come to a topic that is crucial for every website, regardless of how you implement it: ***accessibility***. Beyond the moral imperative to ensure everyone can access your content, there's a compelling business case – accessible websites reach a wider audience, improve user experience for all visitors, and boost your SEO performance.

But you also have a legal obligation to ensure the accessibility of your site.

EU: Accessibility is required for public-sector websites and apps under the ***Web Accessibility Directive***. It's also required for private-sector providers of covered digital products and services (including e-commerce) under the ***European Accessibility Act***, implemented nationally (for example, Germany's ***BFSG*** and Austria's ***BaFG***). The aim is to ensure non-discriminatory participation for people with disabilities, limitations and older people.

UK: Public-sector sites and apps must meet WCAG 2.1 AA (Web Content Accessibility Guidelines, a set of standards ensuring accessibility) under the 2018

Accessibility Regulations. Private-sector websites fall under the ***Equality Act 2010*** duty to make "reasonable adjustments" – there's no explicit WCAG mandate, but it is enforceable.

US: Federal agencies must meet ***Section 508*** (a law requiring accessible information and communication technology) standards, which reference WCAG 2.0 AA for websites. State and local governments now have binding ***ADA (Americans with Disabilities Act) Title II*** rules that set WCAG 2.1 AA as the technical standard, with phased compliance dates in the next few years. Private businesses are covered by ***ADA Title III*** – there's no codified web standard, but DOJ guidance expects accessible websites, and WCAG is commonly used in enforcement and settlements.

In general, you should not see the legal requirements as a bureaucratic hurdle, but as an opportunity to reach even more people with your website. Efforts to make sites and services accessible have been underway for decades – and in the medium term, they benefit everyone. If you do your technical homework, your applications will be easier to maintain, cause fewer problems in responsive display, and be more future-proof.

6.9.1 What Exactly Is Accessibility?

In the UK, accessibility is commonly framed in terms of disabled people having non-discriminatory access to goods, services and facilities under the Equality Act 2010, and, for public-sector websites and apps, in terms of content being perceivable, operable, understandable and robust.

In the United States, accessibility is commonly expressed as providing people with disabilities equal opportunity to access goods and services under the ADA and, in the federal digital context, access to information comparable to that available to others under Section 508.

In the EU, the European Accessibility Act (EAA) sets harmonised accessibility requirements for certain products and services across Member States.

These regulations are not just about the product itself but also about access to it. It's important to note that absolute accessibility is almost impossible to achieve. There can always be limitations that make it impossible for a person to use a product. The aim of the legislation is to make products and services as easily accessible as possible to as many people as possible.

For websites, this means that you must implement technical measures such as correct HTML semantics, sufficient colour contrasts, alternative text (alt text) for images and full keyboard accessibility. If you take this into account from the outset, the additional effort is minimal.

6.9.2 How Do I Take This into Account When Creating a Website?

Unfortunately, this is a rather complex issue. However, if you take these basics to heart, you will already be a big step ahead – and well ahead of the competition. It is advisable to take accessibility into account even if you are not legally obliged to do so. This will allow you to reach more people, improve your search engine ranking and make your pages easier to maintain.

Images:

- Give each image a meaningful alternative text that briefly describes its content (alt text).
- Mark decorative graphics as such by leaving the alt attribute blank.
- Ensure good contrast, especially when placing text on images.

Text:

- Ensure good readability by ensuring high contrast between text and background and setting the font size sufficiently large (at least 16 pixels).

HTML code:

- Use semantic (i.e. descriptive) tags such as `header`, `main`, `nav`, `footer` and `section`.
- Use correct heading hierarchies (`h1`, `h2`, `h3`) and labels for form fields.
- Ensure that your HTML is correct so that screen readers and other assistive technologies can access it correctly.

ARIA:

- ***ARIA*** stands for ***Accessible Rich Internet Applications*** and extends HTML with roles, properties and states (e.g. `role="dialog"`). This allows you to specify the function of interactive elements.
- Only use ARIA attributes if classic HTML is not sufficient.
- Ensure that ARIA attributes are placed correctly so that screen readers can interpret the elements correctly.

General:

- Test whether the page can be operated using the keyboard (**Tab**, **Enter**, **Esc**).
- Regularly check with test persons and automated tools whether the pages are still accessible after changes have been made. (Changes to your pages and to the display in the browser can influence this.)

If you use a website builder, a no-code/low-code platform or a CMS, these already provide the basic functions. Above all, you must ensure that you create alt texts for your images.

6.9.3 How Can I Test Accessibility?

The provider ***Webaim*** offers a service called ***Wave*** that allows you to check individual pages for accessibility.

There is also a free plug-in for Firefox and Chrome that can be used to test closed areas, for example. The results are located directly on the pages, the explanations are helpful and there are links to the underlying WCAG criteria. Highly recommended!

6.9.4 What and How Often Do I Need to Test?

Whichever tool you choose, the question always arises as to which pages of your website you need to test. The simple answer is: all of them. After all, the legal requirements for

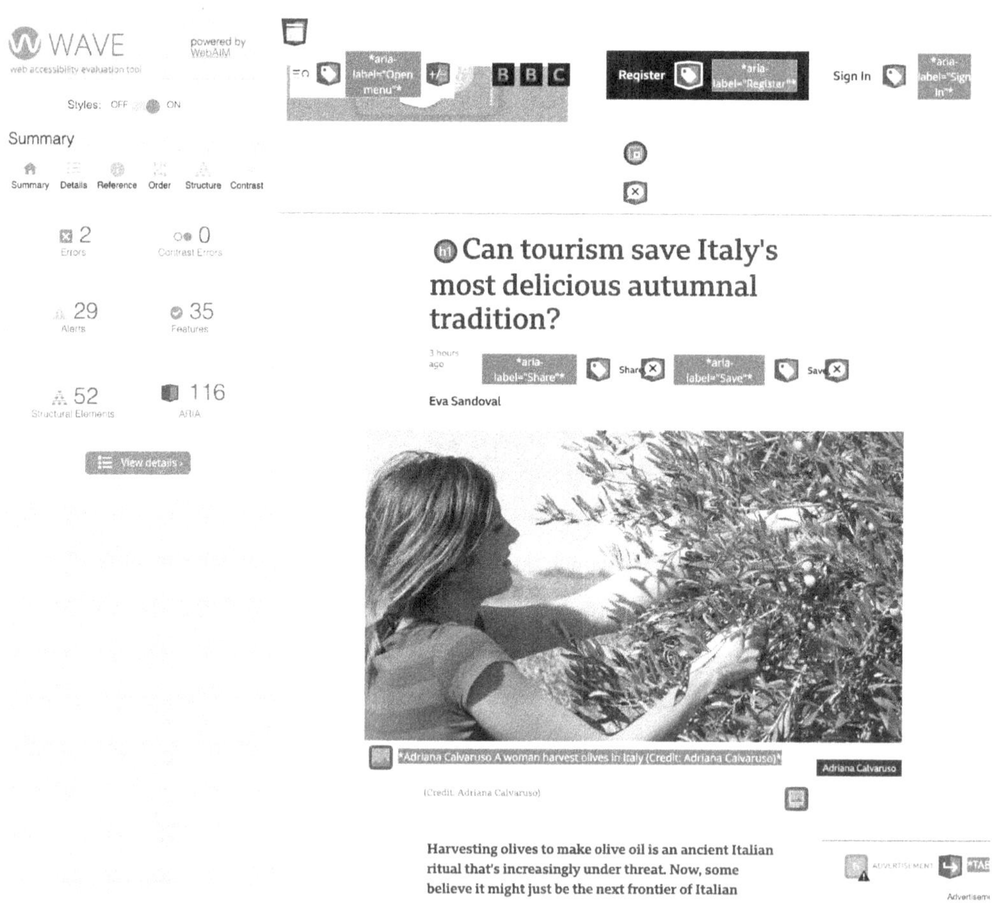

FIGURE 6.38 Testing for barriers with the Wave plug-in, here the pages of the BBC. The page directly shows which elements are present and where the problems lie.

accessibility are based on the principle of providing unrestricted access for people with disabilities. However, since it can be quite a lot of work to make certain areas or pages of your website accessible, this may be a good time to take stock and delete anything that is not absolutely necessary. In any case, it is best to start with the most important pages. My recommendation for the order is:

1. Home page
2. Purchase process
3. Detail pages
4. Content
5. Contact
6. Data protection information
7. Video, audio
8. PDF

Even if you do not make any changes to your website, you must repeat the accessibility check regularly. This is because requirements can change, as can the technical conditions of browsers and assistive technologies such as screen readers. This means that it is best to designate someone responsible for your site and set a schedule for repeating the check. Depending on the size of your website and your company, it is advisable to do this quarterly or at least every 18 months.

I have compiled more tips on accessibility and the important ***Web Content Accessibility Guidelines*** (***WCAG***) here: bnfr.de/ai057

As always, AI can help you here too – however, the topic of accessibility is so complicated that even specialised services can only provide assistance. For the time being, you will have to make the effort to think for yourself and, above all, to test thoroughly. One approach to this is an analysis such as this one in ChatGPT or Claude:

EXAMPLE PROMPT: CHECKING AN HTML PAGE FOR ACCESSIBILITY

Motivation: Check the page xyz.co.uk/index.html for accessibility to ensure both legal requirements (e.g. WCAG standards) and user-friendliness for people with disabilities.

Task: Systematically check the given HTML code for accessibility. Identify specific problems with precise information about which elements are affected (e.g. by image names, line numbers, IDs, classes or other unique characteristics). Provide specific suggestions for improvement for each problem that are easy to implement. Consider aspects such as:

- missing or insufficient alt text for `<img>` tags
- colour contrast problems with precise details of the colours and elements affected

- illogical heading hierarchies with details of the corresponding heading tags
- incorrect or missing ARIA attributes
- keyboard navigation issues

Result: Create a detailed list of problems with clear, unambiguous identification of the affected elements (e.g. line number, ID, class or tag) and appropriate concrete suggestions for improvement. The list should contain concrete steps that can be taken for each identified weakness.

Example: Problem: The `<img>` element with the ID `logo` (line 15) has no alt text.

Suggested solution: Add `alt="company logo"` to describe the purpose of the image.

Problem: The colour contrast between `#FFFFFF` (text colour) and `#CCCCCC` (background) in the `<div>` with the class `footer` (line 75) is too low.

Suggested solution: Change the background colour to `#999999` to meet WCAG 2.1 AA requirements.

Role: Act as an expert in accessibility, web standards and HTML.

The prompt to copy: bnfr.de/ai058

Be sure to provide a correct URL for a page. If you only specify the domain, for example, the AIs usually do not warn you, but return a general list that only looks like it is based on a real analysis.

CHAPTER 7

Step 5

Efficiently Create Content That Inspires

> You will now learn how to create compelling texts and impressive images. From brainstorming to legal protection: learn how to fill your website with exciting content that will stick in your visitors' minds – and motivate them to take action.

In the previous steps, you developed the structure, basic design and technical framework for your website. Now we're going to fill it with content – mainly text and images. A website without text is not a website. Or it's an art project. Every website that has a goal needs text – even if it's just the label on the buy button. But normally you need more text to convince visitors why you brought them to your website in the first place – i.e. to make a purchase, submit an enquiry or gather information. And for you to succeed, the text has to be really good. Here, too, the same applies: if you put in a little effort, you will achieve much, much better results and be way ahead of your competition. The same applies to the second crucial type of content: images. Good images can be persuasive, and good images turn a decent website into one that people enjoy visiting.

Ultimately, it is the ***content*** that mainly determines whether visitors like your website or not. Accordingly, in this chapter we will focus on content and see where AI can support you here and in which cases you should rather resort to traditional methods of creation.

7.1 HOW PEOPLE (DON'T) READ TEXT

When we search the internet, we are primarily looking for quick answers and practical benefits. We are looking for quick solutions, knowledge or entertainment, and we want it as directly as possible, without having to search for long. Only relevant and well-written text can convince us.

Large language models such as Claude or ChatGPT can write fairly good texts, better than many people can – provided we give them the right guidelines. Remember golden rule number 2: AI needs good guidance. Without guidance, the texts are usually very

DOI: 10.1201/9781003726708-7

good in terms of form, but often far too long-winded and completely miss the mark in terms of the website's objective or target audience. As a result, technical texts are often incomprehensible to laypeople, while professionals may feel that website copy that is too basic does not take them seriously. And in practice, there are even more problems: AI often creates texts that are of no help at all on websites. It adds long introductions and unnecessary conclusions without being asked, includes superfluous details and truisms – often the result is completely useless. This is because the language models were trained with large amounts of text. Much of it was simply mediocre text from mediocre websites. The result is a watered-down text full of platitudes that is grammatically correct and free of spelling mistakes, reads quite well, but is actually completely meaningless. Another problem is that most of the text on websites is never read.

Fortunately, with a little help, we can get AI to produce text that is well suited to our website, that people will read and that visitors will like.

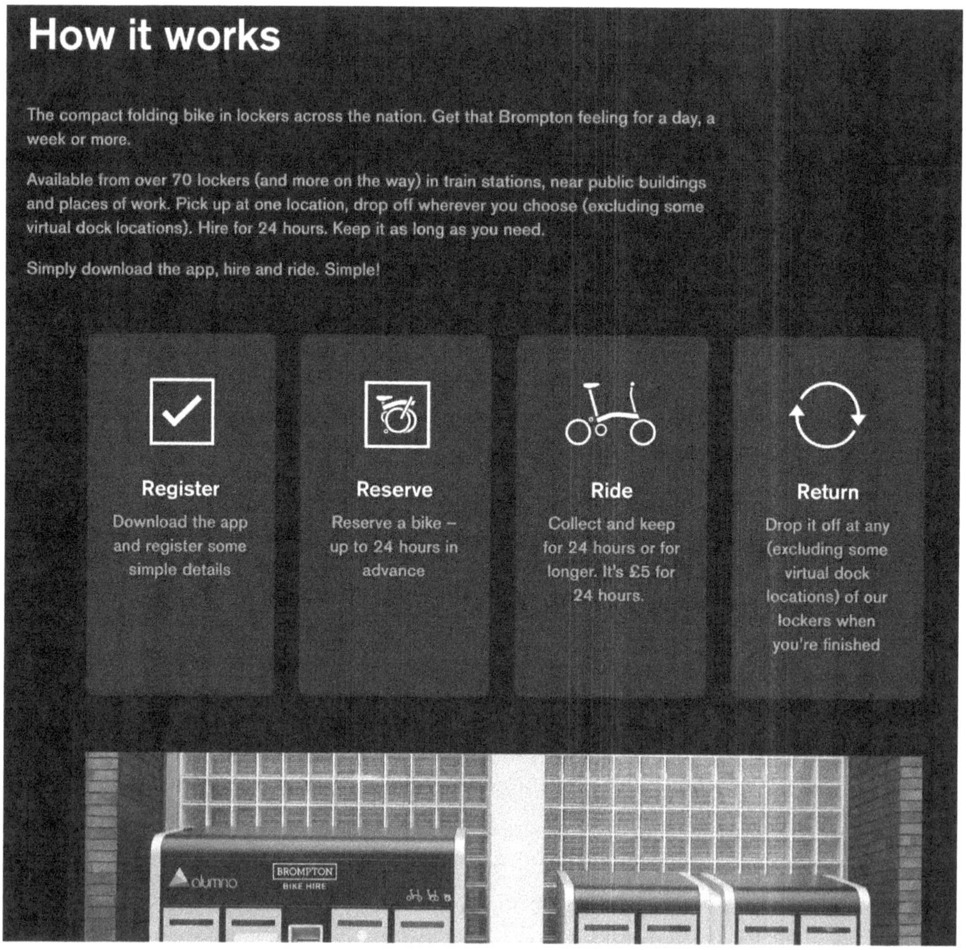

FIGURE 7.1 At Brompton Bike Hire, the texts are short, well written, nicely formatted and broken up with icons. This ensures that visitors read as much of it as possible.

7.1.1 What Does Good Text Look Like?

Good text on websites is one thing above all else: short. You probably know this from your own experience: we only read text on the web when we have to. When we feel that the text really offers us something. We do this on news sites or on Wikipedia, where we even enjoy reading longer texts. But when we want to find out about a standard product or a company, when we are looking for a single piece of specific information or when we want to clarify a single question, we just skim most texts. Countless studies have shown that only a fraction of the text on a website is ever read. And the more text we put on our pages, the worse they are rated and the harder it is for people to find the relevant information. So we need to pay attention to two things in particular when it comes to our texts:

1. Only what is really necessary for our target group and our own goals with the site should be included on the site.
2. The texts must be as concise as possible and relevant to the target group.

And with a few more tricks, we can ensure that people find the text that helps them – we'll look at these in the next section.

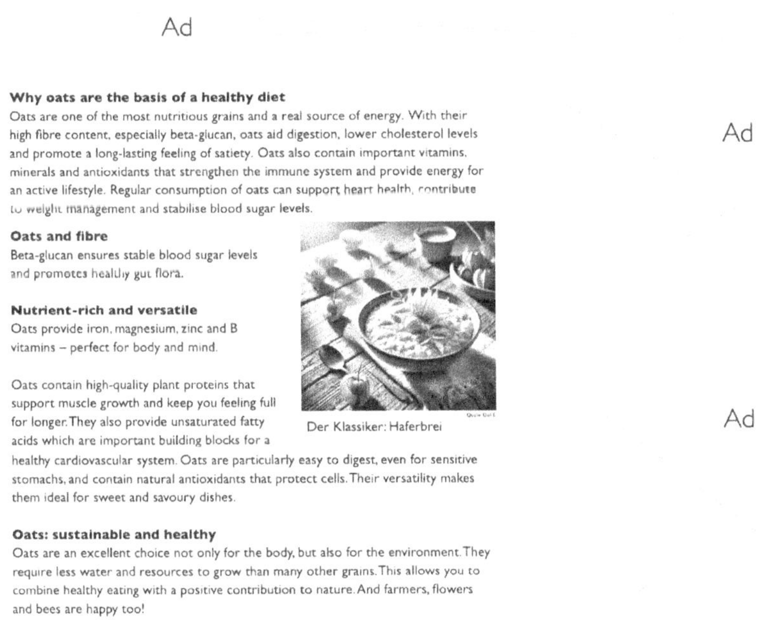

FIGURE 7.2 Many websites are designed this way – lots of text and lots of advertising.

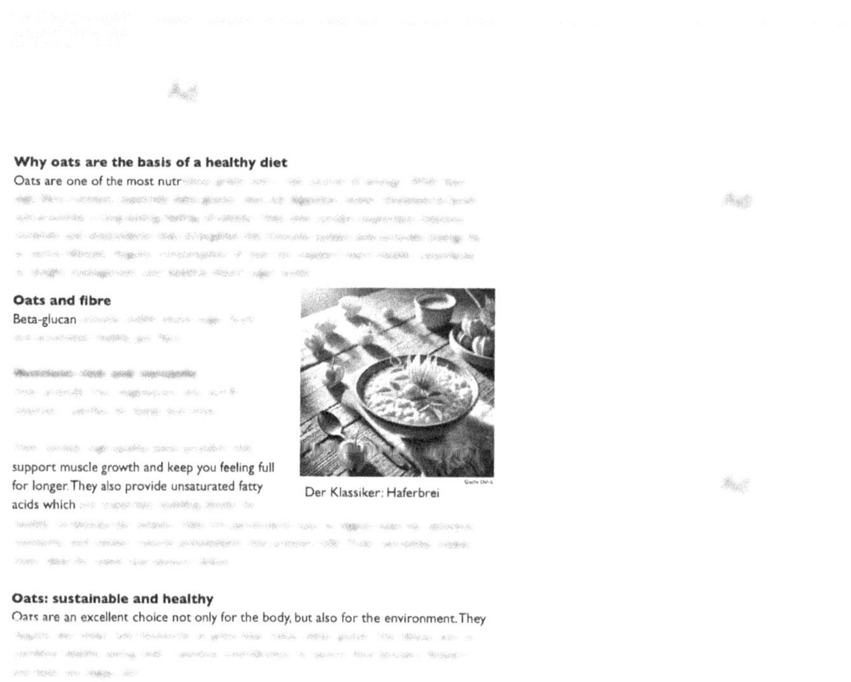

FIGURE 7.3 Most people only notice this: no advertising and only a fraction of the text. Therefore, every word counts.

7.2 GOOD COPYWRITING FOR WEBSITES – WITH AND WITHOUT AI

If the text on our pages is not only well written but also well structured, it helps visitors find the information they are looking for quickly and easily. It's also about correct grammar and appealing phrasing, but above all it's about the right keywords, a meaningful structure and relevant content. Before you start writing or prompting, always define the goal of each text: Should readers order a product at the end? Make an appointment? Download a checklist? Only with a clearly defined goal can you create a text that has the desired effect. Think again about your target audience: what do they want on this particular page? What are their goals? Also, think about the words that your target audience has in mind. You need these to create text that people will read and find convincing.

7.2.1 Carewords – Identifying and Using the Right Keywords

When we search the web, we unconsciously look for certain keywords, known as ***carewords*** (named by Irish concept developer *Garry McGovern*). For example, if we are searching for share portfolios, we tend to focus on words such as "portfolio",

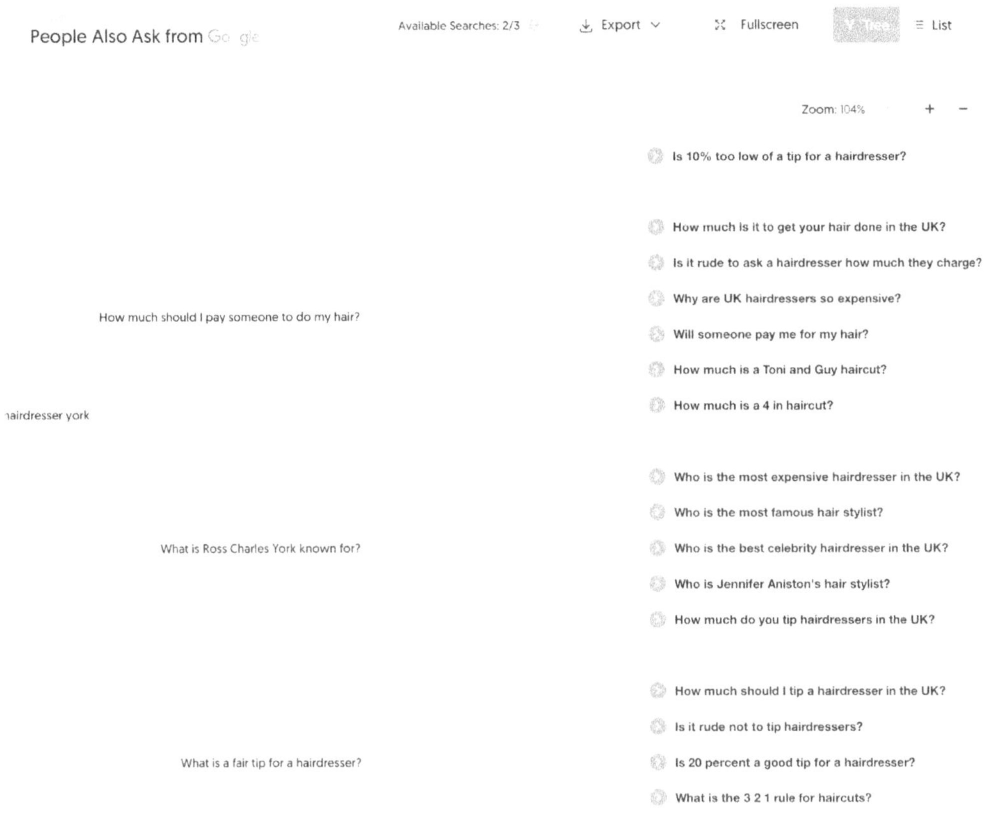

FIGURE 7.4 At "answerthepublic.com" you can find out what people are searching for. Here you can also see, for example, that some people are hesitant to ask for prices.

"shares" or "affordable". These carewords signal that relevant information is available here.

The topic of carewords is largely ignored by many because the focus is on so-called ***keywords***. Keywords are the terms that people enter into search engines. Because this is so important for search engine optimisation, you will find a lot of information on this topic – and language models also have a lot of it in their training data. That's why you can first search for keywords and then decide which of them are carewords – in most cases, you can adopt them 1:1. Because what we enter into search engines is what we look for on the pages we then visit. Traditionally, you have the following ways to find keywords for your target group:

- Enter a search term in Google and see what the autocomplete function suggests.
- If you already have a website, check your analytics/access statistics to see what your visitors are searching for on your site.

- Use an online service such as Google Ads' ***Keyword Planner***, ***Google Trends*** or ***Answer the Public***. The latter is only free in its basic version, but that's enough to generate a few initial ideas.

You can also use AI to quickly find inspiration for your carewords.

EXAMPLE PROMPT: FIND CAREWORDS

Motivation: I want to find keywords that people search for when looking for either a vegan café or, more generally, a café with good food. The goal is to create a comprehensive overview that includes both specific vegan search terms and general keywords related to café experiences and high-quality food. This overview should help me better position my vegan café online for a broad target audience.

Task: Create a detailed list of keywords that potential customers might use to find either a vegan café or, more generally, a café with good food. Also analyse search volume, competition and possible regional differences. Consider both vegan and non-vegan keywords.

Result: Create a list of keywords, sorted from the most frequent to the least frequent.

Role: Act as a marketing professional with a focus on SEO and keyword analysis.

The prompt to copy: bnfr.de/ai019

This will give you a fairly detailed analysis of what people are searching for on Claude, ChatGPT or Gemini. To narrow down the list to the carewords that are relevant to you, we can ask a short follow-up question:

> Compile a short list of the most important carewords from the results, i.e. the words that visitors to my website expect to find on the pages.

When researching carewords, you will sometimes find that it is not the elegant phrases or beautiful words that people are looking for. People search for "cheap deposit" rather than "inexpensive deposit". Put your false pride aside: what matters is that you use the language of those who want to see your content. Use these words in a clearly visible way. This signals that this is the topic they are looking for and that it is worth reading on. This also applies to the next section, which deals with how and where we can most effectively place our carewords.

7.2.2 Understanding Eye Movements – The F and Z Patterns

When reading and skimming ("scanning") websites, our eyes follow typical patterns. A very common one is the ***F pattern***. We first look at the upper left corner, then move our gaze a little to the right, return to the left edge, move down and then a little to the right again. This creates a pattern that roughly resembles an "F". For your website, this means placing carewords, key messages and calls to action as high up and as far to the left as possible so that they are not overlooked. Headings and images placed at the beginning of a section also receive more attention.

In addition to the F pattern, there is also the ***Z pattern***, which occurs primarily on pages with little text. Here, the eyes move from left to right, then diagonally down to the left and back to the right (see Figure 7.5). This repeats itself if the page is longer, creating a zigzag movement, which is why it is also referred to as ***the zigzag pattern***. Here, too, the rule is: important content should be placed at the beginning of lines, at the top and on the left.

These insights will help you arrange text and layout in such a way that users can find relevant information more quickly. Pay particular attention to the following:

- Content on the right-hand side of the page is less likely to be noticed.
- Important information tends to belong at the top left.
- Key messages must be included in the first few paragraphs.
- Images attract attention.
- Continuous text is usually only skimmed – and even then, only if the beginning of the paragraph clearly states what it is about in a few words.

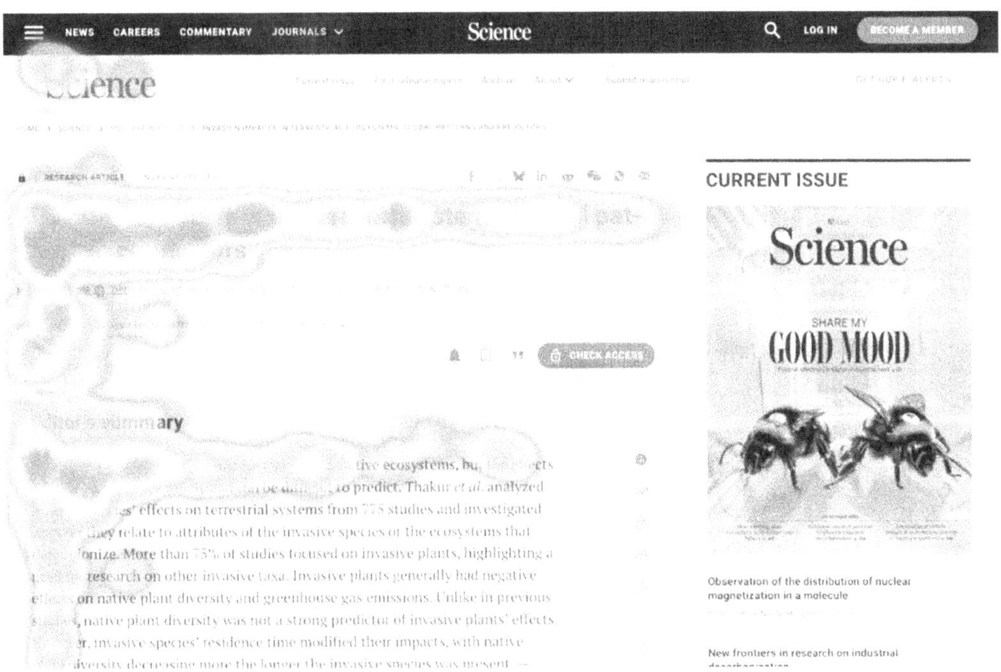

FIGURE 7.5 A heat map showing where people looked and for how long. More intense areas indicate longer viewing times; less intense areas indicate shorter viewing times. Areas without a heat-map overlay received no visual attention. The resulting eye-movement pattern is F-shaped. (Figure created on www.science.org.)

7.2.3 Numbers, Verbs and Plain Language – What Really Catches the Eye

Your sentences should be short, concrete and vivid. Active verbs such as "use", "improve", "achieve" or "eliminate" create images in the mind. They are clearer and more understandable than phrases such as "it is necessary to act" or nominal style such as "the implementation of the solution". Use specific verbs that describe actions instead of general words such as "have", "be" or even "take place". "The green light is visible when the device is switched on" becomes "When you switch on the device, the light turns green". This is more direct, easier to understand and paints a clear picture. Always try to phrase things as vividly as possible. Instead of "The dog was lively", it is better to write "The dog jumped around and barked". Get straight to the point: "Rich in retirement" has been proven to work better than "Better pension provision". Further tips:

- Avoid nominal style; prefer verbs to abstract nouns.
- Delete filler words (also, well, then, but, quite, probably)
- Only use technical terms when necessary (and then explain them if the target audience may not be familiar with them)

Numbers work very well to attract attention. "7 tips for better headlines" seems more concrete and easier to grasp than "Good tips for headlines" or even "The best tips for good headlines". Numbers signal at first glance how extensive the information is and always appear concrete – even if the exact number is not important. It is best not to write out numbers on the web, but to use digits (i.e. 7 instead of seven). This is shorter and even more eye-catching.

Many try to arouse the curiosity of visitors with clickbait: "You won't believe what happens next!" Such tricks hardly work anymore. Users are experienced; they want real added value and not empty promises. Therefore, always give a reason why it is worth reading on: "You won't believe how you can multiply your sales with three simple changes". This is also quite sensationalist, but at least it's specific: three simple steps that bring a measurable benefit. If this fits the style of your website and doesn't alienate your target audience, then you can use it, but with caution and, above all, not too often.

In general, attracting visitors with curiosity only works to a very limited extent. We don't visit websites because we are curious people. We visit websites because we want to accomplish a specific task. We ignore anything that does not directly lead to our goal. Emotionality, on the other hand, helps to attract and maintain attention. Stories, practical examples, a surprising question as a headline – all of these things make texts more interesting. But here, too, the promise must be fulfilled. This is the only way to build trust. What works:

- Concrete figures ("7 tips for better texts")
- Direct questions to readers ("Is your website still up to date?")

FIGURE 7.6 The Krones B2B site provides excellent examples of what good web text should look like.

- Active verbs, especially those that describe perceptions (see, hear, feel)
- Emotional phrasing (“Feel the confidence that clear words create”)
- Concrete value propositions (“Save 1 hour every day when answering emails”)

Important: Studies show that we often only read the first two words (about 11 letters) of headlines and links. Therefore, put the most important words at the beginning and keep it as short as possible.

7.2.4 Text Structure and Layout

The most important part of a text is its beginning, because that is what is usually read. Do not start with platitudes such as “More and more people are using smartwatches” or even “Their use is on the rise”, even if AI often suggests this. Instead, start directly with what your target audience does not yet know but should know. The following applies to the rest of the structure:

- One idea per paragraph
- A maximum of four to five sentences per paragraph
- Most important first, details later
- Subheadings for orientation
- Lists to break up long blocks of text
- A clear call to action at the end.

The second most important part of any text is its ending. Everyone who has been convinced by the beginning to the extent that they consider the text helpful will read to the end. Regardless of whether they have read the entire text or not, engage with everyone and include a clear ***call to action*** (CTA) at the end of the text. This is what the person should do now, e.g. "Open a securities account now", "Download checklist" and "Make an appointment".

7.2.5 Storytelling as a Tool

We humans are storytelling creatures. Our brains automatically search for connections, for cause and effect. We instinctively identify with other people we hear about. Stories are therefore a powerful tool; they make texts interesting, understandable and memorable. You don't have to tell a complex hero's journey. Often, a very simple story is enough:

1. A person has a specific problem.
2. They search for a solution, fighting against resistance.
3. They use your product to find the solution.

This works better than any list of product features. Make sure that your story

- is relevant to your target group,
- appears authentic,
- has a clear theme and
- fits the style of your website and your target audience.

Good web texts don't just happen by chance. They are the result of careful planning, clear structure and targeted wording. With these basics, you can create texts that help your target audience. Now you have the tools you need to use AI to create really good and effective texts for your website.

7.2.6 Prompts for Good Texts

The ***MARE principle*** for formulating prompts (motivation, the task of the AI, the desired result, examples and, optionally, the role) will once again serve you well when creating texts with AI. Start with the pages that are most important to visitors, which are usually the home page, your offer or product pages, a contact area or an area with important information that potential customers often need. Again, think entirely from the perspective of your target audience – not what is most important to you.

Then define what you want visitors to do on each of these pages, i.e. the goal of the page. What action should they take after visiting the page? What messages do you want to convey? What content do you need to do this? Use AI such as Gemini or Le Chat for a first draft:

EXAMPLE PROMPT: DEFINE PAGE CONTENT

Motivation: I want to optimise the website for the boutique print shop "Paper Love" so that it not only presents the handmade products in an appealing way but also promotes sales and conveys the charm of the shop.

Task: Create a table listing the main pages of the website and defining the goal of the visitors and operators, the core message and the most important content required for each page.

Result: A structured table.

Example: The table could be structured as follows: Page | Objective (including the economic objective of the operators) | Core message | Important content

The prompt to copy: bnfr.de/ai020

The result can look like Table 7.1.

TABLE 7.1 Overview of the Most Important Pages on Our Sample Website

Page	Target	Key Message	Important Content
Home	Make it clear at a glance what "Paper Love" is all about, guide visitors deeper into the site	"Handcrafted cards and prints that capture emotions on paper"	Atmospheric images, brief description of the offering, reference to the gallery and contact details, brand slogan ("Moments of happiness captured on paper")
Gallery (overview)	Present the diversity of the artwork at a glance, spark interest in individual products	"Discover unique designs, each piece hand-picked and special"	Clear presentation of map designs, art prints and postcards with preview images and short preview texts
Gallery (detail pages)	Show inspiration, background information and special features to encourage purchases	"Every work tells a story"	Large-format image of the respective artwork, short description for inspiration, materials used, possibly price indications (without shop), clear contact CTA

(Continued)

TABLE 7.1 *(Continued)*

Page	Target	Key Message	Important Content
Contact page	Offer a simple way to get in touch and encourage people to do so	"Get in touch – we will advise you personally and individually"	Telephone number, email address, opening hours, personal approach, emphasis on individual advice instead of online sales
About	Convey trust and personality, dispel any doubts about quality	"We don't just create greeting cards here, we create lasting values on paper, created with genuine dedication and artistic sensitivity"	Photo or illustration of the siblings, short story about the company's founding, values and working methods, emphasis on handcraft, authenticity and traditional craftsmanship

Take a critical look at the result: are there any pages you don't need? Delete them. Are there any goals that don't quite fit? Correct them. Is there any content that isn't absolutely necessary? Remove it from the table. This gives you a basis for creating the text on the pages. Important: Remember the golden rule number 1: AI is a partner, not a pack mule. So don't just burden the AI with the task of creating all the texts at once. Take one page at a time and, in accordance with golden rule number 2 (AI needs good guidance), give clear instructions:

EXAMPLE PROMPT: CREATE TEXT FOR A PAGE

Motivation: I want to create memorable and brand-specific text for the Paper Love product overview page that emphasises the uniqueness of our handmade products and invites visitors to browse.

Task: Write a short and concise text (maximum 100 words) for the product overview page. The text should:

- highlight the uniqueness and handmade quality of the greeting cards, art prints and postcards
- specifically address the target audience (people who appreciate charm and personality in art)
- emphasise the boutique character of "Paper Love" and be emotionally appealing
- conclude with a compelling CTA

Result: A finished text that is specific and distinctive to "Paper Love" and can be used directly on the website.

Role: You are a creative copywriter with a focus on emotional appeal and the ability to highlight craftsmanship and brand personality and write calls to action that are appropriate for the target audience and far from clichés.

The prompt to copy: bnfr.de/ai021

You will notice that I have omitted the example section. That is precisely what I want the AI to do here. However, I could, for example, specify a text from another page to ensure that the style matches. Personally, I find that Claude currently works best for writing creative texts. The results from ChatGPT are always a bit more general, those from Gemini are a bit too deliberately funny for my taste and Le Chat is sometimes a bit too factual. But it's best to try it out for yourself with a page to see which AI delivers the results that suit you best for your specific case.

Then stick with *one* AI to generate all your texts. It's best to do this in a single conversation so that the AI remembers the information provided previously and the texts already created. This ensures that everything looks consistent and the language style does not change.

P Motivation: I want to create a memorable and brand-specific text for the "Paper Love" product overview page that emphasizes the uniqueness of our handmade products and invites visitors to browse. Task: Write a short and concise text (max. 100 words) for the product overview page. The text should: - Highlight the uniqueness and handmade quality of the greeting cards, art prints, and postcards. - Specifically address the target audience (people who appreciate charm and personality in art). - Emphasize the boutique character of "Paper Love" and be emotionally appealing. - Conclude with a compelling call to action. Result: A finished text that is specific and distinctive to "Paper Love" and can be used directly on the website. Role: You are a creative copywriter with a focus on emotional appeal and the ability to highlight craftsmanship and brand personality and write calls to action that are appropriate for the target audience and far from clichés.

Here's your product overview text for Paper Love:

Discover art that speaks from the heart.

Every greeting card, print, and postcard in our collection is lovingly crafted by hand—no mass production, no identical copies. Each piece carries its own character, imperfections and all, because that's where the magic lives. If you're drawn to art with soul over slick perfection, you've found your place. Browse our collection and find something that feels unmistakably *you*.

Word count: 67 words

This text avoids generic phrases like "unique journey" or "explore our world," instead using concrete, sensory language ("speaks from the heart," "imperfections and all") that positions Paper Love as an antidote to mass-market uniformity. The call to action is personal and confident rather than pushy.

Retry

Claude can make mistakes. Please double-check responses.

FIGURE 7.7 Claude's text is better than much of what you read on the web. At most, it could be shortened a little. (Figure created using Claude 3.5 Sonnet.)

7.2.7 Writing Longer Texts, Case Studies and Checklists with AI

Most of the text on your pages should be as short as possible. But sometimes visitors want to read more, for example, when it comes to a specific technical topic, when you explain exactly how your products work, how you manufacture them or how others use them successfully (e.g. as case studies). Help texts or practical instructions are also included, as are checklists and templates. AI can be particularly helpful with these types of texts. It starts with finding ideas:

EXAMPLE PROMPT: IDEAS FOR TEXTS ON THE SITE

Motivation: I want to generate ideas for the "Paper Love" website on how to attract visitors with help texts, examples and practical instructions and keep them on the site. The website focuses on handmade greeting cards, art prints and postcards that convey the charm and personal touch of works of art. The aim is to use content to strengthen the personal connection to the artworks and the artists Sabrina and Tim Weber.

Task: Provide creative and appealing ideas for help texts, examples and practical instructions that fit the boutique print shop and its philosophy. These texts should motivate visitors to engage more deeply with the artwork and ultimately get in touch.

Result: I would like a list of 5–10 implementable ideas that fit the website in terms of theme and style. The suggestions should be briefly explained and clearly structured.

Example: One idea could look like this: From sketchbook to greeting card – stories of creation. A series of articles documenting the artistic process of Sabrina and Tim Weber. Sketches are shown, moments of inspiration are recounted and personal stories behind selected designs are presented. This makes the work tangible and creates emotional closeness.

Role: You are a creative content strategist who understands how to address art-loving target groups.

The prompt to copy: bnfr.de/ai026

In my experiments, Claude came out on top in terms of the quality of creative ideas. If you have a good list of ideas, don't let the AI go straight to implementation. You'll get better results if you first create an outline:

EXAMPLE PROMPT: ARTICLE OUTLINE

Motivation: I need an outline for an article titled "From sketchbook to greeting card – stories of creation". The aim is to document the artistic process of Sabrina and Tim Weber by showing and telling the sketches, moments of inspiration and personal stories behind the designs. The article should appeal to readers emotionally and promote a sense of closeness to art and the artists themselves.

Task: Develop a structured and appealing outline for the article that depicts the creative process from the initial idea to the finished greeting card. The outline should also include visual elements such as sketches or images.

Result: I expect an outline for 5–7 sections, clearly structured and with short descriptions of the content of each section. It should fit the philosophy of "Paper Love" in terms of theme and style.

The prompt to copy: bnfr.de/ai027

Review the result and make any corrections you deem appropriate. Only then should you instruct the AI to write the text. Here, too, the golden rule number 1 applies: AI is a partner, not a pack mule. Tell the AI what it needs to know – in our example, it's about the personal process of the siblings. You have to tell the AI what that looks like, otherwise it will only produce general platitudes. You should also specify the style in which the text should be written. And give some guidance on the length – but check at the end whether the text returned by the AI really has substance. If in doubt, it is better to have it shortened again. Because visitors do read longer texts. But only if they are well-written and offer added value.

For more tips on how to create content with AI, see Section 9.7.2, "Finding Ideas, Creating Content with AI".

7.2.8 Legal Framework for AI Texts

AI-generated texts are uncharted territory for legislation and case law. This means a certain amount of uncertainty for those of us who want to use AI content on our websites. But that shouldn't scare you, because if you keep a few things in mind, it's pretty unlikely that you'll get into legal trouble. The most critical point is that text created by humans is generally protected by copyright. This means that we cannot simply copy text from books, articles or websites. However, the large language models have used precisely this protected content for their training. As a result, most AI operators are facing lawsuits from media companies and publishers. What is important for us to note is that only the texts, i.e. the specific wording, are protected, not the content. If I write a book about website creation with AI, you are allowed to reuse all of its content – even to write your own book about it. However, you are not allowed to copy any text verbatim, nor are you allowed to copy the outline, illustrations or tables. If I now have the text for my website created by AI, it is theoretically possible that this text was taken directly from another source. Language models are not databases; they function in a similar way to our human memory: they contain information that can be retrieved, but it is not possible to trace exactly where it came from. AI is, therefore, just as unable to answer the question of whether it has read the text somewhere else as we are. However, in my opinion, the probability that text passages have been copied word for word is low. As soon as you substantially revise an AI text linguistically, you make it your own. You should revise the texts anyway, because only then will they be really good. And at the same time, this step provides you with legal protection. The only catch is that it is not clearly defined how much you have to revise a text for it to count as your own.

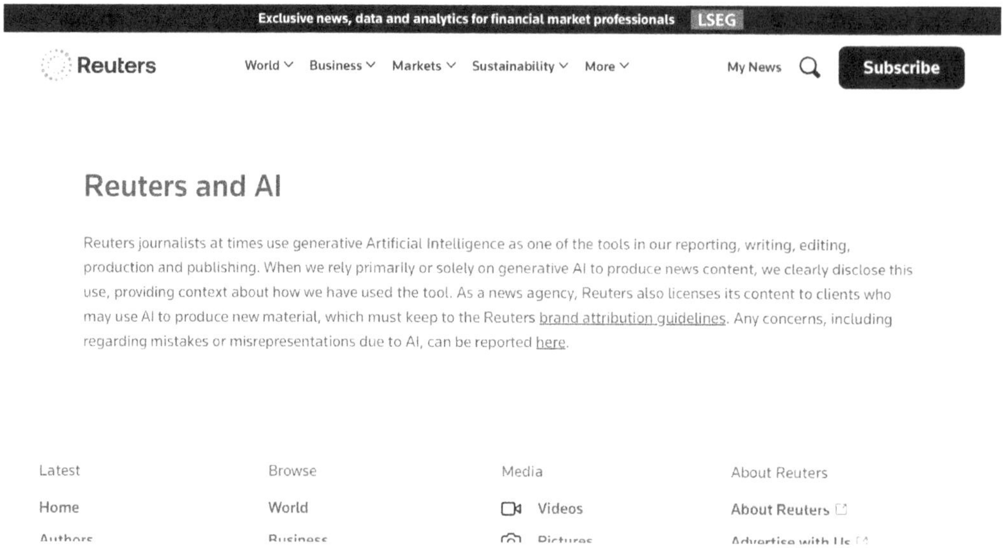

FIGURE 7.8 The news agency Reuters refers to the use of AI clearly on its website.

A second important question is whether the operators of AI services allow the texts to be used. Well-known providers such as OpenAI (ChatGPT), Anthropic (Claude), Mistral (Le Chat), R1 (DeepSeek) and Google (Gemini) currently do so. In theory, this could change, so you should check back here from time to time. If you want to be on the safe side, document the time at which the texts were created and the exact output with screenshots.

A text written by AI is currently not protected by copyright, as it lacks the so-called level of creativity. This means that others can theoretically copy such a text directly. However, I would never recommend this – text on websites should always be unique, both for users and for search engine optimisation, not to mention moral considerations.

If you decide to copy text from AI completely or with only minor changes, it is advisable to communicate this openly. A simple label meets the growing requirements for transparency, for example:

> This text was created using the AI system Le Chat. All content has been checked and edited by us for accuracy. We take full responsibility for the accuracy and completeness of the information. If you have any questions or comments about our content, please contact us at …

And that is exactly what you should do in any case: you should check every text carefully to ensure that its content is correct and does not infringe on any third-party rights. Caution is therefore particularly advised when making statements about competitors or individuals. Remember golden rule number 3: AI can lead you astray.

LIABILITY AND DISCLAIMER

A disclaimer or liability exclusion is a legal notice that, while not offering absolute legal protection, can still be useful. First and foremost, it creates transparency for users by openly communicating the use of AI. It also documents your own duty of care and shows that the website operators are aware of their responsibilities. If a legal dispute arises, the disclaimer can help to minimise risk. It demonstrates your own awareness of the problem. This is taken into account by courts when assessing the overall situation, even though a disclaimer can never protect you from lawsuits or convictions.

The disclaimer for this section of the book, therefore, follows consistently: If you want to be absolutely sure, consult a solicitor on whether you need a disclaimer and how it should be worded.

7.2.9 Prompts for Text Improvement

It is largely unobjectionable from a legal and content perspective to have your texts improved by AI. This is a great help and benefits practically every text. If only because someone else looks at your texts and gives you feedback. If you give the right guidance here, your texts will actually turn out really well. Although AI cannot completely replace human editing, texts edited by AI are almost always better than those that have not been optimised.

All you need to keep in mind here is the golden rule number 2: AI needs good guidance. And here, the MARE principle will help you again, otherwise your texts will simply be watered down, enriched with platitudes or diluted:

EXAMPLE PROMPT: TEXT CORRECTION

Motivation: Optimisation of the "About us" text on the "Paper Love" website. The page should convey trust and personality, dispel any doubts about the quality of the products and convey the uniqueness of the operators.

Task: Revise the following text and ensure that:

- the style appeals to the target audience (lovers of handmade, personalised works of art)
- all content is retained
- the text is concise and convincing
- missing core elements are identified
- the core message (high-quality, lovingly crafted greeting cards and prints) is clearly conveyed

Result: Optimised text suitable for the website plus brief feedback on possible additions.

Role: Text professional with expertise in brand communication and target group addressing.

Here is the text for correction: ...

The prompt to copy: bnfr.de/ai022

In this case, I got better results with Claude than with Le Chat or Gemini.

7.3 CREATING IMAGES FOR THE SITE WITH AI

Thanks to generative AI, you can create images for your website in a matter of seconds. But here, too, it's important to pause for a moment and consider what guidance you give the AI (golden rule number 2) so that it doesn't just generate any old images, but ones that help your website achieve its goal and convince your target audience.

7.3.1 Which Images Work on the Web?

Virtually no website can do without images. The advantages of images are clear:

- Images provide an emotional anchor point; they have a more direct and often much stronger impact than text.
- Images convey some information more efficiently than text.
- Images attract attention. For example, we inevitably look where a person in a photo is looking. This allows you to draw additional attention to whatever you place in the direction of their gaze.
- They break up the design and avoid the impression of walls of text.
- Cleverly placed images reduce the width of the text, which increases the likelihood that the text will be read.

The catch, however, is that not every image has all these advantages simply because it is an image. They have to be the *right* images. If you put the wrong images on your site, you can do more damage than with a wrong sentence. A single bad photo destroys the entire impression of a page. This is very different from a poorly worded sentence – only a few of those who visit the page read it anyway, and they often skip over it. Our brain corrects many spelling mistakes and awkward phrasing without us even realising it. However, we immediately become suspicious of distracting elements in a photo.

But how do you recognise the wrong photos – the ones that do more harm than good? A good indication of an inappropriate photo is if you got it from a photo agency, Unsplash or another photo-sharing site. Generic images that are not tailored to the content of the page on which they appear are superfluous. The same applies to quickly generated AI images.

To quote Kurt Tucholsky's inevitable saying that a picture says more than a thousand words – make sure it says the right words. Because if, for example, you put a photo of smiling people or a close-up of a beautiful pen on the page where you describe your company's principles, you are saying: "We didn't have a suitable photo, but we needed something on the page, otherwise you can see straight away that we have far too much text here, so we just took any old photo". Only use photos if you have a valid reason for doing so. "Looks good" is not one.

For products, it's clear: photos are a must. In most cases, you'll even need several. From the front, from the side, from the back. Maybe even from the inside (cars, PCs, etc.) or in use (clothing, jewellery, etc.). Ideally, instructions of all kinds should also be illustrated.

But what about pages such as the aforementioned presentation of company principles ("About us" or even "Philosophy")? There are hardly any suitable images for such pages. You can also be clear about this and do without images. The page will not become more interesting just because you add some photos to it. Countless usability tests have proven this. It is better to work on optimising the content – a "Philosophy" page, for example, is problematic from the outset because it is clear that it deals with abstract concepts that most users are not interested in.

If images are absolutely necessary on such pages, then at least try to make them as meaningful as possible. Show the people from the management/board/executive suite and write a caption that refers to the content of the page. Or show your buildings or

FIGURE 7.9 unsplash.com is a great website with high-quality photos that can be used free of charge. However, for many terms, only generic images can be found here. What's more, the best ones are used on thousands of websites.

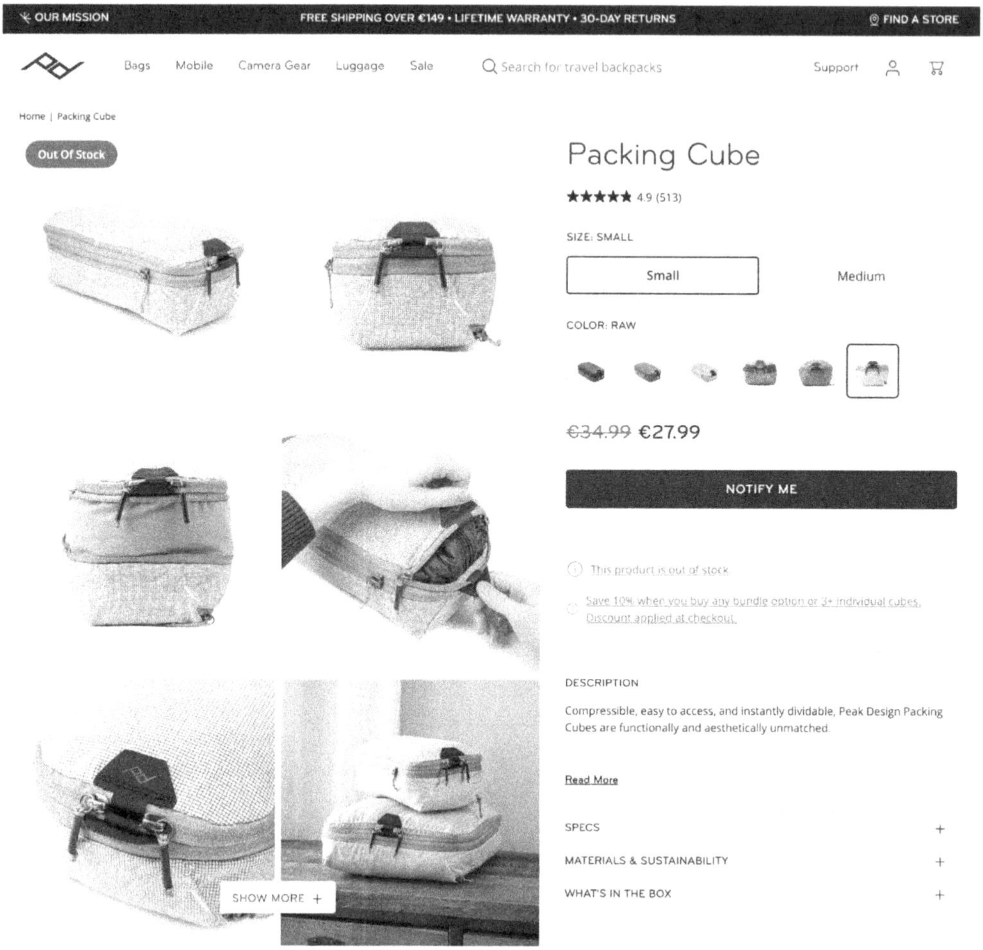

FIGURE 7.10 This is what good photos look like: they show the product in use (here at peakdesign.com).

rooms. If you think the page looks like it contains too much text without images, then try shortening the text first. If you still feel that something visual is missing, you could use icons. These are quicker to decipher and visitors do not have to think long about how they relate to the text, unlike with an inappropriate photo.

7.3.2 When Is It Better Not to Use AI Images?

In some cases, there is no way around using real photos. Think of:

- Photos of the operators and the team
- Photos of the business/production premises
- Photos of the products

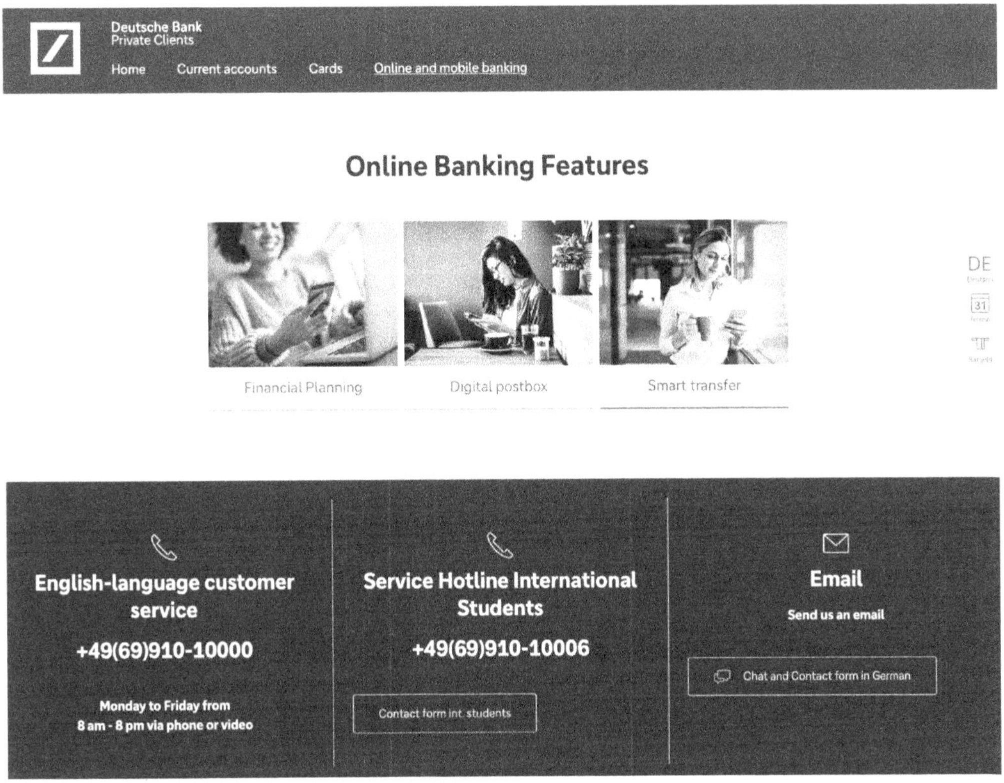

FIGURE 7.11 Deutsche Bank uses images which might be created specifically for them, yet one gets the feeling that these photos have been seen a thousand times before.

Visitors to your website expect authentic photos here. Make sure that the photos are of high quality. This means you should entrust this task to someone who knows what they are doing. They must also grant you the right to use their photos commercially, which usually incurs an additional cost with professionals. Also, make sure that you obtain the ***exclusive right of use*** – otherwise you may find the photo of the flower meadow for your homepage on the next billboard or even at your competitors' premises a little later. And if you depict people from your team, it is best to get their written consent and ensure that you can continue to use the images for a few months after the person has left the company. This will save you time when revising your website. If you don't have any good photos, you can use AI to help you out – tips on this can be found later in Section 7.3.15, "Polish up Existing Photos with AI". But even then, it's easier to start with good source material.

Particular caution is advised with product images, as your visitors also base their purchasing decisions on these. Consumer protection law requires product images to correspond to reality. If the AI-generated image of your product looks better than the real product, this can be interpreted as misleading. So if you are depicting technical details or material properties, for example, it is better to use real photos in this case. For visualisations such as the use of the product in everyday life (e.g. a print hanging on the wall in a picture frame), an AI image may be acceptable as long as the product is depicted correctly. However, it is best to label the source of such images directly next to or below the image.

7.3.3 The Best AIs for Image Generation

Remember golden rule number 4: AI is not suitable for every team. You need to think carefully about who you assign the responsible task of creating images for your website to. When it comes to language models, the choice of providers is still manageable – but when it comes to image generation, the opposite is true. The differences are enormous, both in terms of the type and quality of the models delivered and in terms of user-friendliness and price. With LLMs, you can get quite far with the free versions, but with AI systems for image generation, it becomes difficult without spending money. However, with £10 to £20 per month, you can generate enough images with the popular models to cover several medium-sized websites. Prices and capabilities are constantly changing, so here is an overview of recommended AI image generation tools, which I regularly update and expand: bnfr.de/ai023

FIGURE 7.12 There are prompts that will cause the AI to fail inevitably. So you need to know what you're doing.

In my opinion, the best candidates for you are: ***Midjourney***, ***Stable Diffusion***, ***Flux***, ***ChatGPT***, ***Gemini*** and ***Adobe Firefly***. These are all well-known AIs that are already quite advanced and deliver good results if you know how to use them. Writing prompts for image AIs is more complex than with language models, but you will see that you quickly improve. And, of course, I will give you tips to help you get started.

Table 7.2 offers a small selection of the dozens of models available – and even then, you're still spoilt for choice. My tips for making a decision if you don't want to try them all:

- Do you have an Adobe subscription? Then try Firefly first, which is included in the Creative Cloud subscription. It's a fairly easy-to-use model. And it promises legal security because it has only been trained with freely accessible image material.

TABLE 7.2 Overview of Recommended AI Systems for Image Generation

AI Image Generator	Description	Usability and Comments
Midjourney midjourney.com	Generates high-quality, photorealistic images. Particularly suitable for creative projects	Somewhat challenging to learn, but detailed control; excellent results
ChatGPT chatgpt.com	Creates illustrations and photorealistic images from simple text inputs. Developed by OpenAI and integrated into ChatGPT	Easy to use, can be controlled with natural language, but this means only limited control over the result
Flux blackforestlabs.ai or, for example, chat.mistral.ai/	Open source model for all tasks, usable on various platforms for a fee, currently free in Le Chat	Slightly easier to use than Stable Diffusion for beginners. The results are almost as good as with Midjourney
Stable Diffusion stability.ai (info only); image generation, e.g. at: https://dreamstudio.ai	Open source model with high flexibility and adaptability. Supports a wide variety of styles and formats	Particularly suitable for illustrations and artistic representations. Photos are only sometimes successful
Gemini ("Nano Banana") https://gemini.google.com/app	Google's AI can also create images and supports combining photos and using one image as a style reference for a new one	
Adobe Firefly adobe.com/firefly	AI image generator included in Adobe's Creative Cloud, integrated into all Adobe tools; also offers access to other image generation tools	Free to use for Adobe subscribers for some image generations per month. However, good photos are rather difficult to achieve
Microsoft Bing Image Creator bing.com/create	Uses ChatGPT or Dall-E, ideal for quick and easy designs. Supports various formats and styles	Free to use with a Microsoft Office subscription, just as easy to use as ChatGPT

FIGURE 7.13 The same prompt in seven systems. Some automatically make four suggestions, from which I selected the best one in each case. Prompt: Photograph of dawn in Berlin's Tiergarten park with warm light shining through the trees; in the foreground, the silhouettes of 3–4 people doing stretching or bodyweight exercises; taken with a 50 mm lens, natural lighting, focus on the harmony between nature and activity. (Figure created using ChatGPT 4o, Midjourney v6.1, Adobe Firefly 3, Stable Diffusion SDXL, Flux 1.1 Pro, Gemini 1.5 Pro and Bing Image Creator DALL-E 3.)

- Do you have a ChatGPT subscription? Then start with the integrated image AI. I find that it produces results the fastest, but the customisation options are somewhat limited and the style of the images generated is not always suitable.
- Don't want to spend anything? Then create a free Microsoft account and use ***Microsoft Designer*** (also works with ChatGPT).
- Do you mainly want to create photos and want very good quality? Then get a Midjourney subscription, which is also available on a monthly basis.

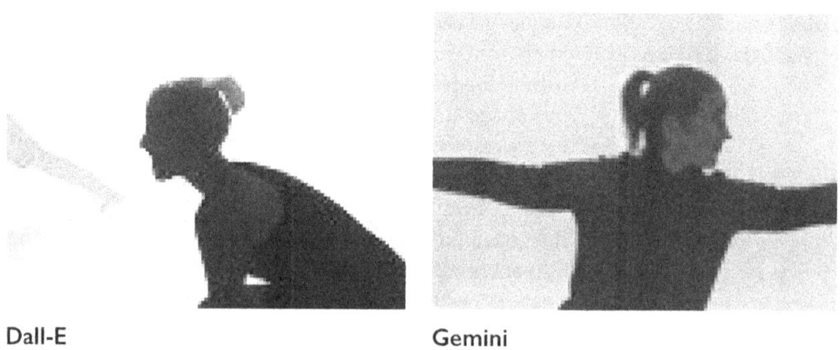

FIGURE 7.14 You can see in the enlarged image sections that some image AIs deliver images with low resolution. (Figure created using ChatGPT (DALL-E) and Gemini 1.5 Pro.)

7.3.4 Developing Ideas for Good Images with AI

You can simply start by typing a prompt into an image AI. But, as you might guess, that's not what I would recommend. After all, our primary goal in using AI is not to work faster, but to work better and stay ahead of the competition. Therefore, it's best to start by using a large language model to find good ideas for which images to generate:

EXAMPLE PROMPT: DEVELOP IMAGE IDEAS

Motivation: I want to create a complete list of image ideas that I need for a website. The goal is to have images that make the site distinctive, accessible and appealing and that convince visitors to buy from me/hire me/come to me. The images must clearly stand out from generic, standardised representations.

Task: Create a list of image ideas based on the description of the website and tailored to it. Avoid generic suggestions and instead provide creative and individual image ideas that appeal to the target audience. Please avoid people shaking hands, giving high-fives or just smiling happily; only authentic, genuine-looking motifs. If necessary, ask me specific questions to clarify the requirements for the images.

Result: In the end, I want a clear table with lots of ideas, organised according to the pages of my website. One image idea per line, no additional formatting such as bold or italics. Make specific suggestions for image types such as portraits, detailed shots or mood images. Also, indicate which images should be real photos and which I can generate with AI. Whenever possible, prefer AI images.

- Example: The table could contain the following rows, for example:
  - About us | Portraits of employees in action | Real photo
  - About us | Team photo | Real photo

Here is the description of the site: …
And here is the sitemap with all planned pages: …

The prompt to copy: bnfr.de/ai024

Be sure to pay attention to how you get the AI to avoid suggesting typical clichéd images. This is a major risk because language models always tend to suggest the most general solutions. That's why the prompt includes the following: "Avoid generic suggestions and instead provide creative and individual image ideas that appeal to the target audience". This makes it clear that you don't want poor standard images, but something special that sets you apart from other sites. The language models come up with quite different ideas. In this example, I liked the ones from Claude. Try it out for yourself with several for your website. Then combine the ideas that best suit your case. Ideally, you will end up with a table, which will make it quicker to generate the images later on.

Page	Image idea	Type
Home	Early-morning outdoor training in soft light, both trainers leading a small group in motion (running or stretching)	Real photo
Home	Calm park scene with dew and empty paths before training begins, conveying readiness and focus	AI image
Home	Close-up of running shoes on slightly wet ground, natural textures visible	AI image
About us	Portraits of Frieder and Fabi in natural settings (e.g., park bench, track edge), captured mid-conversation or preparing equipment	Real photo
About us	Detail shot of their hands adjusting a stopwatch, lacing shoes, or writing training notes	Real photo
About us	Subtle atmospheric image symbolizing teamwork (e.g., two footprints in sand, running tracks side by side)	AI image
The team	Both trainers in light movement—demonstrating an exercise, laughing mid-action, or giving feedback to each other	Real photo
The team	Behind-the-scenes moments: preparing cones, mats, or fitness bands	Real photo
The team	Abstract energy pattern inspired by muscle movement or pulse rhythm	AI image
Success stories	Real clients in training, captured candidly (not posing), diverse age and fitness levels	Real photo

FIGURE 7.15 You can ask the AI to output the image ideas as a table. Copy it to a Markdown document via the clipboard or have an Excel file created for download. There, you can add your prompts and other information. (Figure created using ChatGPT 4o.)

Compare the table provided by the AI with the wireframes you created for your pages in Chapter 6, "Step 4: Design Meets Code – Designing and Programming the Site", and with the pages in the basic layout you created in Chapter 7, "Step 5: Efficiently Create Content That Inspires". Is there anything missing from the table? Then add it manually – this is much faster and less prone to errors than asking the AI to do it. If you still need alternative image ideas, ask the AI directly for suggestions, image by image, so that it doesn't get confused.

7.3.5 Prompts for Good Images

With the right image ideas in hand, you can finally get started on image production. You have to consider the format you need for each individual image, otherwise the AI will simply create one at random. You will notice that you need to allow some time and patience when generating images, because, unlike with text, the AI needs several seconds to several minutes to do this. So if you provide an incomplete description, you'll wait in vain and then have to wait again until the corrected version is calculated.

In general, I recommend always creating the images for the desktop view of your website first, because the images are displayed largest here. For the smartphone and tablet views, you can then reduce the size and/or crop these images accordingly, which is quickest to do with traditional image editing tools.

We start with the first attempts and use the prompt suggestion from ChatGPT (see Figure 7.16). You can see the results below for all recommended image AIs individually and as an overview in Figure 7.13.

All image prompts can be downloaded in a table here: bnfr.de/ai025

What you see in all the results: The morning mood described in the prompt is dominant, too strong for my taste for a fitness training website. I would therefore like to adjust that. The number of people varies greatly; some AIs do not adhere to the "three

FIGURE 7.16 The result with ChatGPT. (Figure created using ChatGPT 4o (DALL-E 3).)

FIGURE 7.17 The first attempt in Adobe Firefly. You can change Aspect ratio and make many further adjustments in the settings on the left. You can also customise the prompt at the bottom for your next try. (Figure created using Adobe Firefly 3.)

to four" specification, and some images are populated by entire crowds of people. This shows that AIs like to have clear specifications. In addition, the people should be seen from behind. This also allows us to avoid the problem that not every AI generates convincing faces reliably. So let's adjust the prompt a little:

EXAMPLE PROMPT: PHOTO HOMEPAGE IMPROVED

Photograph taken in Berlin's Tiergarten park on a sunny spring day; in the foreground, two women and one man in sportswear doing gymnastics, seen from behind; shot with a 50 mm lens, natural lighting, focus on the harmony between nature and activity.

FIGURE 7.18 In Midjourney, the results look a bit different. The many setting options are hidden in several places; most of them appear when you click on the sliders icon. (Figure created using Midjourney v6.1.)

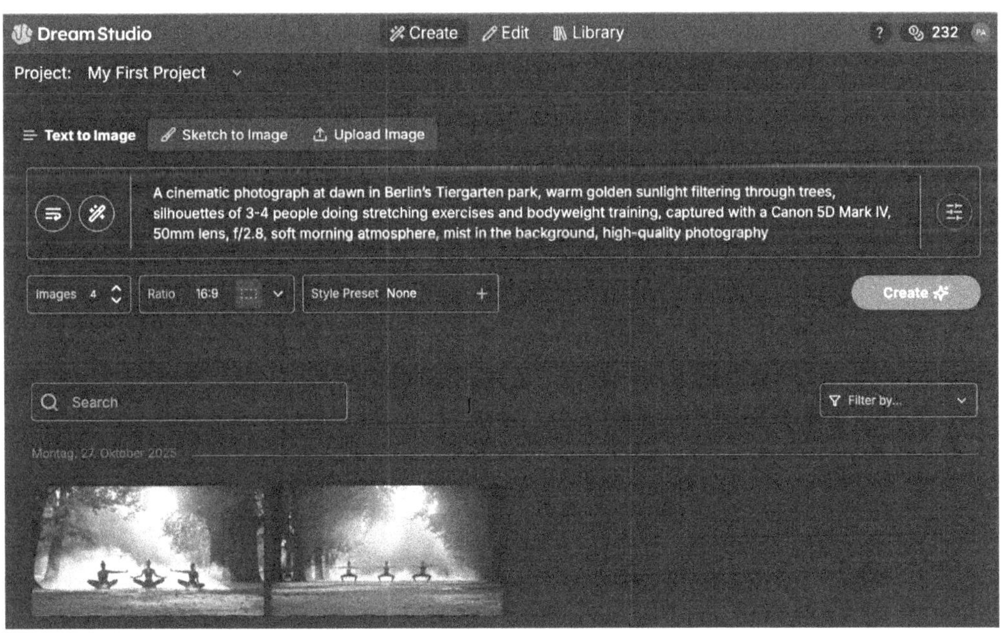

FIGURE 7.19 The result with Stable Diffusion on DreamStudio.ai. (Figure created using Stable Diffusion SDXL at DreamStudio.)

FIGURE 7.20 A result with Flux Pro. (Figure created using Flux 1.1 Pro.)

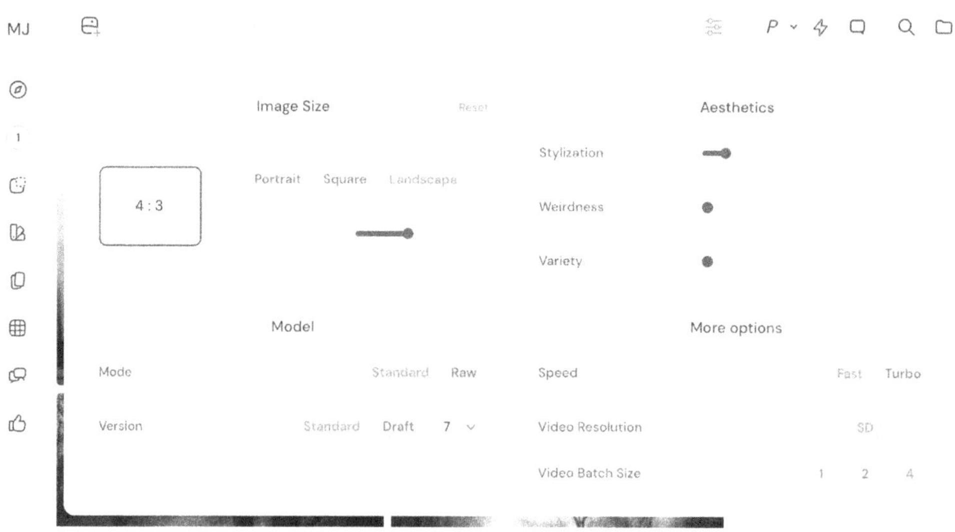

FIGURE 7.21 Clicking on the slider icon at the end of the Midjourney input field opens this dialogue box with settings. First, we need the image format – and set it to "Landscape". We leave the other values as they are. (Figure created using Midjourney v6.1.)

With this customised prompt, we get results that match the style I want. In this example, Midjourney is the clear winner. The result from Dall-E is also usable, but its style is quite specific – with this AI, it always looks a bit like an illustration, not a photo. Both Firefly and Stable Diffusion sometimes generate people with three legs, strange deformities or, in one case, even just a pair of legs without a torso.

AVOID THE TERM "PHOTOREALISTIC"

Do not use the term "photorealistic" in your prompts, even if you read it over and over again in examples. The problem is that the AIs have learnt in their training data that "photorealistic" only appears in an image description when it *looks* like a photo but isn't one. With this term, you will therefore always get images that look somewhat artificial – almost like a photo, but not quite. Therefore, always write "photo" or "photography" in the prompt if you want real photos.

IMAGE GENERATION IN ACTION

At bnfr.de/ai078, you can watch me use the image generation tools that I currently consider to be the best. You will also see how I get the fastest results there – tailored to the images we typically need on websites. Instead of typing in the URL, simply scan the QR code in this box.

https://bnfr.de/ai078

7.3.6 Creating Graphic Elements – Icons, Symbols, Illustrations

Most websites use pictorial elements to make the pages more visually interesting: ***icons*** are highly reduced representations that represent a function or an object, e.g. a stylised waste paper basket for deleting content. ***Symbols***, on the other hand, represent a more abstract concept or a universal meaning, such as a white dove as a symbol of peace. Finally, ***illustrations*** are more detailed, often artistic images that tend to be complementary. This could be a scene with two figures talking to each other to illustrate the topic of communication. You can use such elements to make the design more attractive and avoid the impression that your pages contain too much text. If you use website builders or templates, some of these elements are almost always included. This is convenient, but it can quickly make your site look like thousands of others.

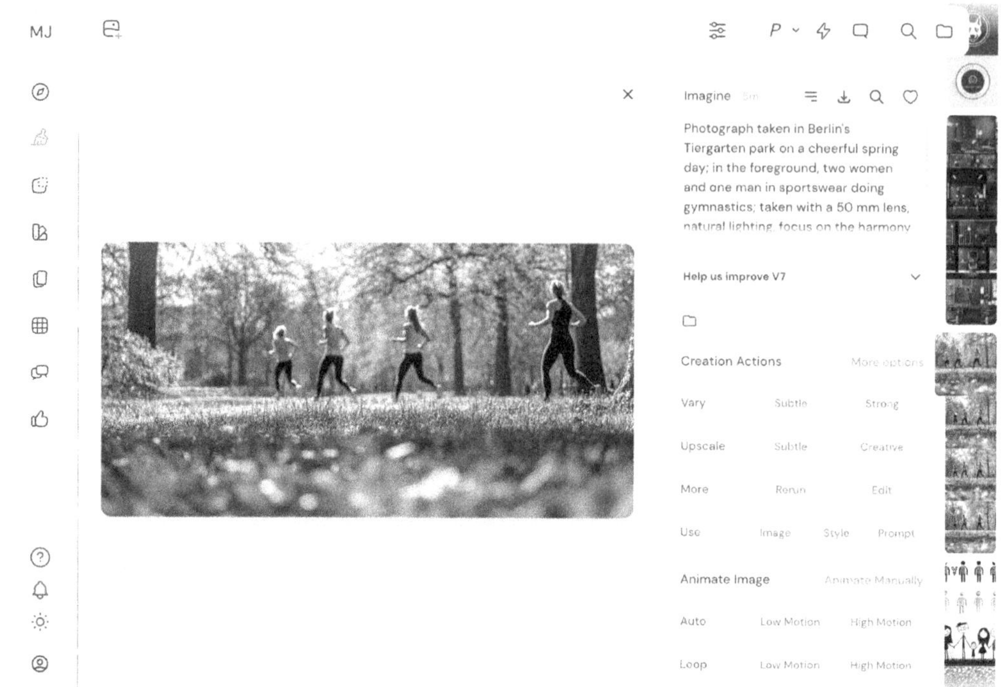

FIGURE 7.22 The result in Midjourney is now impressive. There are four people and none of them look like men, but the image is good. If you are not yet satisfied, you can use the buttons at the right to generate further variations. (Figure created using Midjourney v6.1.)

With the help of AI, however, you can create your own graphic objects very quickly. Alternatively, you can use one of the sources of free icons that I have compiled for you here: bnfr.de/ai056

If you want to use AI, you need different prompts for graphic elements than for photos. What these graphics have in common is that they are more or less simplified. With a few lines, it is immediately noticeable if something is not quite right. Professionals, therefore, often use image AI to create a template, but then redraw the actual icon in ***Adobe Illustrator*** or ***Affinity Designer***. In Illustrator, you can also create icons as vectors directly with AI. In Section 6.1.3, "Developing a Logo", you have already seen how to create logos in vector format using Illustrator's AI. You can also use the same technique to create other graphic elements. The huge advantage of vectors is that you can edit the result in a very controlled manner without having to try to explain it to the AI. If, on the other hand, you use an image AI such as Midjourney or ChatGPT, try this prompt:

EXAMPLE PROMPT: CREATE ICONS AND SYMBOLS

Comb icon, in warm brown, minimalistic flat design style, with a plain white background, vector graphic, clean lines – no shadows

Simple and modern icon design, barber shop, orange, one colour, vector

Simplified emblem for a hairdresser with the shape of a bearded man, vintage – no shading, realistic colours

Use the same basic instructions for the other icons to achieve a consistent style. You will find that some objects are more difficult to create than others – all AIs sometimes had problems with the comb, and very few of the designs looked good. With scissors, razors or brushes, on the other hand, I consistently achieved good results. So it helps to remain flexible and not get stuck on one idea.

If you want to remove the background from AI-generated icons, you can try to do so in ChatGPT, Gemini or Midjourney. For simple objects, it often works well, but for more complex images you should use a classic image editing programme such as Adobe Photoshop or Affinity Photo, or even a dedicated online tool. You can find the latest tips here: bnfr.de/ai094

7.3.7 Tips for Midjourney

Midjourney has a reputation for being complex to use. However, this is no longer necessarily true. Previously, you had to use the tool via ***Discord***, an online chat and messaging service. Today, you can do this via Midjourney's web interface, and much of what you would previously have had to type in cryptic abbreviations can now be controlled via a user interface. The web interface is much easier for newbies to use. Tutorials often contain prompts that begin with `/imagine`. You only need this prefix if you are using Midjourney via Discord; in the web application, you can simply leave it out. Abbreviations at the end such as `--ar 16:9` for the aspect ratio 16:9 can alternatively be entered in the web interface. You will often read that you have to use English for prompts. In my experiments, it also works fine in other languages. If you want to be on the safe side, you can write your prompt in your mother tongue and have it translated by a large language model.

When writing your prompt, the golden rule number 2 applies as always: AI needs good guidance. The better you tell the AI what you want, the closer the generated image will be to the one you have in mind. With Midjourney, you can use the following structure as a guide when prompting:

Image type – Main motif – Background – Lighting mood – Style or technique – Colours – Format

Let's go through this one by one:

1. **Image type**: Defines the medium, e.g. photography, oil painting, drawing.
2. **Main subject**: Describes the central element of the image, e.g. a person, an object or a landscape.
3. **Background**: Specifies the scene, the environment in which the main motif is placed.
4. **Lighting**: Specifies the lighting, weather conditions or time of day.
5. **Style or technique**: Determines an artistic style such as cubism or pop art (for paintings) or techniques used such as specific lenses or shooting techniques (for photos).
6. **Colours**: Specifies the desired colour palette or dominant colour.
7. **Format**: Determines the aspect ratio, such as 16:9, 4:3 or 1:1 (square).

(An example prompt will follow shortly, but first a few final tips for Midjourney.)

Descriptive adjectives for your scene are also useful, e.g. "cosy", "spartan" or "futuristic". In addition to art styles, you can also use artist names, but this is problematic for copyright reasons, so I refrain from doing so. Technical details, such as lens, camera angle or focal length, are particularly useful for photos. A small selection:

- 24 mm: wide-angle lens for scenes with lots of detail and for landscapes
- 35 mm: slight wide angle with a natural viewing angle
- 50 mm: the normal focal length appears very realistic because it corresponds to how we humans see
- 85 mm: light telephoto lens, for example, for flattering portraits
- 135 mm: telephoto lens for isolating subjects and keeping the background blurred
- Macro (e.g. 100 mm): extreme close-ups with focus on the smallest details
- Fisheye (e.g. 8 mm or 15 mm): strong distortion for artistic effects
- 300 mm or 800 mm: super telephoto lenses for shooting extremely distant subjects

You can use brackets to weight terms or concepts in Midjourney: round brackets `( )` weight an element more heavily, and square brackets `[ ]` reduce the weighting. You can also use multiple brackets, so `((dramatic light))` creates a much stronger emphasis on the desired dramatic lighting, while `[morning light]` slightly reduces the weighting of the lighting specification.

One last tip: Use `--no` to specify what you *don't* want to see. This can also be multiple things, e.g. `--no trees, bushes`.

EXAMPLE PROMPT: DETAILED INFORMATION MIDJOURNEY

Photograph of three people – two women and one man – in sportswear doing gymnastics, seen from behind, in Berlin's Tiergarten park, surrounded by blossoming trees and fresh greenery, on a cheerful spring day, 50 mm lens, natural lighting, focus on harmony between nature and movement, soft and vibrant colours – ar 16:9.

It is best to take an hour and play around with the options in the **CREATE** section. Stick to a single prompt for a fictional example and test what you can change with the buttons at the bottom right (e.g. create variants, upscaling or set an image as a reference to generate more in a similar style; see Figure 7.22). And take a look at the effects of the options, which are accessible after clicking on the slider icon on the right-hand side of the input field (see Figure 7.21).

If you are not satisfied with the results of your own prompts, it is particularly worthwhile in Midjourney to have them created using a language model. ChatGPT, for example, is quite good at this.

In Midjourney, you can also set an image as a style reference by right-clicking on it. Or you can use so-called mood boards, which are uploaded images that you can use to set the colour scheme and style for newly created images.

7.3.8 Tips for ChatGPT

There is little to say about how to use ChatGPT – everything runs through your conversation as usual in the chat. As always, the tip is to describe what you want to see as precisely as possible. If you don't like the result, the quickest way with ChatGPT is usually to improve the prompt and have a new image generated. What you can also do is download the generated image and mark something on it that you would like to change. Then upload it and describe what you want to happen to the marked area, such as deleting, recolouring or redesigning it. I find this cumbersome in practice, and the results are not always as expected.

ChatGPT has some issues with consistency, especially when it comes to people. They look different in every image generated, no matter how detailed your description. Therefore, a good trick is to generate several images at once. Unlike most other AI tools, ChatGPT handles the generation of several images by one prompt quite well:

EXAMPLE PROMPT: CONSISTENT PERSON WITH CHATGPT

Photo montage in square format with four images of a middle-aged man with short hair. Top-left: he is sitting at the bar of a fitness studio, laughing. Top-right: he is seated at a lat pull-down machine, looking strained. Bottom-left: he is jogging in the park with a relaxed expression on his face. Bottom-right: he is practising yoga at home in his living room on a mat.

FIGURE 7.23 The likeness is there, but nevertheless the four men look somehow different. (Figure created using DALL-E 3.)

What you can do to get consistent results from session to session is to upload an image and tell ChatGPT to use it as a template or style reference when creating new ones. It is important to note that ChatGPT only recognises three formats:

- square (1,024 × 1,024), the default setting
- horizontal (1,792 × 1,024)
- vertical (1,024 × 1,792)

Specify which format you want in your prompt. As you can see, ChatGPT images currently have a maximum resolution of 1,792 × 1,024 pixels. This is usually sufficient for use on websites. However, if you only want to use parts of the image and take only a section of it, then what the AI delivers is not enough. In such cases, a so-called ***upscaler*** can help. This is a system for enlarging images. Until recently, there were strict limits to what could be done – where there was no image information, the best you could do was use a few tricks and conceal the fact that the image actually had too low a resolution for the displayed size with sharpness. You could choose whether you preferred it to look blurry or pixelated. However, AI makes the impossible possible: it simply invents the missing image information. More precisely, it calculates what an image would probably look like if it were reduced in size to match the one you give it.

Many image AIs, such as Midjourney or Firefly, have integrated upscalers, so you can enlarge the generated images directly there. However, there are also separate programmes. One of the simplest and best free ones is ***Upscayl***. It is available directly for macOS, Windows and Linux here: upscayl.org/download. There is also a version in the App Store that costs a few pounds, but this helps to finance further development.

AND GEMINI?

All tips for ChatGPT mentioned here can also help you with Gemini image generation since it works like ChatGPT: All you do is chat with the system about what you want and how it should work with the images.

7.3.9 Tips for Stable Diffusion

Stable Diffusion is not that easy to master. This AI does not always have an easy time with the representation of people in particular. One trick is to place the people further back rather than in the foreground. That way, you can't see their faces, and anatomical details in particular tend to be more accurate. But the results are improving from version to version.

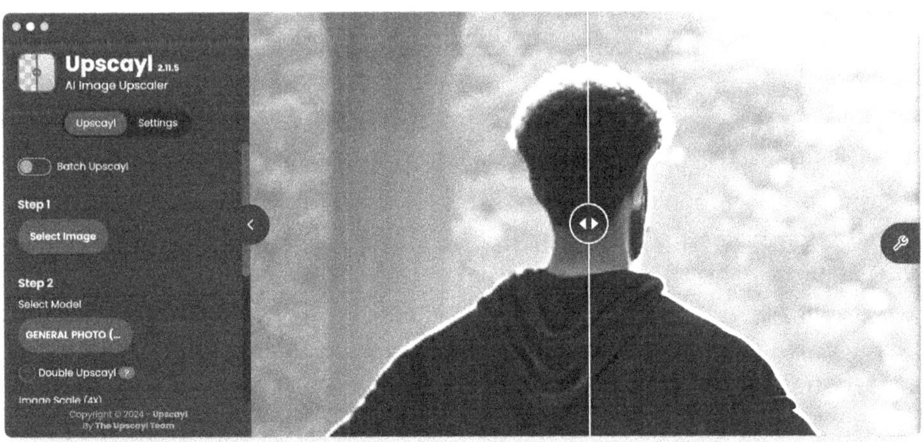

FIGURE 7.24 On the left is the original, and on the right is the upscaled result in Upscayl. Errors remain, but you can see how well the enlargement works, especially on the hair. (Figure created using Midjourney v6.1 and Upscayl 2.11.5.)

FIGURE 7.25 Stable Diffusion often doesn't quite master text rendering, but the caption can be quickly replaced in an image editing programme. (Figure created using Stable Diffusion SDXL.)

In general, the same tips I gave you above for Midjourney apply to Stable Diffusion. Unlike with Midjourney, however, I strongly recommend using English prompts with Stable Diffusion.

As mentioned, Stable Diffusion is open source, meaning you can download the programme free of charge. However, it only runs via the command line, which is not very convenient. There are several graphical user interfaces available, but these also take some getting used to. For macOS, iOS and iPadOS, there is ***Draw Things***, a free programme that is very easy to use. But even here, you will need to invest some time before you can master it. Therefore, my tip is to use Stable Diffusion via a web service if you want to work with it. Here you will find a compilation of free sites with access to Stable Diffusion: bnfr.de/ai079

7.3.10 Tips for Flux

Flux is one of the newer image AIs. It was developed by the German researchers who did the groundwork on which the development of Stable Diffusion is based. Flux is also open source, and here, too, the easiest way to use it is via a web service. You can find my tips here: bnfr.de/ai080

In terms of operation, Flux does not appear to differ greatly from Stable Diffusion at first glance. However, it is noticeable that distortions, deformations or strange excrescences occur less frequently. Flux more often delivers images that look correct. On the other hand, it is often a little more difficult to precisely control the output. Make an extra effort to describe the desired results precisely so that they correspond to what you had in mind.

FIGURE 7.26 The result of the identical prompt in three image AIs: (a) Flux, (b) Midjourney and (c) Stable Diffusion. Flux didn't quite get the ice surface right, and some things don't look quite right on the hands, but the composition is interesting. (Figure created using Flux 1.1 Pro, Midjourney v6.1 and Stable Diffusion SDXL.)

7.3.11 Tips for Adobe Firefly

If you don't already have years of experience with other image AI tools, you'll learn to master Firefly faster than you would with other tools. This is because Firefly has a sidebar where you can set a wide range of parameters that you would normally specify in other image AI tools using text descriptions or abbreviations. This may seem a little cumbersome to professionals, but it is definitely more accessible.

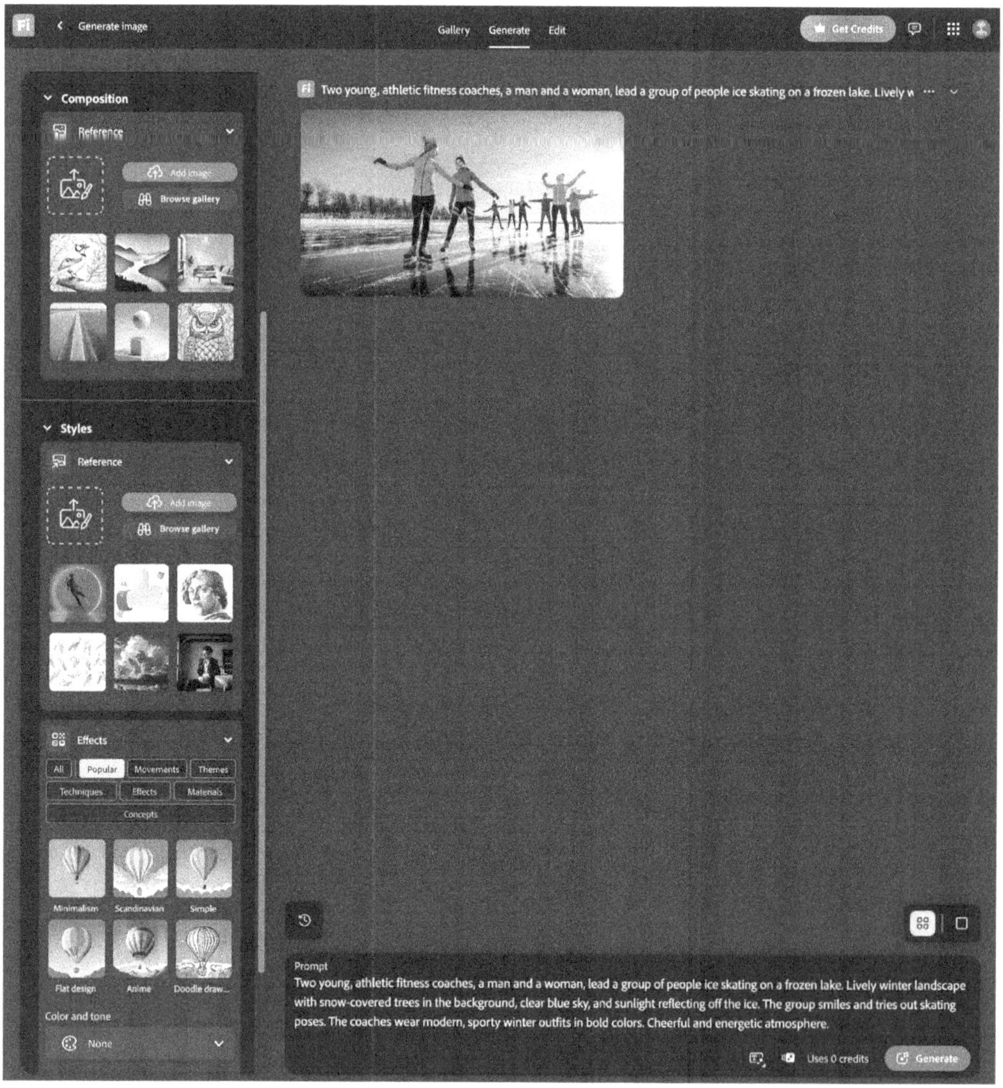

FIGURE 7.27 You can adjust a wide range of details in the sidebar. It's particularly worth trying out different effects – you'll find art styles such as Art Nouveau and Cubism, as well as techniques such as acrylic and linocut. (Figure created using Adobe Firefly 3.)

Personally, I always have great difficulty getting human figures right in Firefly. Portraits work, illustrations and artistic graphics too, but bodies often show distortions, double limbs or similar issues.

Another annoyance: the images you create are not saved, nor are the prompts. This only happens if you add an image to your favourites by clicking on the star icon that appears when you roll over the image. You can access your favourites from the Firefly home page via the main menu. But be careful: your favourites are saved in your browser – if you clear its cache or use a different browser, your favourites will be gone! Add the images to a library so that you can access them permanently. But even that didn't always work for me. So my approach is to save all prompts and settings together with the downloaded images that I created in Firefly. Since this is tedious, I only do this for the images that I actually want to use.

7.3.12 Tips for Adobe Illustrator

As dissatisfied as I am with Adobe Firefly in some respects, I am enthusiastic about Adobe Illustrator. In Section 6.1.3, I showed you how to create logos with its AI. These are created in vector format, which makes it very easy to edit the result. This is also very helpful for more complex illustrations. Let's assume we don't want photos for our hairdressing website, but illustrative images instead.

FIGURE 7.28 Illustrator creates AI-generated images as vectors, so you can highlight details you don't like and correct or delete them with just a few clicks. (Figure created using Adobe Illustrator (v28) Firefly 3.)

This is very, very quick:

1. In Illustrator, use the rectangle tool to drag an object to the size you want your illustration to be.
2. A context-sensitive taskbar appears, where you can select **TO GENERATE VECTOR GRAPHICS**. Enter a short description in the text field.
3. Click on the **CONTENT TYPE** icon next to it to specify whether you want to create a complex **SCENE**, a simpler **MOTIF** without a background or an abstract **SYMBOL**.
4. In the dialogue box that opens with the next icon, **STYLES**, you can influence the style of the display.
5. Finally, under the third icon, the cogwheel, you can open a large pop-up window where you can see and manipulate all the details at a glance.
6. If you are satisfied, click **GENERATE**.

7.3.13 Alternative Image AI

If you search for AI image generators, you will come across hundreds of providers. Many of them have simply installed an AI such as Stable Diffusion on their server and programmed a more or less user-friendly interface that allows you to use it. That's not a bad thing, but it's very difficult to separate the wheat from the chaff. Ultimately, you have to read up on each individual provider to find out what AI is behind it and what the terms of use and prices are. And then you have to try out what the results look like. With the market in flux, this is a Sisyphean task. Even if you've tested them all once, you can start all over again because the models are constantly changing. You can find my current tips on alternatives, such as AIs that are good at placing text on images, here: bnfr.de/ai081

7.3.14 Cropping and Resizing Images

If you want to crop and resize images or make other simple changes, you're almost always better off with classic image editing tools. It's surprisingly difficult to explain such simple tasks to an image AI correctly. If you use a programme like ***Adobe Photoshop*** or ***Affinity Photo*** (my choice), then you already have everything you need. But if you just want to make a few quick adjustments, such as resizing or cropping, free tools are perfectly adequate. On Mac, the ***Preview*** programme is installed with the operating system and can be used to make basic adjustments. It has basic tools such as cropping and basic colour correction. For Windows, it's ***Paint***. If you want a little more, these alternatives are available:

- ***Krita***: This free open-source software is primarily suitable for digital painting, but can also be used for image editing.

- ***Paint.NET***: This is an easy-to-use, free image editing programme for Windows with basic functions, but its style is somewhat outdated. It is well suited for quick and uncomplicated image adjustments.
- ***Photopea:*** This browser-based image editor reads a variety of files (Sketch, PSD, etc.). It is well suited for small, quick changes directly in the browser without installing any programmes. However, some functions, such as exporting as a PSD file, are subject to a fee.

7.3.15 Polish up Existing Photos with AI

There are countless AI tools for image editing – online applications, desktop programmes or apps. Many seemingly free image editing offers have severe limitations, such as allowing only one upload or download per day, having limited resolution or annoying watermarks. Although reliable free solutions can be found in some cases, the search is tedious and time-consuming. If you absolutely need something free, take a look here, where I have collected recommendations for the most suitable tools currently available: bnfr.de/ai028

However, my general recommendation is to choose a professional tool and accept the price in order to be able to work efficiently and without compromise in the long term. Such AI-based image editing tools offer a variety of functions for flexibly adjusting images. For example, you can use them to remove distracting people or objects, fill image areas with completely different patterns or backgrounds using ***generative fill***, add additional elements or completely replace the background, e.g. to place people in a new environment. You can also use them to make customers or team members unrecognisable by turning them so that they have their backs to the camera.

Photoshop has the advantage that you can use the AI capabilities of Adobe Firefly directly in the programme. You can create an image with Firefly directly in a file or remove parts of the image (see Figure 7.29).

Midjourney can do this, for example, using a technique known as ***inpainting***. To do this, select a generated image and click on **EDIT** in the **MORE** section on the right side. Then use the Erase tool, which is selected by default, to mark the unwanted object. If you have accidentally selected too much, you can undo this or use the Restore brush to bring back what you have deleted. Now describe what you want to see instead. But keep in mind that this is meant mainly to change small details or texture in the background. Inserting completely different objects won't work. When you are finished, click **SUBMIT EDIT** (see Figure 7.30).

If you don't like the image section, shrink the image and/or move it in the editor so that the elements are in the desired positions and click **SUBMIT EDIT**. This will give you four variants that add further image elements to match the rest. And here's another great use for this feature: Use the Erase tool in the editor to click on details Midjourney did not quite get right, such as eyes, earrings or hands. You will then be given variants

FIGURE 7.29 In Photoshop, select what you want to remove with the Remove tool. Be sure to paint over it generously, otherwise only a variation will be created, which in our case would be another person. You can also easily remove the shadow by painting over it once. (Figure created using Adobe Photoshop (v25) Firefly 3.)

for these areas, which often look better than the first attempts. You can also upload and edit your own images. Do you only have one good photo of yourself? Then take that and swap out your clothes and background to match what you want to show. You can also turn the photo into a comic or an oil painting in no time at all – in far better quality than any filters that have been available for image editing programmes for years. But despite all the excitement about the possibilities of image manipulation, be sure to stick to the truth! This not only protects you from legal trouble but also safeguards your integrity, which is always evident on the website.

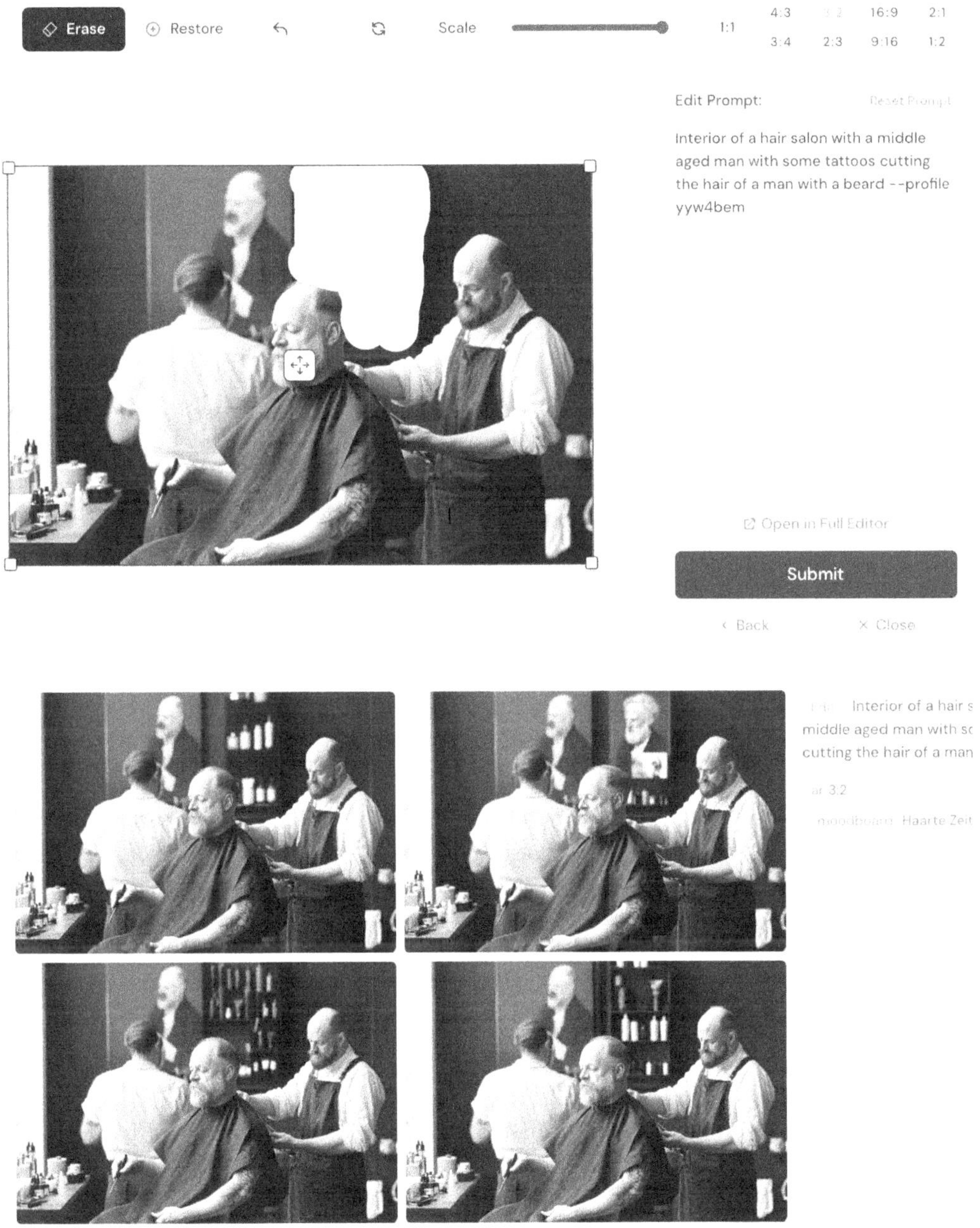

FIGURE 7.30 In the Midjourney editor, select what you want to remove, describe what you want to see in this area, and you will get four suggestions with a different background. (Figure created using Midjourney v6.1.)

7.3.16 Legal Framework for AI Images

The legal situation is even more complex for images generated by AI than it is for text. The uncertainty surrounding images is also based on the fact that AI systems are usually trained using existing, legally protected material. However, the main difference lies in the type of work – the question of originality and creative height is somewhat different for images than it is for text. Unlike with texts, the similarity to existing works is often more obvious with images and, therefore, more problematic from a legal perspective. In addition, AI images can more easily infringe trademark rights or personal rights, for example, if they contain recognisable logos or faces. How can you avoid legal pitfalls when using AI images?

The major image generators such as ChatGPT, Midjourney and Stable Diffusion have been trained with millions of images. Hardly any artists have consented to this use of their works, so various lawsuits are pending against the providers. When we use these image generators, it is particularly problematic if we use artists' names in prompts. For example, if you use "in the style of Keith Haring" as a prompt, this may infringe copyright, personal rights or even trademark rights, depending on the context. A style (such as "pop art") cannot be protected, but if an image we create bears a strong resemblance to a specific image (such as Keith Haring's "Barking Dog"), this is legally problematic. AI cannot recognise this – the responsibility lies entirely with us.

So you need to think about this problem in two places: first, when you enter the prompt, and then when you check the result. Your prompt has a decisive influence: the more specific and individual you make it, the more likely it is that you can argue that you have achieved a certain level of originality. However, you must then look critically at the result and ensure that it does not resemble another specific image too closely, which is difficult without in-depth knowledge of comparable images. Editing the AI image, for example, through retouching, colour correction, cropping and combining it with other images or your own design elements, can help to create an independent work.

Pay particular attention to:

- well-known people (faces, but also typical clothing styles or poses)
- well-known buildings and landmarks
- brands, logos, lettering, symbols
- characters (such as Donald Duck, the Michelin Man, SpongeBob)
- politically sensitive or discriminatory content (symbols of political parties, visual stereotypes of ethnic groups or religions, sexual orientation or gender roles, etc.)

You must also pay attention to the conditions specified by the AI systems. Most of them allow commercial use, but there is a labelling requirement, i.e. you must indicate the source. The terms of use are subject to change, so it is important to document for each image when you created it and with which system. You should also save the exact prompt and what you edited. Finally, it is important that you stay up to date with any changes to the operators' specifications. Your due diligence obligations also include directly citing the source for each image and, for example, indicating the use of AI in the imprint.

SUGGESTED DISCLAIMER

"The AI-generated images used on this website were carefully created and checked by us using [system]. We respect the rights of third parties and have ensured to the best of our knowledge that no property rights have been infringed. However, if you notice any infringement, please contact us immediately at [contact]. We will remove the image in question immediately if there are justified objections".

Here too, the same applies: if you want to be on the safe side, seek advice from legal professionals on what a disclaimer should look like in your specific case.

7.3.17 Photos from Image Agencies and Portals

If you are unable or unwilling to use AI for individual images, then use stock image agencies. You can purchase photos from these on their websites. To be on the safe side, document for each individual image when you purchased it, at what exact time and from whom. I even save the purchase confirmation page as a PDF so that I can prove the purchase later. If others are involved in the implementation of your site, it is best to ask them to provide you with a list of the sources for each individual image. This will save you trouble later on if there is a dispute about an image and no one can remember where it came from.

You need to be careful with the term ***royalty-free***. It does not mean that there are no rights attached to these images, nor that they are free of charge. Rather, it means that you purchase the rights to use such images once and can then use them as often and for as long as you like. In contrast, a ***rights-managed*** image is one for which you must obtain a licence for each individual use. When you purchase such a non-royalty-free image, you usually acquire a temporary licence. If this expires after two years, for example, you must remove the image from your website or purchase a new licence.

The term ***royalty-free*** is often used, but it is not a legally defined term. If an image you want to use is described as such, you should always check what this means.

There are also portals such as ***Unsplash*** or ***Pixabay*** where you can download images free of charge and use them freely. These platforms provide free-to-use images under their own licenses and, on Pixabay, some ***public-domain***-equivalent works. The quality varies, and you can find good images on many other websites as well. But it often takes a long time to find a truly suitable image. In addition, someone may post an image that actually belongs to someone else. Then you will be the one who gets into trouble when the author discovers the image on your website.

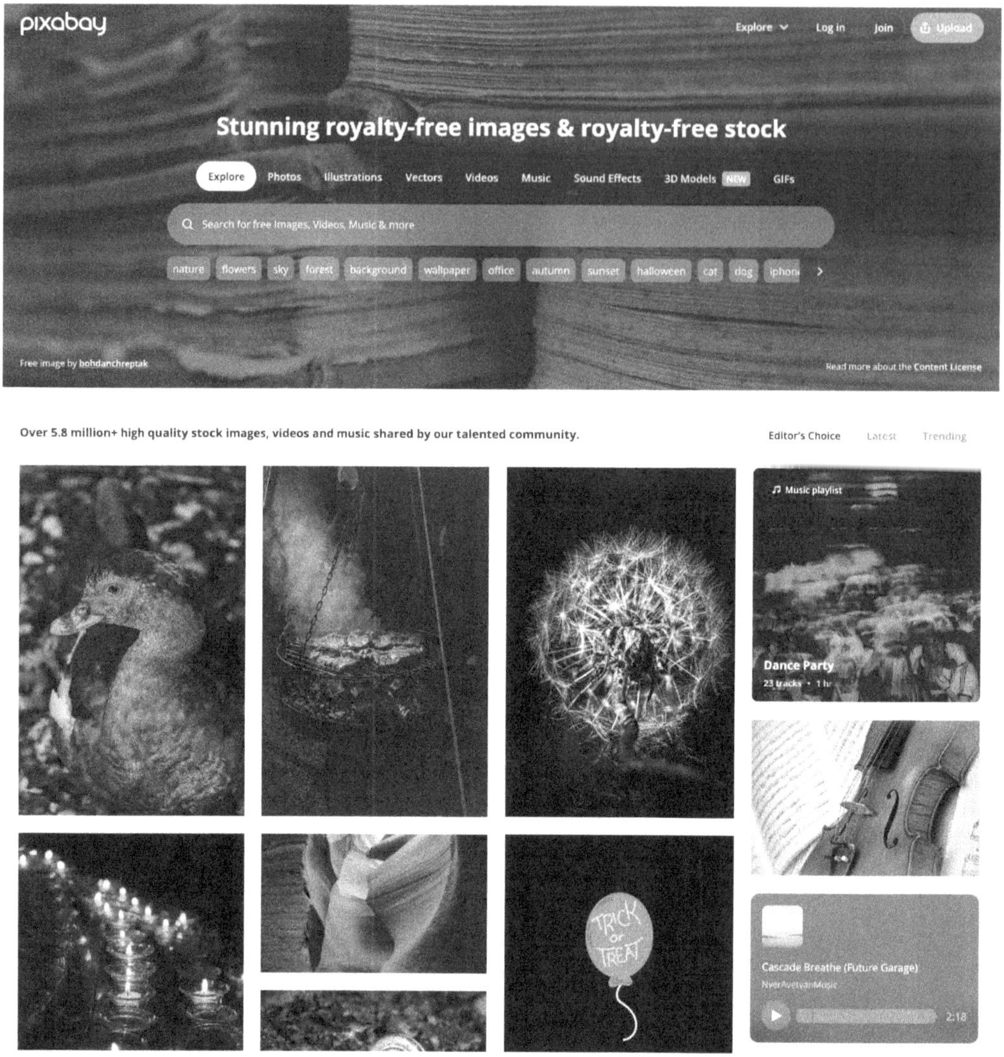

FIGURE 7.31 Thousands of high-quality photos, free to use, are available at pixabay.com, among other sites.

7.4 USE AUDIO AND VIDEO SENSIBLY

Remember: everything you put on the website must be interesting for visitors and help to achieve the site's goals. Otherwise, creating this content is not only a waste of time but can also be harmful because it distracts from the content that is actually relevant. Therefore, when it comes to audio and especially video, we have to consider very carefully whether it is worth the effort to create it, or whether it is just a gimmick that ultimately no one on the site will watch or listen to. Video and audio require more engagement from users: they cannot be skimmed as easily as text, must be actively started, and demand full attention.

Autoplay is not a solution either, as most people find it annoying and patronising. In most cases, visitors to your website are looking for a quick solution to their problem, a piece of information that is easier to find with well-structured text. But of course, audio and video have their strengths; they can be more emotionally appealing and illustrate things that are difficult to explain with text alone. For specific implementation of audio and video, you will find some tips in Section 9.7.3, "Creating Audio and Video with AI".

7.5 INCORPORATING CONTENT INTO THE WEBSITE

Once you have created all the text and images, they need to find their way onto your website. Unfortunately, this is still a process that requires a lot of manual work. In theory, AI can do this for us – to do this, you need to create your own agent that, for example, reads the images from a specific directory and incorporates them into the right places on your site. This is conceivable, but it involves so much effort that it is far less work and far less prone to errors to do it yourself. This is not unpleasant, but rather enjoyable and even a source of pride, because you can see how your website is improving bit by bit and getting closer and closer to the ideal image you may have had in mind from the beginning or developed during the design process.

7.5.1 Check and Copy Text

Before incorporating any text, check it again for consistency, whether everything fits together and whether it matches the style of the other text. Then check whether you have enough paragraphs – only one idea should be formulated per paragraph. If necessary, insert subheadings to make the text easier to understand.

Finally, copy the text for your pages into the respective tool in your browser or into your code if you are creating HTML and CSS yourself. It is essential to ensure that text markup is used ***semantically***. This means, for example, marking headings as such and not simply formatting the text in a larger font and bold. This promotes accessibility and helps search engines to interpret the structure of your content correctly. The same applies to paragraphs, lists, quotations and other mark-ups. This allows readers and technical systems to make optimal use of your content.

7.5.2 Prepare and Insert Images

If you have created a table for your images as shown above, use this as a guide. Alternatively, work your way through the directory on your hard drive where you have stored the images. Be sure to clearly document which images you ultimately used on your website. Otherwise, you will often spend ages searching for them months later. Use meaningful file names, as this will also make your work much easier in the long run. And it also helps with search engine optimisation.

A table is also useful because you need ***alt text*** for each image, which you can then easily add to the table. Alt text is an image description that is necessary for visually impaired users and also for search engine optimisation. This text describes what can be seen in the image. To create these texts, you can make good use of AI if you have the prompts available:

EXAMPLE PROMPT: CREATE ALT TEXT

Motivation: I would like to expand the uploaded table to include prompts, alt texts for the images, and web-safe file names. The goal is to prepare the images optimally for use on a website.

Task: Generate a short, concise alt text for each row in the table based on the file names and prompts. If the file name is unclear or not web-safe, suggest a new file name that complies with best practices (e.g. lower case letters, no special characters or spaces).

Result: An expanded table with two new columns: "Alt text" and "File name". The alt texts should be short, concise and descriptive, and the file names should comply with the requirements for files on a web server.

Example:

- Alt text: "Two people ice skating at the Lankwitz ice rink"
- Web-safe file name: "ice-skating-training-lankwitz.jpg"

Role: Act as an expert in accessible websites and SEO optimisation.

The prompt to copy: bnfr.de/ai082

Then copy the alt texts from the table directly into the fields provided in your website builder or no-code/low-code tool. If you create HTML and CSS yourself, copy the alt texts into the code.

Convert the images into the appropriate formats. The JPG format is suitable for photos. Although this format is lossy, it ensures small file sizes. PNG is better for graphics and logos and often smaller. Vector graphics remain scalable in SVG format without any loss of quality, and these files are almost always very small. Some website builders and no-code platforms automatically convert your images if you upload them in unsuitable formats. But to be on the safe side, you should not leave this to the system, but rather provide the optimal formats right from the start.

Images should only be provided in the size that is actually required on the website. Therefore, scale the images before uploading them using an image editing programme or online tool and reduce them to the maximum size required. This reduces the amount of data that needs to be transferred and thus reduces loading times. If you code your pages yourself, it makes sense to create images in different sizes – for example, a large version for desktop viewing, a medium version for tablets and laptops, and a small version for smartphones. This is because it is particularly important for mobile devices that the files are as small as possible, as the transfer speed is often lowest when users are on the move. You can find more details on this in Section 6.8.5, "Responsive Web Design – Flexibility for All Screen Sizes". With website builders and no-code/low-code systems, you don't have to worry about this, as they take care of it for you. But even here, you should check whether the images are displayed in appropriate sizes on the various end devices. This is a question not only of file size but also of aesthetics and usability.

If you want to see what our sample projects look like with the generated texts and images, you can view them here: bnfr.de/ai083

7.6 ANNOYING, BUT NECESSARY – LEGAL NOTICE AND PRIVACY POLICY

If you operate a website, you have to deal with legal issues. The most relevant, if you have visitors from the European Union, is the ***General Data Protection Regulation*** (***GDPR***). It is an EU-wide regulation that sets out general requirements and basic principles for the protection of personal data. Laws in the member countries specify and concretise these requirements for digital services (i.e. websites, online services, apps) and telecommunications.

In the United Kingdom, the ***UK GDPR*** (which is basically the same as the EU version) and the ***Data Protection Act 2018*** apply; rules for cookies and similar technologies are set by ***PECR*** (***Privacy and Electronic Communications Regulations***). In the United States, there is no single federal equivalent; obligations depend on state privacy laws (notably California's ***CCPA/CPRA***, but other states are following suit) and sectoral rules, so notice and opt-out/-in duties can vary by user location. In general, you should check your local privacy and consumer laws and remember that the GDPR/UK GDPR can still apply extraterritorially if you target or monitor people in the EU/UK.

If you violate the provisions of the GDPR, you may face warnings and fines. In theory, these can run into the millions under the GDPR; however, such sums are primarily intended as a deterrent for globally active companies that do not take data protection very seriously. However, even smaller websites can face costs of a few thousand euros. If

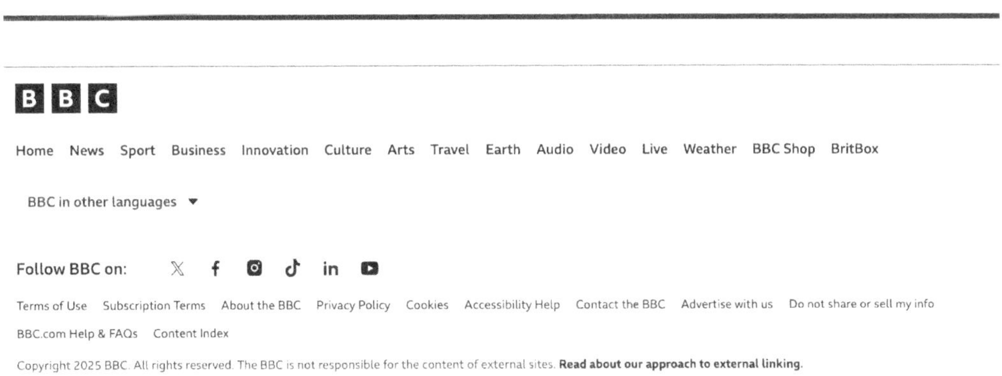

FIGURE 7.32 The footer of bbc.com. As on almost every website, this is where you will find the mandatory links to the legal stuff like terms of use and privacy policy.

you want to be on the safe side, you can use one of the free generators for privacy policies or, better still, consult a solicitor. You should also keep an eye on legal developments, as the requirements may continue to change.

7.6.1 Imprint

Public-facing websites should provide a clearly accessible legal notice/website information page. In the EU, core identification duties come from the E-Commerce Directive (Article 5); in the UK, from the Electronic Commerce (EC Directive) Regulations 2002 and the Companies Act 2006. In some locations, like Germany, every website that is not operated purely for private purposes requires an imprint. As soon as a site pursues commercial purposes – for example, when operating an online shop, a company blog or if income is to be generated in any other way, even indirectly – an imprint is mandatory under § 5 DDG (previously § 5 TMG). Even those who work freelance or are self-employed and have an online presence require this information. You should include at least:

- Name and geographic address of the service provider
- For companies, cooperatives and associations, the name of the authorised representative must also be provided.
- Email address and telephone number
- Commercial register, association register, partnership register or cooperative register with register number (where applicable)
- For certain professions (e.g. skilled trades, legal professions, medical professions), information about the chamber and professional regulations
- For activities requiring a licence, the competent supervisory authority
- VAT identification number and economic identification number (if available)

For the UK: limited companies must also display their registered company name, registration number, place of registration (England and Wales, Scotland, or Northern Ireland) and registered office address under the Companies (Trading Disclosures) Regulations 2008.

For the US, there's no general "imprint" rule. Typical obligations are instead:

Privacy Policy: If you collect any personal information from visitors (names, emails, IP addresses, cookies, etc.), you need a clear privacy policy. California's laws (CalOPPA and CCPA/CPRA) require this for sites with California visitors – which means practically every US website needs one. Several other states, including Virginia, Colorado, Connecticut, Utah, and Texas, have similar rules. Your privacy policy should be easy to find (usually in the footer) and explain what data you collect, how you use it and what rights users have.

Advertising Disclosures: If you earn money through affiliate links, sponsorships or paid promotions, the FTC requires you to disclose this clearly to your visitors – no burying it in fine print.

If your site allows users to add content and you want US DMCA safe-harbor protection, you need to publish a 'DMCA Notice/Copyright Agent' page (agent name, address, email, phone) and register the same details with the U.S. Copyright Office; this needs renewal every three years. This is optional for sites without user uploads/comments.

Even when not legally required, listing your business name and contact details is smart practice. It builds trust and makes it easier for customers to reach you. And in many countries, it is a legal obligation to do so.

7.6.2 Privacy Policy

A privacy policy is required for almost all public-facing websites. In the EU, the GDPR requires transparent privacy information (Articles 13 and 14). In the UK, equivalent duties apply under the UK GDPR. Your policy must clearly explain what data you collect, why you're collecting it, your legal basis for processing, who you share it with, how long you keep it, your contact details (and Data Protection Officer details if you have one) and users' rights (access, deletion, correction, etc.).

Be upfront about automatic data collection like server logs, IP addresses and cookies. Also disclose any third-party tools you use – analytics platforms like ***Google Analytics*** or social media buttons or elements that transfer data to these services (see the following Section 7.6.3), embedded content and similar services. For non-essential cookies and trackers, you must obtain prior consent before they run, and make it easy for users to withdraw that consent later. These consent rules come from the ePrivacy Directive (in the EU) and PECR (in the UK), not the GDPR itself.

When collecting data, it is also important to anonymise the IP address and give users the option to prevent tracking. If you use any processor, you need a ***data processing agreement***. In this agreement, the provider certifies that they comply with EU regulations. When data moves outside the EU or UK – for example, to US-based services – you must rely on an adequacy decision (such as the EU-US Data Privacy Framework) or use appropriate safeguards like EU Standard Contractual Clauses (SCCs), the UK International Data Transfer Agreement (IDTA) or the UK Addendum to EU SCCs.

If you have offers aimed at children and young people, stricter rules apply. In the EU, you need verifiable parental consent to process data of children under 16 for information-society services. But Member States can lower this to 13, which many have. In the UK, the threshold is also 13. Under US law, COPPA requires verifiable parental consent for services directed at children under 13. If you rely on consent from children, build appropriate age-verification and parental-consent mechanisms into your service. If you are targeting this group, I would consult professionals on this issue.

For standard cases, most website operators work with a so-called ***data protection generator***. This is a simple web service that asks you for a few details and then generates a suitable privacy policy. You need to find one which covers the country you operate in and the countries you target customers in. Or you bite the bullet and hire a specialised law firm to create a privacy policy for you.

Place the link to the privacy policy in the footer, just like the link to the legal notice.

7.6.3 Data Protection and Integration of Social Media

If you integrate social media elements into your website, you need to bear a few details in mind with regard to data protection. This is because you are transferring visitors' personal data to the respective platforms – even if users do not interact with the elements. In the EU/UK, loading ***social plug-ins*** (e.g. Facebook "Like", X/Twitter "Tweet") or embeds typically triggers consent requirements for non-essential cookies/trackers under ePrivacy/PECR; outside the EU/UK, rules vary (e.g. in the US the model is generally opt-out for "sale/share" and targeted ads, not universal prior consent).

Social plug-ins such as the "Like" button from Facebook or the "Tweet" button from Twitter/X automatically connect to the operators' servers when the page is loaded. This transfers visitor data such as IP address, browser type and the page visited. In the EU/UK, you should obtain permission (consent) before this happens. One approach is the so-called ***two-click solution***: you initially display the button only as a static image or link. Only when users click on the image or link is the connection to the social network established and data transfer started. This gives users control over the transfer of their data. AI systems such as Le Chat or Claude can easily generate the code for this. In website builders, implementing the two-click solution is not so easy. Most of them come from the US, where data protection regulations are less strict, so they do not offer this as standard. If you want to be on the safe side, do not directly embed Facebook and Twitter buttons or YouTube videos. Instead, you can use screenshots and links to the respective content, which is harmless. To be on the safe side, clearly inform users that the link leads to the respective provider. In addition to standard embedding, YouTube also offers embedding in ***extended privacy mode*** (via the URL youtube-nocookie.com*)*. Cookies are only set and usage data is only stored when visitors play the video – mostly, but in some cases YouTube may still load some tracking/cookies before the video is played (depending on configuration and the user's YouTube account status). With the normal embedding code, data is always transferred when the page is loaded. Privacy-enhanced mode reduces tracking but may still trigger limited storage or requests. So a consent gate/two-click remains preferable for EU/UK compliance.

You must explain every integration of social media in detail in your privacy policy:

- What data do you transfer to which platforms?
- For what purpose?
- On what legal basis?
- How long is the data stored?
- What options do users have to object?

The data protection generators recommended above will help you to create these statements.

You should regularly check both the technical implementation and the legal requirements. Social media services are constantly changing their interfaces and behaviour when it comes to integration, and laws and regulations are also being updated. Document all measures taken to ensure data protection compliance so that, in case of doubt, you can prove that you have exercised the due diligence required by law.

7.6.4 Cookie Banners and Tracking

Cookies are small text files that virtually all websites store on visitors' computers. Many cookies are technically necessary, for example, for shopping baskets or logins. Others are used for personalised advertising and tracking, i.e. analysing what users do on the web. In the EU and UK, you must inform visitors and obtain prior consent before setting any non-essential cookies or similar trackers; the ePrivacy/PECR rules apply alongside (UK) GDPR.

Consent banners should ensure:

- Consent must be obtained *before* cookies are set.
- Consent and rejection must be presented equally (no nudging, no pre-ticked boxes).

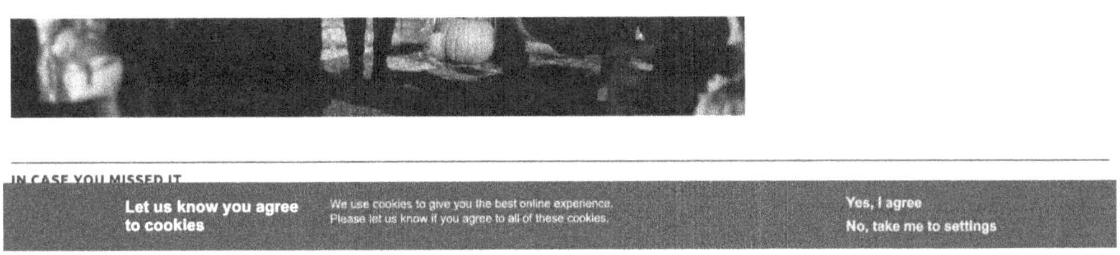

FIGURE 7.33 The cookie banner on bbc.com. Important: The links for rejecting cookies are designed to be equivalent to those for accepting them – in the EU it must even be possible to reject them with one click.

- Revocation must be possible at any time.
- The storage period of the cookies must be specified.
- Information must be provided as to whether third parties can access the cookies.
- The privacy policy and legal notice must be directly accessible (i.e. not only after the banner has been closed, because it obscures the links, for example).

You don't need consent for technically necessary cookies, such as shopping baskets or session cookies that keep users logged in or remember shopping baskets. Everything else, including analytics, typically requires consent.

A few European authorities (e.g. in France, Spain) allow basic analytics without consent under very strict conditions: first-party only, short lifespan, no cross-site tracking, no third-party sharing, and IP anonymization. Most analytics setups don't meet these requirements, so don't assume you qualify.

In the US, no prior consent is required for cookies. Instead, state laws like CCPA/CPRA require clear notice and opt-out mechanisms for selling/sharing data and targeted ads. Covered businesses must honor Global Privacy Control (GPC) – a browser signal that communicates opt-out preferences automatically.

Your best multi-region strategy is: Configure your Cookie Management Platform to show EU/UK visitors consent requests (opt-in) and US visitors disclosure with opt-out options. When in doubt, use the stricter EU/UK model – it keeps you compliant everywhere.

DRAFTING LEGAL TEXTS WITH AI?

Texts written by people who have studied law are often difficult for laypeople to understand, as are those written by other experts. However, such texts are also intended for laypeople, so they should actually be easy to understand or at least not intimidating. So it seems to make sense to let AI write the texts, because language models have also been trained with legal texts on websites, so they should be able to do this quite well. That may be the case, but as a layman, I would steer clear of it. Because I have no way of judging whether the texts are correct. In the field of law, the wording is important, and what may sound to me like the same sentence, only more beautifully phrased, may mean something else. Therefore, my recommendation is: if you revise legal texts with AI or even create them from scratch, always have the result checked by someone who is familiar with the subject matter.

CHAPTER 8

Step 6

Test and Optimise

> The earlier you test, the less work it is to correct errors. With the help of AI and humans, you can find these with little effort and optimise your site before it even goes live. And afterwards, ongoing testing ensures that the site keeps getting better and better.

You have completed your website in the previous steps. You may be wondering why testing comes at this stage. This is because many websites are only tested once they are online – if at all. However, this is a mistake, because the earlier you discover that something is not working, the less effort it takes to fix the problem. A new aeroplane is not tested on its first scheduled flight, but undergoes many test series before the first passengers board.

8.1 TESTING IS ALWAYS WORTHWHILE

Usability expert *Steve Krug* says:

> Testing one user is 100 percent better than testing none. Testing always works. Even the worst test with the wrong user will show you things you can do that will improve your site.

This means that even if you have never tested before, now is the right time to start. Of course, it would be ideal to test as early as possible. To have already carried out dozens of usability tests with preliminary versions, paper prototypes, mock-ups and click dummies. And to have enough time and financial resources to find test subjects who perfectly match the target group. But we practically never have such ideal conditions. Nevertheless, it's best to start testing now if you haven't already done so.

Everyone knows that testing is worthwhile. The story of user experience (UX) expert *Jared Spool's* "300 million dollar button" is often told: he reports on the testing of a

DOI: 10.1201/9781003726708-8

large shopping site that had a classic form for the payment process: two fields for email address and password, two buttons "Log in" and "Register" and a link "Forgot password". So far, nothing unusual and, from a usability perspective, no problem at first glance. However, a usability test revealed that people who had never shopped there before were annoyed by the requirement to register. They didn't want to create another account and feared receiving even more unwanted advertising. Returning customers, on the other hand, often had difficulty remembering their login details or finding them. So the website was redesigned: "Register" became "Continue" and it was possible to place a guest order. This was a new concept at the time – and led to a 45% increase in purchases. This brought the shop operators additional revenue of US$300 million in the first year. Nowadays, almost all shopping websites offer this option of ordering as a guest in order to simplify the purchasing process and reduce abandoned purchases. In this case, testing

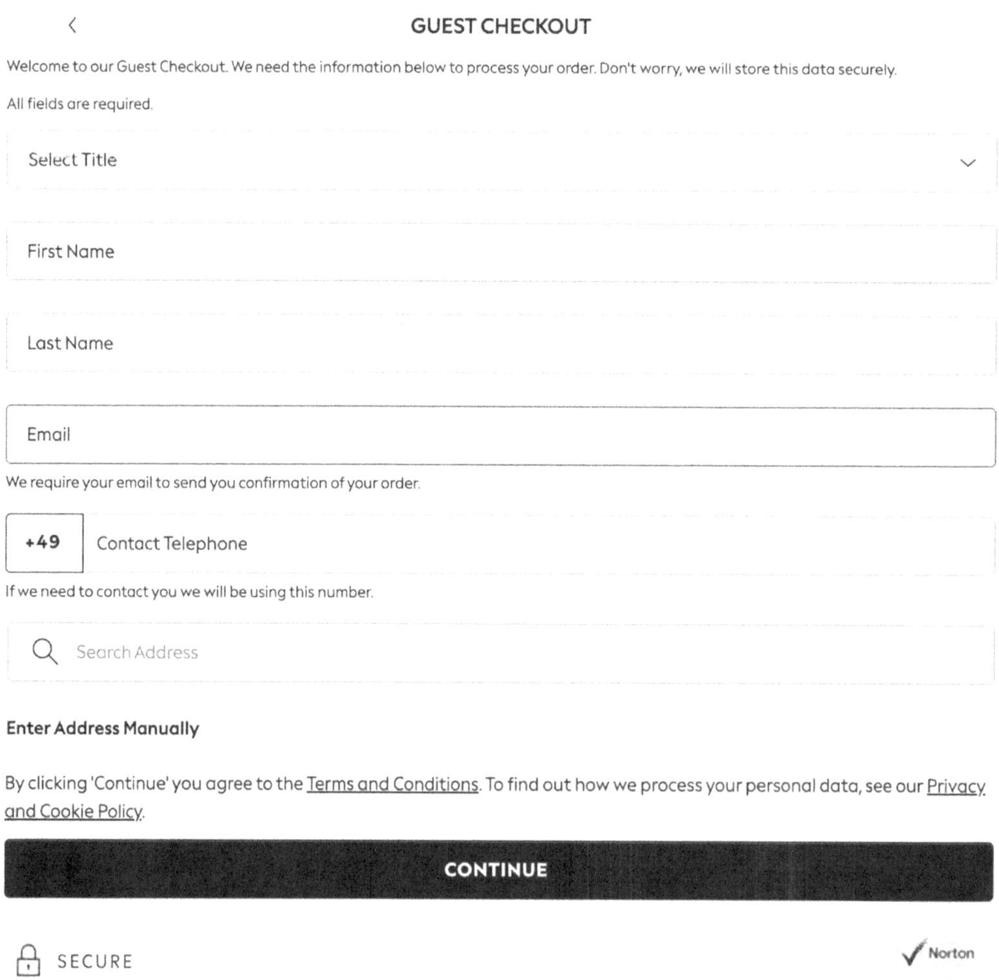

FIGURE 8.1 Guest orders in the Next shop – best practice today, a minor revolution a few years ago.

really paid off, and the ***ROI*** (***return on investment***) was fantastic. But even if your site doesn't generate millions in revenue, testing is always worthwhile.

8.2 EARLY TESTING SAVES TROUBLE LATER

When they hear the word "testing", many people think of technical errors (bugs). But in the case of smaller websites, these are usually found quickly. More difficult to find and often much more crucial to the success of your site are errors in usability. These often creep in unnoticed: navigation that confuses users, texts that no one understands, buttons that are overlooked, forms that frustrate. The most costly mistake is to wait until the website is online before testing it. By then, changes are expensive and time-consuming. What would have been a quick click in the design phase now requires extensive code and graphic adjustments. Even worse, your website is already online and you are annoying visitors and potential customers every day. They leave your website without buying, without registering and without contacting you. Without testing, these problems often remain undetected for years. Visitors simply leave without telling you why. If you collect access statistics, you will see the symptoms in your access figures: high bounce rates, low conversion rates and few returning visitors. To identify and fix these costly usability problems, you need a well-thought-out testing strategy. This chapter shows you how to do this - from simple tests that you can carry out yourself immediately to advanced methods with and without AI support.

8.3 TYPES OF TESTS

What can you test? In principle, everything. But we limit ourselves to what is most useful for small and medium-sized websites. We only do ***qualitative*** tests, not ***quantitative ones***. This means that we do not want to collect statistically reliable data, but only gain (qualitative) insights into what we can improve quickly. You are not interested in exactly *how many* people have problems with a form on your website (you could find this out with quantitative surveys, for example). If you discover during a test that three out of five people do not understand it, then it is definitely worth fixing the problem.

The first thing that comes to mind for many people is traditional ***questionnaires***. These are suitable for collecting structured feedback from a large number of people. They can provide both quantitative data and qualitative insights into the UX and are relatively inexpensive to conduct. The catch: the method *seems* simple, but it is very difficult to master. More on that in a moment.

Usability tests provide deeper insights into the actual behaviour of users, which is why this is the method of choice. Test subjects perform typical tasks on your website while you watch and analyse. Such tests can be conducted both on-site and online and often reveal problems that you would never have discovered with surveys alone.

FIGURE 8.2 When moderating usability tests, you should never let anything show and always remain neutral.

Various specialised testing methods have been established specifically for optimising content and design, which you can use in the early stages of implementation:

- ***First-click tests*** examine which element catches the eye so much that users click on it first. To do this, you show test subjects the mock-up (the visual design) of a website and give them a task, e.g. to contact the company. You do not mention that the site is not yet interactive and simply record where the users' first click goes. This allows you to find out which elements on the page are the most eye-catching and whether users click where you actually intended them to.
- With ***5-second tests***, you can find out what the first impression of a page is. Here, too, you initially keep the test subjects in the dark about the test setup: you give them a task and show them a page. After 5 seconds, the page is hidden and you ask questions such as "What was the page about?", "What did you notice?" or "What does the company offer?". This allows you to quickly and easily check whether your most important messages are being conveyed and whether the design communicates the desired core messages. You will be amazed at how much can be grasped from a page in just 5 seconds.

Of course, AI can also help you with testing. Unfortunately, it doesn't work quite as well as one would like, but when used correctly, it can provide valuable insights into how you can improve. The market for AI testing is in flux, but at present, the promises made by providers are often grandiose, the prices high and the actual benefits low. What is already simple, inexpensive and works well, however, are AI tests for comprehensibility, user appeal and traceability of arguments:

EXAMPLE PROMPT: ANALYSE USER ADDRESS AND REASONING

Motivation: Analyse the website {URL} to determine whether the textual reasoning is convincing for a specific target group. The target group is men aged 20–70 who value efficiency, fair prices and clear information at a hairdresser's. They live a maximum of 15 minutes' walk away and come from all occupational groups.

Task: Examine the website for the following points:

- Is the argumentation convincing to the target group?
- Is there any content missing that the target group would expect?
- Are the texts understandable, appealing and do they fit the company?
- Is the argumentation complete?
- Is there a clear call to action (CTA)? Are any questions or doubts that the target group may have sufficiently addressed and dispelled?

Result: Create a short, bullet-point report with clear evaluations and suggestions for possible improvements.

Prompt to copy: bnfr.de/ai073

Which of the other test methods mentioned is most useful for you depends on various factors, including your budget, project schedule and, most importantly, what exactly you want to test. Let's take a closer look at some of the test methods.

8.4 QUESTIONNAIRES – SEEMINGLY SIMPLE

At first glance, questionnaires seem to be the easiest way to quickly obtain feedback from users. After all, we can all ask questions. The problem is, however, that it is very easy to design a poor questionnaire – even AI is of little help if you don't know how to give it good guidelines. At best, such questionnaires will yield meaningless results and, at worst, results that lead in completely the wrong direction. It is not without reason that truly meaningful surveys are created by people who have studied psychology or otherwise acquired a deep understanding of psychology, statistics and human response behaviour. Or as UX expert Erika Hall puts it:

> Surveys are the most dangerous research tool – misunderstood and misused.

The easiest and safest approach is therefore to rely on established questionnaires. This also gives you a broad database for comparing the results with others. For us, the three most important standardised questionnaires are the ***System Usability Scale*** (***SUS***), the

Net Promoter Score (***NPS***) and the ***AttrakDiff***. All three are scientifically validated and the results are easy to interpret.

The ***SUS*** comprises ten statements that users rate on a scale of 1 to 5. Originally developed for software, it can also be used for websites. The statements range from "I think I would like to use this system more often" to "I found the system very cumbersome to use". Ideally, there should be at least 25 participants, but initial trends can already be identified with as few as five people.

The NPS questionnaire is much quicker to answer, as it consists of just one question: "How likely are you to recommend the website?" The response scale ranges from 0 to 10. Those who give a score of 9 or 10 are counted as ***promoters***, those between 7 and 8 are ***passive*** and those with a score of 6 or below are ***detractors*** (critics). The NPS value is calculated as the difference between promoters and detractors as a percentage; passives are ignored. If you surveyed 100 people and 20 of them are promoters and 10 are detractors, you calculate 20% minus 10% and arrive at an NPS of 10%. A value above 0 is acceptable, above 30 is quite good, and above 70 is excellent, but I have never seen such a value in my practice.

AttrakDiff measures the attractiveness of an application based on perceived usability, inspiration and identification with the website. It is a questionnaire with 28 pairs of opposites, such as "clear – confusing" or "valuable – inferior".

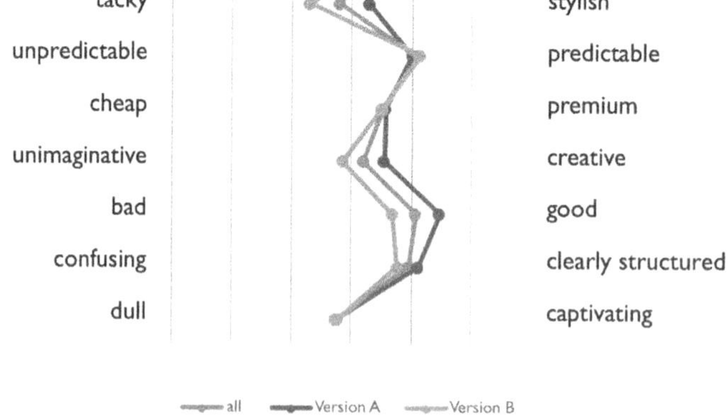

FIGURE 8.3 Some of the word pairs from the AttrakDiff test and their classification by users for two versions of a website.

8.4.1 Develop Your Own Questionnaires

If you don't like any of the established questionnaires, then develop your own. But as mentioned, this is very difficult, even if it doesn't seem so. That doesn't scare you? Then pay attention to the following. The most important rule for designing any survey is: never ask too many questions. What is too many depends on the individual case, but it is usually much less than you think.

Long surveys annoy respondents and cast a bad light on you. Above all, however, the number of people who drop out prematurely increases, and the quality of the answers suffers. Limit yourself to a clear topic. Only ask questions that are actually relevant to your website. Consider: What will we do differently if X comes out of this question? Only ask this question if you would really change something.

A few basic tips for writing good questions:

- Formulate your questions in such a way that your target group understands them, i.e. no technical terms, short sentences.
- Avoid leading questions. Instead of "Did you like it?" or "How much did you like it?", it is better to ask: "How good or bad did you find …?"
- Use text fields very sparingly. Typing text is tedious, and evaluating text is too. Whenever possible, provide a list of possible answers.
- Ask questions as specifically as possible, i.e. not "Would you buy a product that …" but rather "When did you last buy a product that …".

EXAMPLE PROMPT: DEVELOP A QUESTIONNAIRE

Motivation: I want to find out why visitors leave my website for handmade greeting cards without buying anything.

Task: Develop a questionnaire with just a few questions that users see when they leave the site. Consider best practices for online questionnaires to maximise the quality of responses. Make recommendations for the optimal mix of open-ended and closed-ended questions. Formulate the questions in a friendly and motivating way. Explain how visitors will benefit from responding and how long it will take to complete.

Result: A short questionnaire that effectively identifies the main reasons for abandoned purchases and is user-friendly and clearly worded.

Role: You are an expert in UX and online market research with years of experience and know the best practices for questionnaires because you have evaluated hundreds of them.

The prompt to copy: bnfr.de/ai031

Remember the golden rule number 3: AI can lead you astray. Check carefully that the AI does not ask too many questions or use non-neutral wording. If in doubt, have another AI critically review the questionnaire, as this often yields valuable insights.

A proven example of a helpful questionnaire is a short survey that appears when someone wants to leave the website (***exit intent survey***). It consists of just three simple questions.

1. Why did you visit the website today?
2. Did you achieve what you wanted?
3. If not, why not?

These specific questions about actual behaviour provide better insights than subjective assessments such as "How did you like the website?".

Another tip for greater participation: reward participation with vouchers, small gifts or even just free downloads (***incentives***). And as soon as the survey is online, take a look at the initial results. This will help you identify technical problems and any misunderstandings of your questions as early as possible.

8.4.2 How Many People Do I Need to Survey?

It is not easy to answer the question of how many participants you need for your survey. That is why most people simply survey as many people as possible. But that is nonsense. Save your respondents for future surveys. And save yourself the work of evaluating so much data. If you have clearly defined the purpose of your survey, the answer is easier: If, for example, you just want to find out why so many people leave your website without making a purchase, a few responses are usually enough to get to the bottom of it. In such cases, 100 respondents are ideal, but you can also get valuable results with just 20 or 30 responses. You are working purely qualitatively here; you want to know *why* people are not buying.

8.5 USABILITY TESTS

A usability test is something amazingly simple: you put potential users on the website and observe how they interact with it. The trick is to influence the test subjects as little as possible and to get them to describe their impressions and expectations by asking clever questions. You can always do usability tests. If you don't have anything for your own website yet, you can put people on your competitors' websites to learn how they interact with them and what is important to them. With so-called ***paper prototype tests***, you can test the basic structure of individual pages on your site: draw the navigation elements and important page elements such as images, text blocks and buttons on paper and present them to potential users. This allows you to check early on and cost-effectively whether the structure and labels are understood.

FIGURE 8.4 An image of an usability test generated by Midjourney. It's pretty close to how unspectacular such a test looks. The test person works with the website while a moderator sits next to them and watches closely. (Figure created using Midjourney v6.1.)

Prototypes are also useful. These are quickly assembled test versions of your site. They can be created with the help of AI, a website builder or a prototyping programme such as ***Figma*** or ***Adobe XD***. With such programmes, you create images, not web pages, but this is perfectly adequate for initial testing. This allows you to find out whether users understand the structure, can find the elements and whether they can find their way around.

Finally, you can test individual final pages before they are all finished. Changes are much more time-consuming in the production phase, but it is still better to find problems now than after the site has been published.

USABILITY AND USER EXPERIENCE – WHAT IS THE DIFFERENCE?

In everyday language, ***usability*** is sometimes described as "user-friendliness", but that's not how the term is defined in professional practice. According to the ISO 9241-11 standard, usability means that a system can be operated with:

- Effectiveness (the goal is achieved)
- Efficiency (with minimal effort)
- Satisfaction (meets users' needs and expectations)

Usability, therefore, goes beyond mere operability. Of course, pages must be easy to read and buttons must be recognisable as such. However, it is also crucial that the structure of the website is immediately understandable. Visitors must always know where they are. The texts should be prepared in a web-friendly manner, and the content and design must form a user-friendly whole. In short, a website with good usability is consistently geared towards the needs of its users in all aspects.

UX goes one step further. In addition to usability, it encompasses the entire UX from the initial perception to the actual use to later memories and emotions that users associate with the system. Ultimately, UX determines whether you achieve the goal you are pursuing with the website you are creating.

8.6 THE TEST CONCEPT OR TEST SCRIPT

As simple as usability tests are, a well-thought-out test concept is still important. In it, you define:

- Your research questions and hypotheses (i.e. your assumptions about what works well or what could be problematic)
- Applied test methods/methodology
- Number and type of participants
- Duration of the test sessions
- Schedule, participants

The test script builds on this and defines the following for a single test run:

- Welcome and introduction for participants
- Specific test tasks in wording
- Additional questions you may wish to ask

Always start with a simple task so that the test subjects can get used to the situation. AI is a great help when creating a test script. Even if you've never done this before, you can easily achieve good results. In my experience, Le Chat and ChatGPT delivered the best results. The creativity of Claude or Gemini did not help in this regard.

EXAMPLE PROMPT: CREATE TEST SCRIPT

Motivation: I want to find out whether the prototype of my website for the greeting card shop is convincing. Specifically, I want to test whether users are motivated to contact the operators, whether they find the information they are looking for, understand the navigation and find the content (text and images) appealing. I also want to know how they rate the products and their presentation.

Task: Create a complete test script for a 30-minute usability test. The script should contain tasks for the test subjects that specifically check the above-mentioned aspects. Take into account best practices for usability tests and formulate the tasks clearly and comprehensibly, as briefly as possible. Add notes for the moderator and possible observation criteria to the script.
Result: A complete test script with very specific, real-life tasks for the test subjects, starting very simple and gradually increasing in difficulty. Add moderation notes and criteria for evaluation. The script should ensure that I receive meaningful feedback on the points mentioned.
Example: An example of a task could be: "Your godchild is turning 10 next week. Find a card that you want to send them". An observation criterion could be: "Can the test person search through the selection easily? Are they missing information or assistance?"
Role: You are a user researcher who has already moderated and observed hundreds of tests and you are helping me to develop a professional and practical test script that even inexperienced users can use effectively.

The prompt is available for download here: bnfr.de/ai032

8.6.1 How Many Test Subjects Do I Need?

You'll be relieved to know that you only need five test subjects to uncover about 85% of the usability problems on your website. This often-cited figure from the well-known usability expert Jakob Nielsen is, of course, somewhat simplified. It is based on the assumption that these are *common* problems that affect at least a third of all users. Rarer but potentially serious problems may be overlooked. In addition, it is rare to be able to test the entire website in just one test. If your site is extensive or offers many functions, you will need more people. Nevertheless, remember what Steve Krug said earlier: any test is better than no test at all. Five test subjects are a good start, but one test subject is better than none. If you notice that one person trips over your carpet, you don't need to see four more people trip to know that you should change something. On the other hand, you can't be sure that you *don't* have a trip hazard on the floor if five people don't trip over it.

8.7 WHO TO RECRUIT? FINDING SUITABLE PARTICIPANTS

Ideal test subjects come from the target group – for an app that controls a wheelchair, you need people in wheelchairs; for a children's website, you need children. Project participants and company employees are unsuitable because they have too much prior knowledge. For diverse target groups, make sure you have a mix of genders, age groups and professions.

Various channels have proven successful for recruiting: from the use of existing customer databases to social media and specialised recruiting platforms. When selecting participants, different groups of users should be taken into account in order to cover as broad a spectrum as possible. Consider these avenues:

- Existing customers

- People on the newsletter mailing list
- Website visitors (recruited via pop-ups on the site)
- Advertisements in search engines or social media
- Social media followers
- Specialised recruitment agencies

The latter is the most professional approach because it allows you to specify exactly which criteria are important to you when selecting participants. However, it is also the most expensive option. Depending on how difficult your target group is to recruit, you can typically expect to pay between £30 and £100 per test person.

You can find more tips on usability testing at: bnfr.de/ai033

8.7.1 Technology – Remote or On-Site

Nowadays, most usability tests take place online. However, if you have the opportunity, it is definitely worthwhile to conduct usability tests on site, i.e. with the test person in the same room. You can then look at the computer or smartphone together. Personal interaction allows for even deeper insights and better observation. On-site tests are particularly worthwhile if the test environment influences the usage situation, such as in a shop or office.

Online tests (***remote tests***), on the other hand, are easier for you and the test subjects, as well as being more cost-effective and enabling you to reach a broader geographical target group. To do this, use a video conferencing system such as ***Zoom***, ***Microsoft Teams*** or ***Google Meet***. Screen sharing allows you to see what the test subject is doing on the test website. In online tests, test subjects are in their familiar environment, which can reduce influence – or increase it if children or colleagues are in the background.

It is common practice to record the test subject's screen and audio so that you can check later if you were unsure about what the test subject did in certain situations. This can happen because people are often faster than we are at observing, especially if we are the only ones documenting during the session. Remember that you need written consent to do this and that, according to the General Data Protection Regulation (GDPR), you are obliged to delete the recordings at the latest after the project has been completed.

8.7.2 Tips for Moderation

A professional usability test begins with a thorough briefing of the test subject. Explain the procedure to them and emphasise that it is the product that is being tested, not the person, and that they cannot do anything wrong. On the contrary, if problems arise with the website, this is exactly what provides valuable information for improvements.

Explain the ***think-aloud method*** to the test person. For example:

> Before each click, say why you want to click and what you expect the result to be. For example: "I'm now clicking on the red button up here because I think it will close the window." This way, I can understand why you are doing what you are doing.

During the test, your most important tool is silence. Inexperienced moderators tend to talk too much, thereby distorting the test results. For example, if a test subject asks, "Do I have to click here?", this is not actually a question. It is more like thinking aloud. The less you intervene in such moments, the more authentic the test person's behaviour will be. And you will notice that the less you say, the more independent the test person becomes and the more they work as they would if no one were watching them.

If silence does not help, there are three moderation techniques: Echo, Boomerang and Columbo. ***Echo*** means that you simply repeat the test subject's last words with a questioning intonation. Such a minimal intervention is almost always enough to encourage the person to continue.

Test person: I don't know, do I have to click there now?
You: Do I have to click there now?

With the ***boomerang***, you repeat the question in different words:

Test subject: Will that take me to the next page?
You: What do you think?

The ***Columbo*** method, named after the bumbling TV detective of the same name from the 1970s, works with unfinished sentences, which the test subject then usually completes themselves:

Test person: That's strange. Nothing is displayed here.
You: You mean, there, um… there's, uh… nothing… um.

With these three tricks, you communicate, but you don't influence. You don't tell the test subject to just carry on, but you avoid it quite elegantly. Try it out; it's actually really fun.

Avoid making judgemental or supposedly reassuring comments throughout the test. Statements such as "no one has ever done that before" can influence the test subject's behaviour and thus distort the results. It is also best to refrain from making comments about speed or time management. Ideally, you should not even say "good", but only something like "thank you" when a task is completed. The key to a well-moderated usability test lies in restrained, encouraging moderation. Your task is to create a setting in which the test subject feels as comfortable as possible, behaves naturally and shows authentic reactions. The techniques described will help you to react professionally even in difficult situations without distorting the test results.

8.7.3 Guerrilla Tests as an Alternative

If you are short on cash or in a hurry, ***guerrilla testing*** is an option. To do this, you spontaneously approach test subjects in public places such as cafés, libraries or train stations. Or you go to the neighbouring office and ask for volunteers. If there is no other option, recruit from among your friends or relatives. However, try to reveal as little as possible about your involvement in the implementation in order to get the most honest feedback possible. These methods are not ideal, but remember Steve Krug's phrase: any test is better than no test at all.

8.8 TESTING WITH AI?

AI is getting better and better at analysing websites and understanding complex content. That's why there are specialist providers who use AI to test the usability and UX of your site. However, this only works to a limited extent and is so expensive that it's out of the question for smaller projects anyway. There is also a fundamental problem with this: when we let AI test usability, it basically does the same thing I do as a UX professional: we have both seen many websites, we have read a lot about how to create good websites – and in the future, AI may even have analysed many videos of how real people interact with websites (which is currently still missing from the training data of the major AIs). Even if an AI has seen thousands of such videos, it will never have seen all possible design approaches. After all, we can design a simple registration form in an infinite number of ways: you can use different colours, fonts, font sizes, field borders, colour backgrounds, different labels or labels, make the elements larger or smaller, and position them differently. And for pages that offer more than just a simple form, the implementation possibilities increase exponentially. So it will never be possible to know all the design options.

Of course, the more you've seen, the better you get. But no one can know everything, not even AI. It can only derive rules from what it knows and make informed guesses about what works for users and what doesn't. That's also what I do when I write a so-called ***usability review***. I try to put myself in the users' shoes and take a thorough look at a site. I click through it as I imagine a real person from the target group would do. I note down everything that I think could be problematic for this person. This is a first starting point, but it cannot replace a real usability test. Many scientific studies have been conducted on this topic. Even the world's best UX professionals encountered two problems:

1. Some problems experienced by real users were overlooked.
2. Some of the problems identified by the UX professionals were not problems for real users at all.

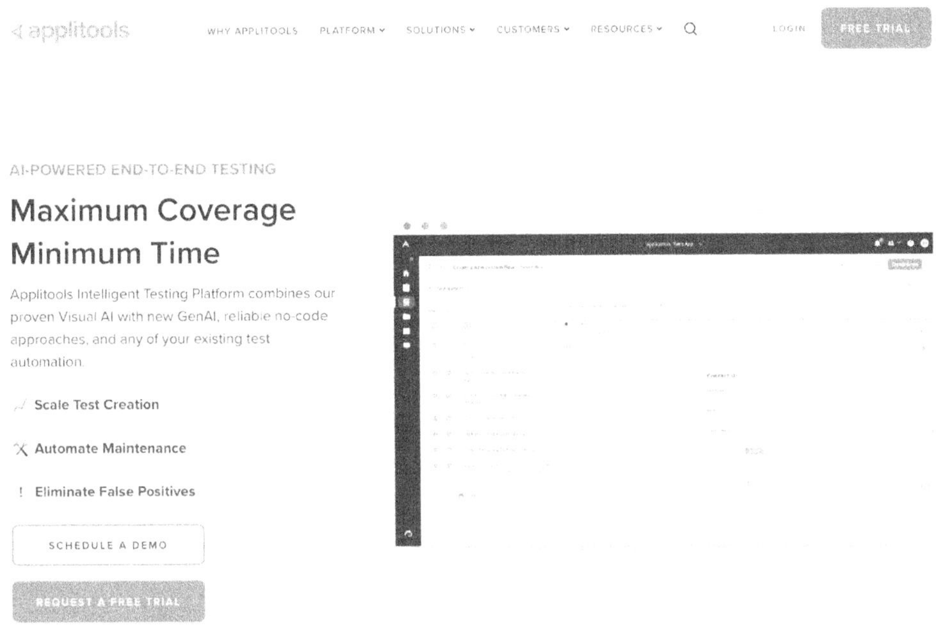

FIGURE 8.5 Applitools uses AI to test websites. It does not claim to replace usability testing, but it should still help to uncover problems.

And AI will be no different in this respect. For this reason, as long as we do not have superintelligence, testing with real users cannot be completely replaced. However, AI tools can provide support in the future, for example, by automating repetitive tasks such as checking forms or analysing large amounts of data from access statistics (***web analytics***) to uncover noticeable patterns in usage behaviour. They can also help identify accessibility issues. Or they can predict eye movements on websites. AI can therefore be used in combination with traditional usability methods to achieve better results.

For anyone developing interactive products, it would generally not be a good idea to completely forego usability testing. Contact with people from the target group is incredibly valuable for a better understanding of their needs and ways of thinking.

8.9 CASE STUDY: TESTING FOR A SMALL SITE

Let's take a look at how to test effectively on a small budget. Let's use the example of fitness coaches Frieder and Fabi again. They had allocated £800 for testing, which quickly paid for itself. First, they determined the most important things they wanted visitors to do on their site:

1. Find a course schedule and book a trial lesson
2. View trainer profiles and get in touch
3. Subscribe to the video service

They decided to start with classic guerrilla testing: they sat down with a tablet in a nearby café and approached guests who might fit the target group. "Would you have 5 minutes to look at a new fitness website? As a thank you, you'll receive a £10 voucher for the café". Of the 15 people they approached, nine agreed. This cost them £90. The volunteers were given a central task to complete: "You're interested in fitness classes, and a friend has recommended this site to you. Find out if there's anything suitable for you and book a trial lesson". They asked the test subjects to think out loud. What they saw was sobering: almost all of the testers initially clicked on "Courses", but then ended up in an overview that confused them. "Where can I find the trial lesson now?" was the most common question. It took several clicks for the testers to find the right path – two of the nine even gave up beforehand.

Frieder and Fabi then optimised the site and wanted to ensure that the problems had been resolved. They also wanted to review the other tasks. They conducted an online usability test. Through a professional provider, they recruited six people from their target group, sports enthusiasts between the ages of 25 and 45. Total cost: £480. They met with them via Google Meet and asked them to share their screens. They gave them the task of booking a trial lesson, followed by another to subscribe to the training videos. One problem quickly became apparent: the pricing structure of the video subscription was unclear to many. "Is that per month or per video?" several test subjects asked. The advantages of the subscription over individual courses were also not immediately apparent.

As the third component of their test strategy, the training duo relied on a short online survey. They rented a tool for one month at a cost of £100. After 30 seconds of visiting the website, a discreet pop-up appeared with the question: "What are you looking for on our website?" The responses from 131 visitors revealed a surprising finding: only 7% were interested in outdoor activities – which is actually the focus of their offering.

These three activities cost a total of £730. However, they quickly paid for themselves: the course schedule page was simplified, and a clear CTA "Book a trial lesson" was placed as a button at the top and bottom of the page. The pricing structure for the video subscription was communicated more clearly, with a clear table comparing the options. The outdoor activities were given a more prominent place in the menu and on the home page. They also planned a separate subpage on the topic of outdoor activities in order to be found even more easily in search engines.

Their success proved them right: the number of trial lesson bookings rose by 27% and the conversion rate for video subscriptions almost tripled.

8.10 CONTINUOUS IMPROVEMENT AND ESTABLISHING FEEDBACK

With larger websites, it unfortunately often happens that valuable insights are gained from user tests or other feedback is collected – but then disappears forever into a folder on the computer. There are many reasons for this. Often, there is simply not enough time for implementation, sometimes the insights are not communicated well or it is unclear who should take care of the improvements.

A structured process for implementing ideas is therefore important. This begins during the tests: document problems and suggestions for improvement immediately after the test. A simple table with three columns is sufficient to start with: What is the problem? How important is it? Who should solve it?

Prioritising the findings is the next critical step. Not everything that stands out in tests needs to be fixed immediately. Focus on what affects many users or what leads to abandoned purchases (or what impairs the core function of your site). What has a big effect but requires little effort comes first. What brings little benefit but means a lot of effort has to wait.

It is also important to communicate the results effectively. The development, design, content and marketing teams all need to understand why certain changes are necessary. Be as specific as possible: "The buy button was overlooked by three of the five test subjects" is more convincing than "the button is poorly placed". Even more convincing are short video clips from the tests that show where users have problems (so-called ***highlight videos***).

When correcting problems, it is best to proceed iteratively, i.e. step by step. This way, everyone can see quick results and you can check the effect of each change and make adjustments if necessary. In addition, you will not overwhelm your team or users with too many changes at once. Always remember to check the changes. Has anything really improved? If not, why not? And sometimes a correction unintentionally causes new problems.

It is best to establish regular reviews. It is always a good idea to conduct a small usability test once a year, or more frequently for larger websites or major changes. Usability optimisation is not a one-off project, but an ongoing process. With each correction, your site gets a little better. Celebrate your successes! Is the conversion rate increasing, are there more enquiries, or are support requests decreasing? This is a credit to the whole team, so they should know about it. This motivates future optimisations and creates support for further tests.

8.10.1 Even Small Sites Can Be Improved

If you run your website on your own, you don't need complex processes to implement feedback. But even for your small site, insights into potential improvements should not be forgotten. Keep a simple list, for example, in a note-taking app on your smartphone or in a to-do list programme. Make a note of problems as soon as you notice them – whether through customer feedback, your own observations or tests.

The most important question you should ask yourself with every problem is: Could this cause me to lose customers? If you receive a call because someone cannot find your opening hours on the website, this is a more critical problem than a link in the footer of your site that is too faint. It is best to set aside one hour a week for optimisation, for example, during a quiet hour in the evening or at the weekend. Also, remember to check after every change: did it work? For example, if you place the booking button more prominently on, will you get more online bookings? You can also always ask your customers. A simple "How did you find out about us?" in a customer conversation often yields valuable insights. Remember: your website is like your shop window – it should always be inviting and up to date. Small, regular improvements are far better than a major relaunch every few years.

8.11 EVALUATE WHAT PEOPLE ARE LOOKING AT – WEB ANALYTICS

It sounds promising: you can see which pages of your site are viewed by how many people, for how long and in what order and use this information to make your site even more successful. That is the basic idea behind the evaluation of web analytics. There is nothing wrong with that; concrete figures enable better decisions to be made. And yet we have to remain realistic when it comes to small and medium-sized websites: if you only have a handful of visits per day, statistics are difficult to use. This is because good and, above all, accurate statistical analysis is based on large amounts of data, which you rarely get with small websites. Some of your pages may even only be visited every few days – the more pages you have, the more the number of visitors is spread out. And yet, even with only a few hundred visits per month, you can still gain valuable insights from the access data. You just need to focus on the essential metrics and interpret them correctly. With only a few visits, you will often see large jumps. A 100% increase in traffic can occur on a day when ten visitors open a page instead of five, which is not a reason to celebrate in absolute terms. However, supposedly poor figures are no reason to be upset either. Instead, always pay attention to longer-term trends and look at monthly figures rather than daily figures.

FIGURE 8.6 Where do visitors come from, where do they go? The analytics tool Matomo answers this question for this page.

It is very important that you always keep your website goal in mind (see Chapter 4, "Step 2: Select the Best Tools"). If you have defined the goal of your website as motivating interested people to visit your shop, then you do not need to have a long dwell time on your pages. It is sufficient for someone to find the address or opening hours and then visit in person – the page visit may then be completed within a few seconds. And yet it was a successful visit, and your site clearly achieved its goal.

8.11.1 How Does Data Collection Work?

The basic principle behind access statistics is that ***cookies*** or so-called ***server logs*** are used to record visitor behaviour. Server logs are created automatically on every web server, unless they have been deactivated. Every time a page on your website is requested, the server logs this. It records the date and time of access, the requested URL, the IP address of the device from which the request came, the browser used and the page from which the link to us came (if the visit was made via a link). This is technically simple and works without cookies. However, it does not allow you to recognise when the same person returns later or how long they view a single page. This is possible if you use cookies.

Cookies are small text files that are stored in the visitor's browser. When you open a website, the analytics tool generates a random identification number on your first visit and stores it in a cookie. Each time you visit another page, your browser sends this ID, which allows the tool to recognise that you are the same person who has already opened a page. Analytics tools such as ***Google Analytics*** also use JavaScript code, which is embedded on every page. This code can collect much more information than server logs: it measures how long you stay on individual pages, tracks your clicks on links and buttons, records how far you scroll on the pages, etc. This way, analytics tools learn not only which pages are opened and how often but also what people do there and how they navigate through the site. They can even analyse when you visit a shop multiple times, compare products there and only decide to buy days later.

8.11.2 Data Protection and Analytics

This description makes it clear that analytics is a data protection issue. I want to be able to decide for myself how much I reveal about myself, and that is exactly what the European GDPR stipulates. That is why websites must obtain the consent of visitors before setting a tracking cookie. As a result, a significant proportion of visits are no longer recorded – between 30% and 70% of visits, depending on the target group. This means that what we measure is no longer reality, but only the behaviour of those who have consented to tracking. In my experience from usability tests, virtually everyone has developed an automatic response to close the typical cookie banners as quickly as possible. Some click on "Reject all" immediately, others on "Accept all".

And the problem is actually getting worse: more and more browsers are blocking tracking cookies by default, and iPhones and increasingly Android smartphones have strict privacy settings. Ad blockers are also being used more and more to avoid tracking.

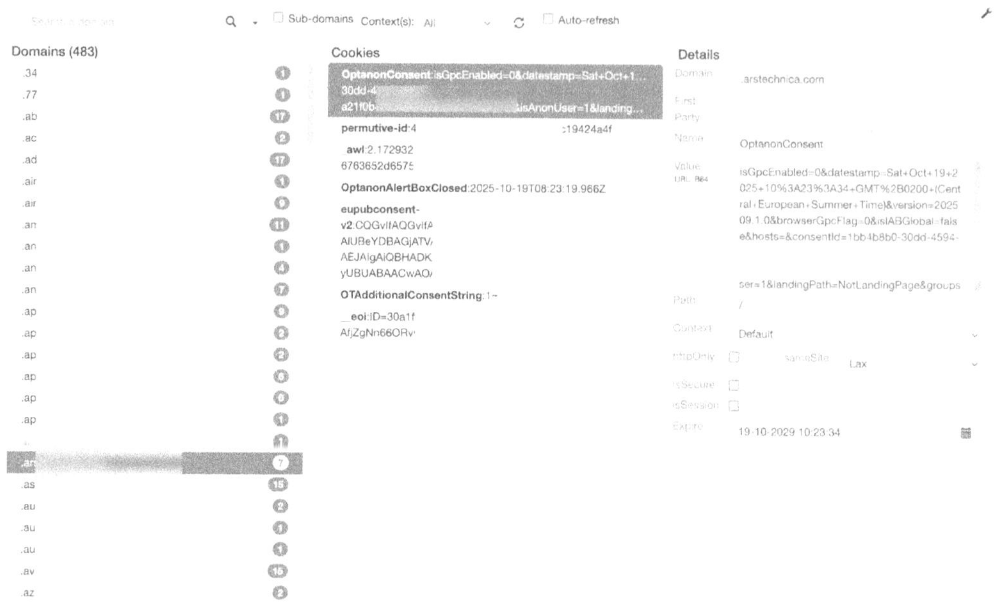

FIGURE 8.7 I have 483 cookies in this browser alone, which I rarely use – almost all of them are for analytics (displayed with the Cookie Quick Manager extension).

This means that the data collected is becoming increasingly incomplete. And the legal requirements are complicated and change frequently. This is another reason why you are well advised to follow the principle of data minimisation: only collect what you really need. We tend to collect all the data first and then never get around to evaluating it all. Not only this is a waste of resources and can give us a guilty conscience, but it also violates the legal principles of data protection.

The standard installation of ***Google Analytics*** activates complete tracking of all visits. This requires the consent of visitors and entails extensive documentation obligations. For example, you must conclude a data processing agreement with Google and

FIGURE 8.8 Ubiquitous – cookie banners. This example from cnn.com shows best practice – the accept button is not more prominent than the others and does not trick visitors into accepting.

FIGURE 8.9 With Matomo, you can see which links visitors have clicked on the page. The percentages indicate how many per cent of the clicks they received.

document the data processing clearly. That is why many sites use the open source solution ***Matomo***. Here, you can activate a mode that does not use cookies and anonymises the IP addresses of visitors. Many lawyers assume that you then do not need the consent of visitors. You can also rely exclusively on the server logs, which are almost always generated automatically, and evaluate them with tools such as ***GoAccess***. Although these provide less detail, they are perfectly adequate for most cases. However, you need some technical background knowledge to install and operate such tools.

8.11.3 What Should We Evaluate?

Take a look at the definition of your site's goals in the rough concept. From this, you can clearly deduce what actions visitors to your website need to take in order for you to achieve these goals. Let's take our barber Lars Schneider from the example: he wants to use his website to attract people to his shop, nothing more. This means that all the visitors should do on the site is look at it, be convinced they want to visit, look up the address and go to the barber. The situation is similar for our café "Bistro Verde". The two fitness coaches, Frieder and Fabi, on the other hand, want a little more from their site: they want to attract participants to their on-site courses. But additionally, they also offer online courses that people can book and use directly. In this case, we can directly determine whether visitors are performing the desired action.

The first figure we always look at is the ***total number of visitors*** (***visits***). This gives an initial impression of your website's reach. However, the trend over time is always more important than the absolute figures: are the numbers rising over time? Are they falling? Are there fluctuations, for example, with the seasons?

The analysis of ***traffic sources*** (***referrers***) shows how people find you. Directly by entering the URL? Via search engines? Via KIs? From blogs or media sites? Here, you may also discover fans who link to you, whom you didn't even know about. It is worth considering maintaining long-term contact with them. The development of the channels over time is also interesting. More traffic from search engines indicates that you have a stronger position there. More direct visits to your site can be a sign of growing awareness or that your flyers, business cards or other advertising materials are well received. Social media traffic shows your visibility on social networks.

Ultimately, what visitors do on your website is crucial. The ***length of stay*** (***duration of visit***) can be a sign of the relevance of your content – although the length of stay also increases if visitors find it difficult to navigate and cannot immediately find what they are looking for.

The ***bounce rate*** is the percentage of visitors who leave the website after viewing only one page. High values for this rate can indicate problems. In our example of the barber and the café, however, a high bounce rate is completely normal: visitors quickly find the information they are looking for and thus have a good UX.

In our example of the fitness site, we can determine the ***conversion rate***. This indicates the percentage of visitors who subscribe to the video courses. However, conversion goals can also be contact enquiries, clicking on the telephone number or even just visiting certain information pages.

In any case, avoid getting annoyed by the metrics. With only a few hits per day, the results often fluctuate greatly. You will have to do without detailed demographic analyses or the examination of usage behaviour for individual segments anyway. Instead, focus on basic trends and combine quantitative data with qualitative insights. In other words, don't forget the people behind the numbers. Even for large websites, analytics only show behaviour patterns. However, they do not provide any clues as to the underlying motivation of visitors or whether they were ultimately satisfied with their visit to your site. That's why we always need qualitative feedback as well.

AI AND ANALYTICS

You would think that AI would be a great help when it comes to website analytics. It is, and sites such as Amazon have been using AI for many years to increase their sales by optimising their website. But in practice, for those of us who run small websites, AI is of little use in this area. Of course, you can use Claude or Le Chat to explain terms and learn about the reasons why certain metrics have changed on your site. But the idea of providing AI with your site's access statistics and then getting tips on how to improve the site in a matter of seconds doesn't work for two reasons:

1. For data protection reasons, you cannot simply upload access data to any AI. The most convenient option is therefore to use the AI tools integrated by the providers, such as Google Analytics. This provides a number of AI tools for evaluation, but then you have to use this solution, which many people do not want to do.
2. The reason why AI can only help you to a limited extent here is that it knows as little as you do. That's just the nature of the beast: analytics tell you what users are doing on the website. But you don't know *why* they are doing it, and AI can only guess. Of course, it can consult statistics on this, and it will certainly get better at this in the future. But the training data of large language models such as ChatGPT contains very little of this, so AI will always come up with an answer to such questions – but, true to golden rule number 3, it can be misleading.

8.12 TEST AND OPTIMISE PERFORMANCE

Fast is good. At least when it comes to websites. This is evident in every user test. If websites take longer than 2 or 3 seconds to appear on the screen, visitors become nervous. This is particularly problematic when they visit our website on a smartphone in an area with poor mobile network coverage or from a moving train. Long loading times annoy people, who then take action and stop loading a site if it does not appear on their screen within 3 or 4 seconds. Countless studies show that people are impatient. A figure from Amazon is often cited: allegedly, improving the loading time of their pages by 100 milliseconds increases sales by 1%.

This makes it clear that loading time is not just a technical issue, but also a crucial UX factor. We have long relied on technology. We assumed that servers, modems, internet connections, computers, graphics cards and browsers would become faster and faster – and that pages would load quickly as a result. But we are undoing these very technical advances by incorporating more and more photos, multiple fonts, videos and other elements. This makes our pages more attractive and improves the UX on the one hand. Unfortunately, however, it also worsens the UX because the pages ultimately take too long to load.

8.13 WHAT REALLY MATTERS – INITIAL RESULTS

It is not the time it takes for *all* content to load completely that is decisive, but how long it takes for visitors to see something they can interact with. A page can take several seconds to load additional elements, as long as the core content appears quickly, creating the *impression* of speed.

For years, search engines such as Google have also been incorporating loading speed into their website rankings. Those that load slowly end up further down in the hit lists. This means that poor performance is also an SEO problem that you need to take seriously. Overloaded pages that are slow to load not only annoy visitors but also have a negative impact on visibility on Google.

FIGURE 8.10 At webpagetest.org, you can test any site for its loading speed. Here we see the results for thetimes.com.

8.13.1 Technical and Conceptual Approaches to Acceleration

You can speed up your pages with a few technical tricks. But you shouldn't rely on them alone, because you can start with the design, graphics and programming and avoid cluttering your pages with unnecessary elements. In general, it also makes sense for the UX to pause and ask yourself for each individual element you want to place on a page: Does this element benefit the user? Does it help me achieve the goals I have for the site?

You can start here, in particular, to make your pages faster:

1. images – number, quality and size
2. the code, i.e. HTML, CSS and JavaScript
3. external files, especially web fonts and external scripts

It is also important to look at how a page is actually transferred. It does not come as a finished piece from the server. The browser has to request many individual parts: HTML, CSS, JavaScript, images and embedded content. Each element requires its own connection. Taken together, this can significantly reduce performance. For performance, it is therefore often better to embed CSS and JavaScript files directly into the HTML code or at least optimise them so that fewer requests are necessary.

8.13.2 Images Are the Biggest Chunk, but Scripts and Fonts Also Play a Role

Images are usually the largest item in terms of data volume. If you want to seriously optimise your website, start with the images. They should not be larger than necessary. If you display images with a maximum width of 1,200 pixels, you should only transfer them in this width. Always save photos in JPG or, even better, WebP format, as these are optimised for this purpose. Increase the compression until the quality is still acceptable. Save line drawings, diagrams and similar content as PNG files. This often saves a lot of bytes without visibly impairing the display for visitors.

Responsive design poses a particular problem: although it is important that our pages look their best on all devices, images are often transferred in their full glory, for example, with a width of 1,200 pixels – even if they are only displayed at a width of 380 pixels on a smartphone. The CSS property `object-fit` and the HTML attribute `srcset` provide a remedy. Details can be found in Section 6.8.5, "Responsive Web Design – Flexibility for All Screen Sizes".

Finally, ***lazy loading*** is an optimisation strategy that speeds up page loading and saves resources. The idea behind it is that users only need to see the elements at the top of the page immediately – they may never see the elements further down because they click on a link and leave the page again soon afterwards. So instead of loading all the content of a page immediately, only the top elements are loaded first. Further content is only loaded when users scroll down. This is particularly advantageous for image-heavy websites or social media with endless scrolling.

When it comes to code, it is important that it is lean, cleanly structured and as free as possible from superfluous definitions. The following often applies: include CSS files in the header (`<head>`) and JavaScript at the end of the page. This is because CSS is needed immediately to display the content correctly, while JavaScript usually provides interactivity or tracking functions that can wait a few moments. Comments, spaces and indentations make code more readable for us humans, but they also increase the file size. In this case, it helps to ***minify*** the code, i.e. remove unnecessary elements. In addition, the code can be compressed on the server (***gzip***), which modern browsers can process effortlessly.

Web fonts are wonderful for making our pages look appealing, but they increase the amount of data to be transferred and make it more complex. The fewer fonts and font styles you use, the better. You can also use tricks, such as assuming that large desktop screens are more likely to have fast internet connections and loading the fonts there, but not on small screens. However, such adaptive techniques are a compromise between aesthetics and performance.

You should also be careful with external ***scripts***. Every integrated library and every additional script for analysis or animation bloats the site. A particularly effective method

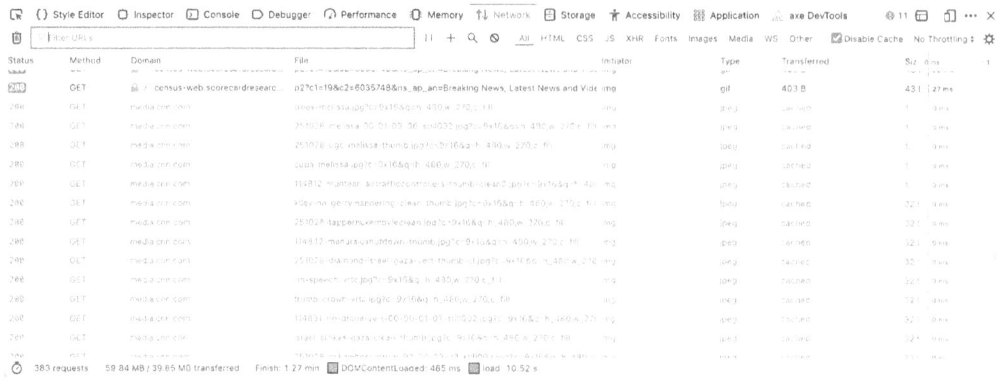

FIGURE 8.11 In Chrome or Firefox (shown here), you can right-click on "Inspect" and select the "Network" tab to see which files the current page has loaded.

of keeping performance under control is to set a ***performance budget***. This means that you specify the maximum time it should take for visitors to be able to use the page. To do this, choose a typical device (e.g. an older smartphone) and a typical connection (e.g. LTE) and use this to determine the maximum number of kilobytes or megabytes your page can have. All elements – HTML, CSS, JavaScript, images, fonts, etc. – must then share this total size. If a website requires a complex tracking script, it may have to do without many images in order not to exceed the budget.

This ties in with the recommendation not to simply always use the most popular CMS (e.g. WordPress) for implementation because it is convenient. Such systems often come with many features that you may not need, but which increase the loading time. (You can find alternatives in Chapter 5, "Step 3: Determine the Optimal Structure of the Website".) Sometimes, a pure HTML page is sufficient if there are only a few subpages. Or you can use a leaner CMS system which is optimised for performance. Similarly, when adding videos, audio, animations or endless images, you need to ask yourself whether visitors will benefit from them. These basic design questions are part of the topic of performance. It's not just about technical tricks, but also about design discipline.

8.13.3 Specific Optimisation Tips and Measurement Methods

To understand how much your measures are helping, you need to measure them. There are a few tools that can help you with this. If you want to get started with this topic, you can take a look at webpagetest.org. Here, you can enter the URL and test conditions and get a detailed breakdown of the loading time. There is also ***Google Lighthouse***, an open-source tool that allows you to check performance, accessibility and SEO aspects. The online service ***PageSpeed Insights***, on the other hand, shows both laboratory data (like Lighthouse) and field data, i.e. real usage data from the Chrome browser, which is collected anonymously. Finally, ***Google Search Console*** also provides insights, but only for sites that you have verified.

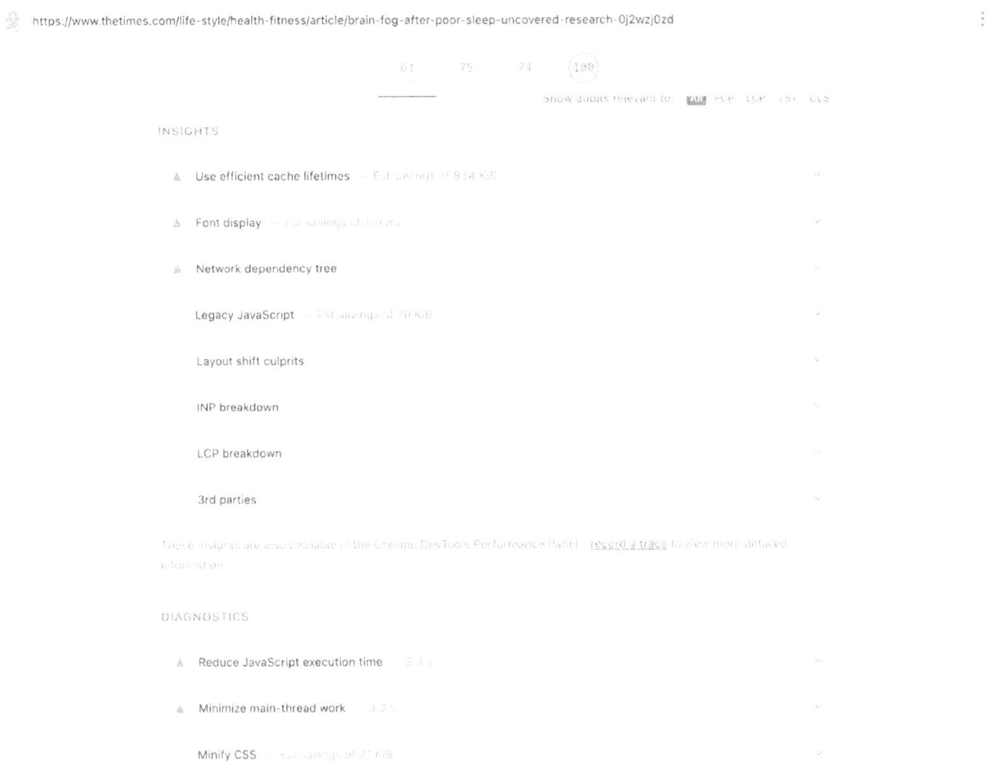

FIGURE 8.12 Google Lighthouse is integrated into Chrome and provides a detailed analysis of the current site with suggestions for improvement.

In all of these tools, you will repeatedly encounter ***Core Web Vitals*** (***CWV***). These are three metrics that show how fast a page is from the user's perspective. This is where it gets really technical, so I have provided additional information online for you: bnfr.de/ai034

As an alternative to all these measuring instruments, you can also carry out real tests under realistic conditions: with your smartphone in a moderately covered network, on the move or in places with poor connection. This will give you first-hand experience of what it feels like to use your website under real conditions.

8.13.4 Caching and CDN

Caching can contribute significantly to the performance and user-friendliness of websites. The idea behind it is to cache frequently used data so that it is available more quickly when accessed repeatedly. The user's browser plays a central role in this by storing static content such as images, stylesheets, JavaScript files and fonts locally on the user's device. When the website is visited again, these resources can be loaded directly from the local storage, which significantly reduces loading times and data volume.

Caching is also used on the server: web servers store frequently requested content in RAM or on fast SSDs. This is particularly useful for dynamic content that has to be generated with every request, such as database queries or calculations. By caching these results, the server can deliver the content much faster, which is especially important for content management systems that use databases.

A special form of caching takes place in ***content delivery networks*** (***CDNs***). These are server networks distributed around the world that store copies of website content. When someone visits the website, the content is not delivered from the actual server, but from the nearest CDN server. This not only significantly reduces loading time but also relieves the actual web server. The combination of these different caching mechanisms leads to significantly improved website performance. Users benefit from faster loading times, while operators can use their server infrastructure more efficiently.

Smaller sites can also use a CDN. The best-known provider, ***Cloudflare***, has a free plan that already offers a lot. The setup takes a little time, but it can be done without any problems, even by laypeople. For websites such as those I give as examples here in the book (hairdresser, fitness site, greeting cards, bistro), I personally wouldn't bother. For these, it is sufficient to set up the pages cleanly and optimise them as described in the previous section.

Ultimately, optimising performance is like optimising usability: you can always keep optimising, but even a few basic measures and good conceptual decisions can lead to noticeable improvements. So don't just think about performance in conceptual terms, but also take into account the most important technical principles of optimisation. Then you'll have the best chance of ensuring that your pages are easy to use even under realistic, tough conditions, offering a good UX – and being rated highly by search engines in terms of performance.

8.13.5 AI Can Optimise

There are specialised providers that use AI to optimise the performance of websites. However, these are usually subject to a fee and are aimed more at professionals. But you can also use large language models for basic optimisation:

EXAMPLE PROMPT: PERFORMANCE OPTIMISATION OF EXISTING PAGES

Motivation: I want to improve the loading time of the website www.xyz.de/index.html in order to optimise the UX and increase performance.

Task: Analyse the HTML, CSS and JavaScript code of the specified page and identify specific factors that affect the loading time. Suggest concrete measures for optimisation.

Result: Create a structured analysis that includes the following points:

1. Identified problems that affect loading time
2. Specific optimisation suggestions to fix the problems
3. Code examples for implementing the optimisations that can be applied directly

Role: You are a performance expert in web development who provides specific and actionable solutions. Ensure that the code of the specified URL is actually analysed and that general information from the web is not simply used.

The prompt to copy: bnfr.de/ai035

Be sure to use a model that has access to web pages. Otherwise, you will only receive general information, not information specifically tailored to your pages.

8.14 CHECKLISTS FOR OPTIMISATION

Here is a list of the most important things you can do to optimise your website:

Simple, inexpensive usability tests

- Test early, before the site goes live, to avoid costly changes later on
- A small number of test subjects are sufficient to identify significant problems
- Ask test subjects to think aloud to understand where ambiguities arise
- Use simple methods such as guerrilla testing in a café or among friends if time or budget is very limited
- Note down problems immediately after the test, prioritise them and fix them promptly

Quick feedback and direct insights

- When leaving the website, display a short, simple pop-up with a very short survey to find out the reasons for abandonment
- Directly track whether change ideas bring improvements (e.g. more bookings, fewer abandonments)

Optimise performance and technical basis

- Only use absolutely necessary content and functions to achieve fast loading times
- Compress images and upload them in the appropriate size to reduce data volume
- Remove unnecessary scripts or plug-ins and use lazy loading where possible
- Find weaknesses with free tools (e.g. PageSpeed Insights) and fix them step by step

Ensure continuous improvement

- Make small adjustments regularly instead of infrequent, large relaunches
- Regularly monitor successes (e.g. conversion rates)
- Keep an eye on sources of feedback (e.g. emails, conversations, mini-surveys) and continuously implement findings

CHAPTER 9

Step 7

Promote and Distribute the Site

Even the best website is useless if no one can find it. Discover effective strategies for greater visibility – from SEO and social media to podcasts. With AI support, you can reach your target audience in a targeted and cost-effective manner.

In the previous steps, you designed, programmed, created and filled your website with content. You have even tested and optimised it. Now it's time to share it with the world. You need to publish it and make sure that your target audience finds and actually visits the website. So let's get started.

9.1 CHOOSE A HOST

If you haven't already done so, you must now decide on a ***host***, i.e. a service provider that provides a server and ensures that others can access your website. You have probably already done this in step 2. If you have opted for a website builder provider such as Wix, the site will be created directly on their server. You can read more about the decision criteria in Chapter 5, "Step 3: Determine the Optimal Structure of the Website".

9.2 DOMAIN NAME – SHORT BUT CRUCIAL

Some people quickly click on a domain name when they book their host. Others make a science out of finding the perfect name. I recommend taking a middle ground. The domain name is important, but ultimately other criteria are far more decisive for your success. On the one hand, people need to remember the name, and on the other hand, a good domain name helps you to be found more easily by search engines.

What do you need to bear in mind? Your own domain always has a so-called ***top-level domain*** (TLD), i.e. an ending such as *.de*, *.at*, *.ch*, *.com* or *.org*. This is preceded by the so-called ***second-level domain***. Together, they form the actual domain name, for

DOI: 10.1201/9781003726708-9

example, benutzerfreun.de. The TLD identifies a country (e.g. *.de* for Germany, *.uk* for the United Kingdom) or a general purpose (e.g. *.com* for commercial sites). Addresses such as benutzerfreunde.provider.de (this is a ***subdomain*** of provider.de) or example.com, example.provider.com and www.provider.com/example (a subdirectory within the domain provider.de) are not separate domains.

You no longer need the *www.* before the domain name. Originally, it was used to distinguish web servers from other services such as mail or FTP servers for file exchange (mail.provider.de and ftp.provider.de). Today, this is no longer technically necessary. Most websites do without the *www.*, as it is shorter and easier to type. However, it is best to set up both versions of your domain – with and without *www.* – and set one version as the default, with the other automatically redirecting to it. This ensures that your website will be found by search engines, AI and users.

9.3 REQUIREMENTS FOR DOMAIN NAMES

If you are looking for a domain name, these are the rules you must follow: The second-level domain name may be between 3 and 63 characters long. Some registrars also offer two-character domains, but these are almost always already taken or very expensive. The name may only contain letters, numbers and hyphens (hyphens should not be at the beginning or end) and may not consist exclusively of numbers.

Many registrars support accented letters, umlauts and non-Latin scripts (Arabic, Cyrillic, etc.). However, it is best to avoid non-ASCII characters in the domain name, as this is less prone to errors. For example, write suesse-sachen.de or cafe-balu.fr. If you want to be on the safe side, you can also register süße-sachen.de and café-balu.fr, but I do not recommend registering all possible spellings or even possible typos. This only costs unnecessary money and, thanks to search engines, you can usually be found regardless of the exact name users type into the search box. Your domain name should be concise and easy to remember. It is therefore a good idea to keep it as short as possible so that users don't have to type too much. But more importantly, your domain name should be catchy. It is best if the name does not contain any little-known abbreviations nor common URL components such as *www, net, com, org* or *edu*. These only lead to confusion.

To find an available domain name, first collect relevant terms that fit your project, company or brand. Think about the carewords of your target group; see Section 7.2.1, "Carewords – Identifying and Using the Right Keywords".

EXAMPLE PROMPT: BRAINSTORMING DOMAIN NAMES

Motivation: I want to find original domain names for my café "Bistro Verde" that include a mix of names with and without the café name. In addition, suggestions should also be made that incorporate place names to emphasise the regional affiliation.

Task: Create 14 domain suggestions that are well thought out and creative. Please consider the following:

- Some of the suggestions should directly incorporate the name "Bistro Verde".
- Other suggestions should choose alternative approaches such as puns, metaphors or themes.
- Another part of the suggestions may incorporate place names such as Oldenburg or regional terms (e.g. Weser) to create a connection to the locality.

Result: A list of 14 domain suggestions offering a balanced mix of names such as "Bistro Verde", creative alternatives and local references.

Examples:

With names: BistroVerdeOldenburg.co.uk, BistroVerdeGenuss.co.uk.
Without names: GreenDelight.co.uk, VeggieMagic.co.uk.
With local references: GenussAmWeserufer.de, OldenburgerBistro.de.
Role: Take on the role of an experienced brand and name consultant who masters creative techniques and develops innovative, tailor-made ideas.

The prompt to copy: bnfr.de/ai036

Once you have a candidate, use online tools such as lookup.icann.org or www.iana.org/whois to check availability. If the domain is already taken, try variations such as different top-level domains (e.g. *.ai*, *.com*, *.net*, *.org*) or alternative spellings. It is essential to ensure that the name does not infringe any trademark rights. Use a search engine to see if anyone is using the name as a brand name – even if no domain has been registered for it, you are not allowed to use it. To be on the safe side, you can check with brand registration offices (***WIPO Global Brand Database*** or ***EUIPO***; for jurisdiction-specific searches, use the official national registries e.g. ***DPMA*** for Germany, ***USPTO*** for the US and ***UKIPO*** for the UK). Registering a trademark yourself is usually not worthwhile, as others are not allowed to use your name even if you can prove that you have been using it for a long time. However, if legal disputes arise, it can be advantageous to have the trademark registered.

It is best to test the impact of your planned domain name: casually mention the name you have come up with to friends and acquaintances. A few days later, ask them to spell the name for you. If there are too many mistakes, you should look for a more catchy name.

Once you have found a suitable domain that is available, register it directly via the domain checker or a host. You can find a checklist to help you choose a host here: bnfr.de/ai037

9.3.1 Being Found in Search Engines – And with AI

What do people need to do before they buy something on your website, contact you or simply find out more about you? First, people have to find your website. Most do this via search engines. Search engines are integrated into all browsers, so suggestions from search engines appear as soon as you start typing something into the browser's address bar. Occasionally, people know a URL and type it in directly, but this is the exception. And even visiting search engines directly is becoming increasingly rare: more and more people are asking a language model such as ChatGPT or Le Chat for information and also using them for web research. Or they use voice control to activate virtual assistants such as Siri, Cortana or Alexa. In the future, we will often use agents to perform tasks that we used to do ourselves in several steps on websites.

But AI also needs to find our content. This means we want to ensure that our website is listed on as many services as possible. Large language models have been trained with data from the internet. Their knowledge is therefore always slightly behind at first, because training takes time and is not done continuously. However, many versions can access the internet or search engines and therefore also include current information. And services such as *perplexity.ai* are even specifically designed for internet research. Little is known about exactly how AI searches work. However, you can assume that most of the things that work well to promote your site on Google and Bing also work with AI search functions.

The good news is that the days when bloggers, marketing professionals and all website operators searched for the holy grail of ***search engine optimisation*** (***SEO***) are over. They spent hours, days and sometimes even weeks finding the perfect keywords to win over the algorithms of Google & Co. What requires much less effort and delivers good results is ***relaxed search engine optimisation***: Instead of racking your brains over which keywords you absolutely must use and how often you should include them in your texts, concentrate on creating content *for people*. You do your technical homework in terms of SEO, but without putting technology, algorithms and supposed best practices above content.

The algorithms from Google and the like. are now so advanced that they understand logical connections and the intent behind search queries (***search intent***), even if these are not particularly well formulated or use similar terms that do not appear directly on the results pages. For you, this means that you should focus less on individual keywords. Instead, you need to make sure that your content is comprehensive and relevant to your target audience. The search engine will then recognise that your text answers users' questions and rate it accordingly. Keywords are no longer the holy grail, but only one part of the big picture. Google continues to rate content that exudes expertise, authority, trustworthiness and experience most highly. This development has been evident for years, but will continue to progress with the advancement of AI models.

9.3.2 Relaxed Search Engine Optimisation in Practice

What does this mean for your own websites? Relaxed SEO means that you focus on high-quality content written for people. You want to inform, entertain or help your visitors – not just satisfy an algorithm or AI. Quantity is less important; quality and uniqueness are what count. The quality of a text is primarily reflected in how well it meets the needs of

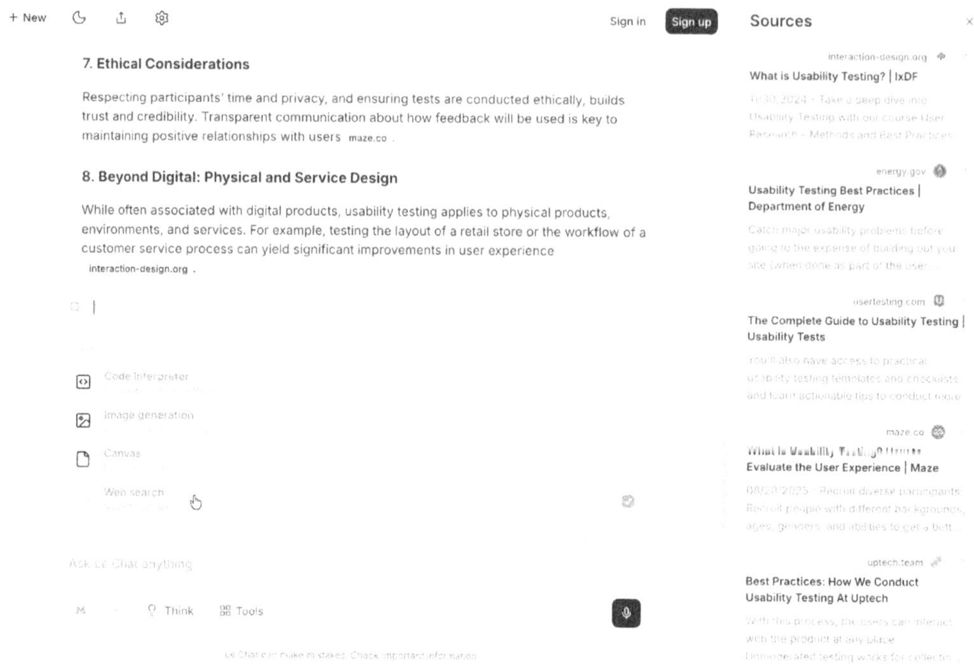

FIGURE 9.1 Web search with source references using Le Chat. (Figure created using Le Chat (Mistral), Mistral Large 2.)

its readers. So you first need to understand the situation your target group is in when they visit your website. Are they looking for a quick solution to a specific problem? Do they want to familiarise themselves with a topic? Or do they need help with an important decision? Depending on their intention, you can offer different types of content:

- Clear step-by-step instructions, specific examples and concise explanations are suitable for **problem solving**. Your text should get to the point quickly and leave out any background information that is not absolutely necessary. Subheadings and lists help readers to quickly find their way around.
- When **imparting knowledge**, a logical structure is important: from the general to the specific, from the familiar to the new. You can clarify complex relationships with analogies and practical examples. Graphics aid understanding. Aim to be as comprehensive and complete as possible in such texts. Include aspects that cannot be found anywhere else. Videos are particularly well suited for this purpose.
- To **aid decision-making**, you need a balanced presentation of the various options with their respective advantages and disadvantages. Concrete comparison criteria and comprehensible evaluations, experience reports and practical examples are also helpful.

Regardless of the specific objective, pay attention to the quality characteristics you already know from Section 7.1.1, "What Does Good Text Look Like?". When writing, it helps to imagine a person from your target group – if you have developed personas, use them (see Section 3.6, "Designing Personas"). Write the text as if you were having a conversation with this person. What questions would they ask? What objections would they have? What examples could help them?

Another proven method is the journalistic ***principle of the inverted pyramid***: you put the most important information first in the text, followed by details and background information that become increasingly specific. This allows readers to decide for themselves how deeply they want to delve into the subject. In addition, search engines assume that your texts are written in this way. They rate things that come earlier more highly than those that come later. Terms that appear in headlines also count for more – the further forward in the headline, the more. If you take all this into account, you will create texts that are not only found by search engines, but above all are enjoyed by people and recommended to others.

EXAMPLE PROMPT: RELAXED SEARCH ENGINE OPTIMISATION

Motivation: I would like to analyse the website xyz.de in terms of its SEO strategy, based on the concept of relaxed SEO. It is important to evaluate the quality and relevance of the content for the target group, rather than focusing solely on technical aspects or keywords.

Task: Analyse the website taking the following points into account:

- How well does it meet the needs of its target audience (e.g. problem solving, knowledge transfer, decision support)?
- Is the content high-quality, well-structured and designed to appeal to people?
- Are principles such as experience, expertise, authoritativeness and trustworthiness (E-E-A-T) taken into account?
- What suggestions for improvement can you make to make the content better for both people and search engines?

Result: Create a detailed analysis report with clear recommendations. The report should include the following points:

- Summary of the strengths and weaknesses of the site
- Specific suggestions for improving the content
- Tips on how to integrate technical SEO measures without overemphasising the technology

Example: The report should be concise and structured, e.g. in sections for analysis, recommendations and conclusion. Example of recommendations: "Use subheadings and lists to better structure the content and increase readability".

Role: You are an experienced SEO analyst with a focus on sustainable and user-centred optimisation strategies.

The prompt to copy: bnfr.de/ai038

GEO, THE NEW SEO?

Generative Engine Optimization (GEO) reframes the goal from earning clicks to being cited inside AI answers – matching how people now ask LLMs specific, question-shaped queries rather than browsing lists of links. The shift is driven by a crawl/traffic imbalance: AI systems ingest massive volumes of pages while sending far fewer or even no visitors to the sources, accelerating a collapse in traditional search-driven traffic.

Act accordingly by structuring your content in clear question-answer formats and covering topics comprehensively so models can lift authoritative passages. Strengthen the technical substrate – fast delivery, semantic HTML, and schema.org markup – and build off-site trust via mentions, reputable media, forums and well-described videos (don't forget subtitles). This way you increase your chances to be found via AI – but the field is nascent, so no best practices have emerged yet.

9.4 TECHNICAL HOMEWORK

You still have to do some technical homework. This applies to every single page of your website. Each one needs unique and meaningful ***meta information***. The title tag and the `description` are the most important of these. This is what search engines not only read but also display in the hit lists. The `title` must describe the page content as specifically as possible and contain important keywords. The `description` is a short summary and should motivate readers to continue reading.

Good pages are structured with headings, which helps readers and is positively evaluated by search engines. There are a few simple rules for this:

- **Headings** are marked with header tags (`h1`, `h2`, `h3`, etc.). The `h1` tag is the most important one, and every single page should have one – and only one. It can be similar to the title tag, as the latter is not displayed on the page itself, only as a window title or tab title in most desktop browsers.

```
▾ <title>
    Rocket Report: Bloomberg calls for SLS cancellation; SpaceX hits century mark - Ars Technica
  </title>
▸ <style> ⋯ </style>
  <link rel="preconnect" href="https://c.arstechnica.com">
  <script async="" src="https://globalservices.conde.digital/p77xzrbz9z.js"></script>
  <script type="text/javascript" async="" src="https://www.googletagmanager.com/gtm.js?id=GTM-PVBXQMCR&gtm=4e5ar0"></script> event
  <script async="" src="https://planebasin.com/dist/25dd01b14_8715a062a12be6f05714ee41f1a252e6e86d0.index.js"></script>
  <script async="" src="https://www.googletagmanager.com/gtm.js?id=GTM-NLXNPCQ"></script>
▸ <script> ⋯ </script>
  <!--The SEO Framework by Sybre Waaijer-->
  <meta name="robots" content="max-snippet:-1,max-image-preview:large,max-video-preview:-1">
  <link rel="canonical" href="https://arstechnica.com/space/2024/10/rocket-report-bloomberg-calls-for-sls-cancellation-spacex-hits-
  century-mark/">
  <meta name="description" content=""For the first time, Canada will host its own homegrown rocket technology."…">
  <meta property="og:type" content="article">
  <meta property="og:locale" content="en_US">
```

FIGURE 9.2 The "title" and "meta" elements with the attribute "name='description'" in the source code of an HTML page (here on arstechnica.com).

- Use the following `h` tags for **subheadings**, arranged in hierarchical order. An `h2` tag is a second-level subheading, `h3` is a third-level subheading and so on. Except for the h1 tag, you can have as many of these as you like on the page; just follow the logical structure of the content.
- Finally, you can make it even easier for search engines and AI by telling them the exact structure of your website. To do this, create a file called **sitemap.xml**. Search engines use it to efficiently understand the structure and content of a website and index it completely. In this file, you list all the URLs of the website. You can include additional information such as the update frequency, the date of the last change and the priority of individual pages. This is particularly important if your website is very extensive, has many subpages, if new content is added frequently or if it is deeply nested. Most CMS platforms create a **sitemap.xml** themselves or with plug-ins (e.g. ***Yoast SEO*** for WordPress). Alternatively, you can use online tools that create a sitemap for medium-sized sites free of charge, which you can then save on your server in the root directory. (Even large language models with online access find it surprisingly difficult to create a **sitemap.**xml file. They know the structure and can answer many questions about it, but when systematically going through all your pages, they usually stop after a few steps.)

If you want to delve deeper into the topic of SEO, you can find lots of additional information here: bnfr.de/ai038

Finally, here is a checklist for SEO of your website:

- **The right keywords**: You should make an effort to use keywords that are as specific as possible and relevant to your target audience in a meaningful way in the text. This also includes related terms. It is not a matter of finding the right word. The aim is to make it as clear as possible to search engines (and AIs) what the page is about.
- **Proper structure, descriptive headings, image texts and links**: You need clearly structured content with descriptive alt texts and meaningful link texts. This makes it easier for machines to read and correctly classify your content.
- **No duplicate content, only one domain**: You should avoid duplicate content at all costs; each text should only be recorded once. Your website should be accessible with and without www, but one variant must be redirected to the other. This prevents the site from being indexed under two URLs (e.g. www.yourdomain.co.uk and yourdomain.co.uk).
- **Use HTTPS**: Your website must be accessible via *https*. To do this, you need an ***SSL certificate***, which you must set up for your site.
- **Individual "title" and "description" tags for each page**: Unique titles and meta descriptions increase relevance and encourage clicks.

- **Crawlable structure, archives for old blog entries or newsletters**: A searchable structure and archives facilitate navigation and findability.
- **Sitemap (XML sitemap)**: Provide an overview of all pages to give a complete and clear overview of all content.
- **Check indexing**: Are all pages being indexed? If not, ensure that no pages are being overlooked or excluded.
- **Valid HTML, proper internal linking**: Clean internal linking and valid HTML improve user-friendliness and search engine friendliness.
- **Meaningful URLs**: Descriptive URLs help search engines to correctly capture the page content.
- **Responsive design**: Use responsive design to ensure that the website works well on different devices.
- **Accessibility**: Ensure accessibility, for example, through clear structures, alternative texts and clear focus elements, so that all visitors can use the content without restriction.
- **Short loading times**: Optimise performance for a better user experience and lower bounce rates. Search engines also reward this with a better ranking (more on this in Section 8.12, "Test and Optimise Performance").

When it comes to SEO, you can once again get help from AI. When it gets technical, I recommend only having the AI examine individual pages, otherwise it can easily become overwhelmed, just like you, because you will end up with a long list of ideas for improvement. Start by analysing the pages that are most important to you and your target audience.

EXAMPLE PROMPT: SEO AT PAGE LEVEL

Motivation: Check the website mywebsite.co.uk/page.html for basic SEO and user-friendliness issues to identify optimisation potential.

Task: Analyse the page in terms of meta information, structure (headings, keywords, image and link texts), technical performance (indexing, loading time, HTML validity) and user-friendliness (responsiveness, accessibility). Provide specific suggestions for improvement.

Result: Deliver a report highlighting strengths, weaknesses and prioritised optimisation suggestions.

Role: You are an experienced SEO analyst.

The prompt to copy: bnfr.de/ai066

9.4.1 Fewer Visits Do Not Necessarily Mean Less Success

Google and other search engine providers are all working on new ways to present search results to us. At Google, this is called ***SGE*** (Search Generative Experience), which is a mixture of AI-generated texts and processed search results. These will lead to more and more questions being answered without us having to visit the results page. In some cases, however, this doesn't matter: if I'm a hairdresser and want people to come to my salon, I don't care whether potential customers find my opening hours via Google, an AI or directly on my website. And if I want to sell something, then perhaps only those who are really interested in my product will come. This means that I will have fewer visitors. But those who do come are genuinely interested. This allows me to tailor my content even better to them.

9.5 COMMUNICATION, CONTACT AND USER RETENTION

Just waiting for someone to randomly enter the right search term in a search engine is not enough. Make sure that the address of your site is well known. It should be included on all letters, documents, goods, gifts, press releases, but also vehicles, etc. that leave the company. Place the URL in the signature of every email. I would advise against direct advertising in blogs, forums and social media. This can trigger angry reactions and ultimately damage your image.

On the other hand, you can score points with good factual contributions. Including the URL of the site at the bottom of your entry is legitimate and can attract readers to the website.

FIGURE 9.3 This is how users feel on many sites – the text is not tailored to their interests.

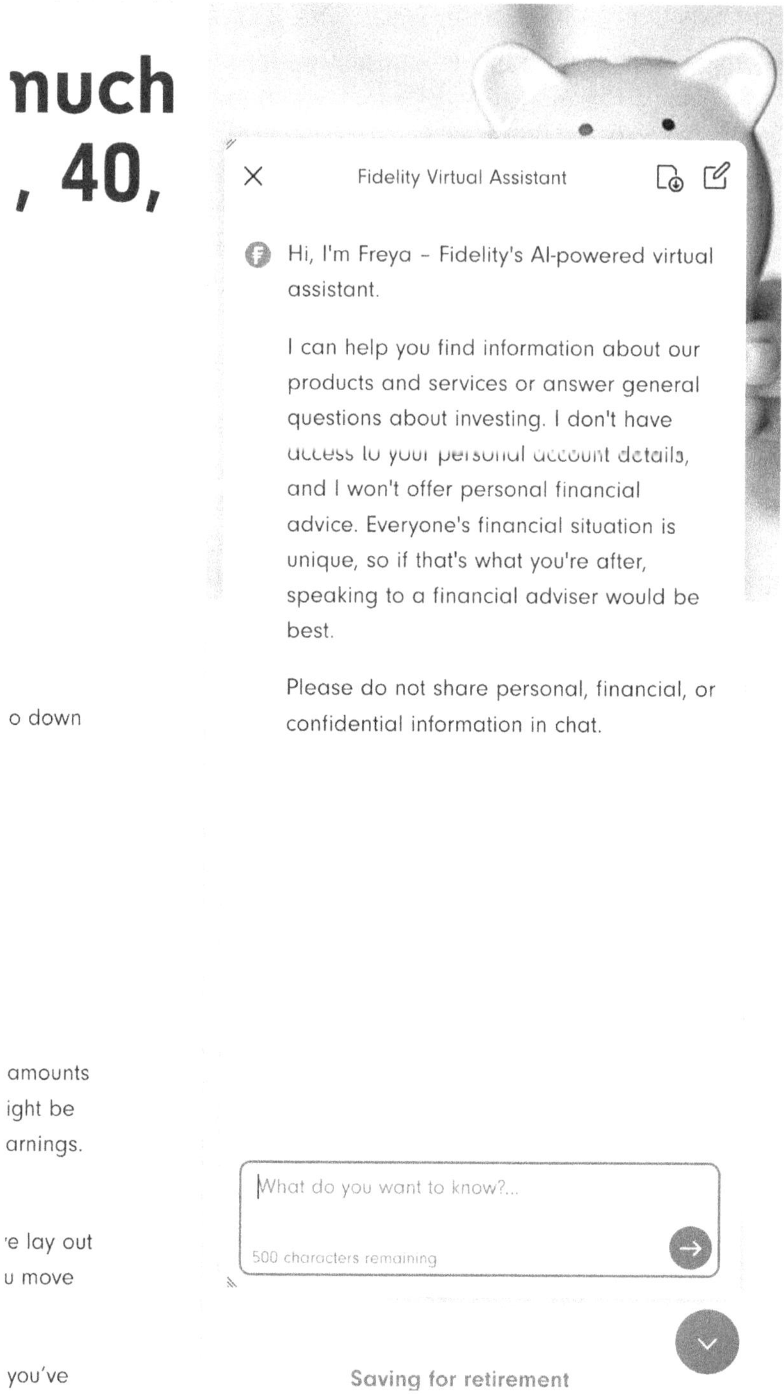

FIGURE 9.4 Chatbot on www.fidelity.co.uk. Users generally have mixed feelings about chatbots on websites. If they work well, they are enthusiastic – but often specific questions cannot be answered. It is therefore essential to provide a way for users to contact real people.

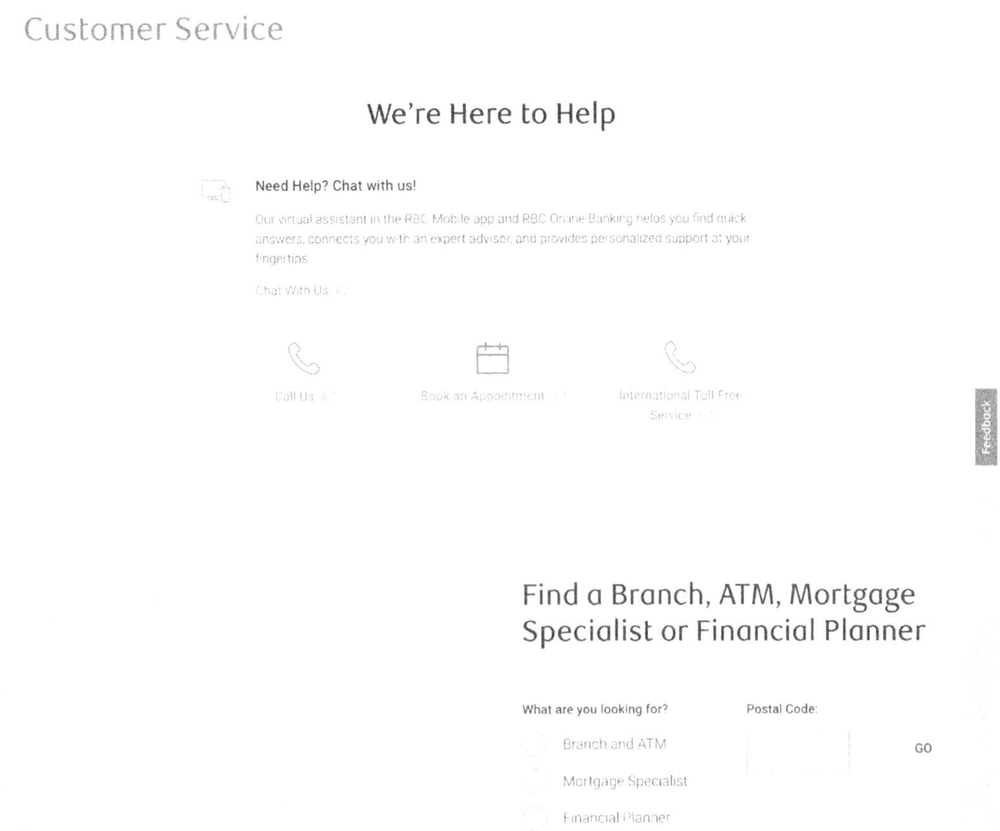

FIGURE 9.5 Exemplary: at rbcroyalbank.com, users can select their preferred contact option among many.

Take advantage of the opportunity to communicate with your visitors. Once again, the good impression you have made with your website is at stake.

Visitors expect your site to include an email address and, if possible, a telephone number. They expect a reply to their emails within one or two days at the latest. Make sure that this happens. An auto-responder is a compromise solution if you cannot reply promptly. This is a programme on the server that sends automatic replies. In this reply, you confirm that the email has been received and that you will deal with it. If at all possible, indicate when a personal reply can be expected.

9.6 SELECT SOCIAL MEDIA FOR MARKETING

Whether it's a blog post, podcast or video – before you create new content, check what goals you want to achieve and whether your target audience actually uses the chosen medium. Just because content is easy to plan and create today thanks to AI, you shouldn't start without a concept. Think carefully about how you want to stand out from the flood of information and entertainment that users are inundated with every day. For example, *several hours* of video material are uploaded to YouTube every single second. The site has over 30 billion visits every month. However, there is hardly any reliable data on how much of the endless amount of video material on YouTube is actually viewed. We can assume, however, that 90% of videos have fewer than 100 views – and most of them are probably abandoned after a few seconds. It's not the production quality or the name that counts – and certainly not the length of the video. A shaky video with poor sound quality often has more credibility than a perfectly produced corporate video. Whether a message is heard is determined by uniqueness, usefulness, entertainment value, marketing and chance. If you want to use video, you shouldn't just say, "My niece does that, she knows TikTok". People tend to overestimate what is actually possible with social media marketing. AI falls into the same trap. Part of its training data consists of countless websites that want to sell social media marketing or give tips on how to do it – it's a huge business.

The very first thing you should do when planning your marketing is to research what your target group wants and find out where they are. Then develop a concept and decide what makes sense for your specific situation. The right decision may be to do nothing. Small and medium-sized businesses in particular have limited time and money for marketing or advertising and need to focus on the most important channels. You don't want to miss out on opportunities, but you also don't want to chase every trend.

When you define a goal, it shouldn't just be to attract attention. A good goal might be: "We want to attract new customers between the ages of 18 and 30 to our website". Or: "We want to remind our existing customers over the age of 30 about us". Such clear goals make it possible to check later whether your activities were successful. Don't forget to define how you will measure success. Activities on social media without success monitoring are a waste of time. Unfortunately, success is not that easy to measure. Simply counting fans, followers, likes, etc. is of little use. Interaction is more important. So if you have a lot of fans on Facebook, that's nice. It's better if you get a lot of likes for a post or if it is shared. It's best if users react and write comments.

The ideal metric is one that directly tracks conversions or even sales: if you can measure how many new sales, enquiries or similar you generate through social media activities, you have the best and most reliable metric. You should always put these goals and metrics in the context of your target group. Do you know which social media platforms have the most users in the UK, the US, and across the EU? In the UK, the largest by monthly adult reach are YouTube (94%), Facebook/Messenger (91%) and Instagram (76%); TikTok reaches 50%. In the US, the most-used platforms are YouTube (83% of adults), Facebook (68%), Instagram (47%) and TikTok (33%). Across the EU, the biggest by average monthly active recipients are YouTube (93%), Instagram and Facebook (both 58%); TikTok reaches only 30%.

Do you know which social media platforms have the most users in German-speaking countries? Currently, these are YouTube (almost 90 million active users per month),

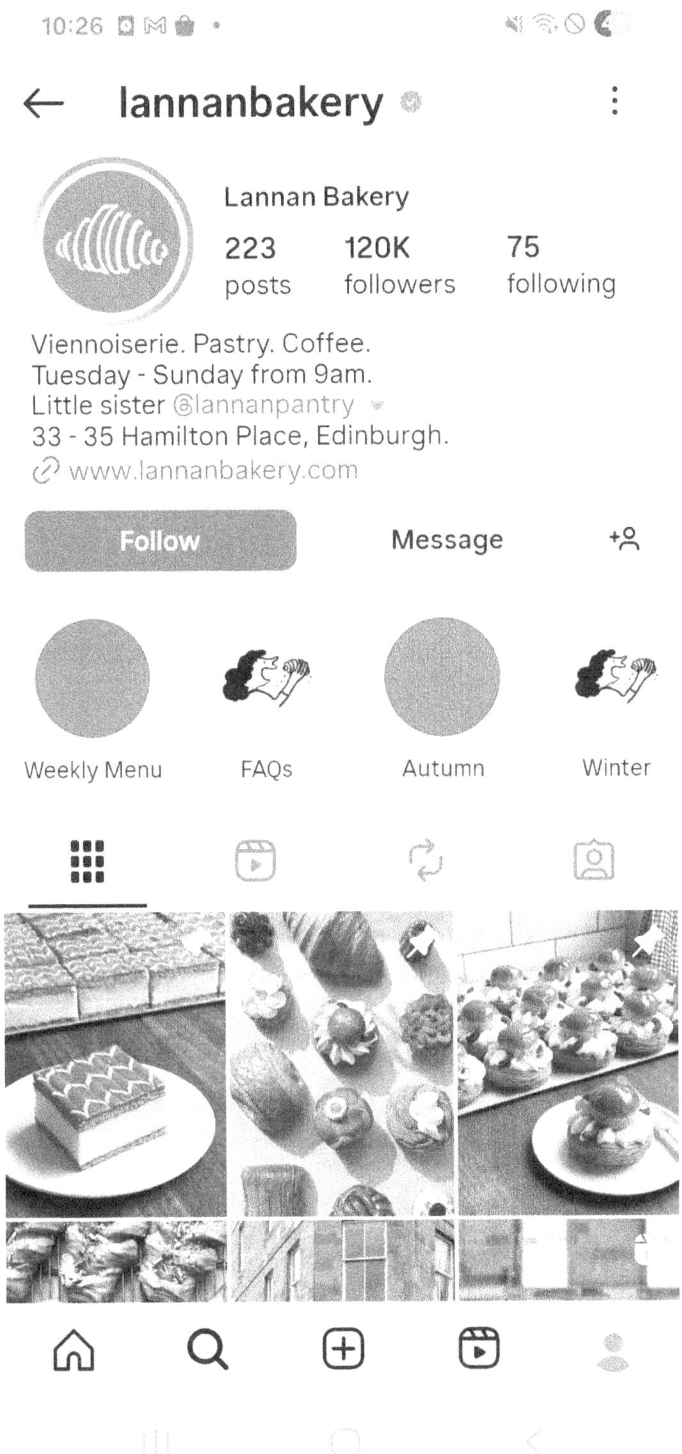

FIGURE 9.6 A bakery may well find it useful to market itself on Instagram.

Instagram (45 million) and Facebook (over 30 million). TikTok, on the other hand, has "only" slightly more than 20 million. You can quickly research the current figures using Perplexity or other language models. But the exact figures are not important. The much more important question is: Do you know where and how to reach *your* target audience? Here, AI with internet access can help you again:

EXAMPLE PROMPT: RESEARCH RELEVANT SOCIAL MEDIA

Motivation: I want to find out which social media platforms my target audience is active on, what they do there and how I can address them with targeted marketing measures. The research should be tailored to the needs of my website.

Task: Conduct a detailed analysis to determine

1. which social media platforms the target audience uses,
2. which activities and content are particularly relevant there and
3. which marketing strategies I can successfully use there.

Use the website description to take the target group's context into account.

Result: Create a structured overview with the following points:

- List of relevant social media, including reasons
- Description of the target group's typical activities there
- Suggestions for specific marketing measures that promise success on these platforms

Example: The result should be an overview in the form of a table or bullet-point list. The language should be precise, technical and clearly understandable.

Role: You are a marketing expert with a focus on social media strategies and target group analysis.

{Insert description of the site's objectives and target group from the rough concept here.}

The prompt to copy: bnfr.de/ai040

As always, critically evaluate the results. Keep in mind that the large language models have been trained with countless websites. This means they have repeatedly read advertising posts from companies that sell social media marketing. And not every measure that is sold is useful. Ask critical questions and treat the AI as a partner, not a pack mule, in accordance with golden rule number 1. Take a look for yourself at the competition in the respective medium. On the one hand, these are your direct competitors. On the other hand, they are also associations, media outlets or individuals who also deal with topics that are important to you. Can you compete with them? How much effort does it take to provide significantly better content than theirs? If you come to the conclusion that your topic is already too crowded, it may make sense to focus on a different channel. The question is always: how do you ensure that your efforts are worthwhile?

Let's take a quick look at each channel and then get started on selecting the right one – and producing the content.

9.6.1 Blog and Background Articles on Your Own Site

Blogs (or ***weblogs***) are websites or parts of a website where content is published regularly. Unlike a news section, for example, the content is usually informal, personal and reports on events or experiences of the authors. They are considered social media because they allow interaction with others through comment functions and links to other blogs. With regular blog posts that entertain people from your target group or provide them with useful content, you can build a community that can be very loyal thanks to the interaction with you and increase your visibility. The catch: you have to bring people to your pages yourself, unlike with Instagram and other social media, where users are suggested your content if the platform thinks it might interest them.

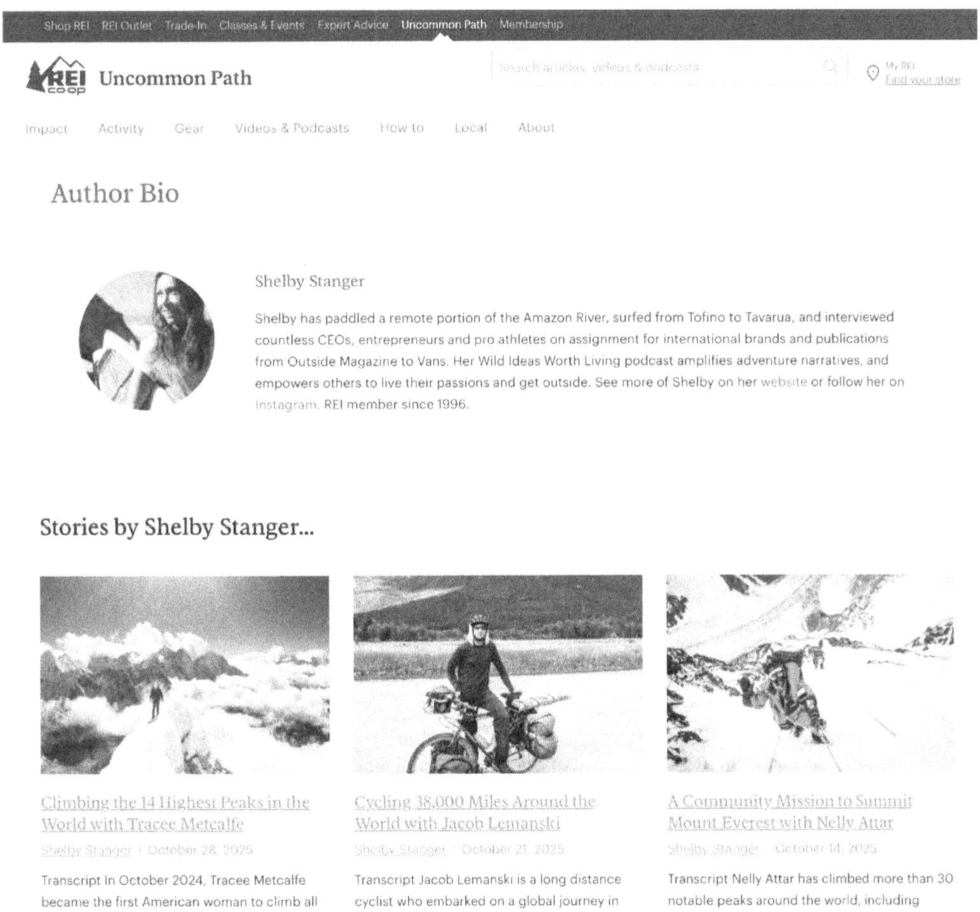

FIGURE 9.7 Outdoor equipment retailer REI runs a blog where named outdoor enthusiasts regularly write personal posts.

9.6.2 Email Newsletters – Not New, but Effective

Email does not actually count as a social medium, but you should not forget about it. The good old email is still a highly effective marketing tool. You may not inspire the very young target group with it, but everyone has an email address, and with good content you can reach many people over the age of 20, especially in a professional environment. Targeted and relevant content helps you build a strong bond with your followers. A newsletter reminds your users about your website or company on a regular basis. Anyone who subscribes to the newsletter voluntarily chooses to receive regular information from you. This makes newsletters a cost-effective and efficient communication method with an excellent ROI (return on investment) – so you get a lot out of the resources you invest.

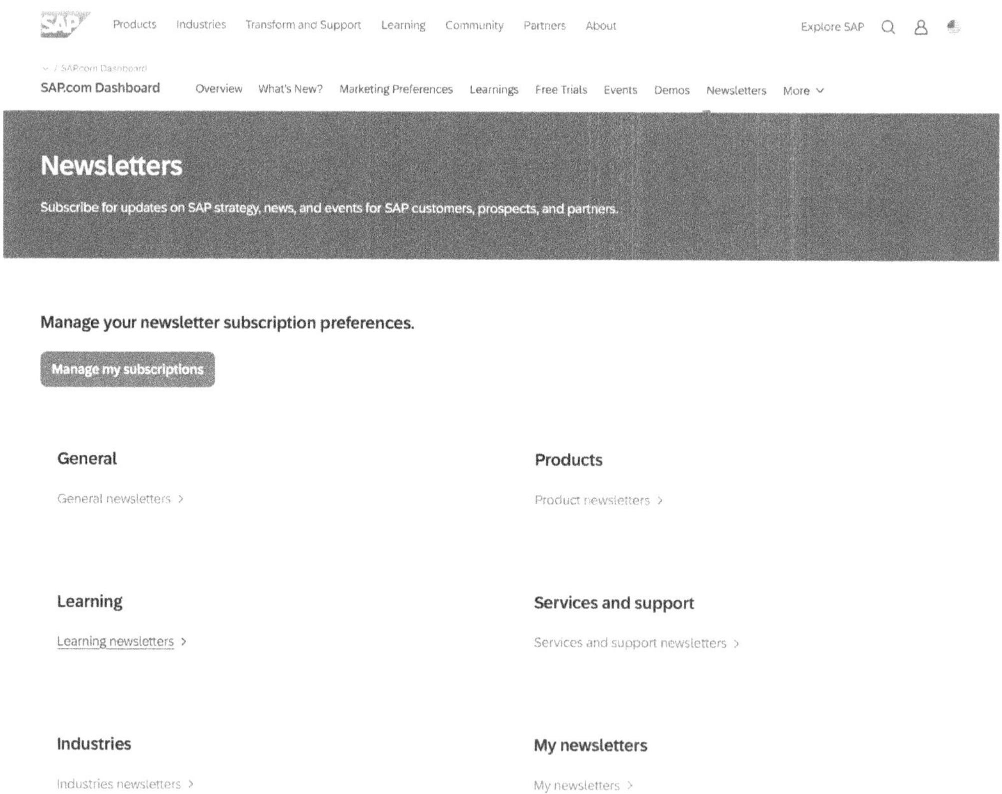

FIGURE 9.8 SAP offers not just one newsletter, but dozens, depending on the interests of the target groups.

However, given the flood of emails that land in our inboxes every day, expectations are high. A successful newsletter is characterised by the following features:

- **Genuine added value**: Your emails must be relevant in terms of content and useful to people. Advertising content should remain the exception. Instead, they should contain information, tips or offers that offer readers a clear benefit.
- **Credibility and trust**: The sender must be clearly identifiable and inspire confidence. Professional design and clear communication are also essential.
- **Meaningful subject line**: The subject line should motivate the recipient to open the email, but should not be sensationalist.
- **Easy unsubscription**: Every email must contain an easily accessible option to unsubscribe (link). This builds trust and complies with legal requirements. A link to the imprint and privacy policy is also mandatory.
- **Data protection and legal security**: Use the ***double opt-in*** procedure to ensure that recipients consciously choose to receive your newsletter. This means that after entering their email address, interested parties must confirm their subscription by clicking on a link in the first email. Only then may you add this person to your mailing list. You must also document this confirmation.
- **Data economy**: You may not force anyone to provide any information other than their email address. However, you can *ask* for additional data if you explain what you intend to do with it and how it will benefit visitors.

A professional newsletter service is essential for sending out newsletters. It makes it easier for you to manage your email lists, ensures that your emails are actually delivered and helps you analyse the success of your campaigns.

9.6.3 Facebook

Although Facebook is no longer the media darling it once was, you can still reach millions of people who visit the platform every day. Facebook is still highly relevant, especially for people over the age of 30. You can attract a lot of attention with entertaining, surprising or helpful posts. An image or video as a visual anchor is a must. And you should definitely participate in discussions. If you don't answer questions here, you might as well not bother posting content at all. Those who only post marketing messages will receive little response. Instead, it's worth providing posts with added value, e.g. short guides, inspiring stories or even exclusive offers.

9.6.4 Instagram

The audience here is slightly younger than on Facebook, with millennials being particularly active. It's all about beautiful images and visually appealing bite-sized content, rather than interaction. Classic corporate marketing is evident here in profiles such as *vodafone_de*, which stand out with lots of red, funny sayings and, above all, beautiful images. There are also numerous creative and unusual examples, such as older laundry operators who pose in clothes that their customers have not picked up, thus engaging in highly appealing marketing. Instagram is a very image-heavy channel that is particularly interesting for lifestyle products, fashion, travel offers or culinary topics. Anyone who is active here must above all be visually convincing and can experiment with authentic stories and reels (see also Figure 9.6).

9.6.5 X/Twitter, Bluesky, Threads, Mastodon

Since the decline of ***Twitter*** and its renaming to ***X***, the world of short message services has become confusing. *X/Twitter* is probably still the largest platform, but its popularity is declining, and ***Threads*** (operated by Facebook) is not far behind in terms of user numbers. ***Bluesky*** currently has only about a tenth as many users, and ***Mastodon*** has even fewer.

If you don't already have a personal connection to one of these services, then I would advise against getting involved at this stage. It's a shame, because the focus is clearly on text and content, and users receive quick, concise information. These services can be particularly useful for specialist information or direct dialogue with users. That's why they are mainly used by people in politics, journalism, science and also companies who want to react quickly to current developments and exchange ideas with their community.

9.6.6 TikTok

The short video platform ***TikTok*** follows its own rules. TikTok is like a quick snack at a bus stop: each video lasts only a few seconds, then it's on to the next one. Teenagers use this platform as a matter of course, while older generations often puzzle over how it works.

You're never done, the stream of content never stops, and many who just want to try it out for a moment suddenly find themselves spending half an hour or more on it. You often see young people performing clever choreography to catchy songs, people doing wild stunts or simply humorous sketches. And animals are always present. What you don't see much of is traditional marketing. It hardly works here, but a few companies (and politicians) are giving it a try. If you don't find that amusing, you shouldn't be active on TikTok yourself. If you want to be successful here, you have to understand the medium and accept that traditional advertising messages don't work. Instead, what counts is entertaining, creative entertainment. Producing original clips is a lot of work, and you need to think carefully about whether this target group is right for you. TikTok can be exciting if you're targeting very young audiences and have a topic that can be conveyed through original short videos.

FIGURE 9.9 Bluesky mainly features news and business topics. But more and more scientists, authors and journalists are joining the crew.

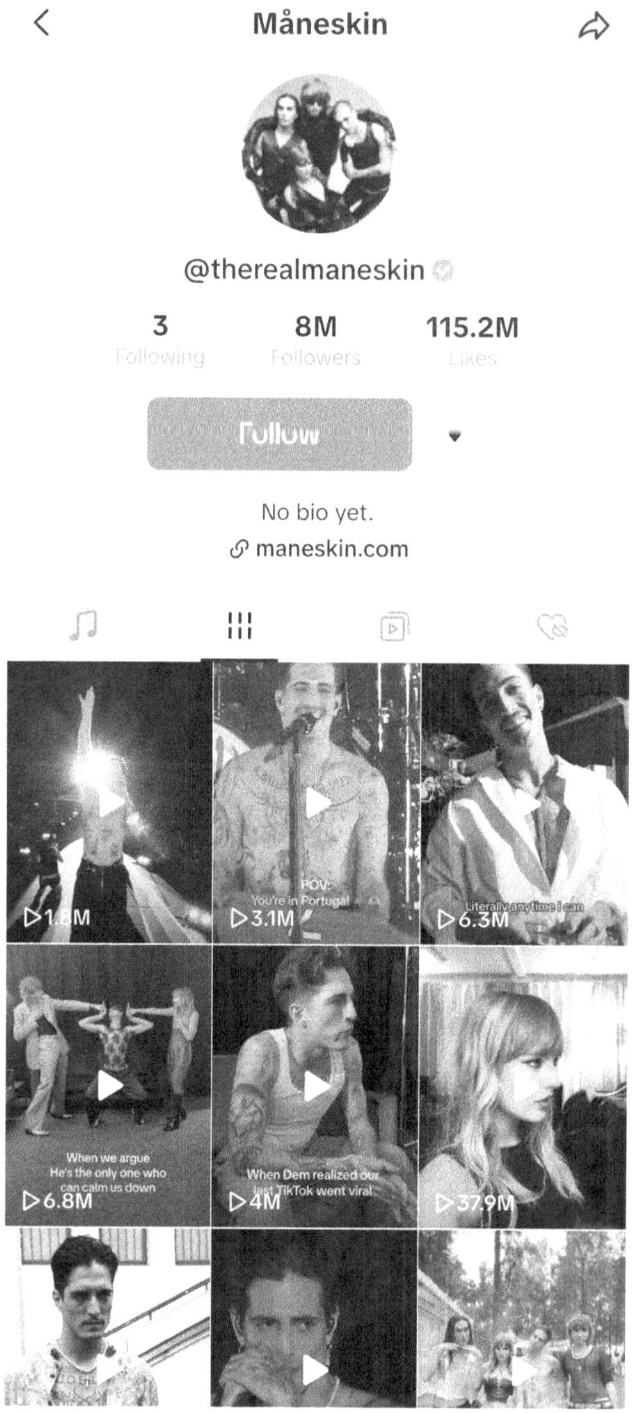

FIGURE 9.10 Bands like Måneskin find it easier on TikTok – they often have good video material anyway, so all they have to do is adapt it to the medium.

9.6.7 YouTube and Vimeo

YouTube is TikTok's supposedly more serious older sibling. YouTube is cross-generational, with users ranging from children looking for help with their homework to millennials giving make-up tips, pensioner hackers showing off their skills and companies posting high-quality videos. But that also means the competition is fierce. You need to have great videos to get attention here. "Great" does not mean expensively produced, but highly relevant, entertaining or useful and tailored to the target audience. The content should take advantage of the medium's strengths. For example, someone presenting a complex product can explain much more with videos on YouTube than with a pure image or text channel. But it is difficult to make your mark here. ***Influencers*** also flock to YouTube (as well as Instagram). Influencers as marketing partners often bring little benefit because they are too expensive, not credible enough or not targeted enough. Here, it is necessary to build up your own channel with added value in the long term. It is also important to maintain the community by responding to comments.

Vimeo is a lesser-known YouTube competitor that focuses entirely on freedom from advertising. The number of users is significantly smaller, but the target groups you address here are more clearly focused and have greater purchasing power. The platform is particularly popular in the creative sector and among providers of premium products.

9.6.8 LinkedIn and Local Business Networks

If you sell to business customers (business-to-business, B2B) or want to present yourself well to potential employees, ***LinkedIn*** is important for you. LinkedIn has one billion users worldwide and focuses primarily on professional topics. What counts here is new, interesting and, above all, useful content relating to jobs, skills, further training and the latest news from the worlds of business, research and further education. No post should be without a visual element. The community is strongly career-oriented and values specialist articles, studies, industry news and background information on products or services. If you offer a software tool for B2B customers, for example, you can share white papers, case studies or short videos with how-to explanations here. Answers to questions, direct dialogue with experts and a professional but relaxed tone are crucial here.

Also, don't forget local networks like ***XING*** (mainly German-speaking countries), ***The Dots*** (UK) or ***InfoJobs*** (Spain, Italy). These often have fewer users, but it can be easier to get noticed there.

9.6.9 Other Platforms

There are several other social media platforms such as ***Pinterest***, ***Snapchat***, ***Reddit*** and ***Twitch***. If you are familiar with and use these yourself, they may also be relevant for your target group. In general, however, you should not let yourself get carried away. Concentrate on creating a good website and accompany this with some social media marketing. The decision as to which social media channels are right for you depends entirely on your goals, your target audience, your budget and your resources. Focus

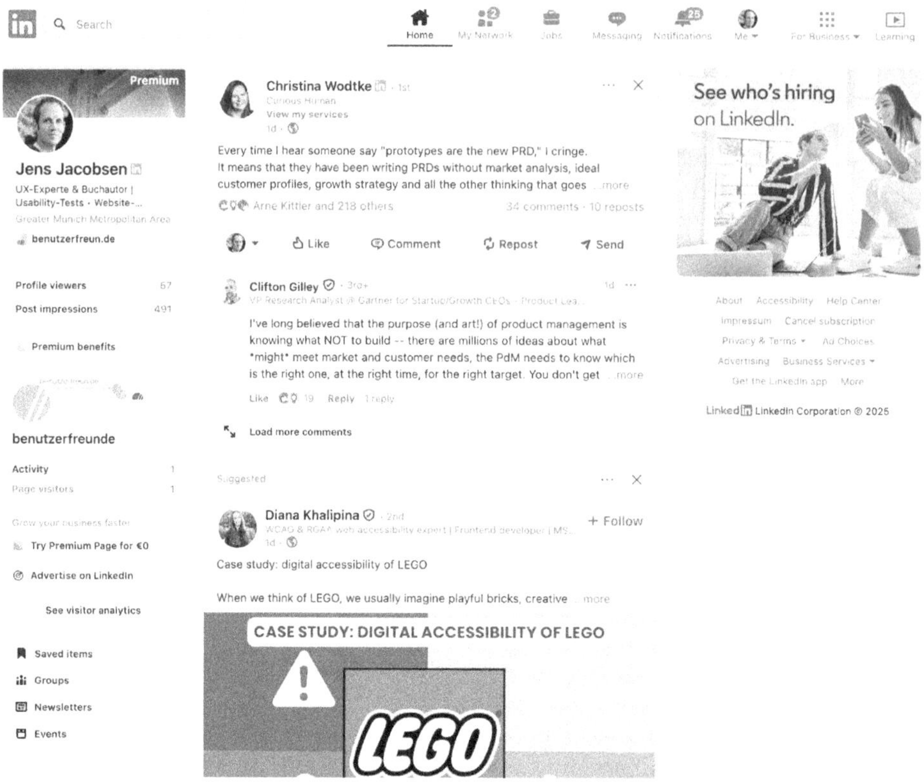

FIGURE 9.11 On LinkedIn, companies and individuals present themselves with helpful posts and engage in discussion.

on the platforms where you have a realistic chance of being noticed, offering added value and measuring your success. If you want to be active everywhere at once, you will quickly realise that you simply don't have the time. Quality over quantity is the motto. It is better to choose fewer channels and really maintain them than to be a little bit present everywhere and nowhere properly.

What is deliberately missing from my list is ***WhatsApp***. In my view, WhatsApp and similar messaging services such as ***Signal*** are not social networks, but messaging services that have replaced email for many people. Communication here takes place in private groups, which is hardly useful for marketing purposes. There are service providers who will tell you otherwise, but sustainable marketing is hardly possible in such channels, apart from information services or service numbers.

9.7 CREATING CONTENT FOR SOCIAL MEDIA AND YOUR OWN WEBSITE

In Chapter 8, "Step 6: Test and Optimise", you have already learnt a lot about the possibilities of using AI to create excellent texts and images. Here are a few additional tips that are particularly helpful for current content that needs to be created frequently.

9.7.1 Content Strategy, Social Media Plan and Editorial Plan

Once you have decided on social media channels, it's time to get down to the nitty-gritty. The first step is to develop a ***content strategy***. What do you want to post and when, what content goes down well, who is responsible for creating the posts and who monitors interactions and communicates with users? Time is a scarce resource for marketing, especially in small and medium-sized businesses. You should therefore clarify internally who is responsible for your social media marketing, what type of content makes sense and how you can create practical workflows for everyday use. Whether your social media content works or not also depends on planning and perseverance. A good ***social media plan*** is crucial for effectively reaching your target audience and successfully conveying your message to them. Let us help you:

EXAMPLE PROMPT: SOCIAL MEDIA PLAN

Motivation: The goal is to increase awareness of the website, improve customer loyalty and ultimately increase sales. Consider content and topics, objectives, target group analysis and the selection of the right platforms.

Task: Develop a comprehensive social media plan that defines goals, selects platforms appropriate for the target audience and creates a content strategy tailored to people's needs and interests.

Result: The social media plan should take the form of a clearly structured table.

Example: The table should be detailed, with clearly defined goals, a comprehensive target group analysis, a well-founded selection of platforms, and specific content ideas and schedules. The information should be presented in a precise and easily understandable manner.

Role: You are an experienced social media consultant who works strategically and practically and designs solutions specifically for small and medium-sized businesses.

Additional information: {Description of the website, objectives and target groups}

The prompt to copy: bnfr.de/ai074

Make sure that the goals are clearly defined and align with your own. When implementing your social media plan, an editorial calendar is useful. This is a calendar that contains all your planned publications on social media and your website. This can range from individual posts on Facebook or X/Twitter to complex campaigns on multiple platforms. The editorial calendar helps you plan topics logically and ensure variety. You should offer a good mix of informational, entertaining and promotional content, which experience shows is the best way to keep your followers interested. Above all, an editorial plan ensures that you publish regularly – this is crucial to your success because it motivates your followers to interact with your content and thus keep your brand in mind. By publishing regularly, you keep your online presence fresh and up to date and maintain people's attention. Regular publishing also helps to increase your visibility on social media. The platforms' algorithms favour content that comes from regularly updated accounts. This allows you to better reach and engage your target audience, ultimately leading to a stronger presence and better communication with your followers. A ***social media posting calendar*** is *part* of the editorial plan and focuses on planning and organising your social media posts. This ensures that you regularly feed all your platforms with fresh content.

EXAMPLE PROMPT: EDITORIAL PLAN

Motivation: Develop an editorial plan for the "Fit mit Frieder und Fabi" team in Berlin. The goal is to strengthen the brand, promote courses and training programmes and attract new customers with minimal effort. The plan should cover content for a period of three months and limit the weekly effort to a maximum of one hour.

Task: Create a table with suggestions for Instagram and YouTube content for the next three months (12 weeks). For each suggestion, we would like:

- Content/topic
- Platform
- Estimated number of characters for texts
- Required media (e.g. photo, short video, story, YouTube video)
- Publication date as a relative time (e.g. "Week 1", "Week 3", ...)

Plan at least one post per week per platform (Instagram and YouTube) and ensure that the content is varied and thematically aligned with the fitness services.

Result: The table should be easy to understand and offer specific suggestions that can be implemented immediately. The descriptions should be detailed enough that we know exactly what we need to depict and write.

Example: The table should contain the following columns:

- Topic
- Number of characters
- Media
- Publication date

Role: You are an expert in social media marketing who knows how to promote fitness services on social media with minimal effort.

The prompt to copy: bnfr.de/ai041

Some AIs still have problems with larger tables. If this is the case for you, have the table output sequentially for weeks 1 to 6, then weeks 7 to 12, etc.

In general, you should keep in mind that social media is not a quick project that you implement once. It is not even something that you start once and then let run. It is a long-term task. You should be prepared to continuously deliver new content, respond to comments and nurture the community. If you ignore questions, don't take complaints seriously or don't publish anything new for months, you will disappoint your followers. After all, one of the great strengths of social media is the direct exchange with your audience. This can be unfamiliar because it means a loss of control. You cannot prevent critical voices from appearing in your comments. But it is precisely this openness that enables you to receive direct feedback and improve your offering. Social media marketing is always a learning process. Observe which posts work and which don't. Try out new formats and analyse the reactions. If a channel isn't working, don't be afraid to abandon it or reduce the frequency of your posts there. Instead, consider investing more energy elsewhere. This is better than desperately clinging to a channel that is simply not relevant to your target audience. Always remember: marketing is not an end in itself; you always want to achieve a specific goal for your website. If you are not doing that, change something.

9.7.2 Finding Ideas, Creating Content with AI

AI is a great help when it comes to finding *ideas* for posts. However, you should make sure that you put a lot of effort into creating the prompt and selecting the suggestions. If you simply write a general prompt, the result will simply be what the AI has seen most often in the training data. This will give you mass-produced content that will attract little attention. A better approach:

EXAMPLE PROMPT: IDEAS FOR A BLOG POST

Motivation: I want to develop original and useful blog post ideas that promote my greeting card shop and offer readers added value by showing creative or helpful ways to use the cards.

Task: Develop eight blog post ideas, consisting of a title and a short description. The ideas should be original, funny or particularly helpful, clearly stand out from typical topics and not contain standard content such as "The best greeting cards for birthdays" or "Why greeting cards are important". Instead, look for unusual perspectives or innovative application ideas that inspire and surprise.

Result: A list of eight blog post ideas, consisting of a title and a short description, presented in a concise and succinct manner.

Example: Each idea should look something like this:

- Title: Card games with a difference: seven games you can make yourself with greeting cards
- Description: Show how to create interactive games from greeting cards – from puzzles and memory games to a unique storytelling game for family and friends.

Role: You are a content marketing expert who specialises in creative and sales-promoting blog content.

The prompt to copy: bnfr.de/ai076

It's worth trying this prompt with different AIs. I don't have a clear favourite – and it's amazing that some ideas appear in several systems. It's worth making sure that this isn't something that's already been done a thousand times in other blogs. And if there's no idea you like, just ask the AI for more suggestions. It's tireless and will keep going longer than you.

The actual writing of the posts with AI assistance is not quite as effective as the brainstorming, but it often provides a solid basic version that you can continue to work with. Personally, I appreciate the language style of Claude's responses:

EXAMPLE PROMPT: CREATE A BLOG POST

Motivation: I want to attract potential participants to my running training by providing valuable tips in a blog post about typical beginner mistakes when running. The post should be motivating and entertaining without seeming promotional. Length approximately 500 words.

Task: Create a detailed outline for a blog post on the most common mistakes made by beginner runners and suggest a title. The outline should include specific examples of typical beginner mistakes and provide a motivating, entertaining structure.

Example: A section could look like this:

Mistake X: "You start off running like a cheetah – and end up like a tortoise".

- Description: Many start too fast and quickly slow down.
- Solution: Why a slow start and a training plan are important.

Role: You are an experienced running coach and blogger who shares your knowledge with humour and enthusiasm. Tailor the outline to an audience that is new to running and needs motivation.

The prompt to copy: bnfr.de/ai075

I cannot recommend copying the generated text directly. If your main goal is to remind people of yourself, then you don't need to change much of what the AI delivers. However, if you want to create truly useful content and encourage users to interact, you will usually need to significantly edit the AI version to get a really good result. You can do this together according to golden rule number 1: AI is a partner, not a pack mule.

COPYRIGHT AND OTHER PLAGIARISM ISSUES

Having your blog texts written entirely by AI can be problematic for several reasons: First, the question of copyright is unclear: Who is the author of a text created by AI? From a legal perspective, only a human being can be the author. This means that, at most, the prompt could be protected by copyright, but even that has not yet been clarified.

Another problem is so-called ***duplicate content***, i.e. duplicated or duplicate content. AI-generated texts could produce similar or identical content that comes from the training data. This is difficult to trace and the AI itself cannot provide any information on this from a purely technical point of view. This is a copyright issue and can also lead to SEO disadvantages, as search engines rate copied content negatively. In addition, large language models tend to generate generic content for technical reasons. They are based on the principle of producing the most probable word combinations. This means that, without additional work, the content is often not very original or personal. You should therefore carefully consider the use of AI for writing. It is always safest to use AI only as a source of ideas and to edit the texts extensively.

9.7.3 Creating Audio and Video with AI

In addition to texts, as just shown, and images (as shown in Chapter 8, "Step 6: Test and Optimise"), AI can also generate audio and video. But just because it's possible doesn't mean you should automatically use it. Consider when these media would benefit your specific target audience and whether they would actually use them. Audio and video are linear media. I have to play them back in the order in which they were recorded. It is difficult for me to get an overview of the content directly – fast-forwarding or rewinding is tedious, and a linked content description is often not directly accessible or even available. The use of audio and video is, therefore, more tedious and time-consuming than skimming through text. Through embedding or presentation, you must also make it clear to users why it is worthwhile to use each individual audio or video.

The advantages lie in authenticity and the possibility of emotional appeal. You can literally address your target group directly; they hear your voice and, in the case of video, they also see you. However, it is also crucial here that the content benefits the user. Entertainment is difficult, but it works very well if you can do it. It is often easier to provide concrete benefits. For example, a conversation in which you interview competent people. One possibility is a podcast in which you regularly give tips, report on your experiences, etc. In a video, you can show your products in action better than with a pure description or with photos or drawings. If you want to reduce support requests, you can explain a lot with short audio clips or ***screencasts*** (usually commented video recordings of the screen content).

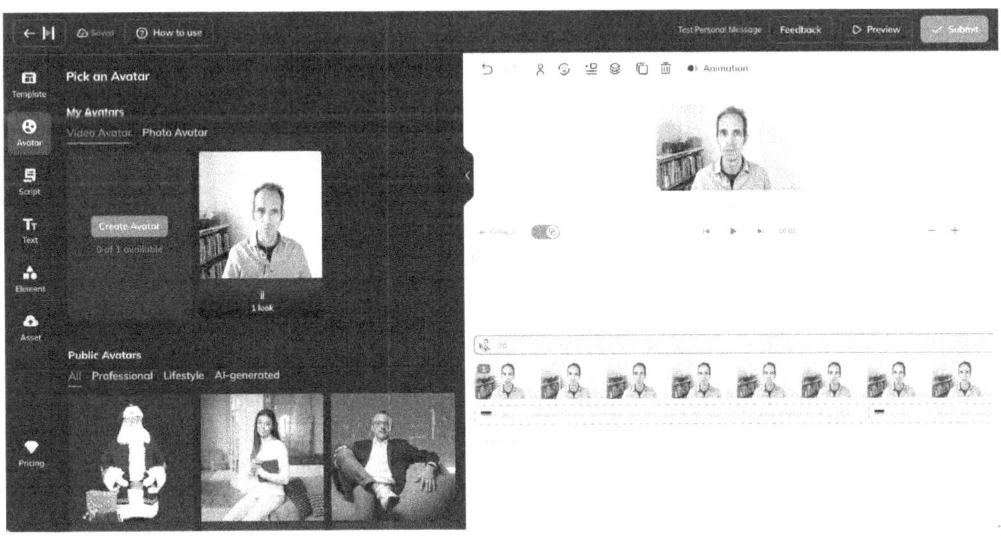

FIGURE 9.12 With HeyGen and similar providers, you can upload a few minutes of video of yourself, and the system will create an avatar that reads out any text. It looks surprisingly real. (Screeshot taken from HeyGen.)

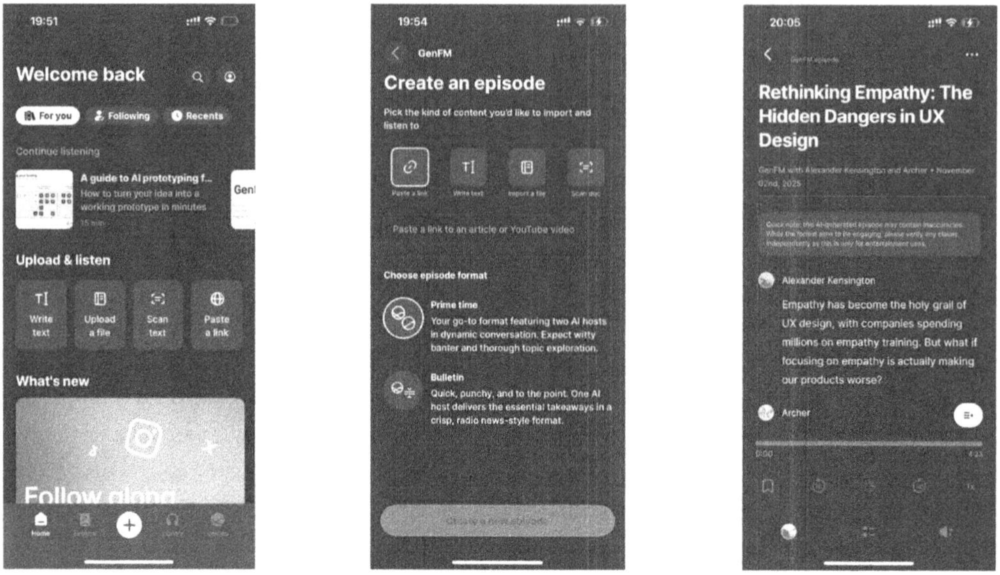

FIGURE 9.13 Create a podcast from a blog article with the ElevenReader app – although initially it is only an audio file, which you then have to add to a podcast. But the quality is impressive. (Screeshot taken from ElevenLabs.)

If a post is too long or lacks content, people will switch off or turn away. Pure advertising messages in the style of "video message from the management" rarely have a motivating effect and often do more harm than good. And at first, people underestimate the effort required to produce good videos and audio recordings. However, AI can help you learn the necessary conceptual and technical skills. Or it can create the content for you.

In addition to embedding audio and video in your website and using YouTube or Vimeo, there is another interesting form of distribution: ***podcasts***, which is "radio to go". With a podcast, you provide your content in regular episodes that interested parties can subscribe to. ***Apple Podcasts*** or the ***Spotify*** app then automatically downloads new episodes as soon as they are released. Users listen to the podcast whenever and wherever they want: on the go, while exercising or doing housework. If you regularly offer relevant topics, users will stay tuned and possibly spread the podcast further. AI can also help here, for example, with automatic editing, generating transcripts or speech recognition. Or you can use a special AI that generates audio files from your texts.

9.8 PAID ADVERTISING

In addition to marketing, which only requires you to invest your time (or pay others to do it), there is also traditional advertising. A major problem with online advertising is that many people simply ignore advertising banners. This phenomenon, also known as "banner blindness", is exacerbated by the fact that more and more people are using ***ad blockers*** to hide advertising completely. According to recent studies, up to a third of internet users do this, which significantly limits the reach and effectiveness of many campaigns.

If you want to advertise, this means you need to adapt your strategies accordingly. Today, online advertising must be not only relevant but also unobtrusive yet compelling. Content that offers added value or is seamlessly integrated into other content, such as sponsored posts, is more likely to be accepted.

Whichever form of advertising you choose, avoid the most serious mistake that a surprising number of advertisers make: simply linking the ad to your home page. Always provide a separate ***landing page***, i.e. a page that is specifically tailored to those who have just clicked on that particular advertisement. Nothing is more frustrating than seeing a beautiful pair of shoes in an advertisement and then, after clicking, being thrown onto the home page of a huge online shoe shop.

9.8.1 Search Engine Advertising

One option in the online sector is search engine advertising, such as ***Google Ads*** (***Paid Search***). This is a proven way to reach people when they use Google. To participate, you bid on specific search terms (***keywords***), and then your ads appear above or next to the list of results in exchange for payment. There is a similar offering for the ***Bing*** search engine. On mobile devices, the list of results in search engines such as Google is designed differently: adverts are placed more prominently and are less likely to be overlooked. This offers opportunities to reach target groups that are particularly mobile-savvy. At the same time, desktop search engine advertising remains an important channel, especially for more complex or work-related search queries. Products that are more likely to be purchased on impulse, such as clothing, books or even baking tins, are ideal for mobile advertising. Larger purchases, such as cars or televisions, are often researched first on a tablet or desktop, where visual elements such as high-quality photos or product videos can be persuasive.

The choice of keywords is crucial: put yourself in the shoes of the searcher and consider specific search queries. Our example café, “Bistro Verde”, should not only choose “vegan café” as a keyword but also consider local additions such as “vegan café Oldenburg”. Similarly, tradespeople such as plumbers should use specific keywords that indicate urgent needs, e.g. “emergency plumber Delmenhorst”.

The beauty of online advertising is that you can tailor your advertising precisely to your target group thanks to ***targeting***. You can specify the location, specific times of use, but also age and gender or device type (e.g. iPhone, Android or desktop). Only those who meet your criteria will then see your ad.

9.8.2 Banner Advertising

Banner advertising is the oldest form of online advertising. It is also the form that is most responsible for the poor reputation of online advertising. As mentioned, many people ignore banners or filter them out with ad blockers. And yet banner advertising can be

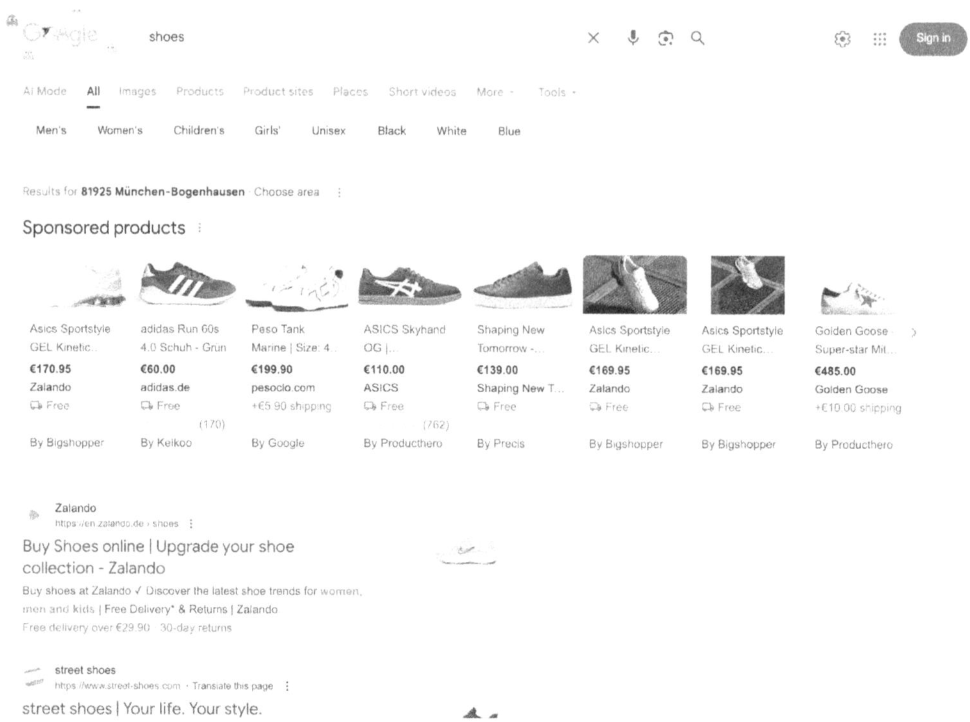

FIGURE 9.14 When I search for “shoes”, I am shown paid advertising from shops. Is this a sensible use of the advertising budget? Do people who enter this search term really want to buy shoes?

useful if used in a targeted manner. You can use it to increase awareness of your brand, even if banners are not clicked on directly. The advantage is that with most models, you don’t pay anything as long as no one clicks on them. Just make sure your advertising isn’t annoying – otherwise you’ll achieve the opposite of what you want.

With precise targeting and by booking banners on thematically relevant websites or in specific networks, you can reach your target group and keep wastage to a minimum. The use of banners is particularly effective in so-called ***retargeting***. This allows you to specifically target users who have already shown interest in your offer by using a cookie to register their previous website visits and then displaying matching advertisements on other websites. This enables you to specifically re-address potential customers who are already familiar with your offer. However, retargeting has been working significantly less well for a few years now, because both ad blockers and the integrated privacy functions of modern browsers are increasingly restricting tracking. In general, this is an advanced option that requires you to delve a little deeper into the technical aspects (and for which you also pay a relatively large amount of money).

On mobile devices, banners benefit from the limited screen size, as they are often integrated directly into the content flow. This makes it almost impossible for users to ignore them. On desktops, on the other hand, banners offer more flexibility in terms of

FIGURE 9.15 They are most commonly found on traditional media sites: banner ads such as this one on the newspaper The Guardian's site.

placement and can display larger content. The ***click-through rate*** (CTR), i.e. the ratio between ad clicks and impressions, is often higher on mobile devices than on desktops. There, a banner usually has to be displayed 500 to 1,000 times before someone clicks on it. With mobile use, it may be enough to show the ad 20 times before someone clicks on it. Nevertheless, desktop banner advertising remains an important element.

It is important that the content of your banners matches the website on which they appear. Otherwise, they may be perceived as intrusive and even have a negative impact on your image. In addition to websites, banners can also be placed in apps. This is particularly common in free app versions, for which advertising serves as a source of income. However, the advertising found here is often of low quality. So check carefully whether the environment suits your offering.

9.8.3 Geotargeting and Location-Based Marketing

With ***geotargeting***, your ad is only displayed in defined geographical regions. For example, an ad for a Berlin gym will not be displayed in other cities. ***Location-based marketing*** goes even further. It uses the location data of users' mobile devices to send them advertisements that are relevant to their current location. For example, an ad for a shop in Google Maps that is just around the corner from my current location.

9.8.4 Advertising on Social Media

Social media platforms know a great deal about the preferences of the people who use them. That's why they are so interesting to advertisers. Facebook, Instagram, LinkedIn and TikTok also earn their money this way. Here, you can target users based on their interests, behaviour patterns and demographic data. For example, you can show your ads only to people who have recently shown interest in products similar to yours or whose online activities indicate potential interest.

When advertising on social media, you should use visually appealing content such as videos, images or interactive formats that are specifically tailored to the platform and its users. Stories, reels or sponsored posts in the feed integrate seamlessly into the consumption of content and thus attract a lot of attention – if they are well done. Interaction rates on social media are far higher than those of traditional banner advertising. Precisely because it is difficult to avoid the ads, they must be creative, informative and entertaining. Authenticity is important, and you need to strike the right tone that is customary on the respective platform. It can be promotional, but then it must entertain. Or it must offer real added value.

Glossary

5-second test A quick method for checking how well a website can convey what users will find there at first glance. → ***Test subjects*** are shown a website for only 5 seconds and then asked questions about its content and functions, as well as their impression of the site.

A/B test In this comparison method, one of two versions of a website or part of it is randomly selected and displayed to a large number of users. Statistical analysis shows which version achieves more clicks or higher → ***conversion rates***. A large number of participants is required to obtain meaningful results.

Accessibility Unrestricted access to applications for all people, regardless of physical or technical limitations.

Adaptive design In this design approach, separate fixed → ***layouts*** are created for different screen sizes, in contrast to → ***responsive design***.

Adobe Firefly The AI programme Firefly can generate content such as images, → ***vector graphics***, text effects and patterns. It is integrated into Adobe applications such as Photoshop and Illustrator, but can also be accessed directly via a web interface.

Adobe Illustrator This graphics programme works with vectors instead of → ***pixels*** and is particularly suitable for logos, → ***illustrations*** and other → ***scalable*** graphics. Thanks to the integrated → ***Adobe Firefly***, it can also generate vector images using AI.

Adobe Photoshop A widely used professional programme for image editing and graphic design. Thanks to the integrated → ***Adobe Firefly***, it can also generate images using AI.

Adobe XD Design and prototyping tool for websites and → ***apps***. Primarily used for → ***mock-ups*** and prototypes.

Affinity Designer Affordable but powerful graphics programme for editing vectors; an alternative to → ***Adobe Illustrator***.

Affinity Photo Affordable but powerful graphics programme for editing photos and → ***pixel graphics***; alternative to → ***Adobe Photoshop***.

Agent (system) The AI system independently performs complex tasks across multiple interfaces, which usually consist of several steps, interacting with websites, services and other agents. For example, searching for the cheapest offer from several providers and placing an order.

AGI, Artificial General Intelligence Refers to AI that not only solves specialised tasks but can also think, learn and adapt to new circumstances as flexibly as a human being. It would be smarter than humans.

Algorithm A clear set of instructions for solving a problem, consisting of a fixed sequence of commands.

Alt text This text description of an image is read aloud by → ***screen readers*** and displayed when images cannot be loaded. It is also read by search engines to index the image content.

Analytics/web analytics Data on visitor behaviour on websites, e.g. page views, → ***dwell time*** and click paths. The term can also refer to tools used to analyse such data, such as Google Analytics or → ***Matomo***.

API, Application Programming Interface The interface enables programmes to communicate with each other and exchange data without revealing their internal structure.

App (application) Refers to a software programme that runs on mobile devices or desktop systems.

ARIA, Accessible Rich Internet Applications This collection of HTML attributes makes web content more accessible to people with disabilities by providing → ***screen readers*** and other assistive technologies with additional information about the structure and functionality of elements in the code.

Artificial intelligence, AI Field of computer science concerned with the development of systems that mimic tasks such as human thinking, learning or problem solving.

Aspect ratio, AR Describes the ratio of width to height of an image or display, e.g. 16:9.

AttrakDiff → ***Questionnaire*** for measuring the perceived hedonic and pragmatic quality of a website or → ***app***, i.e. it measures how appealing and useful people find the application.

Avatar The graphic representation or symbolic figure represents a person in a digital environment.

Backend Refers to the part of a website on the → ***server*** that is responsible for data processing and storage and is not directly visible to users.

Banner This graphic element on a website, usually in the header area or between content areas, is often used for advertising or other messages that website operators want to communicate as directly as possible.

Benchmark This standard or reference is used to evaluate the performance or quality of a product or website.

Best practice This proven method or recommended procedure has proven to be particularly efficient and effective.

Blog, weblog Refers to a website on which posts are simply displayed one after the other, with the most recent ones at the top. Originally, a blog was a web diary in which a person provided subjective observations, comments and bits of information. Today, many company websites also have a blog, for example.

Body text The main text content of a page, for example, which usually consists of several complete sentences.

Bootstrap → ***Framework*** for developing → ***responsive*** websites with ready-made CSS and JavaScript components.

Bounce rate Refers to the percentage of visitors who leave a website immediately after viewing only a single page.

Box model (CSS) This → ***CSS*** concept defines how the space of an HTML element (→ ***element***, → ***HTML***) is calculated by content, inner spacing (→ ***padding***), borders and outer spacing (→ ***margin***).

Breadcrumbs The → ***navigation element*** shows the position of the current page within the website hierarchy and provides links to the parent pages (e.g. Home > Products > Raincoats).

Breakpoint Defines the screen width at which the → ***layout*** of a → ***responsive*** website changes in order to make effective use of the available screen space. In → ***debugging***, the term refers to a point at which the execution of a programme is paused in order to analyse the current status.

Briefing This written or verbal description contains all the important information for a project or task.

Bug Refers to an error or problem in an application that impairs its function.

Call-to-action, CTA In the form of buttons or links, a call to action is intended to lead visitors to a desired action such as "Buy now" or "Learn more".

Card sorting Using this method to develop or review the information architecture of a website or → ***app***, → ***test subjects*** organise content into categories that make sense to them.

Cards Cards are visual elements on websites or in → ***apps*** that present information or functions in a compact form and are usually arranged in a regular grid.

Careword Refers to a term or expression that users have in mind when searching for information on a page. Related to → ***keywords***.

Carousel, slider This interactive element on a web page displays images (and occasionally videos) one after the other in the same position, often changing automatically at fixed intervals. Also known as a slideshow, which usually displays the images in full-screen mode while nothing else is visible on the page.

Cascading The principle of cascading in → ***CSS*** determines which style rules are applied when there are several.

Chain of thought The method in AI uses a logical sequence of thoughts or steps to solve problems, for example, when AIs are asked to explain their "thought processes" step by step.

Chatbot This programme responds automatically to user input and simulates a conversation.

Check-out Refers to the completion of an online purchase, where users review their order once more and then make the final payment.

Churn Usually expressed as a percentage per month or year, this indicates the rate at which users or customers cancel an offer or stop using a service.

Class (CSS) The → ***CSS*** selector of the class allows the same formatting to be assigned to multiple HTML elements (→ ***element***, → ***HTML***).

Click dummy The interactive prototype is used to test the user guidance and design of a website or application. It is clickable like the finished product, but does not yet have full functionality.

Clickbait Clickbait is an attention-grabbing title or content designed to entice users to click on a link, even if the content is of no further use to them.

CMS, content management system This programme for managing and maintaining web content enables even less tech-savvy users to update and maintain a website. The best-known example is → ***WordPress***.

Community Refers to a group of people who share a common interest or goal and interact with each other online or offline.

Compression Refers to the process of reducing the size of data to save storage space or bandwidth.

Confabulate Describes how a → ***language model*** invents facts when it has no information. Some people prefer this term to → ***hallucinating***.

Container (CSS) The → ***HTML*** element serves as a container for other → ***elements*** and is used to structure a web page. It makes it easier to format or control elements together.

Content delivery network, CDN This network of → ***servers*** provides content such as images or videos worldwide to reduce page loading times.

Content marketing The marketing strategy of content marketing aims to attract and retain customers by offering them → ***content*** that is useful or entertaining to them.

Content Refers to all content on a website, such as text, images, videos and other media.

Context window Refers to the maximum amount of content that a → ***language model*** can process at one time.

Conversion rate Quantifies the percentage of visitors to a website who perform a desired action, such as making a purchase.

Cookie This small text file is stored by a website on a user's device to save information such as login status, language settings or preferences, and activities.

Crawler The programme automatically searches and indexes websites, usually for search engines.

CSS, Cascading Style Sheets Language for designing and formatting → ***HTML*** documents.

Customer experience, CX Refers to the totality of all experiences a person has when interacting with a company or product.

Customer journey map See *User Journey Map*.

Data minimization This noble principle of data protection stipulates that only data that is actually necessary should be collected, processed and stored.

Data processing agreement, DPA Contract that defines how a processor may handle personal data on behalf of a controller to meet data protection requirements. It is generally required when personal data is processed on another party's behalf.

Debugging Finding and fixing errors in a software programme.

Declaration (CSS) The statement in → ***CSS*** assigns style rules to a selected HTML element (→ ***element***, → ***HTML***), consisting of a property and a value, e.g. `color: red;`, to colour the text of an element red.

Deep learning In this subfield of → ***machine learning***, artificial → ***neural networks*** with many layers analyse large amounts of data and recognise complex patterns, e.g. in image and speech processing.

Diffusion model The AI model for image generation gradually converts noise into an increasingly precisely defined image based on text prompts (→ ***prompt***) or other specifications.

Disclaimer This legal statement is intended to exclude liability for certain matters.

Domain The unique address of a website on the Internet (e.g. abc.co.uk) consists of the name or → ***second-level domain*** (*abc*) and the → ***top-level domain*** (*.co.uk*).

Dropdown A dropdown menu (→ ***menu***) expands when clicked or tapped and displays additional options.

Dummy text See *Lorem ipsum*.

Dwell time, time on page Time visitors spend on a website or a single page.

E-E-A-T, Experience, Expertise, Authoritativeness, Trustworthiness Refers to Google's quality criteria for web content: experience, expertise, authoritativeness, trustworthiness.

Element (HTML) The basic component of an HTML document consists of a start tag, an end tag and the content in between. Example: `<p>Hello World!</p>`, where `<p>` is the start tag, `</p>` is the end tag and `Hello World!` is the content.

em (CSS) This relative unit of measurement in → ***CSS*** refers to the font size of the respective parent element. Example: `2em` means twice the font size of the surrounding element → ***rem***.

Encoding Describes the conversion of data into a specific format in order to store or transfer it securely and efficiently.

Encryption Process of converting data into a secure format that can only be decoded with a key.

European Accessibility Act, EAA The European Union directive stipulates the → ***accessibility*** of products and services for people with disabilities.

Exit intent The moment when users want to leave a website can be detected with JavaScript on a website by tracking mouse movements. Users can then be shown specific content, such as a special offer or help text, to persuade them to stay.

Eye tracking Method for recording and analysing the eye movements of users. In research, eye tracking is used, for example, to analyse which elements on a website are viewed and which are not ( ).

Fat footer A particularly extensive footer at the bottom of a website. This often contains a number of links and other elements, which makes sense because users often look for orientation at the bottom of the page.

Favicon This is a small → ***symbol*** or logo for a website that is displayed in the browser's address bar and on the tabs next to the → ***URL***.

Few-shot prompting In this → ***prompting*** technique, AI models are given a few examples to show what the result should look like. In → ***one-shot prompting***, only one example is given, while in → ***zero-shot prompting***, no examples are given.

Figma Design programme for creating drafts and prototypes and for collaborating on UI/UX design projects (→ ***User Experience***, → ***UI***).

Filter Mechanism that sorts or displays data according to specific criteria.

Fine-tuning Adaptation of a pre-trained AI model to specific tasks through further → ***training*** with additional data sets.

Firefly See *Adobe Firefly*.

First-click test This → ***usability*** testing method examines where users click first when they are asked to perform a specific task. It shows how effective the calls to action on the page are.

Flat file CMS This content management system (→ ***CMS***) works without a database and stores content in simple files.

Flexbox → ***CSS*** module for flexible and efficient arrangement of elements, especially for → ***responsive designs***.

Fly-out A fly-out menu (→ ***menu***) or element opens when clicked, tapped or → ***hovered*** over.

Focal length (camera) Measure of the distance between a camera lens and the image sensor. Influences the perspective and image section. We perceive a focal length of 50 mm, for example, as natural because the resulting image roughly corresponds to our visual impression. Focal lengths of less than 35 mm, for example, are wide-angle lenses.

Footer This area at the bottom of a website usually contains links such as contact, privacy policy and → ***legal notice***.

F-pattern Typical viewing pattern when viewing websites. Users first read horizontally at the top, jump down a bit and then read horizontally again. This shows that people rarely take in the entire content of a page.

Framer Programme for creating interactive prototypes and → ***UI*** designs.

Framework A collection of predefined functions, libraries and rules. Provides a structured basis for programming, allowing code to be created more efficiently without having to program everything from scratch.

Front end The part of a website or application that is visible to users and displayed in the browser. In contrast, the → ***backend*** handles server-side data processing and business logic and remains invisible to users.

Frontier model An advanced AI model that demonstrates the current limits of what is technically feasible and sets standards in terms of result quality, performance and complexity.

FTP, File Transfer Protocol Protocol for transferring files between computers on the Internet.

Funnel Describes a person's journey through a website, from the first interaction to the completion of a transaction, e.g. a purchase. In marketing, the funnel refers to the path from initial interest to purchase.

Gallery Refers to an area on a website with a collection of images (or videos), usually arranged in a grid.

GAN, Generative Adversarial Network → ***Neural network*** that combines two models – a so-called generative model and a so-called discriminative model. The two networks compete with each other and thus improve each other. Often used for image generation.

General Data Protection Regulation, GDPR EU regulation which establishes uniform rules for the processing of personal data.

Generative AI, genAI This → ***artificial intelligence*** can create content such as code, text, images or videos.

GEO, Generative Engine Optimisation Measures to increase a site's visibility and citations within AI-generated answers and AI search results.

Google Fonts This Google service provides free fonts for use on websites. When using them, you must pay attention to data protection.

GPU, Graphical Processing Unit Specialised hardware for fast graphics processing and parallel computing. Used for computer games as well as AI and scientific simulations.

Grid Generally refers to the (design) grid for the structured arrangement of elements. In → ***CSS***, it refers to a → ***layout system*** for arranging content in rows and columns.

Guardrails The safety mechanisms built into AI systems restrict their use and prevent undesirable outcomes.

gzip The compression process reduces the size of files. It is used to shorten the loading time of web pages.

Hallucinating When an AI provides false or fabricated information, this is called hallucinating or → ***confabulating***.

Header The header area of a website. Usually contains the logo and → ***navigation***.

Heatmap Visually represents, in the form of a colour map, which areas of a website users have frequently interacted with (often shown in warm colours, e.g. red) and which areas have seen less interaction (usually marked in cooler colours, e.g. blue).

Hero banner/section The large-format area, usually at the top of a website, presents important content or actions (→ ***banner***). It often shows a close-up of a product or an important person.

Hex value Specification of a colour shade in hexadecimal format, consisting of six characters (0–9, A–F), for example, `#FF0000` for red or `#00FF00` for green. Used by → ***CSS***.

Highlight video A short video clip summarising important moments or content.

Hover, mouseover, rollover The mouse pointer is moved over an element – without clicking.

HTML, Hypertext Markup Language Standard markup language for creating/programming websites.

HTTP/HTTPS Protocols for transferring data on the web. HTTPS offers → ***encryption*** via → ***SSL***.

Icon This small graphical → ***symbol*** represents a function, application or file, e.g. a stylised magnifying glass for the search function.

id selector (CSS) The → ***CSS*** selector is used to address a specific HTML element (→ ***element***, → ***HTML***) based on its unique ID.

Illustration This graphical representation supports content visually by explaining or artistically interpreting it.

Illustrator See *Adobe Illustrator.*

Image format See *aspect ratio.*

In-depth interview See *interview.*

index.html If no file is specified, this default file is loaded by a web server (→ ***server***).

Information architecture The structuring and organisation of a website's content, pages and navigation.

Inheritance (CSS) Through the mechanism of inheritance, style rules are automatically transferred from parent HTML elements (→ ***element***, → ***HTML***) to their child elements. This reduces the amount of code required, ensures consistent design and facilitates maintenance.

Inpainting AI technique used to fill in missing or unwanted areas of an image based on the surrounding visual context.

Inspector This tool in web browsers allows you to analyse and edit the source code and CSS styles of a web page.

Integrated Development Environment (IDE) This software contains tools such as an editor (for writing code) and a debugger (for troubleshooting) to facilitate code writing.

Interview, in-depth interview These data collection methods involve asking specific questions to gather participants' opinions, experiences or knowledge. A prepared list of questions is usually used for this purpose.

ISO 9241 This collection of international standards sets out guidelines for the design of user-friendly human-computer systems, particularly with regard to ergonomics, → ***usability*** and → ***user experience***.

JavaScript, JS Programming language for interactive and dynamic content on websites.

Jimdo This website builder allows you to create your own websites without any programming knowledge.

Jobs to be Done, JTBD The approach analyses the needs and tasks of users in order to tailor products specifically to their actual requirements.

JPG, JPEG This widely used image format compresses content efficiently. → ***WebP.***

jQuery The JavaScript library simplifies common programming tasks.

Keyword Entered as a term or group of words into a search engine to find relevant content and used by search engines to identify and evaluate suitable results. → ***Careword.***

Landing page Visitors land on this specially optimised web page after clicking on an advertisement, for example.

Language model An AI model (→ ***model***) that processes natural language and generates text, such as GPT-4 or LLaMA, is called a language model.

Large Language Model, LLM This AI model (→ ***model***) has been trained with large amounts of text to understand and generate natural language.

Latent diffusion model A powerful variant of a → ***diffusion model*** that creates images faster with comparable quality and requires less memory.

Layout Arrangement of elements on the page.

Lazy loading By only loading images and other content on a web page when they are visible or needed, this technique reduces loading time.

Legal notice The legally required section of a website provides information about the operator and responsible parties.

LORA, Low-Rank Adaptation The LORA method for fine-tuning pre-trained AI models adjusts only a small portion of the model parameters (→ ***model***, → ***parameters***) in order to learn new tasks with little effort. This allows, for example, an image AI to be trained for a specific style.

Lorem ipsum Dummy text, i.e. meaningless placeholder text such as Lorem ipsum, is used in the development phase to test → ***layouts*** without distracting from the actual content, or because the content has not yet been created.

Low-code platform A low-code development environment allows applications or websites to be created with minimal programming effort, but unlike → ***no-code platforms***, it also allows you to integrate your own code if desired.

Machine learning, ML This subfield of AI enables → ***algorithms*** to recognise patterns in data, learn from them and improve their performance by repeatedly processing new data without being programmed to do so. It is used by large → ***language models*** (→ ***Large Language Model***, → ***Model***) as well as image AIs.

Margin The outer distance of an HTML element (→ ***element***, → ***HTML***) determines the distance to other elements.

Matomo This open-source solution for → ***analytics*** offers better data protection options than most commercial systems.

Media queries The CSS techniques of media queries allow the → ***layout*** of a page to be adapted to different devices and screen sizes.

Menu Provides an interactive list of options or functions that users can select, e.g. for → ***navigation*** on a website.

Meta element This HTML element (→ ***element***, → ***HTML***) defines metadata such as the description, → ***keywords*** or the author of a web page.

Meta navigation The → ***navigation*** at the top of a website contains links to the login page or help section, for example.

Metric Provides clearly measurable values or key figures for evaluating performance, behaviour or quality.

Minifying To improve the loading speed of a website, minifying removes characters that are not required for the function from files such as → ***CSS*** or JavaScript.

Mobile first In this design approach, websites are first developed for mobile devices and then adapted for larger screens based on this design. This takes into account the fact that most websites are most frequently accessed via mobile devices.

Mock-up A mock-up is a detailed visual representation that shows the design, → ***layout*** and structure of a product or user interface. Although a mock-up has no interactive functions, it is often visually indistinguishable from the finished version.

Modal A modal (dialogue box) or window covers the content of the page and requires interaction before you can continue.

Model (AI model) Refers to a trained system that recognises patterns in data and generates predictions or content based on them, e.g. in language and image AI.

Mouseover See *hover*.

MP4 This common video format offers efficient compression with high quality.

Multimodal model This AI model (→ ***model***) can process and/or output various types of data such as text, images or audio.

MySQL See *SQL*.

Navigation This system of links and/or → ***menus*** enables users to navigate and move around a website.

Neural network This → ***model*** of → ***machine learning*** is inspired by the structure and functioning of the human brain.

NLP, Natural Language Processing This area of AI deals with the processing and analysis of natural language.

No-code platform Within a no-code development environment, you can create applications or websites without any programming knowledge.

NPS, Net Promoter Score This metric measures the likelihood of people recommending a product or brand to others.

Ogg (video format) Free and open multimedia container format for audio and video data; alternative to → ***MP4***.

One-pager This website displays all content on a single page.

One-shot prompting Here, the AI is given a single example to show what the desired result should look like. → ***Few-shot prompting***, → ***Zero-shot prompting***.

Open source Software with source code that is publicly available and can be used and modified by anyone.

Outpainting With this technique, image AI extends an existing image beyond its original boundaries. It does this by generating additional matching content. For example, it uses outpainting to supplement a square portrait with a complete scene with a background in landscape format.

Overlay An overlay superimposes additional information, → ***menus*** or interactive content onto the main content of a page without reloading the page.

Padding The inner spacing of an HTML element (→ ***element***, → ***HTML***) defines the distance between the content and the frame.

Page grid Serves as a guide for the arrangement of content on a page in order to achieve a harmonious → ***layout***.

Paper prototype A simple prototype made of paper is used for visualisation and early testing of concepts or ideas.

Parallax scrolling With this web design effect, the background of the page moves more slowly than the foreground, creating a depth effect.

Parameters Parameters are values that are used as input for functions, → ***algorithms*** or AI models and influence their behaviour, output or learning process. In AI, parameters determine how a → ***neural network*** recognises and processes patterns. The more parameters a → ***model*** has, the more powerful and precise it is.

Pattern Patterns refer to recurring design solutions that offer proven methods for specific problems. In contrast, the term ***pattern recognition*** describes characteristic features or structures in data that are recognised and classified by → ***algorithms***.

Performance The speed and efficiency with which a website or application functions or loads.

Personalisation Adaptation of content or functions to the individual needs or preferences of users.

Photoshop See *Adobe Photoshop*.

PHP Scripting language that is executed on the web server (→ ***server***). Used for dynamically generated web pages, basis of many → ***CMS***.

Pixel, Picture Element The smallest unit of a digital image or display, representing colour and brightness. The size of a pixel depends on the screen resolution. In → ***CSS***, the unit px is used to define font sizes, spacing and the dimensions of elements.

Plug-in An extension for a programme that enables additional functions or applications.

PNG The lossless image format PNG supports transparency and is often used for graphics. It is less suitable for photos, as the data files become quite large. → ***JPG***, → ***WebP***

Podcast A series of digital audio or video files that are made available for streaming or downloading. Podcasts can be subscribed to via platforms such as Spotify, Apple Podcasts or RSS feeds.

Pop-over A small window that floats above the main content and is displayed when interacting with an element. It displays additional information, controls or options.

Pop-up A stand-alone window or → ***overlay*** that opens automatically or through interaction to display additional information, advertising or further options for action.

Probabilistic model, probability-based model The AI model (→ ***model***) works with probabilities to take uncertainties into account and make informed predictions, e.g. in weather forecasts or language AI.

Prompt engineering The art and science of designing inputs so that AI models (→ ***model***) deliver optimal results.

Prompt A prompt is an input or instruction that causes an AI model (→ ***model***) to perform a task, e.g. generate text or create an image.

Public domain Works whose copyright has expired or which were never protected by copyright are considered to be in the public domain.

Python Programming language used for web development, data analysis and → ***machine learning***.

Qualitative tests Qualitative studies collect non-numerical data such as opinions, impressions or behaviours in order to better understand user experiences and decision-making processes; one example is in-depth interviews (→ ***interview***).

Quantitative tests Quantitative studies collect measurable numerical data to evaluate systems or processes. In → ***usability*** tests, for example, in addition to qualitative findings, it is possible to measure the exact time users need to complete a task in an → ***app***.

Questionnaire This tool for collecting data consists of a series of questions. It looks simple, but it is difficult to do well.

RAG, retrieval-augmented generation This AI approach combines real-time data retrieval with text generation. This enables it to provide more accurate and up-to-date answers, as it incorporates external knowledge sources.

Recruitment Refers to the process of finding participants for studies, tests or experiments.

Referrer, traffic source The source URL (→ ***URL***) indicates the website from which users were redirected to another page. → ***Analytics***.

rem (CSS) This relative unit of measurement in → ***CSS*** refers to the font size of the root element (i.e. the HTML element). → ***Element***, → ***HTML***, → ***em***.

Responsive design In the responsive approach to web design, pages adapt flexibly to different screen sizes, in contrast to → ***adaptive design***.

Retargeting This marketing strategy attempts to target users with targeted advertising at a later point in time on another website after they have left a website. For example, products that they viewed on the exit page are advertised.

Reverse card sorting See *tree testing.*

Review See *Usability Review.*

Robot The automated programme regularly performs tasks such as data processing or searching the web.

ROI, return on investment This key figure measures profit in relation to the time or money invested.

Rollover See *hover.*

Royalty-free Describes materials such as images or music that can be used without ongoing licence fees. However, a one-time payment is often required.

Ruby on Rails The → ***development environment*** for web applications is based on the Ruby programming language.

Sass (Syntactically Awesome Stylesheets) This extension for ***CSS*** simplifies the writing of CSS. It uses reusable building blocks such as variables and groups. The code is later translated into normal CSS so that it can be read by browsers.

Scaling Refers to adjusting the size of an element or system, e.g. enlarging or reducing an image.

Screen reader This tool for people with visual impairments reads the text of a website aloud or outputs it in Braille.

Scribble The mostly hand-drawn, rough draft visually represents the ideas and structure of web pages in a sketch.

Search engine optimization See *SEO.*

Search intent Describes the intention with which users perform a search query, e.g. searching for information or wanting to buy a product.

Second-level domain Refers to the part of a → ***domain*** that comes directly before the → ***top-level domain*** (e.g. *.com*), e.g. *abc* in abc.de.

Seed Random-based → ***algorithms*** or → ***models*** use this initial value to obtain reproducible results. In image AIs, the same seed value can produce identical images.

Selector (HTML) This part of → ***CSS*** defines the HTML elements (→ ***element***, → ***HTML***) to which a rule is applied.

Semantic HTML Semantic HTML uses → ***elements*** in such a way that their meaning describes the content, e.g. `<article>` or `<header>`.

SEO, Search Engine Optimisation Measures to improve the ranking of a website in search engine results.

Server logs These files record the activities and requests on a → ***server***, e.g. accesses to web pages.

Server Refers to a computer that provides data, services or content via a network.

Sidebar The side area on a website or → ***app*** displays additional information, → ***navigation elements*** or widgets. The sidebar can be shown or hidden, particularly on mobile devices.

Sitemap The overview of a website's page structure is used both for search engine optimisation (→ ***SEO***) and for developing a clear information architecture.

Sketch Design programme primarily used to create UI/UX layouts (→ ***UI***, → ***user experience***, → ***layout***) and prototypes; only for macOS.

Slider See *Carousel*.

Slideshow See *Carousel*.

Snippets Search engines display these short text excerpts above or next to the hit lists to give users a quick overview.

Social media marketing This marketing strategy uses social networks to promote products, services or brands.

SQL, Structured Query Language Language for managing and querying data in databases for storing, retrieving and editing data. A well-known database-based system that uses SQL is MySQL.

Squarespace → ***Website builder*** with design templates and tools for creating websites.

SSL, Secure Sockets Layer Protocol for → ***encrypting*** and securely transmitting data over the Internet → ***HTTPS***.

styles.css The file contains the ***CSS*** style rules for a website.

Subdomain This part of a → ***domain*** precedes the main domain, e.g. *blog* in blog.abc.de.

Survey Method of collecting data or opinions by asking specific questions, for example, in an → ***interview*** or → ***questionnaire.***

SVG, Scalable Vector Graphics The SVG image format is based on → ***vector graphics*** and therefore allows lossless enlargement. It is particularly suitable for logos, → ***icons*** and line drawings.

Symbol Such a graphic element represents an idea, action or function.

System Usability Scale, SUS This is a standardised → ***questionnaire*** for evaluating the user-friendliness of a product or application.

Tag Refers to an HTML element (→ ***element***, → ***HTML***) that marks the beginning or end of a block, e.g. <p> for a paragraph.

Tailwind (framework) This CSS library provides a large collection of predefined → ***classes*** for efficiently designing → ***layouts*** and designs without having to write your own CSS rules.

Targeting The marketing technique of targeting is used to address clearly defined target groups with relevant content or advertisements.

Teaser A short text or preview on a website is intended to arouse users' curiosity and encourage them to view further content.

Template Defined as a template for the basic layout (→ ***layout***) and design of a website or document.

Test subjects People who take part in tests or experiments to provide data or feedback.

Theme This pre-designed template, usually in a → ***CMS***, determines the appearance and structure of a website.

Thinking aloud In this method of → ***usability*** research, → ***test subjects*** voice their thoughts aloud while using a product. This reveals what people think and feel while interacting with the product.

Thumbnail Small preview image of larger content, e.g. book covers or video previews.

Tiles Tiles are the rectangular elements on a web page that display information or functions in a grid-based → ***layout***.

Toggle Use this switch or control panel to switch between two states, e.g. to show or hide elements.

Token Refers to the smallest unit of text or data that an AI model (→ ***model***) processes, e.g. a word, punctuation mark or part of a word.

Tooltip A small window or text element that appears when users hover over an element with the mouse to display additional information.

Top-level domain, TLD The last part of a → ***domain*** indicates the type or origin of the domain, e.g. *.com* or *.de*.

Tracking Collection of data about user behaviour, e.g. page views or clicks → ***Analytics***.

Traffic Quantifies the volume of data transferred or the number of visitors who visit a website.

Training data The data used to train an AI model and improve its performance largely determines what the → ***model*** will later be able to recognise and reproduce.

Training Refers to the process in which an AI model (→ ***model***) is fed with data in order to learn specific tasks.

Transformer This → ***neural network*** processes language and other data efficiently by recognising connections between words or elements. Used in modern AI models (→ ***model***) such as GPT.

Tree testing This method is used to test the effectiveness of website navigation. To do this, → ***test subjects*** are asked to find specific content in the → ***navigation*** of a website.

Turing test An experiment for evaluating AI, named after the mathematician Alan Turing, who proposed it in 1950. AI is considered intelligent if it cannot be distinguished from a human being in a text-based dialogue.

UI, user interface Refers to the user interface of an application or website through which users communicate with the system, for example, via buttons, → ***menus*** or input fields.

Upscaling The process of upscaling increases the resolution of an image or video to make it sharper and/or larger.

URL, Uniform Resource Locator Unique address of a resource on the Internet, e.g. benutzerfreun.de/index.html.

Usability review Evaluation of the user-friendliness of a product or system, usually by several UX experts.

Usability A measure of the ease, efficiency and satisfaction with which users can operate a system or product.

Usage research, user research Area of → ***user experience*** that deals with the behaviour and needs of users. Tools such as → ***surveys*** and → ***usability tests*** are used for this purpose.

User experience, UX Describes the totality of experiences that users have when interacting with a product or service.

User journey map, customer journey map Visual representation of the steps users go through when interacting with a product or service.

User-friendliness See *usability*.

UTF-8 The standard for encoding text supports umlauts, special characters and characters from almost all writing systems.

Vector graphics A vector graphic is based on mathematical formulas and can therefore be → ***scaled*** without loss of quality.

Visits Number of visits to a website within a specific period of time.

WCAG, Web Content Accessibility Guidelines Guidelines for improving the → ***accessibility*** of web content. In the EU, compliance with these guidelines is required by law in some cases.

Web fonts These fonts are downloaded from the Internet and integrated into web pages instead of being installed on the user's device.

Webflow A tool for creating and managing websites that combines design and hosting with minimal programming. → ***No-code platform***, → ***Low-code platform***.

Weblog See *blog*.

WebP This image format allows both lossless and lossy → ***compression***, resulting in smaller file sizes than → ***JPG*** or → ***PNG*** with comparable quality.

Website builder This tool or service allows websites to be created without programming knowledge.

Wireframe A simple, schematic representation of → ***the layout*** of a web page.

Wix The → ***website builder*** offers templates and tools for creating websites.

WordPress The best-known → ***CMS*** for websites.

XD See *Adobe XD*.

XML, Extensible Markup Language Markup language used to store and exchange data in a hierarchical structure. Used to present information in a clear, cross-platform readable format, e.g. in configuration files or for data exchange between systems.

Z pattern, zigzag pattern In this reading pattern, the user's eyes follow a zigzag or Z pattern on the page.

Zero-shot prompting With this → ***prompting*** technique, the AI is simply given an instruction. With → ***one-shot prompting***, an example is also provided, while with → ***few-shot prompting***, several examples are provided.

Index

Note: Locators in *italics* represent figures and **bold** indicate tables in the text.

For Product Safety Concerns and Information please contact our EU representative GPSR@taylorandfrancis.com
Taylor & Francis Verlag GmbH, Kaufingerstraße 24, 80331 München, Germany

www.ingramcontent.com/pod-product-compliance
Lightning Source LLC
Chambersburg PA
CBHW080326290726
48947CB00043B/846
9781041213307